DAILY LIGHT *on the* DAILY PATH

DAILY LIGHT *on the* DAILY PATH

FROM THE NEW INTERNATIONAL VERSION

OVER 500,000 COPIES IN PRINT

ZONDERVAN®

ZONDERVAN.com/
AUTHORTRACKER
follow your favorite authors

ZONDERVAN

Daily Light on the Daily Path
Copyright © 1981 by The Zondervan Corporation

This title is also available as a Zondervan ebook. Visit www.zondervan.com/ebooks.

Requests for information should be addressed to:

Zondervan, *Grand Rapids, Michigan 49530*

ISBN 978-0-310-32912-1

Cover design: Michelle Lenger
Interior design: Mark Sheeres

Printed in the United States of America

09 10 11 12 13 14 • 20 19 18 17 16 15 14 13 12 11 10 9 8 7 6 5 4 3 2 1

FOREWORD

DAILY LIGHT ON the Daily Path has become a virtual legend in the publishing world, and a much imitated pattern as other arrangements of Scripture portions have appeared in print.

This devotional book offers two Bible passages for each day of the year, morning and evening. A single daily theme helps to emphasize a particular Bible truth so that after one progresses through the book he has completed a Bible doctrine course to help him in his daily Christian walk.

This edition gives new expression to the cherished readings of *Daily Light on the Daily Path* by its use of the New International Version of the Bible, a contemporary translation of distinctive clarity and beauty in its language.

"But as for you, continue in what you have learned and have become convinced of, because you know those from whom you learned it, and how from infancy you have known the holy Scriptures, which are able to make you wise for salvation through faith in Christ Jesus. All Scripture is God-breathed and is useful for teaching, rebuking, correcting and training in righteousness, so that the man of God may be thoroughly equipped for every good work" (2 Tim. 3:14–17).

—THE PUBLISHER

JANUARY 1

MORNING

But one thing I do: Forgetting what is behind,... I press on toward the goal to win the prize for which God has called me heavenward in Christ Jesus.

"FATHER, I WANT those you have given me to be with me where I am, and to see my glory, the glory you have given me." — I know whom I have believed, and am convinced that he is able to guard what I have entrusted to him for that day. — He who began a good work in you will carry it on to completion until the day of Christ Jesus.

Do you not know that in a race all the runners run, but only one gets the prize? Run in such a way as to get the prize. Everyone who competes in the games goes into strict training. They do it to get a crown that will not last; but we do it to get a crown that will last forever. — Let us throw off everything that hinders and the sin that so easily entangles, and let us run with perseverance the race marked out for us. Let us fix our eyes on Jesus.

PHIL. 3:13–14. John 17:24. 2 Tim. 1:12. Phil. 1:6. 1 Cor. 9:24–25. Heb. 12:1–2.

EVENING

The LORD himself goes before you and will be with you; he will never leave you nor forsake you.

IF YOUR PRESENCE does not go with us, do not send us up from here. — I know, O LORD, that a man's life is not his own; it is not for man to direct his steps.

The LORD delights in the way of the man whose steps he has made firm; though he stumble, he will not fall, for the LORD upholds him with his hand.

I am always with you; you hold me by my right hand. You guide me with your counsel, and afterward you will take me into glory. — For I am convinced that neither death nor life, neither angels nor demons, neither the present nor the future, nor any powers, neither height nor depth, nor anything else in all creation, will be able to separate us from the love of God that is in Christ Jesus our Lord.

DEUT. 31:8. Exod. 33:15. Jer. 10:23. Pss. 37:23–24; 73:23–24. Rom. 8:38–39.

JANUARY 2

MORNING

Sing to the Lord a new song.

SING FOR JOY to God our strength; shout aloud to the God of Jacob! Begin the music, strike the tambourine, play the melodious harp and lyre.... He put a new song in my mouth, a hymn of praise to our God. Many will see and fear and put their trust in the LORD.

"Be strong and courageous. Do not be terrified; do not be discouraged, for the LORD your God will be with you wherever you go." — "For the joy of the LORD is your strength." — Paul thanked God and was encouraged.

And do this, understanding the present time. The hour has come for you to wake up from your slumber, because our salvation is nearer now than when we first believed. The night is nearly over; the day is almost here. So let us put aside the deeds of darkness and put on the armor of light. Let us behave decently, as in the daytime, not in orgies and drunkenness, not in sexual immorality and debauchery, not in dissension and jealousy. Rather, clothe yourselves with the Lord Jesus Christ, and do not think about how to gratify the desires of the sinful nature.

ISA. 42:10. Pss. 81:1–2; 40:3. Josh. 1:9. Neh. 8:10. Acts 28:15. Rom. 13:11–14.

EVENING

May my prayer be set before you like incense; may the lifting up of my hands be like the evening sacrifice.

MAKE AN ALTAR of acacia wood for burning incense.... Put the altar in front of the curtain that is before the ark of the Testimony — before the atonement cover that is over the Testimony — where I will meet with you. Aaron must burn fragrant incense on the altar every morning when he tends the lamps. He must burn incense again when he lights the lamps at twilight so incense will burn regularly before the LORD for the generations to come.

[Jesus] is able to save completely those who come to God through him, because he always lives to intercede for them. — The smoke of the incense, together with the prayers of the saints, went up before God from the angel's hand.

You also, like living stones, are being built into a spiritual house to be a holy priesthood, offering spiritual sacrifices acceptable to God through Jesus Christ.

Pray continually.

PS. 141:2. Exod. 30:1, 6–8. Heb. 7:25. Rev. 8:4. 1 Peter 2:5. 1 Thess. 5:17.

JANUARY 3

MORNING

He led them by a straight way.

IN A DESERT land he found him [Jacob], in a barren and howling waste. He shielded him and cared for him; he guarded him as the apple of his eye, like an eagle that stirs up its nest and hovers over its young, that spreads its wings to catch them and carries them on its pinions. The LORD alone led him; no foreign god was with him. — "Even to your old age and gray hairs I am he, I am he who will sustain you. I have made you and I will carry you; I will sustain you and I will rescue you."

He restores my soul. He guides me in paths of righteousness for his name's sake. Even though I walk through the valley of the shadow of death, I will fear no evil, for you are with me; your rod and your staff, they comfort me.

The LORD will guide you always; he will satisfy your needs in a sun-scorched land and will strengthen your frame. You will be like a well-watered garden, like a spring whose waters never fail. — For this God is our God for ever and ever; he will be our guide even to the end. — Who is a teacher like him?

PS. 107:7. Deut. 32:10 – 12. Isa. 46:4. Ps. 23:3 – 4. Isa. 58:11. Ps. 48:14. Job 36:22.

EVENING

"What do you want me to do for you?" ... "Lord, I want to see."

OPEN MY EYES that I may see wonderful things in your law.

Then he opened their minds so they could understand the Scriptures. — But the Counselor, the Holy Spirit, whom the Father will send in my name, will teach you all things. — Every good and perfect gift is from above, coming down from the Father of the heavenly lights.

The God of our Lord Jesus Christ, the glorious Father, may give you the Spirit of wisdom and revelation, so that you may know him better. I pray also that the eyes of your heart may be enlightened in order that you may know the hope to which he has called you, the riches of his glorious inheritance in the saints, and this incomparably great power for us who believe. That power is like the working of his mighty strength.

LUKE 18:41. Ps. 119:18. Luke 24:45. John 14:26. James 1:17. Eph. 1:17 – 19.

JANUARY 4

MORNING

Since you have not yet reached the resting place and the inheritance the LORD your God is gluing you.

THIS IS NOT your resting place. — There remains, then, a Sabbath-rest for the people of God.... It enters the inner sanctuary behind the curtain, where Jesus, who went before us, has entered on our behalf.

In my Father's house are many rooms; if it were not so, I would have told you. I am going there to prepare a place for you. And if I go and prepare a place for you, I will come back and take you to be with me that you also may be where I am. — With Christ, which is better by far.

[God] will wipe every tear from their eyes. There will be no more death or mourning or crying or pain, for the old order of things has passed away. — There the wicked cease from turmoil, and there the weary are at rest.

But store up for yourselves treasures in heaven, where moth and rust do not destroy, and where thieves do not break in and steal. For where your treasure is, there your heart will be also. — Set your minds on things above, not on earthly things.

DEUT. 12:9. Mic. 2:10. Heb. 4:9; 6:19 – 20. John 14:2 – 3. Phil. 1:23. Rev. 21:4. Job 3:17. Matt. 6:20 – 21. Col. 3:2.

EVENING

"Where, O death, is your victory? Where, O death, is your sting?"

THE STING OF death is sin. — Then Christ would have had to suffer many times since the creation of the world. But now he has appeared once for all at the end of the ages to do away with sin by the sacrifice of himself. Just as man is destined to die once, and after that to face judgment, so Christ was sacrificed once to take away the sins of many people; and he will appear a second time, not to bear sin, but to bring salvation to those who are waiting for him.

Since the children have flesh and blood, he too shared in their humanity so that by his death he might destroy him who holds the power of death — that is, the devil — and free those who all their lives were held in slavery by their fear of death.

For I am already being poured out like a drink offering, and the time has come for my departure. I have fought the good fight, I have finished the race, I have kept the faith. Now there is in store for me the crown of righteousness.

1 COR. 15:55. 1 Cor. 15:56. Heb. 9:26 – 28; 6:14 – 15. 2 Tim. 4:6 – 8.

JANUARY 5

MORNING

We who have believed enter that rest.

THEY WEARY THEMSELVES with sinning. — I see another law at work in the members of my body, waging war against the law of my mind and making me a prisoner of the law of sin at work within my members. What a wretched man I am! Who will rescue me from this body of death?

"Come to me, all you who are weary and burdened, and I will give you rest." — Therefore, since we have been justified through faith, we have peace with God through our Lord Jesus Christ, through whom we have gained access by faith into this grace in which we now stand. And we rejoice in the hope of the glory of God.

For anyone who enters God's rest also rests from his own work. — Not having a righteousness of my own that comes from the law, but that which is through faith in Christ — the righteousness that comes from God and is by faith. — "This is the resting place, let the weary rest" and, "This is the place of repose."

HEB. 4:3. Jer. 9:5. Rom. 7:23–24. Matt. 11:28. Rom. 5:1–2. Heb. 4:10. Phil. 3:9. Isa. 28:12.

EVENING

Set a guard over my mouth, O LORD; keep watch over the door of my lips.

IF YOU, O LORD, kept a record of sins, O LORD, who could stand?... For they rebelled against the Spirit of God, and rash words came from Moses' lips.

"What goes into a man's mouth does not make him 'unclean,' but what comes out of his mouth, that is what makes him 'unclean.'"

A gossip separates close friends.... Reckless words pierce like a sword, but the tongue of the wise brings healing. Truthful lips endure forever, but a lying tongue lasts only a moment. — But no man can tame the tongue. It is a restless evil, full of deadly poison.... Out of the same mouth come praise and cursing. My brothers, this should not be.

But now you must rid yourselves of all such things as these: anger, rage, malice, slander, and filthy language from your lips. Do not lie to each other, since you have taken off your old self with its practices. — It is God's will that you should be holy. — No lie was found in their mouths; they are blameless.

PS. 141:3. Pss. 130:3; 106:33. Matt. 15:11. Prov. 16:28; 12:18–19. James 3:8, 10. Col. 3:8–9. 1 Thess. 4:3. Rev. 14:5.

JANUARY 6

MORNING

May the favor of the Lord our God rest upon us; establish the work of our hands for us.

AND YOUR FAME spread among the nations on account of your beauty, because the splendor I had given you made your beauty perfect, declares the Sovereign LORD. — And we, who with unveiled faces all reflect the Lord's glory, are being transformed into his likeness with ever-increasing glory, which comes from the Lord, who is the Spirit. — The Spirit of glory and of God rests on you.

Blessed are all who fear the LORD, who walk in his ways. You will eat the fruit of your labor; blessings and prosperity will be yours. Commit to the LORD whatever you do, and your plans will succeed.

Continue to work out your salvation with fear and trembling, for it is God who works in you to will and to act. — May our Lord Jesus Christ himself and God our Father, who loved us and by his grace gave us eternal encouragement and good hope, encourage your hearts and strengthen you in every good deed and word.

PS. 90:17. Ezek. 16:14. 2 Cor. 3:18. 1 Peter 4:14. Ps. 128:1–2. Prov. 16:3. Phil. 2:12–13. 2 Thess. 2:16–17.

EVENING

The apostles gathered around Jesus and reported to him all they had done and taught.

THERE IS A friend who sticks closer than a brother. — The LORD would speak to Moses face to face, as a man speaks with his friend. — "You are my friends if you do what I command. I no longer call you servants, because a servant does not know his master's business. Instead, I have called you friends, for everything that I learned from my Father I have made known to you."

"When you have done everything you were told to do, [you] should say, 'We are unworthy servants; we have only done our duty.'"

For you did not receive a spirit that makes you a slave again to fear, but you received the Spirit of sonship. And by him we cry, "Abba, Father."

In everything, by prayer and petition, with thanksgiving, present your requests to God. — The prayer of the upright pleases him.

MARK 6:30. Prov. 18:24. Exod. 33:11. John 15:14–15. Luke 17:10. Rom. 8:15. Phil. 4:6. Prov. 15:8.

JANUARY 7

MORNING

Remember me with favor, O my God.

"I REMEMBER THE devotion of your youth, how as a bride you loved me and followed me through the desert, through a land not sown." — "Yet I will remember the covenant I made with you in the days of your youth, and I will establish an everlasting covenant with you." — "I will come to you and fulfill my gracious promise to bring you back to this place. For I know the plans I have for you," declares the LORD, "plans to prosper you and not to harm you, plans to give you hope and a future."

"As the heavens are higher than the earth, so are my ways higher than your ways and my thoughts than your thoughts. — "But if it were I, I would appeal to God; I would lay my cause before him. He performs wonders that cannot be fathomed, miracles that cannot be counted." — Many, O LORD my God, are the wonders you have done. The things you planned for us no one can recount to you; were I to speak and tell of them, they would be too many to declare.

NEH. 5:19. Jer. 2:2. Ezek. 16:60. Jer. 29:10–11. Isa. 55:9. Job 5:8–9. Ps. 40:5.

EVENING

I will never leave you or forsake you.

NOT ONE OF all the LORD's good promises to the house of Israel failed; every one was fulfilled. — God is not a man, that he should lie, nor a son of man, that he should change his mind. Does he speak and then not act? Does he promise and not fulfill? — Know therefore that the LORD your God is God; he is the faithful God, keeping his covenant of love to a thousand generations of those who love him and keep his commands. He remembers His covenant forever.

"Can a mother forget the baby at her breast and have no compassion on the child she has borne? Though she may forget, I will not forget you! See, I have engraved you on the palms of my hands.

"The LORD your God is with you, he is mighty to save. He will take great delight in you, he will quiet you with his love, he will rejoice over you with singing."

JOSH. 1:5. Josh. 21:45. Num. 23:19. Deut. 7:9. Ps. 111:5. Isa. 49:15–16. Zeph. 3:17.

JANUARY 8

MORNING

Those who know your name will trust in you, for you, LORD,
have never forsaken those who seek you.

THE NAME OF the LORD is a strong tower; the righteous run to it and are safe. — "I will trust and not be afraid. The LORD, the LORD, is my strength and my song; he has become my salvation."

I was young and now I am old, yet I have never seen the righteous forsaken or their children begging bread.... For the LORD loves the just and will not forsake his faithful ones. They will be protected forever, but the offspring of the wicked will be cut off. — For the sake of his great name the LORD will not reject his people, because the LORD was pleased to make you his own. — He has delivered us from such a deadly peril, and he will deliver us. On him we have set our hope that he will continue to deliver us.

Be content with what you have, because God has said, "Never will I leave you; never will I forsake you." — So we say with confidence, "The Lord is my helper, I will not be afraid."

PS. 9:10. Prov. 18:10. Isa. 12:2. Ps. 37:25, 28. 1 Sam. 12:22. 2 Cor. 1:10. Heb. 13:5 – 6.

EVENING

No lie was found in their mouths; they are blameless.

"SEARCH WILL BE made for Israel's guilt, but there will be none, and for the sins of Judah, but none will be found, for I will forgive the remnant I spare." — Who is a God like you, who pardons sin and forgives the transgression of the remnant of his inheritance? You do not stay angry forever but delight to show mercy. You will again have compassion on us; you will tread our sins underfoot and hurl all our iniquities into the depths of the sea.

He has freely given us in the One he loves. — To present you holy in his sight, without blemish and free from accusation.

To him who is able to keep you from falling and to present you before his glorious presence without fault and with great joy — to the only God our Savior be glory, majesty, power and authority, through Jesus Christ our Lord, before all ages, now and forevermore! Amen.

REV. 14:5. Jer. 50:20. Mic. 7:18 – 19. Eph. 1:6. Col. 1:22. Jude 24 – 25.

JANUARY 9

MORNING

*But for those who fear you, you have raised a banner to be
unfurled against the bow.*

THE LORD IS my Banner. — For he will come like a pent-up flood that the breath of the LORD drives along.

We will shout for joy when you are victorious and will lift up our banners in the name of our God. — "The LORD has vindicated us; come, let us tell in Zion what the LORD our God has done." — No, in all these things we are more than conquerors through him who loved us. — But thanks be to God! He gives us the victory through our Lord Jesus Christ. — The author of their salvation.

Finally, be strong in the Lord and in his mighty power. — By truth they triumph. — Fight the battles of the LORD. — "Be strong, all you people of the land," declares the LORD, "and work. For I am with you." — "Open your eyes and look at the fields! They are ripe for harvest." — For in just a very little while, "He who is coming will come and will not delay."

PS. 60:4. Exod. 17:15. Isa. 59:19. Ps. 20:5. Jer. 51:10. Rom. 8:37. 1 Cor. 15:57.
Heb. 2:10. Eph. 6:10. Jer. 9:3. Isa. 18:17. Hag. 2:4–5. John 4:35. Heb. 10:37.

EVENING

Only one thing is needed.

MANY ARE ASKING, "Who can show us any good?" Let the light of your face shine upon us, O LORD. You have filled my heart with greater joy than when their grain and new wine abound.

As the deer pants for streams of water, so my soul pants for you, O God. My soul thirsts for God, for the living God.... O God, you are my God, earnestly I seek you; my soul thirsts for you, my body longs for you, in a dry and weary land where there is no water.

"I am the bread of life. He who comes to me will never go hungry, and he who believes in me will never be thirsty.... "Sir," they said, "from now on give us this bread." — Mary ... sat at the Lord's feet listening to what he said. — One thing I ask of the LORD, this is what I seek: that I may dwell in the house of the LORD all the days of my life, to gaze upon the beauty of the LORD and to seek him in his temple.

LUKE 10:42. Pss. 4:6–7; 42:1–2; 63:1. John 6:35. 34. Luke 10:39. Ps. 27:4.

JANUARY 10

MORNING

May your whole spirit, soul and body be kept blameless at the coming of our Lord Jesus Christ.

CHRIST LOVED THE church and gave himself up for her, . . . to present her to himself as a radiant church, without stain or wrinkle or any other blemish, but holy and blameless. — We proclaim him, admonishing and teaching everyone with all wisdom, so that we may present everyone perfect in Christ.

The peace of God . . . transcends all understanding. — Let the peace of Christ rule in your hearts, since as members of one body you were called to peace.

May our Lord Jesus Christ himself and God our Father, who loved us and by his grace gave us eternal encouragement and good hope, encourage your hearts and strengthen you in every good deed and word. — He will keep you strong to the end, so that you will be blameless on the day of our Lord Jesus.

1 THESS. 5:23. Eph. 5:25, 27. Col. 1:28. Phil. 4:7. Col. 3:15. 2 Thess. 2:16–17. 1 Cor. 1:8.

EVENING

"But will God really dwell on earth with men?"

"THEN HAVE THEM make a sanctuary for me, and I will dwell among them." . . . There also I will meet with the Israelites, and the place will be consecrated by my glory. . . . Then I will dwell among the Israelites and be their God. — When you ascended on high, you led captives in your train; you received gifts from men, even from the rebellious — that you, O LORD God, might dwell there.

For we are the temple of the living God. As God has said: "I will live with them and walk among them, and I will be their God, and they will be my people." — Your body is a temple of the Holy Spirit, who is in you. — And in him you too are being built together to become a dwelling in which God lives by his Spirit.

"Then the nations will know that I the LORD make Israel holy, when my sanctuary is among them forever."

2 CHRON. 6:18. Exod. 25:8; 29:43, 45. Ps. 68:18. 2 Cor. 6:16. 1 Cor. 6:19. Eph. 2:22. Ezek. 37:28.

JANUARY 11

MORNING

Praise awaits you, O God, in Zion.

FOR US THERE is but one God, the Father, from whom all things came and for whom we live; and there is but one Lord, Jesus Christ, through whom all things came and through whom we live. — That all may honor the Son just as they honor the Father. He who does not honor the Son does not honor the Father, who sent him. — Through Jesus, therefore, let us continually offer to God a sacrifice of praise — the fruit of lips that confess his name. — "He who sacrifices thank offerings honors me, and he prepares the way so that I may show him the salvation of God."

After this I looked and there before me was a great multitude that no one could count, from every nation, tribe, people and language, standing before the throne and in front of the Lamb. They were wearing white robes and were holding palm branches in their hands. And they cried out in a loud voice: "Salvation belongs to our God, who sits on the throne, and to the Lamb." ... "Amen! Praise and glory and wisdom and thanks and honor and power and strength be to our God for ever and ever. Amen!"

PS. 65:1. 1 Cor. 8:6. John 5:23. Heb. 13:15. Ps. 50:23. Rev. 7:9 – 10, 12.

EVENING

He redeems my life from the pit.

YET THEIR REDEEMER is strong; the LORD Almighty is his name. — "I will ransom them from the power of the grave; I will redeem them from death. Where, O death, are your plagues? Where, O grave, is your destruction?"

Since the children have flesh and blood, he too shared in their humanity so that by his death he might destroy him who holds the power of death — that is, the devil — and free those who all their lives were held in slavery by their fear of death.

"Whoever believes in the Son has eternal life, but whoever rejects the Son will not see life, for God's wrath remains on him."

For you died and your life is now hidden with Christ in God. When Christ, who is your life, appears, then you also will appear with him in glory. — On the day he comes to be glorified in his holy people and to be marveled at among all those who have believed.

PS. 103:4. Jer. 50:34. Hos. 13:14. Heb. 2:14 – 15. John 3:36. Col. 3:3 – 4. 2 Thess. 1:10.

January 12

Morning

The only God our Savior.

Christ Jesus ... has become for us wisdom from God—that is, our righteousness, holiness and redemption.—Can you fathom the mysteries of God? Can you probe the limits of the Almighty? They are higher than the heavens—what can you do? They are deeper than the depths of the grave—what can you know?

No, we speak of God's secret wisdom, a wisdom that has been hidden and that God destined for our glory before time began.—This mystery, which for ages past was kept hidden in God, who created all things. His intent was that now, through the church, the manifold wisdom of God should be made known to the rulers and authorities in the heavenly realms.

If any of you lacks wisdom, he should ask God, who gives generously to all without finding fault, and it will be given to him.... But the wisdom that comes from heaven is first of all pure; then peace loving, considerate, submissive, full of mercy and good fruit, impartial and sincere.

JUDE 25. 1 Cor. 1:30. Job 11:7–8. 1 Cor. 2:7. Eph. 3:9–10. James 1:5; 3:17.

Evening

"When I lie down I think, 'How long before I get up?'"

"Watchman, what is left of the night?" The watchman replies, "Morning is coming."

For in just a very little while, "He who is coming will come and will not delay."—He is like the light of morning at sunrise on a cloudless morning.

"I am going there to prepare a place for you. And if I go and prepare a place for you, I will come back and take you to be with me that you also may be where I am.... Do not let your hearts be troubled and do not be afraid. You heard me say, 'I am going away and I am coming back to you.'"

"So may all your enemies perish, O Lord! But may they who love you be like the sun when it rises in its strength."—You are all sons of the light and sons of the day. We do not belong to the night or to the darkness.—There will be no night there.

JOB 7:4. Isa. 21:11–12. Heb. 10:37. 2 Sam. 23:4. John 14:2–3. 27–28. Judg. 5:31.
1 Thess. 5:5. Rev. 21:25.

JANUARY 13

MORNING

You will keep in perfect peace him whose mind is steadfast,
because he trusts in you.

CAST YOUR CARES on the Lord and he will sustain you; he will never let the righteous fall. — "I will trust and not be afraid. The Lord, the LORD, is my strength and my song; he has become my salvation."

"You of little faith, why are you so afraid?" — Do not be anxious about anything, but in everything, by prayer and petition, with thanksgiving, present your requests to God. And the peace of God, which transcends all understanding, will guard your hearts and your minds in Christ Jesus. — In quietness and trust is your strength.

The effect of righteousness will be quietness and confidence forever. — "Peace I leave with you; my peace I give you. I do not give to you as the world gives. Do not let your hearts be troubled and do not be afraid." — Grace and peace to you from him who is, and who was, and who is to come.

ISA. 26:3. Ps. 55:22. Isa. 12:2. Matt. 8:26. Phil. 4:6–7. Isa. 30:15; 32:17. John 14:27. Rev. 1:4.

EVENING

Do not let the sun go down while you are still angry.

"IF YOUR BROTHER sins against you, go and show him his fault, just between the two of you. If he listens to you, you have won your brother over." ... "Lord, how many times shall I forgive my brother when he sins against me? Up to seven times?" Jesus answered, "I tell you, not seven times, but seventy-seven times." — When you stand praying, if you hold anything against anyone, forgive him, so that your Father in heaven may forgive you your sins."

Therefore, as God's chosen people, holy and dearly loved, clothe yourselves with compassion, kindness, humility, gentleness and patience. Bear with each other and forgive whatever grievances you may have against one another. Forgive as the Lord forgave you. — Be kind and compassionate to one another, forgiving each other, just as in Christ God forgave you.

The apostles said to the Lord, "Increase our faith!"

EPH. 4:26. Matt. 18:15, 21–22. Mark 11:25. Col. 3:12–13. Eph. 4:32. Luke 17:5.

JANUARY 14

MORNING

"The Father is greater than I."

"WHEN YOU PRAY, say: 'Father, hallowed be your name, your kingdom come.'" — "My Father and your Father, ... my God and your God." — "I do exactly what my Father has commanded me." ... The words I say to you are not just my own. Rather, it is the Father, living in me, who is doing his work."

"The Father loves the Son and has placed everything in his hands." ... "For you granted him authority over all people that he might give eternal life to all those you have given him."

"Lord, show us the Father and that will be enough for us." Jesus answered: "Don't you know me, Philip, even after I have been among you such a long time? Anyone who has seen me has seen the Father. How can you say, 'Show us the Father'?" ... "Don't you believe that I am in the Father, and that the Father is in me?" ... "I and the Father are one." ... "As the Father has loved me, so have I loved you. Now remain in my love. If you obey my commands, you will remain in my love, just as I have obeyed my Father's commands and remain in his love."

JOHN 14:28. Luke 11:2. John 20:17; 14:31, 10; 3:35; 17:2; 14:8 – 10; 10:30; 15:9 – 10.

EVENING

"He will crush your head, and you will strike his heel."

HIS APPEARANCE WAS so disfigured beyond that of any man and his form marred beyond human likeness.... But he was pierced for our transgressions, he was crushed for our iniquities; the punishment that brought us peace was upon him, and by his wounds we are healed.

"But this is your hour — when darkness reigns." — "You would have no power over me if it were not given to you from above.

The reason the Son of God appeared was to destroy the devil's work. — He also drove out many demons, but he would not let the demons speak because they knew who he was.

"All authority in heaven and on earth has been given to me." — The God of peace will soon crush Satan under your feet.

GEN. 3:15. Isa. 52:14; 53:5. Luke 22:53. John 19:11. 1 John 3:8. Mark 1:34. Matt. 28:18. Mark 16:17. Rom. 16:20.

JANUARY 15

MORNING

I am hid low in the dust; renew my life according to your word.

SINCE, THEN, YOU have been raised with Christ, set your hearts on things above, where Christ is seated at the right hand of God. — Set your minds on things above, not on earthly things. For you died, and your life is now hidden with Christ in God. — But our citizenship is in heaven. And we eagerly await a Savior from there, the Lord Jesus Christ, who, by the power that enables him to bring everything under his control, will transform our lowly bodies so that they will be like his glorious body.

For the sinful nature desires what is contrary to the Spirit, and the Spirit what is contrary to the sinful nature. They are in conflict with each other, so that you do not do what you want. — Brothers, we have an obligation — but it is not to the sinful nature to live according to it. For if you live according to the sinful nature, you will die; but if by the Spirit you put to death the misdeeds of the body, you will live. I urge you, as aliens and strangers in the world, to abstain from sinful desires, which war against your soul.

PS. 119:25. Col. 3:1–3. Phil. 3:20–21. Gal. 5:17. Rom. 8:12–13. 1 Peter 2:11.

EVENING

The measure of faith.

HIM WHOSE FAITH is weak.... Strengthened in his faith and gave glory to God. "You of little faith," he said, "why did you doubt?" ... "Woman, you have great faith! Your request is granted."

"Do you believe that I am able to do this?" "Yes, Lord," they replied. "According to your faith will it be done to you."

"Lord, increase our faith." — Build yourselves up in your most holy faith — rooted and built up in him, strengthened in the faith as you were taught, and overflowing with thankfulness.

Now it is God who makes both us and you stand firm in Christ. — And the God of all grace, who called you to his eternal glory in Christ, after you have suffered a little while, will himself restore you and make you strong, firm and steadfast.

We who are strong ought to bear with the failings of the weak and not to please ourselves.... Therefore let us stop passing judgment on one another. Instead, make up your mind not to put any stumbling block or obstacle in your brother's way.

ROM. 12:3. Rom. 14:1; 4:20. Matt. 14:31; 15:28; 9:28–29. Luke 17:5. Jude 20. Col. 2:7. 2 Cor. 1:21. 1 Peter 5:10. Rom. 15:1; 14:13.

January 16

Morning

For God was pleased to have all his fullness dwell in him.

THE FATHER LOVES the Son and has placed everything in his hands.—God exalted him to the highest place and gave him the name that is above every name, that at the name of Jesus every knee should bow, in heaven and on earth and under the earth, and every tongue confess that Jesus Christ is Lord, to the glory of God the Father.—Far above all rule and authority, power and dominion, and every title that can be given, not only in the present age but also in the one to come.—For by him all things were created: things in heaven and on earth, visible and invisible, whether thrones or powers or rulers or authorities; all things were created by him and for him.

Christ died and returned to life so that he might be the Lord of both the dead and the living.—You have been given fullness in Christ, who is the head over every power and authority.—From the fullness of his grace we have all received one blessing after another.

COL. 1:19. John 3:35. Phil. 2:9–11. Eph. 1:21. Col. 1:16. Rom. 14:9. Col. 2:10. John 1:16.

Evening

"Write, therefore, what you have seen, what is now and what will take place later."

BUT MEN SPOKE from God as they were carried along by the Holy Spirit.—We proclaim to you what we have seen and heard, so that you also may have fellowship with us. And our fellowship is with the Father and with his Son, Jesus Christ. "Look at my hands and my feet. It is I myself! Touch me and see; a ghost does not have flesh and bones, as you see I have." When he had said this, he showed them his hands and feet.—The man who saw it has given testimony, and his testimony is true. He knows that he tells the truth, and he testifies so that you also may believe.

We did not follow cleverly invented stories when we told you about the power and coming of our Lord Jesus Christ, but we were eyewitnesses of his majesty.—So that your faith might not rest on men's wisdom, but on God's power.

REV. 1:19. 2 Peter 1:21. 1 John 1:3. Luke 24:39–40. John 19:35. 2 Peter 1:16. 1 Cor. 2:5.

JANUARY 17

MORNING

In your love you kept me from the pit of destruction.

HE SENT HIS one and only Son into the world that we might live through him. This is love: not that we loved God, but that he loved us and sent his Son as an atoning sacrifice for our sins.

Who is a God like you, who pardons sin and forgives the transgression of the remnant of his inheritance? You do not stay angry forever but delight to show mercy. You will again have compassion on us; you will tread our sins underfoot and hurl all our iniquities into the depths of the sea. — O LORD my God, I called to you for help and you healed me. O LORD, you brought me up from the grave; you spared me from going down into the pit.

"When my life was ebbing away, I remembered you, LORD, and my prayer rose to you, to your holy temple." — I waited patiently for the LORD; he turned to me and heard my cry. He lifted me out of the slimy pit, out of the mud and mire; he set my feet on a rock.

ISA. 38:17. 1 John 4:9 – 10. Mic. 7:18 – 19. Ps. 30:2 – 3. John 2:7. Ps. 40:1 – 2.

EVENING

What is now.

NOW WE SEE but a poor reflection. — At present we do not see everything subject to him.

And we have the word of the prophets made more certain, and you will do well to pay attention to it, as to a light shining in a dark place, until the day dawns and the morning star rises in your hearts. — Your word is a lamp to my feet and a light for my path.

But, dear friends, remember what the apostles of our Lord Jesus Christ foretold. They said to you, "In the last times mere will be scoffers who will follow their own ungodly desires." — The Spirit clearly says that in later times some will abandon the faith and follow deceiving spirits and things taught by demons.

Dear children, this is the last hour. — The night is nearly over; the day is almost here. So let us put aside the deeds of darkness and put on the armor of light.

REV. 1:19. 1 Cor. 13:12. Heb. 2:8. 2 Peter 1:19. Ps. 119:105. Jude 17 – 18. 1 Tim. 4:1. 1 John 2:18. Rom. 13:12.

JANUARY 18

MORNING

The one to come.

JESUS, WHO WAS made a little lower than the angels, now crowned with glory and honor because he suffered death, so that by the grace of God he might taste death for everyone.—One died for all.—For just as through the disobedience of the one man the many were made sinners, so also through the obedience of the one man the many will be made righteous.

"The first man Adam became a living being"; the last Adam, a life-giving spirit. The spiritual did not come first, but the natural, and after that the spiritual.—God said, "Let us make man in our image, in our likeness." ... So God created man in his own image, in the image of God he created him.—But in these last days he has spoken to us by his Son, whom he appointed heir of all things, and through whom he made the universe. The Son is the radiance of God's glory and the exact representation of his being.—For you granted him authority over all people.

ROM. 5:14. Heb. 2:9. 2 Cor. 5:14. Rom. 5:19. 1 Cor. 15:45–46. Gen. 1:26–27. Heb. 1:2–3. John 17:2.

EVENING

What will take place later.

IT IS WRITTEN: "No eye has seen, nor ear has heard, no mind has conceived what God has prepared for those who love him."—But God has revealed it to us by his Spirit.

Look, he is coming with the clouds, and every eye will see him, even those who pierced him; and all the peoples of the earth will mourn because of him. So shall it be! Amen.

Brothers, we do not want you to be ignorant about those who fall asleep, or to grieve like the rest of men, who have no hope. We believe that Jesus died and rose again and so we believe that God will bring with Jesus those who have fallen asleep in him.... For the Lord himself will come down from heaven, with a loud command, with the voice of the archangel and with the trumpet call of God, and the dead in Christ will rise first. After that, we who are still alive and are left will be caught up with them in the clouds to meet the Lord in the air. And so we will be with the Lord forever.

REV. 1:19. 1 Cor. 2:9–10. John 16:13. Rev. 1:7. 1 Thess. 4:13–14, 16–17.

JANUARY 19

MORNING

I served the Lord with great humility.

"WHOEVER WANTS TO become great among you must be your servant, and whoever wants to be first must be your slave — just as the Son of Man did not come to be served, but to serve, and to give his life as a ransom for many."

If anyone thinks he is something when he is nothing, he deceives himself. — For by the grace given me I say to every one of you: Do not think of yourself more highly than you ought, but rather think of yourself with sober judgment, in accordance with the measure of faith God has given you. — When you have done everything you were told to do, [you] should say, 'We are unworthy servants; we have only done our duty.'"

Now this is our boast: ... we have conducted ourselves in the world ... in the holiness and sincerity that are from God. We have done so not according to worldly wisdom but according to God's grace.... But we have this treasure in jars of clay to show that this all-surpassing power is from God and not from us.

ACTS 20:19. Matt. 20:26–28. Gal. 6:3. Rom. 12:3. Luke 17:10. 2 Cor. 1:12; 4:7.

EVENING

Each of us has turned to his own way.

NOAH, A MAN of the soil, proceeded to plant a vineyard. When he drank some of its wine, he became drunk.... Abram ... said to his wife Sarai,... "Say you are my sister, so that I will be treated well for your sake." ... Then Isaac said to Jacob,... "Are you really my son Esau?"...

"I am," he replied. — And rash words came from Moses' lips.

The men of Israel sampled their provisions but did not inquire of the LORD. Then Joshua made a treaty of peace with them. — For David had done what was right in the eyes of the LORD and had not failed to keep any of the LORD's commands all the days of his life — except in the case of Uriah the Hittite.

These were all commended for their faith. — And are justified freely by his grace through the redemption that came by Christ Jesus. — For the transgression of my people he was stricken.

I am not doing this for your sake, declares the Sovereign LORD. Be ashamed and disgraced for your conduct.

ISA. 53:6. Gen. 9:20–21; 12:11. 13; 27:21, 24. Ps. 106:33. Josh. 9:14–15. 1 Kings 15:5. Heb. 11:39. Rom. 3:24. Isa. 53:8. Ezek. 36:32.

JANUARY 20

MORNING

And he will be called Wonderful.

THE WORD BECAME flesh and lived for a while among us. We have seen his glory, the glory of the one and only Son, who came from the Father, full of grace and truth. — For you have exalted above all things your name and your word.

"They will call him Immanuel" — which means, "God with us," . . . "Jesus, because he will save his people from their sins."

All may honor the Son just as they honor the Father. — Therefore God exalted him to the highest place and gave him the name that is above every name. — Far above all rule and authority, power and dominion, and every title that can be given, not only in the present age but also in the one to come. And God placed all things under his feet. — He has a name written on him that no one but he himself knows. . . . king of kings and lord of lords.

The Almighty is beyond our reach. — What is his name, and the name of his son? Tell me if you know!

ISA. 9:6. John 1:14. Ps. 138:2. Matt. 1:23, 21. John 5:23. Phil. 2:9. Eph. 1:21 – 22. Rev. 19:12, 16. Job 37:23. Prov. 30:4.

EVENING

The LORD'S portion is his people.

YOU ARE OF Christ, and Christ is of God. — I belong to my lover, and his desire is for me. . . . I am his. — The Son of God, who loved me and gave himself for me.

You are not your own; you were bought at a price. Therefore honor God with your body. — But as for you, the LORD took you and brought you out of the iron-smelting furnace, out of Egypt, to be the people of his inheritance, as you now are.

For we are God's fellow workers; you are God's field, God's building. — Christ is faithful as a son over God's house. And we are his house, if we hold on to our courage and the hope of which we boast. — A spiritual house to be a holy priesthood.

"They will be mine," says the LORD Almighty, "in the day when I make up my treasured possession." — "All I have is yours, and all you have is mine. And glory has come to me through them." — The riches of his glorious inheritance in the saints.

DEUT. 32:9. 1 Cor. 3:23. Song of Songs 7:10; 2:16. Gal. 2:20. 1 Cor. 6:19 – 20. Deut. 4:20. 1 Cor. 3:9. Heb. 3:6. 1 Peter 2:5. Mal. 3:17. John 17:10. Eph. 1:18.

JANUARY 21

MORNING

"He cuts off every branch in me that bears no fruit."

FOR HE WILL be like a refiner's fire or a launderer's soap. He will sit as a refiner and purifier of silver; he will purify the Levites and refine them like gold and silver. Then the LORD will have men who will bring offerings in righteousness.

But we also rejoice in our sufferings, because we know that suffering produces perseverance; perseverance, character; and character, hope. And hope does not disappoint us, because God has poured out his love into our hearts by the Holy Spirit, whom he has given us.

Endure hardship as discipline; God is treating you as sons. For what son is not disciplined by his father? If you are not disciplined (and everyone undergoes discipline), then you are illegitimate children and not true sons.... No discipline seems pleasant at the time, but painful. Later on, however, it produces a harvest of righteousness and peace for those who have been trained by it. Therefore, strengthen your feeble arms and weak knees.

JOHN 15:2. Mal. 3:2–3. Rom. 5:3–5. Heb. 12:7–8, 11–12.

EVENING

But now we call the arrogant blessed.

FOR THIS IS what the high and lofty One says—he who lives forever, whose name is holy: "I live in a high and holy place, but also with him who is contrite and lowly in spirit, to revive the spirit of the lowly and to revive the heart of the contrite."

Better to be lowly in spirit and among the oppressed than to share plunder with the proud.—"Blessed are the poor in spirit, for theirs is the kingdom of heaven."

There are six things the LORD hates, seven that are detestable to him: haughty eyes, a lying tongue, hands that shed innocent blood.... The LORD detests all the proud of heart.

Search me, O God, and know my heart; test me and know my anxious thoughts. See if there is any offensive way in me, and lead me in the way everlasting.

Grace and peace to you from God our Father and the Lord Jesus Christ. I thank my God every time I remember you.—"Blessed are the meek, for they will inherit the earth."

MAL. 3:15. Isa. 57:15. Prov. 16:19. Matt. 5:3. Prov. 6:16–17; 16:5. Ps. 139:23–24.
    Phil. 1:2–3. Matt. 5:5.

JANUARY 22

MORNING

*For this God is our God for ever and ever; he will be our
guide even to the end.*

O LORD, YOU are my God; I will exalt you and praise your name, for in perfect
faithfulness you have done marvelous things, things planned long ago. — LORD,
you have assigned me my portion and my cup.

He guides me in paths of righteousness for his name's sake. Even though I
walk through the valley of the shadow of death, I will fear no evil, for you are with
me; your rod and your staff, they comfort me.... You hold me by my right hand.

You guide me with your counsel, and afterward you will take me into glory.
Whom have I in heaven but you? And being with you, I desire nothing on
earth.... My flesh and my heart may fail, but God is the strength of my heart
and my portion forever.... In him our hearts rejoice, for we trust in his holy
name.... The LORD will fulfill his purpose for me; your love, O LORD, endures
forever—do not abandon the works of your hands.

PS. 48:14. Isa. 25:1. Pss. 16:5; 23:3–4; 73:23–26; 33:21; 138:8.

EVENING

*When anxiety was great within me, your consolation brought
joy to my soul.*

I CALL AS my heart grows faint; lead me to the rock that is higher than I.

I am troubled; O Lord, come to my aid!" — Cast your cares on the LORD and
he will sustain you.

I am only a little child and do not know how to carry out my duties. — If any
of you lacks wisdom, he should ask God, who gives generously to all without
finding fault.

And who is equal to such a task? — I know that nothing good lives in
me. — "My grace is sufficient for you, for my power is made perfect in weakness." — "Take heart, son, your sins are forgiven." — "Take heart, daughter," he
said, "your faith has healed you."

My soul will be satisfied as with the richest of foods. — On my bed I remember you; I think of you through the watches of the night.

**PS. 94:19. Ps. 61:2. Isa. 38:14. Ps. 55:22. 1 Kings 3:7. James 1:5. 2 Cor. 2:16. Rom. 7:18.
2 Cor. 12:9. Matt. 9:2, 22. Ps. 63:5–6.**

JANUARY 23

MORNING

Hope does not disappoint us.

"I am the Lord; those who hope in me will not be disappointed." — "But blessed is the man who trusts in the Lord, whose confidence is in him. You will keep in perfect peace him whose mind is steadfast, because he trusts in you."

Trust in the Lord forever, for the Lord, the Lord, is the Rock eternal. — Find rest, O my soul, in God alone, my hope comes from him. He alone is my rock and my salvation; he is my fortress, I will not be shaken. — I am not ashamed, because I know whom I have believed.

Because God wanted to make the unchanging nature of his purpose very clear to the heirs of what was promised, he confirmed it with an oath. God did this so that, by two unchangeable things in which it is impossible for God to lie, we who have fled to take hold of the hope offered to us may be greatly encouraged. We have this hope as an anchor for the soul, firm and secure. It enters the inner sanctuary behind the curtain, where Jesus, who went before us, has entered on our behalf.

ROM. 5:5. Isa. 49:23. Jer. 17:7. Isa. 26:3–4. Ps. 62:5–6. 2 Tim. 1:12. Heb. 6:17–20.

EVENING

The offense of the cross.

"If anyone would come after me, he must deny himself and take up his cross and follow me."

Don't you know that friendship with the world is hatred toward God? Anyone who chooses to be a friend of the world becomes an enemy of God. — "We must go through many hardships to enter the kingdom of God."

"The one who trusts in him will never be put to shame." — Now to you who believe, this stone is precious. But to those who do not believe, "The stone the builders rejected has become the capstone," and, "A stone that causes men to stumble and a rock that makes them fall."

May I never boast except in the cross of our Lord Jesus Christ, through which the world has been crucified to me, and I to the world.... I have been crucified with Christ.... Those who belong to Christ Jesus have crucified the sinful nature with its passions and desires.

If we endure, we will also reign with him. If we disown him, he will also disown us.

GAL. 5:11. Matt. 16:24. James 4:4. Acts 14:22. Rom. 9:33. 1 Peter 2:7–8. Gal. 6:14; 2:20; 5:24. 2 Tim. 2:12.

January 24

Morning

The Lord is near.

For the Lord himself will come down from heaven, with a loud command, with the voice of the archangel and with the trumpet call of God, and the dead in Christ will rise first. After that, we who are still alive and are left will be caught up with them in the clouds to meet the Lord in the air. And so we will be with the Lord forever. Therefore encourage each other with these words. — He who testifies to these things says, "Yes, I am coming soon." — Amen. Come, Lord Jesus.

So then, dear friends, since you are looking forward to this, make every effort to be found spotless, blameless and at peace with him. — Avoid every kind of evil. — May God himself, the God of peace, sanctify you through and through. May your whole spirit, soul and body be kept blameless at the coming of our Lord Jesus Christ. The one who calls you is faithful and he will do it.

You too, be patient and stand firm, because the Lord's coming is near.

PHIL. 4:5. 1 Thess. 4:16–18. Rev. 22:20. 2 Peter 3:14. 1 Thess. 5:22–24. James 5:8.

Evening

The choicest branch.

My loved one had a vineyard on a fertile hillside. He dug it up and cleared it of stones and planted it with the choicest vines.... Then he looked for a crop of good grapes, but it yielded only bad fruit. — I had planted you like a choice vine of sound and reliable stock. How then did you turn against me into a corrupt, wild vine?

The acts of the sinful nature are obvious: sexual immorality, impurity and debauchery; ... and envy; drunkenness, orgies, and the like. I warn you, as I did before, that those who live like this will not inherit the kingdom of God. But the fruit of the Spirit is love, joy, peace, patience, kindness, goodness, faithfulness, gentleness and self-control.

"I am the true vine and my Father is the gardener. He cuts off every branch in me that bears no fruit, while every branch that does bear fruit he trims clean so that it will be even more fruitful.... Remain in me, and I will remain in you.... This is to my Father's glory, that you bear much fruit, showing yourselves to be my disciples."

GEN. 49:11. Isa. 5:1–2. Jer. 2:21. Gal. 5:19, 21–23. John 15:1–2, 4, 8.

January 25

Morning

This righteousness from God comes through faith in Jesus Christ to all who believe.

God made him who had no sin to be sin for us, so that in him we might become the righteousness of God. — Christ redeemed us from the curse of the law by becoming a curse for us. — Who has become for us wisdom from God — that is, our righteousness, holiness and redemption. — He saved us, not because of righteous things we had done, but because of his mercy. He saved us through the washing of rebirth and renewal by the Holy Spirit, whom he poured out on us generously through Jesus Christ our Savior.

I consider everything a loss compared to the surpassing greatness of knowing Christ Jesus my Lord, for whose sake I have lost all things. I consider them rubbish, that I may gain Christ and be found in him, not having a righteousness of my own that comes from the law, but that which is through faith in Christ — the righteousness that comes from God and is by faith.

ROM. 3:22. 2 Cor. 5:21. Gal. 3:13. 1 Cor. 1:30. Titus 3:5–6. Phil. 3:8–9.

Evening

The Spirit of sonship. And by him we cry, "Abba, Father."

After Jesus said this, he looked toward heaven and prayed: "Father,... Holy Father,... Righteous Father." — "*Abba,* Father." he said. — Because you are sons, God sent the Spirit of his Son into our hearts, the Spirit who calls out, "*Abba, Father.*" — For through him we both have access to the Father by one Spirit. Consequently, you are no longer foreigners and aliens, but fellow citizens with God's people and members of God's household.

But you are our Father, though Abraham does not know us or Israel acknowledge us; you, O Lord, are our Father, our Redeemer from of old is your name.

"I will set out and go back to my father and say to him: Father, I have sinned against heaven and against you. I am no longer worthy to be called your son; make me like one of your hired men." So he got up and went to his father.

Be imitators of God, therefore, as dearly loved children.

ROM. 8:15. John 17:1, 11, 25. Mark 14:36. Gal. 4:6. Eph. 2:18–19. Isa. 63:16.
Luke 15:18–20. Eph. 5:1.

JANUARY 26

MORNING

*Let us, then, go to him outside the camp, bearing the disgrace
he bore. For here we do not have an enduring city, but we are
looking for the city that is to come.*

DEAR FRIENDS, DO not be surprised at the painful trial you are suffering, as though something strange were happening to you. But rejoice that you participate in the sufferings of Christ, so that you may be overjoyed when his glory is revealed.—As you share in our sufferings, so also you share in our comfort.

If you are insulted because of the name of Christ, you are blessed, for the Spirit of glory and of God rests on you.

The apostles left the Sanhedrin, rejoicing because they had been counted worthy of suffering disgrace for the Name.—He chose to be mistreated along with the people of God rather than to enjoy the pleasures of sin for a short time. He regarded disgrace for the sake of Christ as of greater value than the treasures of Egypt, because he was looking ahead to his reward.

HEB. 13:13–14. 1 Peter 4:12–13. 2 Cor. 1:7. 1 Peter 4:14. Acts 5:41. Heb. 11:25–26.

EVENING

*The Lord Jesus Christ ... will transform our lowly bodies so
that they will be like his glorious body.*

ABOVE THE EXPANSE over their heads was what looked like a throne of sapphire, and high above on the throne was a figure like that of a man. I saw that from what appeared to be his waist up he looked like glowing metal, as if full of fire, and that from there down he looked like fire; and brilliant light surrounded him. Like the appearance of a rainbow in the clouds on a rainy day, so was the radiance around him.

This was the appearance of the likeness of the glory of the LORD.

And we, who with unveiled faces all reflect the Lord's glory, are being transformed into his likeness with ever-increasing glory, which comes from the Lord, who is the Spirit.—What we will be has not yet been made known. But we know that when he appears, we shall be like him, for we shall see him as he is.

Never again will they hunger; never again will they thirst.... And [they] sang the song of Moses the servant of God and the song of the Lamb.

PHIL. 3:20–21. Ezek. 1:26–28. 2 Cor. 3:18. 1 John 3:2. Rev. 7:16; 15:3.

January 27

Morning

*But you know that he appeared so that he might take away
our sins. And in him is no sin.*

BUT IN THESE last days he has spoken to us by his Son, whom he appointed heir
of all things, and through whom he made the universe. The Son is the radiance
of God's glory and the exact representation of his being, sustaining all things by
his powerful word. After he had provided purification for sins, he sat down at
the right hand of the Majesty in heaven. — God made him who had no sin to be
sin for us, so that in him we might become the righteousness of God.

Live your lives as strangers here in reverent fear. For you know that it was not
with perishable things such as silver or gold that you were redeemed from the
empty way of life handed down to you from your forefathers, but with the precious blood of Christ, a lamb without blemish or defect. He was chosen before
the creation of the world, but was revealed in these last times for your sake.

For Christ's love compels us, because we are convinced that one died for all,
and therefore all died. And he died for all, that those who live should no longer
live for themselves but for him who died for them and was raised again.

1 JOHN 3:5. Heb. 1:1–3. 2 Cor. 5:21. 1 Peter 1:17–20. 2 Cor. 5:14–15.

Evening

*I have set before you life and death, blessings and curses. Now
choose life, so that you and your children may live.*

FOR I TAKE no pleasure in the death of anyone, declares the Sovereign LORD.
Repent and live!

If I had not come and spoken to them, they would not be guilty of sin. Now,
however, they have no excuse for their sin. — "That servant who knows his master's will and does not get ready or does not do what his master wants will be
beaten with many blows."

The wages of sin is death, but the gift of God is eternal life in Christ Jesus
our Lord. — "Whoever believes in the Son has eternal life, but whoever rejects
the Son will not see life, for God's wrath remains on him." — Don't you know
that when you offer yourselves to someone to obey him as slaves, you are slaves
to the one whom you obey — whether you are slaves to sin, which leads to death,
or to obedience, which leads to righteousness?

DEUT. 30:19. Ezek. 18:32. John 15:22. Luke 12:47. Rom. 6:23. John 3:36. Rom. 6:16.

January 28

Morning

And your strength will equal your days.

"Whenever you are arrested and brought to trial, do not worry beforehand about what to say. Just say whatever is given you at the time, for it is not you speaking, but the Holy Spirit." — "Therefore do not worry about tomorrow, for tomorrow will worry about itself. Each day has enough trouble of its own."

The God of Israel gives power and strength to his people. Praise be to God! — He gives strength to the weary and increases the power of the weak.

"My grace is sufficient for you, for my power is made perfect in weakness." Therefore I will boast all the more gladly about my weaknesses, so that Christ's power may rest on me.... That is why, for Christ's sake, I delight in weaknesses, in insults, in hardships, in persecutions, in difficulties. For when I am weak, then I am strong. — I can do everything through him who gives me strength. — March on, my soul; be strong!

DEUT. 33:25. Mark. 13:11. Matt. 6:34. Ps. 68:35. Isa. 40:29. 2 Cor. 12:9–10. Phil. 4:13. Judg. 5:21.

Evening

Awake, north wind, and ... blow on my garden, that its
fragrance may spread abroad.

No discipline seems pleasant at the time, but painful. Later on, however, it produces a harvest of righteousness and peace for those who have been trained by it. — The fruit of the Spirit.

With his fierce blast he drives her out, as on a day the east wind blows. — As a father has compassion on his children, so the Lord has compassion on those who fear him.

Though outwardly we are wasting away, yet inwardly we are being renewed day by day. For our light and momentary troubles are achieving for us an eternal glory that far outweighs them all. So we look for what is unseen. For what is seen is temporary, but what is unseen is eternal.

Although he [Jesus] was a son, he learned obedience from what he suffered.... But we have one who has been tempted in every way, just as we are — yet was without sin.

SONG OF SONGS 4:16. Heb. 12:11. Gal. 5:22. Isa. 27:8. Ps. 103:13. 2 Cor. 4:16–18. Heb. 5:8; 4:15.

JANUARY 29

MORNING

"You are the God who sees me."

O LORD, YOU have searched me and you know me. You know when I sit and when I rise; you perceive my thoughts from afar. You discern my going out and my lying down; you are familiar with all my ways. Before a word is on my tongue you know it completely, O LORD. Such knowledge is too wonderful for me, too lofty for me to attain.

The eyes of the LORD are everywhere, keeping watch on the wicked and the good.... For a man's ways are in full view of the LORD, and he examines all his paths. — God knows your hearts. What is highly valued among men is detestable in God's sight. — For the eyes of the LORD range throughout the earth to strengthen those whose hearts are fully committed to him.

[Jesus] knew all men. He did not need man's testimony about man, for he knew what was in a man.... "Lord, you know all things; you know that I love you."

GEN. 16:13. Ps. 139:1 – 4, 6. Prov. 15:3; 5:21. Luke 16:15. 2 Chron. 16:9. John 2:24 – 25; 21:17.

EVENING

I will praise you, O Lord my God, with all my heart; I will glorify your name forever.

HE WHO SACRIFICES thank offerings honors me.... It is good to praise the LORD and make music to your name, O Most High, to proclaim your love in the morning and your faithfulness at night. Let everything that has breath praise the LORD.

Therefore, I urge you, brothers, in view of God's mercy, to offer your bodies as living sacrifices, holy and pleasing to God — which is your spiritual worship. — And so Jesus also suffered outside the city gate to make the people holy through his own blood.... Through Jesus, therefore, let us continually offer to God a sacrifice of praise — the fruit of lips that confess his name. — Always giving thanks to God the Father for everything, in the name of our Lord Jesus Christ.

"Worthy is the Lamb, who was slain, to receive power and wealth and wisdom and strength and honor and glory and praise!"

PS. 86:12. Pss. 50:23; 92:1 – 2; 150:6. Rom. 12:1. Heb. 13:12, 15. Eph. 5:20. Rev. 5:12.

JANUARY 30

MORNING

Let us run with perseverance the race marked out for us. Let us fix our eyes on Jesus, the author and perfecter of our faith.

"IF ANYONE WOULD come after me, he must deny himself and take up his cross daily and follow me." ... "In the same way, any of you who does not give up everything he has cannot be my disciple."—Let us put aside the deeds of darkness and put on the armor of light.

Everyone who competes in the games goes into strict training. They do it to get a crown that will not last; but we do it to get a crown that will last forever. ... No, I beat my body and make it my slave so that after I have preached to others, I myself will not be disqualified for the prize.

Brothers, I do not consider myself yet to have taken hold of it. But one thing I do: Forgetting what is behind and straining toward what is ahead, I press on toward the goal to win the prize for which God has called me heavenward in Christ Jesus.—Let us acknowledge the LORD; let us press on to acknowledge him.

HEB. 12:1 – 2. Luke 9:23; 14:33. Rom. 13:12. 1 Cor. 9:25. 27. Phil. 3:13 – 14. Hosea 6:3.

EVENING

It is good for a man to bear the yoke while he is young.

TRAIN A CHILD in the way he should go, and when he is old he will not turn from it.

We have all had human fathers who disciplined us and we respected them for it. How much more should we submit to the Father of our spirits and live! Our fathers disciplined us for a little while as they thought best; but God disciplines us for our good, that we may share in his holiness.

Before I was afflicted I went astray, but now I obey your word. ... It was good for me to be afflicted so that I might learn your decrees.

"I know the plans I have for you," declares the LORD, "plans to prosper you and not to harm you, plans to give you hope and a future."—Humble yourselves, therefore, under God's mighty hand, that he may lift you up in due time.

LAM. 3:27. Prov. 22:6. Heb. 12:9 – 10. Ps. 119:67, 71. Jer. 29:11. 1 Peter 5:6.

JANUARY 31

MORNING

"If you do not drive out the inhabitants of the land, those you allow to remain will become barbs in your eyes and thorns in your sides. They will give you trouble in the land where you will live."

FIGHT THE GOOD fight of faith. — The weapons we fight with are not the weapons of the world. On the contrary, they have divine power to demolish strongholds.... And we take captive every thought to make it obedient to Christ. Therefore, brothers, we have an obligation — but it is not to the sinful nature, to live according to it. For if you live according to the sinful nature, you will die; but if by the Spirit you put to death the misdeeds of the body, you will live.

For the sinful nature desires what is contrary to the Spirit, and the Spirit what is contrary to the sinful nature. They are in conflict with each other, so that you do not do what you want. — But I see another law at work in the members of my body, waging war against the law of my mind and making me a prisoner of the law of sin at work within my members.... We are more than conquerors through him who loved us.

NUM. 33:55. 1 Tim. 6:12. 2 Cor. 10:4–5. Rom. 8:12–13. Gal. 5:17. Rom. 7:23; 8:37.

EVENING

"If a man sins against the LORD, who will intercede for him?"

IF ANYBODY DOES sin, we have one who speaks to the Father in our defense — Jesus Christ, the Righteous One. He is the atoning sacrifice for our sins, and not only for ours but also for the sins of the whole world. — God presented him as a sacrifice of atonement, through faith in his blood. He did this to demonstrate his justice, because in his forbearance he had left the sins committed beforehand unpunished — he did it to demonstrate his justice at the present time, so as to be just and the one who justifies the man who has faith in Jesus.

"To be gracious to him and say, 'Spare him from going down to the pit, I have found a ransom for him.'"

What, then shall we say in response to this? If God is for us, who can be against us?... It is God who justifies. Who is he that condemns? Christ Jesus, who died — more than that, who was raised to life — is at the right hand of God and is also interceding for us.

1 SAM. 2:25. 1 John 2:1–2. Rom. 3:25–26. Job 33:24. Rom. 8:31. 33–34.

FEBRUARY 1

MORNING

You have not seen him.

WE LIVE BY faith, not by sight. — We love because he first loved us.... And so we know and rely on the love God has for us. God is love. Whoever lives in love lives in God, and God in him.

And you also were included in Christ when you heard the word of truth, the gospel of your salvation. Having believed, you were marked in him with a seal, the promised Holy Spirit. — To them God has chosen to make known among the Gentiles the glorious riches of this mystery, which is Christ in you, the hope of glory.

If anyone says, "I love God," yet hates his brother, he is a liar. For anyone who does not love his brother, whom he has seen, cannot love God, whom he has not seen.

Then Jesus told him, "Because you have seen me, you have believed; blessed are those who have not seen and yet have believed." — Blessed are all who take refuge in him.

1 PETER 1:8. 2 Cor. 5:7. 1 John 4:19, 16. Eph. 1:13. Col. 1:27. 1 John 4:20. John 20:29. Ps. 2:12.

EVENING

The LORD Our Righteousness.

ALL OF US have become like one who is unclean, and all our righteous acts are like filthy rags.

I will come and proclaim your mighty acts, O Sovereign LORD; I will proclaim your righteousness, yours alone. — I delight greatly in the LORD; my soul rejoices in my God. For he has clothed me with garments of salvation and arrayed me in a robe of righteousness, as a bridegroom adorns his head like a priest, and as a bride adorns herself with her jewels.

Bring the best robe and put it on him. — "Fine linen, bright and clean, was given to her to wear." (Fine linen stands for the righteous acts of the saints.)

I consider everything a loss compared to the surpassing greatness of knowing Christ Jesus my Lord, for whose sake I have lost all things. I consider them rubbish, that I may gain Christ and be found in him, not having a righteousness of my own that comes from the law, but that which is through faith in Christ — the righteousness that comes from God and is by faith.

JER. 23:6. Isa. 64:6. Ps. 71:16. Isa. 61:10. Luke 15:22. Rev. 19:8. Phil. 3:8–9.

FEBRUARY 2

MORNING

"Oh that you would keep me from harm."

"WHY ARE YOU sleeping?" he asked them. "Get up and pray so that you will not fall into temptation." — "The spirit is willing, but the body is weak."

"Two things I ask of you, O LORD; do not refuse me before I die: Keep falsehood and lies far from me; give me neither poverty nor riches, but give me only my daily bread. Otherwise, I may have too much and disown you and say, 'Who is the LORD?' Or I may become poor and steal, and so dishonor the name of my God."

The LORD will keep you from all harm — he will watch over your life. — "I will save you from the hands of the wicked and redeem you from the grasp of the cruel." — The one who was born of God keeps him safe, and the evil one does not touch him.

Since you have kept my command to endure patiently, I will also keep you from the hour of trial that is going to come upon the whole world to test those who live on the earth. — The Lord knows how to rescue godly men from trials.

1 CHRON. 4:10. Luke 22:46. Matt. 26:41. Prov. 30:7–9. Ps. 121:7. Jer. 15:21. 1 John 5:18. Rev. 3:10. 2 Peter 2:9.

EVENING

Star differs from star in splendor.

ON THE WAY they had argued about who was the greatest. Sitting down, Jesus called the Twelve and said, "If anyone wants to be first, he must be the very last, and the servant of all." — Clothe yourselves with humility toward one another, because, "God opposes the proud but gives grace to the humble." Humble yourselves, therefore, under God's mighty hand, that he may lift you up in due time.

Your attitude should be the same as that of Christ Jesus: Who, being in very nature God, did not consider equality with God something to be grasped, but made himself nothing, taking the very nature of a servant, being made in human likeness.... Therefore God exalted him to the highest place and gave him the name that is above every name, that at the name of Jesus every knee should bow.

Those who are wise will shine like the brightness of the heavens, and those who lead many to righteousness, like the stars for ever and ever.

1 COR. 15:41. Mark 9:34–35. 1 Peter 5:5–6. Phil. 2:5–7, 9–10. Dan. 12:3.

FEBRUARY 3

MORNING

> *"'Be strong, all you people of the land,' declares the LORD, 'and work. For*
> *I am with you,' declares the LORD Almighty."*

"I AM THE vine; you are the branches. If a man remains in me and I in him, he will bear much fruit; apart from me you can do nothing. — I can do everything through him who gives me strength. — Be strong in the Lord and in his mighty power. — "The joy of the LORD is your strength."

This is what the LORD Almighty says: "You who now hear these words spoken by the prophets, ... let your hands be strong." — Strengthen the feeble hands, steady the knees that give way; say to those with fearful hearts, "Be strong, do not fear." — The LORD turned to him and said, "Go in the strength you have."

If God is for us, who can be against us? — Therefore, since through God's mercy we have this ministry, we do not lose heart.

Let us not become weary in doing good, for at the proper time we will reap a harvest if we do not give up. — But thanks be to God! He gives us the victory through our Lord Jesus Christ.

HAG. 2:4. John 15:5. Phil. 4:13. Eph. 6:10. Neh. 8:10. Zech. 8:9. Isa. 35:3–4. Judg. 6:14. Rom. 8:31. 2 Cor. 4:1. Gal. 6:9. 1 Cor. 15:57.

EVENING

> *The darkness will not be dark to you.*

"HIS EYES ARE on the ways of men; he sees their every step. There is no dark place, no deep shadow, where evildoers can hide." — "Can anyone hide in secret places so that I cannot see him?" ... "Do not I fill heaven and earth?" declares the LORD.

You will not fear the terror of night, ... nor the pestilence that stalks in the darkness.... If you make the Most High your dwelling — even the LORD, who is my refuge — then no harm will befall you, no disaster will come near your tent.... He who watches over you will not slumber.... The LORD watches over you — the LORD is your shade at your right hand; the sun will not harm you by day, nor the moon by night. The LORD will keep you from all harm.

Even though I walk through the valley of the shadow of death, I will fear no evil, for you are with me.

PS. 139:12. Job 34:21–22. Jer. 23:24. Pss. 91:5–6, 9–10; 121:3, 5–7; 23:4.

FEBRUARY 4

MORNING

The LORD has told you, "You are not to go back that way again."

IF THEY HAD been thinking of the country they had left, they would have had opportunity to return. Instead, they were longing for a better country — a heavenly one.... He chose to be mistreated along with the people of God rather than to enjoy the pleasures of sin for a short time. He regarded disgrace for the sake of Christ as of greater value than the treasures of Egypt.

"But my righteous one will live by faith. And if he shrinks back, I will not be pleased with him." But we are not of those who shrink back and are destroyed, but of those who believe and are saved. — "No one who puts his hand to the plow and looks back is fit for service in the kingdom of God."

May I never boast except in the cross of our Lord Jesus Christ, through which the world has been crucified to me, and I to the world. — "Therefore come out from them and be separate," says the Lord. "Touch no unclean thing, and I will receive you."

He who began a good work in you will carry it on to completion until the day of Christ Jesus.

DEUT. 17:16. Heb. 11:15 – 16, 25 – 26; 10:38 – 39. Luke 9:62. Gal. 6:14. 2 Cor. 6:17.
   Phil. 1:6.

EVENING

Talk about the pain of those you hurt.

"I WAS ONLY a little angry, but they added to the calamity."

Brothers, if someone is caught in a sin, you who are spiritual should restore him gently. But watch yourself, or you also may be tempted.

Whoever turns a sinner away from his error will save him from death and cover over a multitude of sins. — Encourage the timid, help the weak, be patient with everyone.

Let us stop passing judgment on one another. Instead, make up your mind not to put any stumbling block or obstacle in your brother's way.... We who are strong ought to bear with the failings of the weak and not to please ourselves.

Love does not delight in evil. — So, if you think you are standing firm, be careful that you don't fall!

PS. 69:26. Zech. 1:15. Gal. 6:1. James 6:20. 1 Thess. 5:14. Rom. 14:13; 15:1.
   1 Cor. 13:6; 10:12.

February 5

Morning

"I have come that they may have life, and have it to the full."

"When you eat of it you will surely die." . . . She took some and ate it. She also gave some to her husband, who was with her, and he ate it.

The wages of sin is death, but the gift of God is eternal life in Christ Jesus our Lord. . . . For if, by the trespass of one man, death reigned through that one man, how much more will those who receive God's abundant provision of grace and of the gift of righteousness reign in life through the one man, Jesus Christ. — For since death came through a man, the resurrection of the dead comes also through a man. For as in Adam all die, so in Christ all will be made alive. — Our Savior, Christ Jesus, . . . has destroyed death and has brought life and immortality to light through the gospel.

God has given us eternal life, and this life is in his Son. He who has the Son has life; he who does not have the Son of God does not have life. — For God did not send his Son into the world to condemn the world, but to save the world through him.

JOHN 10:10. Gen. 2:17; 3:6. Rom. 6:23; 5:17. 1 Cor. 15:21–22. 2 Tim. 1:10.
1 John 5:11–12. John 3:17.

Evening

The judgment seat.

Now we know that God's judgment against those who do such things is based on truth. — "When the Son of Man comes in his glory, and all the angels with him, he will sit on his throne in heavenly glory. All the nations will be gathered before him, and he will separate the people one from another as a shepherd separates the sheep from the goats."

Then the righteous will shine like the sun in the kingdom of their Father. — Who will bring any charge against those whom God has chosen? It is God who justifies. Who is he that condemns? Christ Jesus, who died — more than that, who was raised to life — is at the right hand of God and is also interceding for us. . . . Therefore, there is now no condemnation for those who are in Christ Jesus.

When we are judged by the Lord, we are being disciplined so that we will not be condemned with the world.

2 COR. 5:10. Rom. 2:2. Matt. 25:31–32; 13:43. Rom. 8:33–34, 1. 1 Cor. 11:32.

FEBRUARY 6

MORNING

The grace of our Lord was poured out on me abundantly,
along with the faith and love that are in Christ Jesus.

FOR YOU KNOW the grace of our Lord Jesus Christ, that though he was rich, yet for your sakes he became poor, so that you through his poverty might become rich. — But where sin increased, grace increased all the more.

In order that in the coming ages he might show the incomparable riches of his grace, expressed in his kindness to us in Christ Jesus. For it is by grace you have been saved, through faith — and this not from yourselves, it is the gift of God — not by works, so that no one can boast. — Know that a man is not justified by observing the law, but by faith in Jesus Christ. So we, too, have put our faith in Christ Jesus that we may be justified by faith in Christ and not by observing the law, because by observing the law no one will be justified.

He saved us ... because of his mercy. He saved us through the washing of rebirth and renewal by the Holy Spirit, whom he poured out on us generously through Jesus Christ our Savior.

1 TIM. 1:14. 2 Cor. 8:9. Rom. 5:20. Eph. 2:7 – 9. Gal. 2:16. Titus 3:5 – 6.

EVENING

"I am ... the bright Morning Star."

A STAR WILL come out of Jacob. — The night is nearly over; the day is almost here. So let us put aside the deeds of darkness and put on the armor of light. — Until the day break, and the shadows flee away, turn, my beloved, and be thou like a roe or a young hart upon the mountains of Bether.

"Watchman, what is left of the night? Watchman, what is left of the night?" The watchman replies, "Morning is coming, but also the night. If you would ask, then ask; and come back yet again."

"I am the light of the world." — I will also give him the morning star.

"Be on guard! Be alert! You do not know when that time will come. It's like a man going away: He leaves his house in charge of his servants, each with his assigned task, and tells the one at the door to keep watch. Therefore keep watch. ... If he comes suddenly, do not let him find you sleeping. What I say to you, I say to everyone: 'Watch!' "

REV. 22:16. Num. 24:17. Rom. 13:12. Song of Songs 2:17. Isa. 21:11 – 12. John 8:12.
Rev. 2:28. Mark 13:33 – 37.

FEBRUARY 7

MORNING

When you have eaten and are satisfied, praise the LORD your God for the good land he has given you.

BE CAREFUL THAT you do not forget the LORD your God. — One of them, when he saw he was healed, came back, praising God in a loud voice. He threw himself at Jesus' feet and thanked him — and he was a Samaritan. Jesus asked, "Were not all ten cleansed? Where are the other nine? Was no one found to return and give praise to God except this foreigner?"

For everything God created is good, and nothing is to be rejected if it is received with thanksgiving, because it is consecrated by the word of God and prayer. — He who eats meat, eats to the Lord, for he gives thanks to God. — The blessing of the LORD brings wealth, and he adds no trouble to it.

Praise the LORD, O my soul; all my inmost being, praise his holy name. Praise the LORD, O my soul, He forgives all my sins and crowns me with love and compassion.

DEUT. 8:10. Deut. 8:11. Luke 17:15 – 18. 1 Tim. 4:4 – 5. Rom. 14:6. Prov. 10:22. Ps. 103:1 – 4.

EVENING

Jesus had compassion on them.

JESUS CHRIST IS the same yesterday and today and forever.... For we do not have a high priest who is unable to sympathize with our weaknesses, but we have one who has been tempted in every way, just as we are — yet was without sin.... He is able to deal gently with those who are ignorant and are going astray. — He returned to his disciples and found them sleeping. "Simon," he said to Peter, "are you asleep? Could you not keep watch for one hour? Watch and pray so that you will not fall into temptation. The spirit is willing, but the body is weak."

As a father has compassion on his children, so the LORD has compassion on those who fear him; for he knows how we are formed, he remembers that we are dust.

But you, O Lord, are a compassionate and gracious God, slow to anger, abounding in love and faithfulness. Turn to me and have mercy on me; grant your strength to your servant and save the son of your maidservant.

MATT. 14:14. Heb. 13:8; 4:15; 5:2. Mark 14:37 – 38. Pss. 103:13 – 14; 86:15 – 16.

FEBRUARY 8

MORNING

"I no longer call you servants, because a servant does not know his master's business. Instead, I have called you friends."

THEN THE LORD said, "Shall I hide from Abraham what I am going to do?"—"The knowledge of the secrets of the kingdom of heaven has been given to you, but not to them."—God has revealed it to us by his Spirit. The Spirit searches all things, even the deep things of God.... We speak of God's secret wisdom, a wisdom that has been hidden and that God destined for our glory before time began.

Blessed is the man you choose and bring near to live in your courts! We are filled with the good things of your house, of your holy temple.

The LORD confides in those who fear him; he makes his covenant known to them.—"For I gave them the words you gave me and they accepted them. They knew with certainty that I came from you, and they believed that you sent me."

"You are my friends if you do what I command."

JOHN 15:15. Gen. 18:17. Matt. 13:11. 1 Cor. 2:10, 7. Pss. 65:4; 25:14. John 17:8; 15:14.

EVENING

But you will call your walls Salvation and your gates Praise.

THE WALL OF the city had twelve foundations, and on them were the names of the twelve apostles of the Lamb.

You are no longer foreigners and aliens, but fellow citizens with God's people and members of God's household, built on the foundation of the apostles and prophets, with Christ Jesus himself as the chief cornerstone. In him the whole building is joined together and rises to become a holy temple in the Lord. And in him you too are being built together to become a dwelling in which God lives by his Spirit.—Now that you have tasted that the Lord is good. As you come to him, the living Stone—rejected by men but chosen by God and precious to him—you also, like living stones, are being built into a spiritual house to be a holy priesthood, offering spiritual sacrifices acceptable to God through Jesus Christ.

Praise awaits you, O God, in Zion.

ISA. 60:18. Rev. 21:4. Eph. 2:19–22. 1 Peter 2:3–5. Ps. 65:1.

FEBRUARY 9

MORNING

Now he is comforted.

YOUR SUN WILL never set again, and your moon will wane no more; the LORD will be your everlasting light, and your days of sorrow will end.... He will swallow up death forever. The Sovereign LORD will wipe away the tears from all faces; he will remove the disgrace of his people from all the earth.

"These are they who have come out of the great tribulation; they have washed their robes and made them white in the blood of the Lamb. Therefore, they are before the throne of God and serve him day and night in his temple; and he who sits on the throne will spread his tent over them. Never again will they hunger; never again will they thirst. The sun will not beat upon them, nor any scorching heat. For the Lamb at the center of the throne will be their shepherd; he will lead them to springs of living water. And God will wipe away every tear from their eyes." ... "There will be no more death or mourning or crying or pain, for the old order of things has passed away."

LUKE 16:25. Isa. 60:20; 25:8. Rev. 7:14–17; 21:4.

EVENING

"Night is coming, when no one can work."

"BLESSED ARE THE dead who die in the Lord from now on." ... "They will rest from their labor, for their deeds will follow them." — There the wicked cease from turmoil, and there the weary are at rest. — Samuel said to Saul, "Why have you disturbed me by bringing me up?"

Whatever your hand finds to do, do it with all your might, for in the grave, where you are going, there is neither working nor planning nor knowledge nor wisdom. It is not the dead who praise the LORD, those who go down to silence.

For I am already being poured out like a drink offering, and the time has come for my departure. I have fought the good fight, I have finished the race, I have kept the faith. Now there is in store for me the crown of righteousness, which the Lord, the righteous Judge, will award to me on that day.

There remains, then, a Sabbath-rest for the people of God; for anyone who enters God's rest also rests from his own work, just as God did from his.

JOHN 9:4. Rev. 14:13. Job 3:17. 1 Sam. 28:15. Eccl. 9:10. Ps. 115:17. 2 Tim. 4:6–8. Heb. 4:9–10.

FEBRUARY 10

MORNING

When your eyes are good, your whole body also is full of light.

THE MAN WITHOUT the Spirit does not accept the things that come from the Spirit of God, for they are foolishness to him, and he cannot understand them, because they are spiritually discerned. — Open my eyes that I may see wonderful things in your law.

"I am the light of the world. Whoever follows me will never walk in darkness, but will have the light of life." — And we, who with unveiled faces all reflect the Lord's glory, are being transformed into his likeness with ever-increasing glory, which comes from the Lord, who is the Spirit. . . . For God, who said, "Let light shine out of darkness," made his light shine in our hearts to give us the light of the knowledge of the glory of God in the face of Christ.

God of our Lord Jesus Christ, the glorious Father, . . . give you the Spirit of wisdom and revelation, so that you may know him better. I pray also that the eyes of your heart may be enlightened in order that you may know the hope to which he has called you, the riches of his glorious inheritance in the saints.

LUKE 11:34. 1 Cor. 2:14. Ps. 119:18. John 8:12. 2 Cor. 3:18; 4:6. Eph. 1:17–18.

EVENING

When he struck the rock, water gushed out, and streams
flowed abundantly.

OUR FOREFATHERS WERE all under the cloud and . . . they all passed through the sea. They were all baptized into Moses in the cloud and in the sea. They all ate the same spiritual food and drank the same spiritual drink; for they drank from the spiritual rock that accompanied them, and that rock was Christ. — One of the soldiers pierced Jesus' side with a spear, bringing a sudden flow of blood and water. — But he was pierced for our transgressions, he was crushed for our iniquities; the punishment that brought us peace was upon him, and by his wounds we are healed.

You refuse to come to me to have life. — "My people have committed two sins: They have forsaken me, the spring of living water, and have dug their own cisterns, broken cisterns that cannot hold water." — "If a man is thirsty, let him come to me and drink." — Whoever wishes, let him take the free gift of the water of life.

PS. 78:20. 1 Cor. 10:1–4. John 19:34. Isa. 53:5. John 5:40. Jer. 2:13. John 7:37.
Rev. 22:17.

FEBRUARY 11

MORNING

Those who feared the LORD talked with each other, and the LORD listened and heard. A scroll of remembrance was written in his presence concerning those who feared the LORD and honored his name.

AS THEY TALKED and discussed these things with each other, Jesus himself came up and walked along with them. — "For where two or three come together in my name, there am I with them." — Many fellow workers, whose names are in the book of life.

Let the word of Christ dwell in you richly as you teach and admonish one another with all wisdom, and as you sing psalms, hymns and spiritual songs with gratitude in your hearts to God. — But encourage one another daily, as long as it is called Today, so that none of you may be hardened by sin's deceitfulness.

"Men will have to give account on the day of judgment for every careless word they have spoken. For by your words you will be acquitted, and by your words you will be condemned." — "See, it stands written before me."

MAL. 3:16. Luke 24:15. Matt. 18:20. Phil. 4:3. Col. 3:16. Heb. 3:13. Matt. 12:36–37. Isa. 65:6.

EVENING

The trees of the LORD are well watered.

I WILL BE like the dew to Israel; he will blossom like a lily. Like a cedar of Lebanon he will send down his roots; his young shoots will grow. His splendor will be like an olive tree, his fragrance like a cedar of Lebanon. — "But blessed is the man who trusts in the LORD, whose confidence is in him. He will be like a tree planted by the water that sends out its roots by the stream. It does not fear when heat comes; its leaves are always green. It has no worries in a year of drought and never fails to bear fruit."

"I the LORD bring down the tall tree and make the low tree grow tall. I dry up the green tree and make the dry tree flourish."

The righteous will flourish like a palm tree, they will grow like a cedar of Lebanon; planted in the house of the LORD, they will flourish in the courts of our God. They will still bear fruit in old age, they will stay fresh and green.

PS. 104:16. Hos. 14:5–6. Jer. 17:7–8. Ezek. 17:24. Ps. 92:12–14.

FEBRUARY 12

MORNING

*"They will be mine," says the LORD Almighty, "in the day
when I make up my treasured possession."*

"I HAVE REVEALED you to those whom you gave me out of the world. They were yours; you gave them to me and they have obeyed your word.... I pray for them. I am not praying for the world, but for those you have given me, for they are yours. All I have is yours, and all you have is mine. And glory has come to me through them.... Father, I want those you have given me to be with me where I am, and to see my glory, the glory you have given me because you loved me before the creation of the world."

"I will come back and take you to be with me." — On the day he comes to be glorified in his holy people and to be marveled at among all those who have believed. — We who are still alive and are left will be caught up with them in the clouds to meet the Lord in the air. And so we will be with the Lord forever. — You will be a crown of splendor in the LORD's hand, a royal diadem in the hand of your God.

MAL. 3:17. John 17:6, 9–10, 24; 14:3. 2 Thess. 1:10. 1 Thess. 4:17. Isa. 62:3.

EVENING

"Now show me your glory."

FOR GOD, WHO said, "Let light shine out of darkness," made his light shine in our hearts to give us the light of the knowledge of the glory of God in the face of Christ. — The Word became flesh and lived for a while among us. We have seen his glory, the glory of the one and only Son, who came from the Father, full of grace and truth.... No one has ever seen God, but God the only Son, who is at the Father's side, has made him known.

My soul thirsts for God, for the living God. When can I go and meet with God?... My heart says of you, "Seek his face!" Your face, LORD I will seek.

And we, who with unveiled faces all reflect the Lord's glory, are being transformed into his likeness with every-increasing glory, which comes from the Lord, who is the Spirit. — "Father, I want those you have given me to be with me where I am, and to see my glory, the glory you have given me because you loved me before the creation of the world."

EXOD. 33:18. 2 Cor. 4:6. John 1:14, 18. Pss. 42:2; 27:8. 2 Cor. 3:18. John 17:24.

February 13

Morning

Above the expanse over their heads was what looked like a throne of sapphire, and high above on the throne was a figure like that of a man.

THE MAN CHRIST JESUS. — Being made in human likeness. And being found in appearance as a man. — Since the children have flesh and blood, he too shared in their humanity so that by his death he might destroy him who holds the power of death.

"I am the Living One; I was dead, and behold I am alive for ever and ever!" — For we know that since Christ was raised from the dead, he cannot die again; death no longer has mastery over him. The death he died, he died to sin once for all; but the life he lives, he lives to God. — What if you see the Son of Man ascend to where he was before! — He raised him from the dead and seated him at his right hand in the heavenly realms. — For in Christ all the fullness of the Deity lives in bodily form.

He was crucified in weakness, yet he lives by God's power. Likewise, we are weak in him, yet by God's power we will live.

EZEK. 1:26. 1 Tim. 2:5. Phil. 2:7–8. Heb. 2:14. Rev. 1:18. Rom. 6:9–10. John 6:62. Eph. 1:20. Col. 2:9. 2 Cor. 13:4.

Evening

Your promise renews my life.

"THE FIRST MAN Adam became a living being"; the last Adam, a life-giving spirit.

For as the Father has life in himself, so he has granted the Son to have life in himself.... "I am the resurrection and the life. He who believes in me will live, even though he dies; and whoever lives and believes in me will never die."

In him was life, and that life was the light of men.... Yet to all who received him, to those who believed in his name, he gave the right to become children of God — children born not of natural descent, nor of human decision or a husband's will, but born of God.

"The Spirit gives life; the flesh counts for nothing. The words I have spoken to you are spirit and they are life." — The word of God is living and active. Sharper than any double-edged sword, it penetrates even to dividing soul and spirit, joints and marrow; it judges the thoughts and attitudes of the heart.

PS. 119:50. 1 Cor. 15:45. John 5:26; 11:25–26; 1:4, 12–13; 6:63. Heb. 4:12.

FEBRUARY 14

MORNING

"Let it be so now; it is proper for us to do this to fulfill all righteousness."

"To DO YOUR will, O my God, is my desire; your law is within my heart."

"Do not think that I have come to abolish the Law or the Prophets; I have not come to abolish them but to fulfill them. I tell you the truth, until heaven and earth disappear, not the smallest letter, not the least stroke of a pen, will by any means disappear from the Law until everything is accomplished." — It pleased the LORD for the sake of his righteousness to make his law great and glorious. — "Unless your righteousness surpasses that of the Pharisees and the teachers of the law, you will certainly not enter the kingdom of heaven."

For what the law was powerless to do in that it was weakened by the sinful nature, God did by sending his own Son in the likeness of sinful man to be a sin offering. And so he condemned sin in sinful man, in order that the righteous requirements of the law might be fully met in us, who do not live according to the sinful nature but according to the Spirit.... Christ is the end of the law so that there may be righteousness for everyone who believes.

MATT. 3:15. Ps. 40:8. Matt. 5:17 – 18. Isa. 42:21. Matt. 5:20. Rom. 8:3 – 4; 10:4.

EVENING

I am your share and your inheritance.

WHOM HAVE I in heaven but you? And being with you, I desire nothing on earth. My flesh and my heart may fail, but God is the strength of my heart and my portion forever.

LORD, you have assigned me my portion and my cup; you have made my lot secure. The boundary lines have fallen for me in pleasant places; surely I have a delightful inheritance.

I say to myself, "The LORD is my portion; therefore I will wait for him." — Your statutes are my heritage forever; they are the joy of my heart.

O God, you are my God, earnestly I seek you; my soul thirsts for you, my body longs for you, in a dry and weary land where there is no water.... Because you are my help, I sing in the shadow of your wings.

My beloved is mine, and I am his.

NUM. 18:20. Pss. 73:25 – 26; 16:5 – 6. Lam. 3:24. Pss. 119:111; 63:1, 7.
Song of Songs 2:16.

FEBRUARY 15

MORNING

Who can say, "I have kept my heart pure"?

THE LORD LOOKS down from heaven on the sons of men to see if there are any who understand, any who seek God. All have turned aside, they have together become corrupt; there is no one who does good, not even one.

Those controlled by the sinful nature cannot please God.... I know that nothing good lives in me, that is, in my sinful nature. For I have the desire to do what is good, but I cannot carry it out. For what I do is not the good I want to do; no, the evil I do not want to do—this I keep on doing.—All of us have become like one who is unclean, and all our righteous acts are like filthy rags; we all shrivel up like a leaf, and like the wind our sins sweep us away.

But the Scripture declares that the whole world is a prisoner of sin, so that what was promised, being given through faith in Jesus Christ, might be given to those who believe.—That God was reconciling the world to himself in Christ, not counting men's sins against them.

If we claim to be without sin, we deceive ourselves and the truth is not in us.... If we confess our sins, he is faithful and just and will forgive us our sins and purify us from all unrighteousness.

PROV. 20:9. Ps. 14:2–3. Rom. 8:8; 7:18–19. Isa. 64:6. Gal. 3:22. 2 Cor. 5:19.
1 John 1:8–9.

EVENING

The seas have lifted up their pounding waves.

MIGHTIER THAN THE thunder of the great waters, mightier than the breakers of the sea—the LORD on high is mighty.... O LORD God Almighty, who is like you? You are mighty O LORD, and your faithfulness surrounds you. You rule over the surging sea; when its waves mount up, you still them.

"Should you not fear me?" declares the LORD. "Should you not tremble in my presence? I made the sand a boundary for the sea, an everlasting barrier it cannot cross."—"When you pass through the waters, I will be with you; and when you pass through the rivers, they will not sweep over you."

Peter got down out of the boat and walked on the water to Jesus. But when he saw the wind, he was afraid and, beginning to sink, cried out, "Lord, save me!" Immediately Jesus reached out his hand and caught him. "You of little faith," he said, "why did *you* doubt?"

PS. 93:3. Pss. 93:4; 89:8–9. Jer. 5:22. Isa. 43:2. Matt. 14:29–31.

FEBRUARY 16

MORNING

Your name is like perfume poured out.

CHRIST LOVED US and gave himself up for us as a fragrant offering and sacrifice to God. — Now to you who believe, this stone is precious. — Therefore God exalted him to the highest place and gave him the name that is above every name, that at the name of Jesus every knee should bow.

"If you love me, you will obey what I command." — God has poured out his love into our hearts by the Holy Spirit, whom he has given us. — And the house was filled with the fragrance of the perfume. — They took note that these men had been with Jesus.

O LORD, our Lord, how majestic is your name in all the earth! You have set your glory above the heavens. — "Immanuel" — which means, "God with us." — And he will be called Wonderful Counselor, Mighty God, Everlasting Father, Prince of Peace. — The name of the LORD is a strong tower, the righteous run to it and are safe.

SONG OF SONGS 1:3. Eph. 5:2. 1 Peter 2:7. Phil. 2:9–10. Col. 2:9. John 14:15. Rom. 5:5. John 12:3. Acts 4:13. Ps. 8:1. Matt. 1:23. Isa. 9:6. Prov. 18:10.

EVENING

For while we are in this tent, we groan and are burdened.

ALL MY LONGINGS lie open before you, O Lord; my sighing is not hidden from you.... My guilt has overwhelmed me like a burden too heavy to bear. — What a wretched man I am! Who will rescue me from this body of death?

We know that the whole creation has been groaning as in the pains of childbirth right up to the present time. Not only so, but we ourselves, who have the firstfruits of the Spirit, groan inwardly as we wait eagerly for our adoption as sons, the redemption of our bodies. — For a little while you may have had to suffer grief in all kinds of trials.

Because I know that I will soon put it [my body] aside. — For the perishable must clothe itself with the imperishable, and the mortal with immortality. When the perishable has been clothed with the imperishable, and the mortal with immortality, then the saying that is written will come true: "Death has been swallowed up in victory."

2 COR. 5:4. Ps. 38:9, 4. Rom. 7:24; 8:22–23. 1 Peter 1:6. 2 Peter 1:14. 1 Cor. 15:53–54.

FEBRUARY 17

MORNING

All the rest of the bull—he must take outside the camp to a place ceremonially clean, where the ashes are thrown, and burn it in a wood fire on the ash pile.

SO THE SOLDIERS took charge of Jesus.... Carrying his own cross, he went out to The Place of the Skull (which in Aramaic is called Golgotha). Here they crucified him.—The high priest carries the blood of animals into the Most Holy Place as a sin offering, but the bodies are burned outside the camp. And so Jesus also suffered outside the city gate to make the people holy through his own blood. Let us, then, go to him outside the camp, bearing the disgrace he bore.—The fellowship of sharing in his sufferings.

But rejoice that you participate in the sufferings of Christ, so that you may be overjoyed when his glory is revealed.—For our light and momentary troubles are achieving for us an eternal glory that far outweighs them all.

LEV. 4:12. John 19:16, 18. Heb. 13:11–13. Phil. 3:10. 1 Peter 4:13. 2 Cor. 4:17.

EVENING

God created man in his own image.

"THEREFORE SINCE WE are God's offspring, we should not think that the divine being is like gold or silver or stone—an image made by man's design and skill."

God, who is rich in mercy, made us alive with Christ even when we were dead in transgressions.... For we are God's workmanship, created in Christ Jesus to do good works, which God prepared in advance for us to do.—For those God foreknew he also presdestined to be conformed to the likeness of his Son, that he might be the firstborn among many brothers.

We know that when he appears, we shall be like him, for we shall see him as he is.—When I awake, I will be satisfied with seeing your likeness.

He who overcomes will inherit all this, and I will be his God and he will be my son.—Now if we are children, then we are heirs—heirs of God and co-heirs with Christ.

GEN. 1:27. Acts 17:29. Eph. 2:4–5, 10. Rom. 8:29. 1 John 3:2. Ps. 17:15. Rev. 21:7. Rom. 8:17.

FEBRUARY 18

MORNING

You are my refuge in the day of disaster.

MANY ARE ASKING, "Who can show us any good?" Let the light of your face shine upon us, O LORD.... But I will sing of your strength, in the morning I will sing of your love; for you are my fortress, my refuge in times of trouble.

When I felt secure, I said, "I will never be shaken." ... To you, O LORD, I called; to the Lord I cried for mercy: "What gain is there in my destruction, if I go down into the pit? Will the dust praise you? Will it proclaim your faithfulness? Hear, O LORD, and be merciful to me; O LORD, be my help."

"For a brief moment I abandoned you, but with deep compassion I will bring you back. In a surge of anger I hid my face from you for a moment, but with everlasting kindness I will have compassion on you," says the LORD your Redeemer.

You will grieve, but your grief will turn to joy. — Weeping may remain for a night, but rejoicing comes in the morning.

JER. 17:17. Pss. 4:6; 59:16; 30:6, 8 – 10. Isa. 54:7 – 8. John 16:20. Ps. 30:5.

EVENING

Adam had a son in his own likeness.

WHO CAN BRING what is pure from the impure? — Surely I have been a sinner from birth, sinful from the time my mother conceived me.

As for you, you were dead in your transgressions and sins.... Like the rest, we were by nature objects of wrath. — I am unspiritual, sold as a slave to sin.... I do not understand what I do. For what I want to do I do not do, but what I hate I do.... I know that nothing good lives in me, that is, in my sinful nature.

Sin entered the world through one man.... Through the disobedience of the one man the many were made sinners.... For if the many died by the trespass of the one man, how much more did God's grace and the gift that came by the grace of the one man, Jesus Christ, overflow to the many!

The law of the Spirit of life set me free from the law of sin and death. — But thanks be to God! He gives us the victory through our Lord Jesus Christ.

GEN. 5:3. Job 14:4. Ps. 51:5. Eph. 2:1, 3. Rom. 7:14 – 15, 18; 5:12, 19, 15; 8:2. 1 Cor. 15:57.

FEBRUARY 19

MORNING

For the L{ORD} gives wisdom, and from his mouth come knowledge and understanding.

T{RUST} I{N THE} L{ORD} with all your heart and lean not on your own understanding. — If any of you lacks wisdom, he should ask God, who gives generously to all without finding fault, and it will be given to him. — For the foolishness of God is wiser than man's wisdom, and the weakness of God is stronger than man's strength.... But God chose the foolish things of the world to shame the wise.... So that no one may boast before him.

The entrance of your words gives light; it gives understanding to the simple.... I have hidden your word in my heart that I might not sin against you.

All spoke well of him and were amazed at the gracious words that came from his lips. — "No one ever spoke the way this man does." — It is because of him that you are in Christ Jesus, who has become for us wisdom from God — that is, our righteousness, holiness and redemption.

PROV. 2:6. Prov. 3:5. James 1:5. 1 Cor. 1:25, 27, 29; Ps. 119:130, 11. Luke 4:22. 1 John 7:46. 1 Cor. 1:30.

EVENING

The year of my redemption has come.

C{ONSECRATE THE FIFTIETH} year and proclaim liberty throughout the land to all its inhabitants. It shall be a jubilee for you; each one of you is to return to his family property and each to his own clan.

But your dead will live; their bodies will rise. You who dwell in the dust, wake up and shout for joy. Your dew is like the dew of the morning; the earth will give birth to her dead.

For the Lord himself will come down from heaven, with a loud command, with the voice of the archangel and with the trumpet call of God, and the dead in Christ will rise first. After that, we who are still alive and are left will be caught up with them in the clouds to meet the Lord in the air. And so we will be with the Lord forever.

"I will ransom them from the power of the grave; I will redeem them from death. Where, O death, are your plagues? Where, O grave, is your destruction?"

Yet their Redeemer is strong; the L{ORD} Almighty is his name.

ISA. 63:4. Lev. 25:10. Isa. 26:19. 1 Thess. 4:16–17. Hos. 13:14. Jer. 50:34.

FEBRUARY 20

MORNING

He will see the light of life and be satisfied.

JESUS SAID, "IT IS FINISHED." With that, he bowed his head and gave up his spirit. — God made him who had no sin to be sin for us, so that in him we might become the righteousness of God.

The people I formed for myself that they may proclaim my praise. — His intent was that now, through the church, the manifold wisdom of God should be made known to the rulers and authorities in the heavenly realms, according to his eternal purpose which he accomplished in Christ Jesus our Lord.... In order that in the coming ages he might show the incomparable riches of his grace, expressed in his kindness to us in Christ Jesus.

Having believed, you were marked in him with a deposit guaranteeing our inheritance until the redemption of those who are God's possession — to the praise of his glory. — But you are a chosen people, a royal priesthood, a holy nation, a people belonging to God, that you may declare the praises of him who called you out of darkness into his wonderful light.

ISA. 53:11. John 19:30. 2 Cor. 5:21. Isa. 43:21. Eph. 3:10–11; 2:7; 1:13–14. 1 Peter 2:9.

EVENING

The time of testing in the desert.

WHEN TEMPTED, NO ONE should say, "God is tempting me." For God cannot be tempted by evil, nor does he tempt anyone; but each one is tempted when, by his own evil desire, he is dragged away and enticed. Then, after desire has conceived, it gives birth to sin.

In the desert they gave in to their craving; in the wasteland they put God to the test.

Jesus, full of the Holy Spirit, returned from the Jordan and was led by the Spirit in the desert, where for forty days he was tempted by the devil. He ate nothing during those days, and at the end of them he was hungry. The devil said to him, "If you are the Son of God, tell this stone to become bread."

He himself suffered when he was tempted, he is able to help those who are being tempted. — "Simon, Simon, Satan has asked to sift you as wheat. But I have prayed for you, Simon, that your faith may not fail."

HEB. 3:8. James 1:3–15. Ps. 106:14. Luke 4:1–3. Heb. 2:18. Luke 22:31–32.

FEBRUARY 21

MORNING

I am the LORD, who makes you holy.

I AM THE LORD your God, who has set you apart from the nations.... You are to be holy to me because I, the LORD, am holy, and I have set you apart from the nations to be my own.

Who are loved by God the father. — Sanctify them by the truth; your word is truth. — May God himself, the God of peace, sanctify you through and through. May your whole spirit, soul and body be kept blameless at the coming of our Lord Jesus Christ.

Jesus also suffered outside the city gate to make people holy through his own blood. Our great God and Savior, Jesus Christ, ... gave himself for us to redeem us from all wickedness and to purify for himself a people that are his very own, eager to do what is good. — Both the one who makes men holy and those who are made holy are of the same family. So Jesus is not ashamed to call them brothers. — "For them I sanctify myself, that they too may be truly sanctified." — By the sanctifying work of the Spirit, for obedience to Jesus Christ and sprinkling by his blood.

LEV. 20:8. Lev. 20:24, 26. Jude 1. John 17:17. 1 Thess. 5:23. Heb. 13:12. Titus 2:13–14. Heb. 2:11. John 17:19. 1 Peter 1:2.

EVENING

Light is shed upon the righteous and joy on the upright in heart.

THOSE WHO SOW in tears will reap with songs of joy. He who goes out weeping, carrying seed to sow, will return with songs of joy, carrying sheaves with him.

For he "has put everything under his feet." Now when it says that "everything" has been put under him, it is clear that this does not include God himself, who put everything under Christ.

Praise be to the God and Father of our Lord Jesus Christ! In his great mercy he has given us new birth into a living hope through the resurrection of Jesus Christ from the dead.... In this you greatly rejoice, though now for a little while you may have had to suffer grief in all kinds of trials. These have come so that your faith — of greater worth than gold, which perishes even though refined by fire — may be proved genuine and may result in praise, glory and honor when Jesus Christ is revealed.

PS. 97:11. Ps. 126:5–6. 1 Cor. 15:27. 1 Peter 1:3, 6–7.

FEBRUARY 22

MORNING

Who, then, is the man that fears the LORD? He will instruct
him in the way chosen for him.

"THE EYE IS the lamp of the body. If your eyes are good, your whole body will
be full of light."

Your word is a lamp to my feet and a light for my path. — Whether you turn
to the right or to the left, your ears will hear a voice behind you, saying, "This
is the way; walk in it."

I will instruct you and teach you in the way you should go; I will counsel
you and watch over you. Do not be like the horse or the mule, which have no
understanding but must be controlled by bit and bridle or they will not come to
you. Many are the woes of the wicked, but the LORD's unfailing love surrounds
the man who trusts in him. Rejoice in the LORD and be glad, you righteous; sing,
all you who are upright in heart!

I know, O LORD, that a man's life is not his own; it is not for man to direct
his steps.

PS. 25:12. Matt. 6:22. Ps. 119:105. Isa. 30:21. Ps. 32:8 – 11. Jer. 10:23.

EVENING

When you lie down, you will not be afraid; when you lie
down, your sleep will be sweet.

A FURIOUS SQUALL came up, and the waves broke over the boat, so that it was
nearly swamped. Jesus was in the stern, sleeping on a cushion.

Do not be anxious about anything, but in everything, by prayer and petition, with thanksgiving, present your requests to God. And the peace of God,
which transcends all understanding, will guard your hearts and your minds in
Christ Jesus.

I will lie down and sleep in peace, for you alone, O LORD, make me dwell in
safety. . . . He grants sleep to those he loves.

While they were stoning him, Stephen prayed, "Lord Jesus, receive my spirit."
Then he fell on his knees and cried out, "Lord, do not hold this sin against
them." When he had said this, he fell alseep. — Away from the body and at home
with the Lord.

PROV. 3:24. Mark 4:37 – 38. Phil. 4:6 – 7. Pss. 4:8; 127:2. Acts 7:59 – 60. 2 Cor. 5:8.

FEBRUARY 23

MORNING

The sprinkled blood that speaks a better word than the blood of Abel.

"LOOK, THE LAMB of God, who takes away the sin of the world! — The Lamb that was slain from the creation of the world. — It is impossible for the blood of bulls and goats to take away sins. Therefore, when Christ came into the world, he said: "Sacrifice and offering you did not desire, but a body you prepared for me." ... And by that will, we have been made holy through the sacrifice of the body of Jesus Christ once for all.

But Abel brought fat portions from some of the firstborn of his flock. The LORD looked with favor on Abel and his offering. — Just as Christ loved us and gave himself up for us as a fragrant offering and sacrifice to God.

Let us draw near to God with a sincere heart in full assurance of faith, having our hearts sprinkled to cleanse us from a guilty conscience and having our bodies washed with pure water.... We have confidence to enter the Most Holy Place by the blood of Jesus.

HEB. 12:24. John 1:29. Rev. 13:8. Heb. 10:4 – 5, 10. Gen. 4:4. Eph. 5:2. Heb. 10:22, 19.

EVENING

Who knows the power of your anger?

FROM THE SIXTH hour until the ninth hour darkness came over all the land. About the ninth hour Jesus cried out in a loud voice, *"Eloi, Eloi, lama sabachthani?"* — which means, "My God, my God, why have you forsaken me?" — And the LORD has laid on him the iniquity of us all.

Therefore, there is now no condemnation for those who are in Christ Jesus.... Since we have been justified through faith, we have peace with God through our Lord Jesus Christ. — Christ redeemed us from the curse of the law by becoming a curse for us.

This is how God showed his love among us: He sent his one and only Son into the world that we might live through him. This is love: not that we loved God, but that he loved us and sent his Son as an atoning sacrifice for our sins. — So as to be just and the one who justifies the man who has faith in Jesus.

PS. 90:11. Matt. 27:45 – 46. Isa. 53:6. Rom. 8:1; 5:1. Gal. 3:13. 1 John 4:9 – 10. Rom. 3:26.

FEBRUARY 24

MORNING

"This is what the Sovereign LORD says: Once again I will yield to the plea."

YOU DO NOT have, because you do not ask God.

"Ask and it will be given to you; seek and you will find; knock and the door will be opened to you. For everyone who asks receives; he who seeks finds; and to him who knocks, the door will be opened." — This is the assurance we have in approaching God: that if we ask anything according to his will, he hears us. And if we know that he hears us — whatever we ask — we know that we have what we asked of him. — If any of you lacks wisdom, he should ask God, who gives generously to all without finding fault, and it will be given to him. — Open wide your mouth and I will fill it. — They should always pray and not give up.

The eyes of the LORD are on the righteous and his ears are attentive to their cry.... The righteous cry out, and the LORD hears them; he delivers them from all their troubles. — You will ask in my name. I am not saying that I will ask the Father on your behalf. No, the Father himself loves you because you have loved me.... Ask and you will receive, and your joy will be complete.

EZEK. 36:37. James 4:2. Matt. 7:7–8. 1 John 5:14–15. James 1:5. Ps. 81:10. Luke 18:1. Ps. 34:15, 17. John 16:26–27, 24.

EVENING

"Shall we accept good from God, and not trouble?"

I KNOW, O Lord, that your laws are righteous, and in faithfulness you have afflicted me. — Yet, O LORD, you are our Father. We are the clay, you are the potter; we are all the work of your hand. — "He is the LORD; let him do what is good in his eyes."

He will sit as a refiner and purifier of silver. — "Because the Lord disciplines those he loves, and he punishes everyone he accepts as a son." — It is enough for the student to be like his teacher, and the servant like his master. — Although he was a son, he learned obedience from what he suffered.

But rejoice that you participate in the sufferings of Christ, so that you may be overjoyed when his glory is revealed. — "These are they who have come out of the great tribulation; they have washed their robes and made them white in the blood of the Lamb."

JOB 2:10. Ps. 119:75. Isa. 64:8. 1 Sam. 3:18. Mal. 3:3. Heb. 12:6. Matt 10:25. Heb. 5:8. 1 Peter 4:13. Rev. 7:14.

FEBRUARY 25

MORNING

Resist the devil, and he will flee from you.

FOR HE WILL come like a pent-up flood that the breath of the LORD drives along. — Jesus said to him, "Away from me, Satan! For it is written: 'Worship the Lord your God, and serve him only.'" Then the devil left him, and angels came and attended him.

Finally, be strong in the Lord and in his mighty power. Put on the full armor of God so that you can take your stand against the devil's schemes.... Have nothing to do with the fruitless deeds of darkness, but rather expose them. — In order that Satan might not outwit us. For we are not unaware of his schemes.

Be self-controlled and alert. Your enemy the devil prowls around like a roaring lion looking for someone to devour. Resist him, standing firm in the faith, because you know that your brothers throughout the world are undergoing the same kind of sufferings. — This is the victory that has overcome the world, even our faith.

Who will bring any charge against those whom God has chosen? It is God who justifies.

JAMES 4:7. Isa. 59:19. Matt. 4:10–11. Eph. 6:10–11; 5:11. 2 Cor. 2:11. 1 Peter 5:8–9. 1 John 5:4. Rom. 8:33.

EVENING

If only I knew where to find him.

WHO AMONG YOU fears the LORD and obeys the word of his servant? Let him who walks in the dark, who has no light, trust in the name of the LORD and rely on his God.

"You will seek me and find me when you seek me with all your heart." — "Ask and it will be given to you; seek and you will find; knock and the door will be opened to you. For everyone who asks receives; he who seeks finds; and to him who knocks, the door will be opened."

And our fellowship is with the Father and with his Son, Jesus Christ. — But now in Christ Jesus you who once were far away have been brought near through the blood of Christ.... For through him we both have access to the Father by one Spirit.

If we claim to have fellowship with him yet walk in the darkness, we lie and do not live by the truth.

"I will be with you always." — "Never will I leave you; never will I forsake you." — "Counselor ... he lives with you and will be in you."

JOB 23:3. Isa. 50:10. Jer. 29:13. Luke 11:9–10. 1 John 1:3. Eph. 2:13, 18. 1 John 1:6. Matt. 28:20. Heb. 13:5. John 14:16–17.

FEBRUARY 26

MORNING

Let us examine our ways and test them.

TEST ME, O LORD, and try me, examine my heart and my mind.... Surely you desire truth in the inner parts; you teach me wisdom in the inmost place.... I have considered my ways and have turned my steps to your statutes. I will hasten and not delay to obey your commands. — A man ought to examine himself before he eats of the bread and drinks of the cup.

If we confess our sins, he is faithful and just and will forgive us our sins and purify us from all unrighteousness. — We have one who speaks to the Father in our defense — Jesus Christ, the Righteous One.

Therefore, brothers, since we have confidence to enter the Most Holy Place by the blood of Jesus, by a new and living way opened for us through the curtain, that is, his body, and since we have a great priest over the house of God, let us draw near to God with a sincere heart in full assurance of faith, having our hearts sprinkled to cleanse us from a guilty conscience and having our bodies washed with pure water.

LAM. 3:40. Pss. 26:2; 51:6; 119:59–60. 1 Cor. 11:28. 1 John 1:9; 2:1. Heb. 10:19–22.

EVENING

A rainbow, resembling an emerald, encircled the throne.

"THIS IS THE sign of the covenant I am making between me and you and every living creature with you, a covenant for all generations to come: I have set my rainbow in the clouds,... I will see it and remember the everlasting covenant between God and all living creatures of every kind on the earth." — Has he not made with me an everlasting covenant, arranged and secured in every part? — God did this so that, by two unchangeable things in which it is impossible for God to lie, we who have fled to take hold of the hope offered to us may be greatly encouraged.

"We tell you the good news: What God promised our fathers he has fulfilled for us, their children, by raising up Jesus."

Jesus Christ is the same yesterday and today and forever.

REV. 4:2. Gen. 9:12–13, 16. 2 Sam. 23:5. Heb. 6:18. Acts 13:32–33. Heb. 13:8.

FEBRUARY 27

MORNING

Count yourselves dead to sin but alive to God in Christ Jesus.

"WHOEVER HEARS MY word and believes him who sent me has eternal life and will not be condemned; he has crossed over from death to life." — For through the law I died to the law so that I might live for God. I have been crucified with Christ and I no longer live, but Christ lives in me. The life I live in the body, I live by faith in the Son of God, who loved me and gave himself for me.

"Because I live, you also will live." ... "I give them eternal life, and they shall never perish; no one can snatch them out of my hand. My Father, who has given them to me, is greater than all; no one can snatch them out of my Father's hand. I and the Father are one."

Since, then, you have been raised with Christ, set your hearts on things above, where Christ is seated at the right hand of God.... For you died, and your life is now hidden with Christ in God.

ROM. 6:11. John 5:24. Gal. 2:19 – 20. John 14:19; 10:28 – 30. Col 3:1, 3.

EVENING

God ... gives generously ... without finding fault.

"WOMAN, WHERE ARE they? Has no one condemned you?" "No one, sir," she said. "Then neither do I condemn you," Jesus declared. "Go now and leave your life of sin."

God's grace and the gift that came by the grace of the one man, Jesus Christ, overflow to the many!...

The gift followed many trespasses and brought justification. But because of his great love for us, God, who is rich in mercy, made us alive with Christ even when we were dead in transgressions — it is by grace you have been saved. And God raised us up with Christ and seated us with him in the heavenly realms in Christ Jesus, in order that in the coming ages he might show the incomparable riches of his grace, expressed in his kindness to us in Christ Jesus.

He who did not spare his own Son, but gave him up for us all — how will he not also, along with him, graciously give us all things?

JAMES 1:5. John 8:10 – 11. Rom. 5:15 – 16. Eph. 2:4 – 7. Rom. 8:32.

FEBRUARY 28

MORNING

"For God so loved the world that he gave his one and only Son, that whoever believes in him shall not perish but have eternal life."

ALL THIS IS from God, who reconciled us to himself through Christ and gave us the ministry of reconciliation: that God was reconciling the world to himself in Christ, not counting men's sins against them. And he has committed to us the message of reconciliation. We are therefore Christ's ambassadors, as though God were making his appeal through us. We implore you on Christ's behalf: Be reconciled to God. God made him who had no sin to be sin for us, so that in him we might become the righteousness of God.

God is love. This is how God showed his love among us: He sent his one and only Son into the world that we might live through him. This is love: not that we loved God, but that he loved us and sent his Son as an atoning sacrifice for our sins. Dear friends, since God so loved us, we also ought to love one another.

JOHN 3:16. 2 Cor. 5:18–21. 1 John 4:8–11.

EVENING

The lamp of the LORD searches the spirit of a man.

"IF ANY ONE of you is without sin, let him be the first to throw a stone at her." ... Those who heard began to go away one at a time, the older ones first, until only Jesus was left, with the woman still standing there.

"Who told you that you were naked? Have you eaten from the tree that I commanded you not to eat from?"

Anyone, then, who knows the good he ought to do and doesn't do it, sins. — Whenever our hearts condemn us. For God is greater than our hearts, and he knows everything. Dear friends, if our hearts do not condemn us, we have confidence before God.

All food is clean, but it is wrong for a man to eat anything that causes someone else to stumble.... Blessed is the man who does not condemn himself by what he approves.

Search me, O God, and know my heart; test me and know my anxious thoughts. See if there is any offensive way in me, and lead me in the way everlasting.

PROV. 20:27. John 8:7, 9. Gen. 3:11. James 4:17. 1 John 3:20–21. Rom. 14:20, 22. Ps. 139:23–24.

FEBRUARY 29

MORNING

Do not boast about tomorrow, for you do not know what a day may bring forth.

I TELL YOU, now is the time of God's favor, now is the day of salvation. — "You are going to have the light just a little while longer. Walk while you have the light, before darkness overtakes you. The man who walks in the dark does not know where he is going. Put your trust in the light while you have it, so that you may become sons of light."

Whatever your hand finds to do, do it with all your might, for in the grave, where you are going, there is neither working nor planning nor knowledge nor wisdom.

" 'You have plenty of good things laid up for many years. Take life easy; eat, drink and be merry.' ... 'You fool! This very night your life will be demanded from you. Then who will get what you have prepared for yourself?' This is how it will be with anyone who stores up things for himself but is not rich toward God."

What is your life? You are a mist that appears for a little while and then vanishes. — The world and its desires pass away, but the man who does the will of God lives forever.

PROV. 27:1. 2 Cor. 6:2. John 12:35 – 36. Eccl. 9:10. Luke 12:19 – 21. James 4:14. 1 John 2:17.

EVENING

But you remain the same, and your years will never end.

BEFORE THE MOUNTAINS were born or you brought forth the earth and the world, from everlasting to everlasting you are God.

"I the LORD do not change. So you, O descendants of Jacob, are not destroyed." — The same yesterday and today and forever.

Every good and perfect gift is from above, coming down from the Father of the heavenly lights, who does not change like shifting shadows. — For God's gifts and his call are irrevocable.

God is not a man, that he should lie, nor a son of man, that he should change his mind. — Because of the LORD's great love we are not consumed, for his compassions never fail.

But because Jesus lives forever, he has a permanent priesthood. Therefore he is able to save completely those who come to God through him, because he always lives to intercede for them. — "Do not be afraid. I am the First and the Last."

PS. 102:27. Ps. 90:2. Mal. 3:6. Heb. 13:8. James 1:17. Rom. 11:29. Num. 23:19. Lam. 3:22. Heb. 1:24 – 25. Rev. 1:17.

MARCH 1

MORNING

The fruit of the Spirit is love.

GOD IS LOVE. Whoever lives in love lives in God, and God in him. — God has poured out his love into our hearts by the Holy Spirit, whom he has given us. — Now to you who believe, this stone is precious. — We love because he first loved us. — For Christ's love compels us, because we are convinced that one died for all, and therefore all died. And he died for all, that those who live should no longer live for themselves but for him who died for them and was raised again.

You yourselves have been taught by God to love each other. — "My command is this: Love each other as I have loved you." — Above all, love each other deeply, because love covers over a multitude of sins. — Live a life of love, just as Christ loved us and gave himself up for us as a fragrant offering and sacrifice to God.

GAL. 5:22. 1 John 4:16. Rom. 5:5. 1 Peter 2:7. 1 John 4:19. 2 Cor. 5:14–15. 1 Thess. 4:9. John 15:12. 1 Peter 4:8. Eph. 5:2.

EVENING

The LORD is my Banner.

IF GOD IS for us, who can be against us? — The LORD is with me; I will not be afraid. What can man do to me? . . . But for those who fear you, you have raised a banner.

The LORD is my light and my salvation — whom shall I fear? The LORD is the stronghold of my life — of whom shall I be afraid? . . . Though an army besiege me, my heart will not fear; though war break out against me, even then will I be confident.

God is with us; he is our leader. — The LORD Almighty is with us; the God of Jacob is our fortress.

They will make war against the Lamb, but the Lamb will overcome them. — Why do the nations rage and the peoples plot in vain? . . . The One enthroned in heaven laughs; the Lord scoffs at them. — Propose your plan, but it will not stand, for God is with us.

EXOD. 17:15. Rom. 8:31. Pss. 118:6; 60:4; 27:1, 3. 2 Chron. 13:12. Ps. 46:7. Rev. 17:14. Ps. 2:1, 4. Isa. 8:10.

MARCH 2

MORNING

"God has made me fruitful in the land of my suffering."

PRAISE BE TO the God and Father of our Lord Jesus Christ, the Father of compassion and the God of all comfort, who comforts us in all our troubles, so that we can comfort those in any trouble with the comfort we ourselves have received from God. For just as the sufferings of Christ flow over into our lives, so also through Christ our comfort overflows.

In this you greatly rejoice, though now for a little while you may have had to suffer grief in all kinds of trials. These have come so that your faith—of greater worth than gold, which perishes even though refined by fire—may be proved genuine and may result in praise, glory and honor when Jesus Christ is revealed.—But the Lord stood at my side and gave me strength.

So then, those who suffer according to God's will should commit themselves to their faithful Creator and continue to do good.

GEN. 41:52. 2 Cor. 1:3–5. 1 Peter 1:6–7. 2 Tim. 4:17. 1 Peter 4:19.

EVENING

There remains, then, a Sabbath-rest for the people of God.

THERE THE WICKED cease from turmoil, and there the weary are at rest. Captives also enjoy their ease; they no longer hear the slave driver's shout.

"Blessed are the dead who die in the Lord from now on." ... "They will rest from their labor, for their deeds will follow them."

"Our friend Lazarus has fallen asleep"; ... Jesus had been speaking of his death, but his disciples thought he meant natural sleep.

For while we are in this tent, we groan and are burdened.—We ourselves, who have the firstfruits of the Spirit, groan inwardly as we wait eagerly for our adoption as sons, the redemption of our bodies. For in this hope we were saved. But hope that is seen is no hope at all. Who hopes for what he already has? But if we hope for what we do not yet have, we wait for it patiently.

HEB. 4:9. Job 3:17–18. Rev. 14:13. John 11:11, 13. 2 Cor. 5:4. Rom. 8:23–25.

MARCH 3

MORNING

Trust in the LORD with all your heart and lean not on your own understanding; in all your ways acknowledge him, and he will make your paths straight.

TRUST IN HIM at all times, O people; pour out your hearts to him, for God is our refuge.

I will instruct you and teach you in the way you should go; I will counsel you and watch over you. Do not be like the horse or the mule, which have no understanding but must be controlled by bit and bridle or they will not come to you. Many are the woes of the wicked, but the LORD's unfailing love surrounds the man who trusts in him. — Whether you turn to the right or to the left, your ears will hear a voice behind you, saying, "This is the way; walk in it."

"My Presence will go with you, and I will give you rest." Then Moses said to him, "If your Presence does not go with us, do not send us up from here. How will anyone know that you are pleased with me and with your people unless you go with us? What else will distinguish me and your people from all the other people on the face of the earth?"

PROV. 3:5–6. Pss. 62:8; 32:8–10. Isa. 30:21. Exod. 33:15–16.

EVENING

The prize for which God has called me heavenward in Christ Jesus.

"YOU WILL HAVE treasure in heaven. Then come, follow me." — "I am your shield, your very great reward."

"Well done, good and faithful servant! You have been faithful with a few things; I will put you in charge of many things. Come and share your master's happiness!" — And they will reign for ever and ever.

You will receive the crown of glory that will never fade away. — The crown of life. — A crown of righteousness. — A crown that will last forever.

"Father, I want those you have given me to be with me where I am, and to see my glory, the glory you have given me." — And so we will be with the Lord forever.

I consider that our present sufferings are not worth comparing with the glory that will be revealed in us.

PHIL. 3:14. Matt. 19:21. Gen. 15:1. Matt. 25:21. Rev. 22:5. 1 Peter 5:4. James 1:12.
2 Tim. 4:8. 1 Cor. 9:25. John 17:24. 1 Thess. 4:17. Rom. 8:18.

MARCH 4

MORNING

Set your minds on things above, not on earthly things.

DO NOT LOVE the world or anything in the world. If anyone loves the world, the love of the Father is not in him. — "Do not store up for yourselves treasures on earth, where moth and rust destroy, and where thieves break in and steal. But store up for yourselves treasures in heaven, where moth and rust do not destroy, and where thieves do not break in and steal. For where your treasure is, there your heart will be also."

We live by faith, not by sight.... Therefore we do not lose heart. Though outwardly we are wasting away, yet inwardly we are being renewed day by day. For our light and momentary troubles are achieving for us an eternal glory that far outweighs them all. So we fix our eyes not on what is seen, but on what is unseen. For what is seen is temporary, but what is unseen is eternal.

An inheritance that can never perish, spoil or fade — kept in heaven for you.

COL. 3:2. 1 John 2:15. Matt. 6:19 – 21. 2 Cor. 5:7; 4:16 – 18. 1 Peter 1:4.

EVENING

He will bend his shoulder to the burden.

BROTHERS, AS AN example of patience in the face of suffering, take the prophets who spoke in the name of the Lord. — These things happened to them as examples and were written down as warnings for us, on whom the fulfillment of the ages has come.

"Shall we accept good from God, and not trouble?" — In all this, Job did not sin in what he said. — Aaron remained silent. — "He is the LORD; let him do what is good in his eyes."

Cast your cares on the LORD and he will sustain you. — Surely he took up our infirmities and carried our sorrows.

"Come to me, all you who are weary and burdened, and I will give you rest. Take my yoke upon you and learn from me, for I am gentle and humble in heart, and you will find rest for your souls. For my yoke is easy and my burden is light."

GEN. 49:15. James 5:10. 1 Cor. 10:11. Job 2:10. Lev. 10:3. 1 Sam. 3:18. Ps. 55:22. Isa. 53:4. Matt. 11:28 – 30.

MORNING

"I am troubled; O Lord, come to my aid!"

I LIFT UP my eyes to you, to you whose throne is in heaven. As the eyes of slaves look to the hand of their master, as the eyes of a maid look to the hand of her mistress, so our eyes look to the LORD our God, till he shows us his mercy.

Hear my cry, O God; listen to my prayer. From the ends of the earth I call to you, I call as my heart grows faint; lead me to the rock that is higher than I. For you have been my refuge, a strong tower against the foe. I long to dwell in your tent forever and take refuge in the shelter of your wings. — You have been a refuge for the poor, a refuge for the needy in his distress, a shelter from the storm.

Christ suffered for you, leaving you an example, that you should follow in his steps. — "He committed no sin, and no deceit was found in his mouth." — When they hurled their insults at him, he did not retaliate; when he suffered, he made no threats. Instead, he entrusted himself to him who judges justly.

ISA. 38:14. Pss. 123:1 – 2; 61:1 – 4. Isa. 25:4. 1 Peter 2:21 – 23.

EVENING

Fight the good fight of the faith.

BUT WE WERE harassed at every turn — conflicts on the outside, fears within. — "Don't be afraid.... Those who are with us are more than those who are with them." — Be strong in the Lord and in his mighty power.

"You come against me with sword and spear and javelin, but I come against you in the name of the LORD Almighty, the God of the armies of Israel, whom you have defied." — It is God who arms me with strength. — He trains my hands for battle; my arms can bend a bow of bronze. — Our competence comes from God.

The angel of the LORD encamps around those who fear him, and he delivers them. — He looked and saw the hills full of horses and chariots of fire all around Elisha.

I do not have time to tell about ... [those] who through faith conquered kingdoms, ... whose weakness was turned to strength; and who became powerful in battle and routed foreign armies.

1 TIM. 6:12. 2 Cor. 7:5. 2 Kings 6:16. Eph. 6:10. 1 Sam. 17:45. 2 Sam. 22:33, 35. 2 Cor. 3:5. Ps. 34:7. 2 Kings 6:17. Heb. 11:32 – 34.

MARCH 6

MORNING

He ... protects the way of his faithful ones.

THE LORD YOUR God ... went ahead of you on your journey, in fire by night and in a cloud by day.... Like an eagle that stirs up its nest and hovers over its young, that spreads its wings to catch them and carries them on its pinions. The LORD alone led him. — The LORD delights in the way of the man whose steps he has made firm; though he stumble, he will not fall, for the LORD upholds him with his hand.

A righteous man may have many troubles, but the LORD delivers him from them all.... For the LORD watches over the way of the righteous, but the way of the wicked will perish. — And we know that in all things God works for the good of those who love him, who have been called according to his purpose. — "With us is the LORD our God to help us and to fight our battles."

"The LORD your God is with you, he is mighty to save. He will take great delight in you, he will quiet you with his love, he will rejoice over you with singing."

PROV. 2:8. Deut. 1:32 – 33; 32:11 – 12. Pss. 37:23 – 24; 34:19; 1:6. Rom. 8:28. 2 Chron. 32:8. Zeph. 3:17.

EVENING

"My God, my God, why have you forsaken me?"

HE WAS PIERCED for our transgressions, he was crushed for our iniquities; the punishment that brought us peace was upon him.... The LORD has laid on him the iniquity of us all.... For the transgression of my people he was stricken.... Yet it was the LORD's will to crush him and cause him to suffer.

Jesus our Lord ... was delivered over to death for our sins and was raised to life for our justification. — For Christ died for our sins once for all, the righteous for the unrighteous, to bring you to God.... He himself bore our sins in his body on the tree, so that we might die to sins and live for righteousness; by his wounds you have been healed.

God made him who had no sin to be sin for us, so that in him we might become the righteousness of God. — Christ redeemed us from the curse of the law by becoming a curse for us.

MATT. 27:46. Isa. 53:5 – 6, 8, 10. Rom. 4:24 – 25. 1 Peter 3:18; 2:24. 2 Cor. 5:21. Gal. 3:13.

MARCH 7

MORNING

For your Maker is your husband—the LORD Almighty is his name.

THIS IS A profound mystery—but I am talking about Christ and the church.—No longer will they call you Deserted, or name your land Desolate. But you will be called Hephzibah, and your land Beulah; for the LORD will take delight in you.

He has sent me to bind up the brokenhearted, to proclaim freedom for the captives and release for the prisoners, to proclaim the year of the LORD's favor and the day of vengeance of our God, to comfort all who mourn, and provide for those who grieve in Zion—to bestow on them a crown of beauty instead of ashes, the oil of gladness instead of mourning, and a garment of praise instead of a spirit of despair.

I delight greatly in the LORD; my soul rejoices in my God. For he has clothed me with garments of salvation and arrayed me in a robe of righteousness, as a bridegroom adorns his head like a priest, and as a bride adorns herself with her jewels.

I will betroth you to me forever; I will betroth you in righteousness and justice, in love and compassion.—Who shall separate us from the love of Christ?

ISA. 54:5. Eph. 5:32. Isa. 62:4–5; 61:1–3, 10. Hos. 2:19. Rom. 8:35.

EVENING

My times are in your hands.

ALL THE HOLY ones are in your hand.—Then the word of the LORD came to Elijah: "Leave here, turn eastward and hide in the ravine of Kerith, east of the Jordan. You will drink from the brook, and I have ordered the ravens to feed you there." ... Then the word of the LORD came to him [Elijah]: "Go at once to Zarephath of Sidon and stay there. I have commanded a widow in that place to supply you with food."

"Therefore I tell you, do not worry about your life, what you will eat or drink; or about your body, what you will wear. ... Your heavenly Father knows that you need them."

Trust in the LORD with all your heart and lean not on your own understanding; in all your ways acknowledge him, and he will make your paths straight.—Cast all your anxiety on him because he cares for you.

PS. 31:15. Deut. 33:3. 1 Kings 17:2–4, 8–9. Matt. 6:25, 32. Prov. 3:5–6. 1 Peter 5:7.

MARCH 8

MORNING

You have put all my sins behind your back.

WHO IS A God like you, who pardons sins and forgives the transgression of the remnant of his inheritance? You do not stay angry forever but delight to show mercy. You will again have compassion on us; you will tread our sins underfoot and hurl all our iniquities into the depths of the sea.

"For a brief moment I abandoned you, but with deep compassion I will bring you back. In a surge of anger I hid my face from you for a moment, but with everlasting kindness I will have compassion on you," says the LORD your Redeemer. — "For I will forgive their wickedness and will remember their sins no more."

Blessed is he whose transgressions are forgiven, whose sins are covered. Blessed is the man whose sin the LORD does not count against him and in whose spirit is no deceit. — The blood of Jesus, his Son, purifies us from every sin.

ISA. 38:17. Mic. 7:18 – 19. Isa. 54:7 – 8. Jer. 31:34. Ps. 32:1 – 2. 1 John 1:7.

EVENING

I know whom I have believed, and am convinced that he is able.

ABLE TO DO immeasurably more than all we ask or imagine. — Able to make all grace abound to you, so that in all things at all times, having all that you need, you will abound in every good work. — Able to help those who are being tempted.

Able to save completely those who come to God through him, because he always lives to intercede for them. — Able to keep you from falling and to present you before his glorious presence without fault and with great joy. — Able to guard what I have entrusted to him for that day.

Who, by the power that enables him to bring everything under his control, will transform our lowly bodies so that they will be like his glorious body.

"Do you believe that I am able to do this?" ... "Yes, Lord." ... "According to your faith will it be done to you."

2 TIM. 1:12. Eph. 3:20. 2 Cor. 9:8. Heb. 2:18; 7:25. Jude 24. 2 Tim. 1:12. Phil. 3:21. Matt. 9:28 – 29.

MARCH 9

MORNING

God, who richly provides us with everything for our enjoyment.

BE CAREFUL THAT you do not forget the LORD your God, failing to observe his commands, his laws and his decrees that I am giving you this day. — Otherwise, when you eat and are satisfied, when you build fine houses and settle down, . . . then your heart will become proud and you will forget the LORD your God. . . . But remember the LORD your God, for it is he who gives you the ability to produce wealth.

Unless the LORD builds the house, its builders labor in vain. Unless the LORD watches over the city, the watchmen stand guard in vain. In vain you rise early and stay up late, toiling for food to eat — for he grants sleep to those he loves. . . . It was not by their sword that they won the land, nor did their arm bring them victory; it was your right hand, your arm, and the light of your face, for you loved them.

Many are asking, "Who can show us any good?" Let the light of your face shine upon us, O LORD.

1 TIM. 6:17. Deut. 8:11 – 12, 14, 18. Pss. 127:1 – 2; 44:3; 4:6.

EVENING

They sang a new song

BY A NEW and living way opened for us through the curtain, that is, his body. — He saved us, not because of righteous things we had done, but because of his mercy. He saved us through the washing of rebirth and renewal by the Holy Spirit, whom he poured out on us generously through Jesus Christ our Savior. — For it is by grace you have been saved, through faith — and this not from yourselves, it is the gift of God — not by works, so that no one can boast.

Not to us, O LORD, not to us but to your name be the glory.

To him who loves us and has freed us from our sins by his blood, and has made us to be a kingdom and priests to serve his God and Father — to him be glory and power for ever and ever! Amen. . . . Because you were slain, and with your blood you purchased men for God from every tribe and language and people and nation. . . . Before me was a great multitude that no one could count, from every nation, tribe, people and language, standing before the throne and in front of the Lamb.

REV. 14:3. Heb. 10:20. Titus 3:5 – 6. Eph. 2:8 – 9. Ps. 115:1. Rev. 1:5 – 6; 5:9; 7:9 – 10.

MARCH 10

MORNING

"The LORD will provide."

"GOD HIMSELF WILL provide the lamb for the burnt offering, my son."

Surely the arm of the LORD is not to short to save, nor his ear to dull to hear. — "The deliverer will come from Zion; he will turn godlessness away from Jacob."

Blessed is he whose help is the God of Jacob, whose hope is in the LORD his God.... But the eyes of the LORD are on those who fear him, on those whose hope is in his unfailing love, to deliver them from death.

My God will meet all your needs according to his glorious riches in Christ Jesus. — "Never will I leave you; never will I forsake you." So we say with confidence, "The Lord is my helper; I will not be afraid.

The LORD is my strength and my shield; my heart trusts in him, and I am helped. My heart leaps for joy and I will give thanks to him in song."

GEN. 22:14. Gen. 22:8. Isa. 59:1. Rom. 11:26. Pss. 146:5; 33:18 – 19. Phil. 4:19. Heb. 13:5 – 6. Ps. 28:7.

EVENING

He browses among the lilies.

FOR WHERE TWO or three come together in my name, there am I with them." — "If anyone loves me, he will obey my teaching. My Father will love him, and we will come to him and make our home with him."

"If you obey my commands, you will remain in my love, just as I have obeyed my Father's commands and remain in his love."

Let my lover come into his garden and taste its choice fruits.... I have come into my garden, my sister, my bride; I have gathered my myrrh with my spice. I have eaten my honeycomb and my honey. — The fruit of the Spirit is love, joy, peace, patience, kindness, goodness, faithfulness, gentleness and self-control.

"This is to my Father's glory, that you bear much fruit, showing yourselves to be my disciples." ... "Every branch that does bear fruit he trims clean so that it will be even more fruitful." — Filled with the fruit of righteousness that comes through Jesus Christ — to the glory and praise of God.

SONG OF SONGS 2:16. Matt. 18:20. John 14:23; 15:10. Song of Songs 4:16; 5:1. Gal. 5:22 – 23. John 15:8, 2. Phil. 1:11.

MARCH 11

MORNING

"The LORD bless you and keep you."

THE BLESSING OF the LORD brings wealth, and he adds no trouble to it. — For surely, O LORD, you bless the righteous; you surround them with your favor as with a shield.

He will not let your foot slip — he who watches over you will not slumber; indeed, he who watches over Israel will neither slumber nor sleep. The LORD watches over you — the LORD is your shade at your right hand.... The LORD will keep you from all harm — he will watch over your life; the LORD will watch over you coming and going both now and forevermore.

"I, the LORD, watch over it; I water it continually. I guard it day and night." — "Holy Father, protect them by the power of your name — the name you gave me — so that they may be one as we are one. While I was with them, I protected them and kept them safe by that name you gave me."

The Lord will rescue me from every evil attack and will bring me safely to his heavenly kingdom. To him be glory for ever and ever. Amen.

NUM. 6:24. Prov. 10:22. Pss. 5:12; 121:3–5, 7–8. Isa. 27:3. John 17:11–12. 2 Tim. 4:18.

EVENING

Jesus wept.

A MAN OF sorrows, and familiar with suffering. — For we do not have a high priest who is unable to sympathize with our weaknesses.... In bringing many sons to glory, it was fitting that God, for whom and through whom everything exists, should make the author of their salvation perfect through suffering.

Although he was a son, he learned obedience from what he suffered. — I have not been rebellious; I have not drawn back. I offered my back to those who beat me, my cheeks to those who pulled out my beard; I did not hide my face from mocking and spitting.

"See how he loved him!" — For this reason he had to be made like his brothers in every way, in order that he might become a merciful and faithful high priest in service to God, and that he might make atonement for the sins of the people.

JOHN 11:35. Isa. 53:3. Heb. 4:15; 2:10; 5:8. Isa. 50:5–6. John 11:36. Heb. 2:16–17.

MARCH 12

MORNING

"The LORD make his face shine upon you and be gracious to you; the LORD turn his face toward you and give you peace."

NO ONE HAS ever seen God, but God the only Son, who is at the Father's side, has made him known. — The Son is the radiance of God's glory and the exact representation of his being. — The god of this age has blinded the minds of unbelievers, so that they cannot see the light of the gospel of the glory of Christ, who is the image of God.

Let your face shine on your servant; save me in your unfailing love. Let me not be put to shame, O LORD, for I have cried out to you.... O LORD, when you favored me, you made my mountain stand firm; but when you hid your face, I was dismayed.... Blessed are those who have learned to acclaim you, who walk in the light of your presence, O LORD.

The LORD gives strength to his people; the LORD blesses his people with peace. — "Take courage! It is I. Don't be afraid."

NUM. 6:25–26. John 1:18. Heb. 1:3. 2 Cor. 4:4. Pss. 31:16–17; 30:7; 89:15; 29:11. Matt. 14:27.

EVENING

Do what pleases him.

WITHOUT FAITH IT is impossible to please God. — Those controlled by the sinful nature cannot please God. — For the LORD takes delight in his people.

For it is commendable if a man bears up under the pain of unjust suffering because he is conscious of God.... But if you suffer for doing good and you endure it, this is commendable before God.... The unfading beauty of a gentle and quiet spirit, ... is of great worth in God's sight.

"He who sacrifices thank offerings honors me, and he prepares the way so that I may show him the salvation of God." ... I will praise God's name in song and glorify him with thanksgiving. This will please the LORD more than an ox, more than a bull with its horns and hoofs.

Therefore, I urge you, brothers, in view of God's mercy, to offer your bodies as living sacrifices, holy and pleasing to God — which is your spiritual worship.

1 JOHN 3:22. Heb. 11:6. Rom. 8:8. Ps. 149:4. 1 Peter 2:19–20, 3:4. Pss. 50:23; 69:30–31. Rom. 12:1.

MARCH 13

MORNING

*For there is one God and one mediator between God and men,
the man Christ Jesus.*

SINCE THE CHILDREN have flesh and blood, he too shared in their humanity.

"Turn to me and be saved, all you ends of the earth; for I am God, and there is no other."

We have one who speaks to the Father in our defense — Jesus Christ, the Righteous One. — But now in Christ Jesus you who once were far away have been brought near through the blood of Christ. For he himself is our peace.

He entered the Most Holy Place once for all by his own blood, having obtained eternal redemption.... For this reason Christ is the mediator of a new covenant, that those who are called may receive the promised eternal inheritance.... Therefore he is able to save completely those who come to God through him, because he always lives to intercede for them.

1 TIM. 2:5. Heb. 2:14. Isa. 45:22. 1 John 2:1. Eph. 2:13–14. Heb. 9:12, 15; 7:25.

EVENING

My God. My soul is downcast within me.

YOU WILL KEEP in perfect peace him whose mind is steadfast, because he trusts in you. Trust in the LORD forever, for the LORD, the LORD, is the Rock eternal.

Cast your cares on the LORD and he will sustain you.... For he has not despised or disdained the suffering of the afflicted one; he has not hidden his face from him but has listened to his cry for help. — Is any one of you in trouble? He should pray.

Do not let your hearts be troubled and do not be afraid. — "Therefore I tell you, do not worry about your life, what you will eat or drink; or about your body, what you will wear. Is not life more important than food, and the body more important than clothes? Look at the birds of the air, they do not sow or reap or store away in barns, and yet your heavenly Father feeds them. Are you not much more valuable than they?" — "Stop doubting and believe." — "And surely I will be with you always."

**PS. 42:6. Isa. 26:3–4. Pss. 55:22; 22:24. James 5:13. John 14:27. Matt. 6:25–26.
John 20:27. Matt. 28:20.**

MARCH 14

MORNING

In every way they will make the teaching about God our Savior attractive.

CONDUCT YOURSELVES IN a manner worthy of the gospel of Christ. — Avoid every kind of evil. — If you are insulted because of the name of Christ, you are blessed.... If you suffer, it should not be as a murderer or thief or any other kind of criminal, or even as a meddler. — You may become blameless and pure, children of God without fault in a crooked and depraved generation, in which you shine like stars in the universe. — Let your light shine before men, that they may see your good deeds and praise your Father in heaven.

Let love and faithfulness never leave you; bind them around your neck, write them on the tablet of your heart. Then you will win favor and a good name in the sight of God and man. — Finally, brothers, whatever is true, whatever is noble, whatever is right, whatever is pure, whatever is lovely, whatever is admirable — if anything is excellent or praiseworthy — think about such things.

TITUS 2:10. Phil. 1:27. 1 Thess. 5:22. 1 Peter 4:14 – 15. Phil. 2:15. Matt. 5:16. Prov. 3:3 – 4. Phil. 4:8.

EVENING

The words I have spoken to you are spirit and they are life.

HE CHOSE TO give us birth through the word of truth. — The letter kills, but the Spirit gives life.

Christ loved the church and gave himself up for her to make her holy, cleansing her by the washing with water through the word, and to present her to himself as a radiant church, without stain or wrinkle or any other blemish.

How can a young man keep his way pure? By living according to your word.... Your promise renews my life.... I have hidden your word in my heart that I might not sin against you.... I delight in your decrees; I will not neglect your word.... I trust in your word.... The law from your mouth is more precious to me than thousands of pieces of silver and gold.... I will never forget your precepts, for by them you have renewed my life.... How sweet are your promises to my taste, sweeter than honey to my mouth! I gain understanding from your precepts; therefore I hate every wrong path.

JOHN 6:63. James 1:18. 2 Cor. 3:6. Eph. 5:25 – 27. Pss. 119:9, 50, 11, 16, 42, 72, 93, 103 – 104.

MARCH 15

MORNING

Perfect through suffering.

"MY SOUL IS overwhelmed with sorrow to the point of death. Stay here and keep watch with me." Going a little further, he fell with his face to the ground and prayed. "My Father, if it is possible, may this cup be taken from me. Yet not as I will, but as you will."—And being in anguish, he prayed more earnestly, and his sweat was like drops of blood falling to the ground.

The cords of death entangled me, the anguish of the grave came upon me; I was overcome by trouble and sorrow.... Scorn has broken my heart and has left me helpless; I looked for sympathy, but there was none, for comforters, but I found none.... Look to my right and see; no one is concerned for me. I have no refuge; no one cares for my life.

He was despised and rejected by men, a man of sorrows, and familiar with suffering. Like one from whom men hide their faces he was despised, and we esteemed him not.

HEB. 2:10. Matt. 26:38–39. Luke 22:44. Pss. 116:3; 69:20; 142:4. Isa. 53:3.

EVENING

The LORD made the heavens and the earth, the sea,
and all that is in them.

THE HEAVENS DECLARE the glory of God; the skies proclaim the work of his hands.... By the word of the LORD were the heavens made, their starry host by the breath of his mouth.... For he spoke, and it came to be; he commanded, and it stood firm.—Surely the nations are like a drop in a bucket; they are regarded as dust on the scales; he weighs the islands as though they were fine dust.

By faith we understand that the universe was formed at God's command, so that what is seen was not made out of what was visible.

When I consider your heavens, the work of your fingers, the moon and the stars, which you have set in place, what is man that you are mindful of him, the son of man that you care for him?

EXOD. 20:11. Pss. 19:1; 33:6, 9. Isa. 40:15. Heb. 11:3. Ps. 8:3–4.

MARCH 16

MORNING

What is your life? You are a mist that appears for a little while and then vanishes.

"My DAYS ARE swifter than a runner; they fly away without a glimpse of joy. They skim past like boats of papyrus, like eagles swooping down on their prey." — You sweep men away in the sleep of death; they are like the new grass of the morning — though in the morning it springs up new, by evening it is dry and withered. — "Man born of woman is of few days and full of trouble. He springs up like a flower and withers away."

The world and its desires pass away, but the man who does the will of God lives forever. — They will perish, but you remain; they will all wear out like a garment. Like clothing you will change them and they will be discarded. But you remain the same, and your years will never end. — Jesus Christ is the same yesterday and today and forever.

JAMES 4:14. Job. 9:25–26. Ps. 90:5–6. Job 14:2. 1 John 2:17. Ps. 102:26–27. Heb. 13:8.

EVENING

I will sing with my spirit, but I will also sing with my mind.

BE FILLED WITH the Spirit. Speak to one another with psalms, hymns and spiritual songs. Sing and make music in your heart to the Lord. — Let the word of Christ dwell in you richly as you teach and admonish one another with all wisdom, and as you sing psalms, hymns and spiritual songs with gratitude in your hearts to God.

My mouth will speak in praise of the LORD. Let every creature praise his holy name for ever and ever.

Praise the LORD. How good it is to sing praises to our God, how pleasant and fitting to praise him!... Sing to the LORD with thanksgiving; make music to our God on the harp.

And I heard a sound from heaven like the roar of rushing waters and like a loud peal of thunder. The sound I heard was like that of harpists playing their harps.

1 COR. 14:15. Eph. 5:18–19. Col 3:16. Pss. 145:21; 147:1, 7. Rev. 14:2.

MARCH 17

MORNING

*He is to lay his hand on the head of the burnt offering, and it
will be accepted on his behalf to make atonement for him.*

FOR YOU KNOW that it was not with perishable things such as silver or gold that you
were redeemed from the empty way of life handed down to you from your forefathers, but with the precious blood of Christ, a lamb without blemish or defect....
He himself bore our sins in his body on the tree, so that we might die to sins.

He has freely given us in the One he loves. — You also, like living stones, are
being built into a spiritual house to be a holy priesthood, offering spiritual sacrifices acceptable to God through Jesus Christ. — Therefore, I urge you, brothers,
in view of God's mercy, to offer your bodies as living sacrifices, holy and pleasing
to God — which is your spiritual worship.

To him who is able to keep you from falling and to present you before his
glorious presence without fault and with great joy — to the only God our Savior
be glory, majesty, power and authority, through Jesus Christ our Lord, before all
ages, now and forevermore! Amen.

LEV. 1:4. 1 Peter 1:18–19; 2:24. Eph. 1:6. 1 Peter 2:5. Rom. 12:1. Jude 24–25.

EVENING

*One who has been tempted in every way, just as we are —
yet was without sin.*

WHEN THE WOMAN saw that the fruit of the tree was good for food and pleasing
to the eye, and also desirable for gaining wisdom, she took some and ate it. She
also gave some to her husband, who was with her, and he ate it.

The tempter came to him and said, "If you are the Son of God, tell these stones
to become bread." Jesus answered, "It is written: 'Man does not live on bread alone,
but on every word that comes from the mouth of God.'" ... The devil ... showed
him all the kingdoms of the world and their splendor. "All this I will give you,"
he said, "if you will bow down and worship me." Jesus said to him, "Away from
me, Satan!"

Because he himself suffered when he was tempted, he is able to help those
who are being tempted.

Blessed is the man who perseveres under trial.

HEB. 4:15. Gen. 3:6. Matt. 4:3–4, 8–10. Heb. 2:18. James 1:12.

MARCH 18

MORNING

My eyes grew weak as I looked to the heavens.

BE MERCIFUL TO me, LORD, for I am faint; O LORD, heal me, for my bones are in agony. My soul is in anguish. How long, O LORD, how long? Turn, O LORD, and deliver me; save me because of your unfailing love.... My heart is in anguish within me; the terrors of death assail me. Fear and trembling have beset me; horror has overwhelmed me. I said, "Oh, that I had the wings of a dove! I would fly away and be at rest—I would flee far away and stay in the desert."

You need to persevere.

They were looking intently up into the sky as he was going, when suddenly two men dressed in white stood beside them. "Men of Galilee," they said, "why do you stand here looking into the sky? This same Jesus, who has been taken from you into heaven, will come back in the same way you have seen him go into heaven."—But our citizenship is in heaven. And we eagerly await a Savior from there, the Lord Jesus Christ.—While we wait for the blessed hope—the glorious appearing of our great God and Savior, Jesus Christ.

ISA. 38:14. Pss. 6:2–4; 55:4–6. Heb. 10:36. Acts 1:10–11. Phil. 3:20. Titus 2:13.

EVENING

His name will be on their foreheads.

"I AM THE good shepherd; I know my sheep."—God's solid foundation stands firm, sealed with this inscription: "The Lord knows those who are his," and, "Everyone who confesses the name of the Lord must turn away from wickedness."

The LORD is good, a refuge in times of trouble. He cares for those who trust in him.—"Do not harm the land or the sea or the trees until we put a seal on the foreheads of the servants of our God."—Having believed, you were marked in him with a seal, the promised Holy Spirit, who is a deposit guaranteeing our inheritance.—Now it is God who makes both us and you stand firm in Christ. He anointed us, set his seal of ownership on us, and put his Spirit in our hearts.

I will write on him the name of my God and the name of the city of my God, the new Jerusalem, which is coming down out of heaven from my God; and I will also write on him my new name.—"This is the name by which it will be called: The LORD Our Righteousness."

REV. 22:4. John 10:14. 2 Tim. 2:19. Nah. 1:7. Rev. 7:3. Eph. 1:13–14. 2 Cor. 1:21–22. Rev. 3:12. Jer. 33:16.

MARCH 19

MORNING

*"When God raised up his servant, he sent him first to you to
bless you by turning each of you from your wicked ways."*

PRAISE BE TO the God and Father of our Lord Jesus Christ! In his great mercy
he has given us new birth into a living hope through the resurrection of Jesus
Christ from the dead. — Saved through his life!

Our great God and Savior, Jesus Christ, who gave himself for us to redeem
us from all wickedness and to purify for himself a people that are his very own,
eager to do what is good. — But just as he who called you is holy, so be holy in
all you do; for it is written: "Be holy, because I am holy."

The God and Father of our Lord Jesus Christ, who has blessed us in the
heavenly realms with every spiritual blessing in Christ. — For in Christ all the
fullness of the Deity lives in bodily form, and you have been given fullness in
Christ, who is the head over every power and authority. — From the fullness of
his grace we have all received one blessing after another.

He who did not spare his own Son, but gave him up for us all — how will he
not also, along with him, graciously give us all things?

ACTS 3:26. 1 Peter 1:3. Rom. 5:10. Titus 2:13 – 14. 1 Peter 1:15 – 16. Eph. 1:3.
Col. 2:9 – 10. John 1:16. Rom. 8:32.

EVENING

Strengthen me according to your word.

REMEMBER YOUR WORD to your servant, for you have given me hope. — "I am
troubled; O Lord, come to my aid!"

"Heaven and earth will pass away, but my words will never pass away." — You
know with all your heart and soul that not one of all the good promises the LORD
your God gave you has failed. Every promise has been fulfilled; not one has failed.

"Do not be afraid, O man highly esteemed," he said. "Peace! Be strong now;
be strong."

When he spoke to me, I was strengthened and said, "Speak, my lord, since
you have given me strength." — "Be strong, all you people of the land," declares
the LORD, "and work. For I am with you," declares the LORD Almighty.

"Not by might nor by power, but by my Spirit," says the LORD Almighty. — Be
strong in the Lord and in his mighty power.

PS. 119:28. Ps. 119:49. Isa. 38:14. Luke 21:33. Josh. 23:14. Dan. 10:19. Hag. 2:4.
Zech. 4:6. Eph. 6:10.

MARCH 20

MORNING

The entrance of your words gives light.

THIS IS THE message we have heard from him and declare to you: God is light; in him there is no darkness at all. — For God, who said, "Let light shine out of darkness," made his light shine in our hearts to give us the light of the knowledge of the glory of God in the face of Christ. — The Word was God.... In him was life, and that life was the light of men. — But if we walk in the light, as he is in the light, we have fellowship with one another, and the blood of Jesus, his Son, purifies us from every sin.

I have hidden your word in my heart that I might not sin against you. — "You are already clean because of the word I have spoken to you."

For you were once darkness, but now you are light in the Lord. Live as children of light. — But you are a chosen people, a royal priesthood, a holy nation, a people belonging to God, that you may declare the praises of him who called you out of darkness into his wonderful light.

PS. 119:130. 1 John 1:5. 2 Cor. 4:6. John 1:1, 4. 1 John 1:7. Ps. 119:11. John 15:3. Eph. 5:8. 1 Peter 2:9.

EVENING

Noah was a righteous man.

"THE RIGHTEOUS WILL live by faith." — Then Noah built an altar to the LORD and, taking some of all the clean animals and clean birds, he sacrificed burnt offerings on it. The LORD smelled the pleasing aroma. — The Lamb that was slain from the creation of the world. — Since we have been justified through faith, we have peace with God through our Lord Jesus Christ.

Therefore no one will be declared righteous in his sight by observing the law; rather, through the law we become conscious of sin. But now a righteousness from God, apart from law, has been made known, to which the Law and the Prophets testify. This righteousness from God comes through faith in Jesus Christ to all who believe. There is no difference.

We also rejoice in God through our Lord Jesus Christ, through whom we have now received reconciliation.

Who will bring any charge against those whom God has chosen?... And those he predestined, he also called.

GEN. 6:9. Gal. 3:11. Gen. 8:20–21. Rev. 13:8. Rom. 5:1; 3:20–22; 5:11; 8:33, 30.

MARCH 21

MORNING

Wake up! Strengthen what remains and is about to die.

THE END OF all things is near. Therefore be clear minded and self-controlled so that you can pray.... Be self-controlled and alert. Your enemy the devil prowls around like a roaring lion looking for someone to devour. — Only be careful, and watch yourselves closely so that you do not forget the things your eyes have seen or let them slip from your heart as long as you live.

"But my righteous one will live by faith. And if he shrinks back, I will not be pleased with him." But we are not of those who shrink back and are destroyed, but of those who believe and are saved.

"What I say to you, I say to everyone: 'Watch!'" — "So do not fear, for I am with you, do not be dismayed, for I am your God. I will strengthen you and help you; I will uphold you with my righteous right hand.... For I am the LORD, your God, who takes hold of your right hand."

REV. 3:2. 1 Peter 4:7; 5:8. Deut. 4:9. Heb. 10:38 – 39. Mark 13:37. Isa. 41:10, 13.

EVENING

Has his unfailing love vanished forever?

HIS LOVE ENDURES forever — "The LORD is slow to anger, abounding in love." — Who is a God like you, who pardons sin and forgives the transgression of the remnant of his inheritance? You do not stay angry forever but delight to show mercy. You will again have compassion on us; you will tread our sins underfoot and hurl all our iniquities into the depths of the sea. — He saved us, not because of righteous things we had done, but because of his mercy.

Praise be to the God and Father of our Lord Jesus Christ, the Father of compassion and the God of all comfort, who comforts us in all our troubles, so that we can comfort those in any trouble with the comfort we ourselves have received from God. — A merciful and faithful high priest in service to God, and that he might make atonement for the sins of the people. Because he himself suffered when he was tempted, he is able to help those who are being tempted.

PS. 77:8. Ps. 136:23. Num. 14:18. Mic. 7:18 – 19. Titus 3:5. 2 Cor. 1:3 – 4. Heb. 2:17 – 18.

MARCH 22

MORNING

*Lot looked up and saw that the whole plain of the Jordan
was well watered, like the garden of the LORD, like the land
of Egypt, toward Zoar. (This was before the LORD destroyed
Sodom and Gomorrah.) So Lot chose for himself the whole
plain of the Jordan.*

LOT ... that righteous man.

Do not be deceived: God cannot be mocked. A man reaps what he sows. — "Remember Lot's wife?"

Do not be yoked together with unbelievers. For what do righteousness and wickedness have in common? Or what fellowship can light have with darkness?

"Therefore come out from them and be separate, says the Lord. Touch no unclean thing." — Therefore do not be partners with them. For you were once darkness, but now you are light in the Lord. Live as children of light ... and find out what pleases the Lord. Have nothing to do with the fruitless deeds of darkness, but rather expose them.

GEN. 13:10–11. 2 Peter 2:7–8. Gal. 6:7. Luke 17:32. 2 Cor. 6:14, 17. Eph. 5:7–8, 10–11.

EVENING

"But, the LORD helping me, I will drive them out just as he said."

BECAUSE GOD HAS said, "Never will I leave you; never will I forsake you." So we say with confidence, "The Lord is my helper; I will not be afraid." — I will come and proclaim your mighty acts, O Sovereign LORD; I will proclaim your righteousness, yours alone.

The fruit of righteousness will be peace; the effect of righteousness will be quietness and confidence forever.

Stand firm then, with the belt of truth buckled around your waist, with the breastplate of righteousness in place.... For our struggle is not against flesh and blood, but against the rulers, against the authorities, against the powers of this dark world and against the spiritual forces of evil in the heavenly realms. Therefore put on the full armor of God, so that when the day of evil comes, you may be able to stand your ground, and after you have done everything, to stand.

"The LORD is with you ... Go in the strength you have."

JOSH. 14:12. Heb. 13:5–6. Ps. 71:16. Isa. 32:17. Eph. 6:14, 12–13. Judg. 6:12, 14.

MARCH 23

MORNING

"Holy, holy, holy is the Lord God Almighty."

YET YOU ARE enthroned as the Holy One; you are the praise of Israel. — "Do not come any closer," God said. "Take off your sandals, for the place where you are standing is holy ground." ... "I am the God of your father, the God of Abraham, the God of Isaac and the God of Jacob." At this, Moses hid his face, because he was afraid to look at God.

"To whom will you compare me? Or who is my equal?" says the Holy One.... "For I am the LORD, your God, the Holy One of Israel, your Savior." ... "I, even I, am the LORD, and apart from me there is no savior."

But just as he who called you is holy, so be holy in all you do; for it is written: "Be holy, because I am holy." — Do you not know that your body is a temple of the Holy Spirit, who is in you, whom you have received from God? — For we are the temple of the living God. As God has said: "I will live with them and walk among them, and I will be their God, and they will be my people." — Do two walk together unless they have agreed to do so?

REV. 4:8. Ps. 22:3. Exod. 3:5 – 6. Isa. 40:25; 43:3, 11. 1 Peter 1:15 – 16. 1 Cor. 6:19. 2 Cor. 6:16. Amos 3:3.

EVENING

But they urged him strongly, "Stay with us."

"HERE I AM! I stand at the door and knock. If anyone hears my voice and opens the door, I will go in and eat with him, and he with me." — Tell me, you whom I love, where you graze your flock and where you rest your sheep at midday. Why should I be like a veiled woman beside the flocks of your friends? ... I found the one my heart loves. I held him and would not let him go.... Let my lover come into his garden and taste its choice fruits.... I have come into my garden.

"I have not said to Jacob's descendants, 'Seek me in vain.' " — "I will be with you always, to the very end of the age."

"Never will I leave you; never will I forsake you." — "For where two or three come together in my name, there am I with them." — "The world will not see me anymore, but you will see me."

LUKE 24:29. Rev. 4:20. Song of Songs 1:7; 3:4; 4:16; 5:1. Isa. 45:19. Matt. 28:20. Heb. 13:5. Matt. 18:20. John 14:19.

MARCH 24

MORNING

Abram believed the LORD, and he credited it to him as righteousness.

YET HE DID not waver through unbelief regarding the promise of God, but was strengthened in his faith and gave glory to God, being fully persuaded that God had power to do what he had promised. This is why "it was credited to him as righteousness." The words "it was credited to him" were written not for him alone, but also for us, to whom God will credit righteousness — for us who believe in him who raised Jesus our Lord from the dead.

It was not through law that Abraham and his offspring received the promise that he would be heir of the world, but through the righteousness that comes by faith.... "The righteous will live by faith." — Let us hold unswervingly to the hope we profess, for he who promised is faithful. — Our God is in heaven; he does whatever pleases him.

"For nothing is impossible with God.... Blessed is she who has believed that what the Lord has said to her will be accomplished!"

GEN. 15:6. Rom. 4:20 – 24, 13; 1:17. Heb. 10:23. Ps. 115:3. Luke 1:37, 45.

EVENING

God ... calls you into his kingdom and glory.

"MY KINGDOM IS not of this world. If it were, my servants would fight to prevent my arrest by the Jews. But now my kingdom is from another place." — He waits for his enemies to be made his footstool.

"The kingdom of the world has become the kingdom of our Lord and of his Christ, and he will reign for ever and ever." — "You have made them to be a kingdom and priests to serve our God, and they will reign on the earth."

I saw thrones on which were seated those who had been given authority to judge.... They came to life and reigned with Christ a thousand years. — "Then the righteous will shine like the sun in the kingdom of their Father."

"Do not be afraid, little flock, for your Father has been pleased to give you the kingdom." ... "And I confer on you a kingdom, just as my Father conferred one on me, so that you may eat and drink at my table in my kingdom and sit on thrones, judging the twelve tribes of Israel."

1 THESS. 2:12. John 18:36. Heb. 10:13. Rev. 11:15; 5:10; 20:4. Matt. 13:43. Luke 12:32; 22:29 – 30.

MARCH 25

MORNING

"Never will I leave vow, never will I forsake you."

So we say with confidence, "The Lord is my helper; I will not be afraid."

"I am with you and will watch over you wherever you go, and I will bring you back to this land. I will not leave you until I have done what I have promised you."—"Be strong and courageous. Do not be afraid or terrified because of them, for the LORD your God goes with you; he will never leave you nor forsake you."

Demas, because he loved this world, has deserted me.... At my first defense, no one came to my support, but everyone deserted me. May it not be held against them. But the Lord stood at my side and gave me strength.—Though my father and mother forsake me, the LORD will receive me.

"And surely I will be with you always, to the very end of the age."—"I am the Living One; I was dead, and behold I am alive for ever and ever!"—"I will not leave you as orphans; I will come to you.... My peace I give you."

HEB. 13:5. Heb. 13:6. Gen. 28:15. Deut. 31:6. 2 Tim. 4:10, 16–17. Ps. 27:10. Matt. 28:20. Rev. 1:18. John 14:18, 27.

EVENING

"Master, we've worked hard all night and haven't caught anything. But because you say so, I will let down the nets."

"All authority in heaven and on earth has been given to me. Therefore go and make disciples of all nations, baptizing them in the name of the Father and of the Son and of the Holy Spirit.... And surely I will be with you always, to the very end of the age."

"The kingdom of heaven is like a net that was let down into the lake."—Yet when I preach the gospel, I cannot boast, for I am compelled to preach. Woe to me if I do not preach the gospel!... I have become all things to all men so that by all possible means I might save some.

Let us not become weary in doing good, for at the proper time we will reap a harvest if we do not give up.—My word ... will not return to me empty, but will accomplish what I desire. So neither he who plants nor he who waters is anything, but only God, who makes things grow.

LUKE 5:5. Matt. 28:18–20; 13:47. 1 Cor. 9:16, 22. Gal. 6:9. Isa. 55:11. 1 Cor. 3:7.

MARCH 26

MORNING

"Again, [heaven] will be like a man going on a journey, who called his servants and entrusted his property to them, ... each according to his ability."

DON'T YOU KNOW that when you offer yourselves to someone to obey him as slaves, you are slaves to the one whom you obey?

All these are the work of one and the same Spirit, and he gives them to each man, just as he determines.... Now to each one the manifestation of the Spirit is given for the common good. — Each one should use whatever gift he has received to serve others, faithfully administering God's grace in its various forms. — Now it is required that those who have been given a trust must prove faithful.

"From everyone who has been given much, much will be demanded; and from the one who has been entrusted with much, much more will be asked." — And who is equal to such a task? — I can do everything through him who gives me strength.

MATT. 25:14–15. Rom. 6:16. 1 Cor. 12:11, 7. 1 Peter 4:10. 1 Cor. 4:2. Luke 12:48. 2 Cor. 2:16. Phil. 4:13.

EVENING

Share with God's people who are in need.

DAVID ASKED, "Is there anyone still left of the house of Saul to whom I can show kindness for Jonathan's sake?"

"Come, you who are blessed by my Father; take your inheritance, the kingdom prepared for you since the creation of the world. For I was hungry and you gave me something to eat, I was thirsty and you gave me something to drink, I was a stranger and you invited me in, I needed clothes and you clothed me, I was sick and you looked after me, I was in prison and you came to visit me.... Whatever you did for one of the least of these brothers of mine, you did for me.

"And if anyone gives a cup of cold water to one of these little ones because he is my disciple, I tell you the truth, he will certainly not lose his reward."

And do not forget to do good and to share with others, for with such sacrifices God is pleased.... God is not unjust; he will not forget your work and the love you have shown him as you have helped his people and continue to help them.

ROM. 12:13. 2 Sam. 9:1. Matt. 25:34–36, 40; 10:42. Heb. 13:16; 6:10.

MARCH 27

MORNING

He who sows righteousness reaps a sure reward.

"AFTER A LONG time the master of those servants returned and settled accounts with them. The man who had received the five talents brought the other five. 'Master,' he said, 'you entrusted me with five talents. See, I have gained five more.' His master replied, 'Well done, good and faithful servant! You have been faithful with a few things; I will put you in charge of many things. Come and share your master's happiness!'"

For we must all appear before the judgment seat of Christ, that each one may receive what is due him for the things done while in the body, whether good or bad. — I have fought the good fight, I have finished the race, I have kept the faith. Now there is in store for me the crown of righteousness, which the Lord, the righteous Judge, will award to me on that day — and not only to me, but also to all who have longed for his appearing.

"I am coming soon. Hold on to what you have, so that no one will take your crown."

PROV. 11:18. Matt. 25:19–21. 2 Cor. 5:10. 2 Tim. 4:7–8. Rev. 3:11.

EVENING

God is faithful.

GOD IS NOT a man, that he should lie, nor a son of man, that he should change his mind. — Does he speak and then not act? Does he promise and not fulfill? — "The Lord has sworn and will not change his mind."

Because God wanted to make the unchanging nature of his purpose very clear to the heirs of what was promised, he confirmed it with an oath. God did this so that, by two unchangeable things in which it is impossible for God to lie, we who have fled to take hold of the hope offered to us may be greatly encouraged. — So then, those who suffer according to God's will should commit themselves to their faithful Creator and continue to do good.

I know whom I have believed, and am convinced that he is able to guard what I have entrusted to him for that day. — The one who calls you is faithful and he will do it. — For no matter how many promises God has made, they are "Yes" in Christ. And so through him the "Amen" is spoken by us to the glory of God.

1 COR. 10:13. Num. 23:19. Heb. 7:21; 6:17–18. 1 Peter 4:19. 2 Tim. 1:12. 1 Thess. 5:24. 2 Cor. 1:20.

MARCH 28

MORNING

"Be strong and courageous!"

THE LORD IS my light and my salvation—whom shall I fear? The LORD is the stronghold of my life—of whom shall I be afraid?—He gives strength to the weary and increases the power of the weak. Even youths grow tired and weary, and young men stumble and fall; but those who hope in the LORD will renew their strength. They will soar on wings like eagles; they will run and not grow weary, they will walk and not be faint.

My flesh and my heart may fail, but God is the strength of my heart and my portion forever.—If God is for us, who can be against us?—The LORD is with me; I will not be afraid. What can man do to me?—Through you we push back our enemies; through your name we trample our foes.

We are more than conquerors through him who loved us.—"Now begin the work, and the LORD be with you."

JOSH. 1:18. Ps. 27:1. Isa. 40:29–31. Ps. 73:26. Rom. 8:31. Pss. 118:6; 44:5. Rom. 8:37. 1 Chron. 22:16.

EVENING

"Our friend . . . has fallen asleep."

BROTHERS, WE DO not want you to be ignorant about those who fall asleep, or to grieve like the rest of men, who have no hope. We believe that Jesus died and rose again and so we believe that God will bring with Jesus those who have fallen asleep in him.

For if the dead are not raised, then Christ has not been raised either. And if Christ has not been raised, your faith is futile; you are still in your sins. Then those also who have fallen asleep in Christ are lost. . . . But Christ has indeed been raised from the dead, the firstfruits of those who have fallen asleep.

When the whole nation had finished crossing the Jordan, the LORD said to Joshua, . . . "Tell them to take up twelve stones from the middle of the Jordan from right where the priests stood and to carry them over with you and put them down at the place where you stay tonight." . . . "These stones are to be a memorial to the people of Israel forever."—"God has raised this Jesus to life, and we are all witnesses of the fact." . . . "Witnesses whom God had already chosen—by us who ate and drank with him after he rose from the dead."

JOHN 11:11. 1 Thess. 4:13–14. 1 Cor. 15:16–18, 20. Josh. 4:1, 3, 7. Acts 2:32; 10:41.

MARCH 29

MORNING

"Come, you who are blessed by my Father, take your inheritance, the kingdom prepared for you since the creation of the world."

"Do NOT BE afraid, little flock, for your Father has been pleased to give you the kingdom." — Listen, my dear brothers: Has not God chosen those who are poor in the eyes of the world to be rich in faith and to inherit the kingdom he promised those who love him? — Now if we are children, then we are heirs — heirs of God and co-heirs with Christ.

"The Father himself loves you because you have loved me." — Therefore God is not ashamed to be called their God, for he has prepared a city for them.

"He who overcomes will inherit all this, and I will be his God and he will be my son." — Now there is in store for me the crown of righteousness, which the Lord, the righteous Judge, will award to me on that day — and not only to me, but also to all who have longed for his appearing. — He who began a good work in you will carry it on to completion until the day of Christ Jesus.

MATT. 25:34. Luke 12:32. James 2:5. Rom. 8:17. John 16:27. Heb. 11:16. Rev. 21:7. 2 Tim. 4:8. Phil. 1:6.

EVENING

For riches do not endure forever, and a crown is not secure for all generations.

MAN IS A mere phantom as he goes to and fro: He bustles about, but only in vain; he heaps up wealth, not knowing who will get it. — Set your minds on things above, not on earthly things. — "Do not store up for yourselves treasures on earth, where moth and rust destroy, and where thieves break in and steal. But store up for yourselves treasures in heaven, where moth and rust do not destroy, and where thieves do not break in and steal. For where your treasure is, there your heart will be also."

They do it to get a crown that will not last; but we do it to get a crown that will last forever. — So we fix our eyes not on what is seen, but on what is unseen. — But he who sows righteousness reaps a sure reward.

Now there is in store for me the crown of righteousness, which the Lord, the righteous Judge, will award to me on that day — and not only to me, but also to all who have longed for his appearing. — The crown of glory that will never fade away.

PROV. 27:24. Ps. 39:6. Col. 3:2. Matt. 6:19–21. 1 Cor. 9:25. 2 Cor. 4:18. Prov. 11:18. 2 Tim. 4:8. 1 Peter 5:4.

MARCH 30

MORNING

He went out to the field one evening to meditate.

MAY THE WORDS of my mouth and the meditation of my heart be pleasing in your sight, O LORD, my Rock and my Redeemer.

When I consider your heavens, the work of your fingers, the moon and the stars, which you have set in place, what is man that you are mindful of him, the son of man that you care for him? ... Great are the works of the LORD; they are pondered by all who delight in them.

Blessed is the man who does not walk in the counsel of the wicked or stand in the way of sinners or sit in the seat of mockers. But his delight is in the law of the LORD, and on his law he meditates day and night. — Do not let this Book of the Law depart from your mouth; meditate on it day and night.

My soul will be satisfied as with the richest of foods; with singing lips my mouth will praise you. On my bed I remember you; I think of you through the watches of the night.

GEN. 24:63. Pss. 19:14; 8:3 – 4; 111:2; 1:1 – 2. Josh. 1:8. Ps. 63:5 – 6.

EVENING

How long, O LORD? Will you forget me forever? How long
will you hide your face from me?

EVERY GOOD AND perfect gift is from above, coming down from the Father of the heavenly lights, who does not change like shifting shadows.

But Zion said, "The LORD has forsaken me, the Lord has forgotten me." "Can a mother forget the baby at her breast and have no compassion on the child she has borne? Though she may forget, I will not forget you!" ... "O Israel, I will not forget you. I have swept away your offenses like a cloud, your sins like the morning mist."

Jesus loved Martha and her sister and Lazarus. Yet when he heard that Lazarus was sick, he stayed where he was two more days. — A Canaanite woman from that vicinity came to him, crying out, "Lord, Son of David, have mercy on me!" ... Jesus did not answer a word.

Your faith — of greater worth than gold, which perishes.

PS. 13:1. James 1:17. Isa. 49:14 – 15; 44:21 – 22. John 11:5 – 6. Matt. 15:22 – 23. 1 Peter 1:7.

MARCH 31

MORNING

*And my God will meet all your needs according to his glorious
riches in Christ Jesus.*

"BUT SEEK FIRST his kingdom and his righteousness, and all these things will be
given to you as well." — He who did not spare his own Son, but gave him up for
us all — how will he not also, along with him, graciously give us all things? — All
things are yours, whether Paul or Apollos or Cephas or the world or life or death
or the present or the future — all are yours, and you are of Christ, and Christ is
of God. — Having nothing, and yet possessing everything.

The LORD is my shepherd, I shall lack nothing. . . . For the LORD God is a sun
and shield; the LORD bestows favor and honor; no good thing does he withhold
from those whose walk is blameless.

God . . . who richly provides us with everything for our enjoyment. — And
God is able to make all grace abound to you, so that in all things at all times,
having all that you need, you will abound in every good thing.

**PHIL. 4:19. Matt. 6:33. Rom. 8:32. 2 Cor. 3:21 – 23. 2 Cor. 6:10. Pss. 23:1; 84:11.
1 Tim. 6:17. 2 Cor. 9:8.**

EVENING

What do righteousness and wickedness have in common?

MEN LOVED DARKNESS instead of light because their deeds were evil. — You are
all sons of the light and sons of the day. We do not belong to the night or to the
darkness.

Darkness has blinded him. — Your word is a lamp to my feet and a light for
my path.

Haunts of violence fill the dark places of the land. — For love comes from
God. Everyone who loves has been born of God and knows God. Whoever does
not love does not know God, because God is love.

But the way of the wicked is like deep darkness; they do not know what
makes them stumble. . . . The path of the righteous is like the first gleam of
dawn, shining ever brighter till the full light of day.

I have come into the world as a light, so that no one who believes in me
should stay in darkness. — For you were once darkness, but now you are light in
the Lord. Live as children of light.

**2 COR. 6:14. John 3:19. 1 Thess. 5:5. 1 John 2:11. Pss. 119:105; 74:20. 1 John 4:7 – 8.
Prov. 4:19, 18. John 12:46. Eph. 5:8.**

APRIL 1

MORNING

But the fruit of the Spirit is ... joy.

JOY IN THE Holy Spirit. — You believe in him and are filled with an inexpressible and glorious joy.

Sorrowful, yet always rejoicing.... In all our troubles my joy knows no bounds. — We ... rejoice in our sufferings.

Fix our eyes on Jesus, the author and perfecter of our faith, who for the joy set before him endured the cross, scorning its shame. — I have told you this so that my joy may be in you and that your joy may be complete. — For just as the sufferings of Christ flow over into our lives, so also through Christ our comfort overflows.

Rejoice in the Lord always. I will say it again: Rejoice! — "The joy of the LORD is your strength."

You will fill me with joy in your presence, with eternal pleasures at your right hand. — "For the Lamb at the center of the throne will be their shepherd; he will lead them to springs of living water. And God will wipe away every tear from their eyes."

GAL. 5:22. Rom. 14:17. 1 Peter 1:8. 2 Cor. 6:10; 7:4. Rom. 5:3. Heb. 12:2. John 15:11. 2 Cor. 1:5. Phil. 4:4. Neh. 8:10. Ps. 16:11. Rev. 7.17.

EVENING

"The LORD is Peace."

BUT YOU WILL have a son who will be a man of peace and rest, and I will give him rest from all his enemies on every side. His name will be Solomon, and I will grant Israel peace and quiet during his reign.

"One greater than Solomon is here." — For to us a child is born, to us a son is given, and the government will be on his shoulders. And he will be called Wonderful Counselor, Mighty God, Everlasting Father, Prince of Peace.... My people will live in peaceful dwelling places, in secure homes, in undisturbed places of rest. Though hail flattens the forest and the city is leveled completely.

For he himself is our peace. — And he will be their peace. When the Assyrian invades our land. — They will make war against the Lamb, but the Lamb will overcome them because he is Lord of lords and King of kings.

"Peace I leave with you; my peace I give you."

JUDG. 6:24. 1 Chron. 22:9. Matt. 12:42. Isa. 9:6; 32:18 – 19. Eph. 2:14. Mic. 5:5. Rev. 17:14. John 14:27.

April 2

Morning

"If you are returning to the LORD with all your hearts, then rid yourselves of the foreign gods and the Ashtoreths and commit yourselves to the LORD and serve him only."

DEAR CHILDREN, KEEP yourselves from idols. — "Therefore come out from them and be separate, says the Lord. Touch no unclean thing, and I will receive you." — "I will be a Father to you, and you will be my sons and daughters, says the Lord Almighty." — You cannot serve both God and Money.

Do not worship any other god, for the LORD, whose name is Jealous, is a jealous God. — Serve him with wholehearted devotion and with a willing mind, for the LORD searches every heart and understands every motive behind the thoughts.

Surely you desire truth in the inner parts; you teach me wisdom in the inmost place. — "Man looks at the outward appearance, but the LORD looks at the heart." — Dear friends, if our hearts do not condemn us, we have confidence before God.

1 SAM. 7:3. 1 John 5:21. 2 Cor. 6:17 – 18. Matt. 6:24. Exod. 34:14. 1 Chron. 28:9. Ps. 51:6. 1 Sam. 16:7. 1 John 3:21.

Evening

"When the Son of Man comes, will he find faith on the earth?"

HE CAME TO that which was his own, but his own did not receive him. — The Spirit clearly says that in later times some will abandon the faith.

Preach the Word; be prepared in season and out of season; correct, rebuke and encourage — with great patience and careful instruction. For the time will come when men will not put up with sound doctrine. Instead, to suit their own desires, they will gather around them a great number of teachers to say what their itching ears want to hear. They will turn their ears away from the truth and turn aside to myths.

"No one knows about that day or hour, not even the angels in heaven, nor the Son, but only the Father. Be on guard! Be alert! You do not know when that time will come." — "It will be good for those servants whose master finds them watching when he comes." — While we wait for the blessed hope — the glorious appearing of our great God and Savior, Jesus Christ.

LUKE 18:8. John 1:11. 1 Tim. 4:1. 2 Tim. 4:2 – 4. Mark 13:32 – 33. Luke 12:37. Titus 2:13.

APRIL 3

MORNING

But do not forget this one thing, dear friends: With the Lord
a day is like a thousand years, and a thousand years are like
a day. The Lord is not slow in keeping his promise, as some
understand slowness.

"FOR MY THOUGHTS are not your thoughts, neither are your ways my ways," declares the LORD. "As the heavens are higher than the earth, so are my ways higher than your ways and my thoughts than your thoughts. As the rain and the snow come down from heaven, . . . so is my word that goes out from my mouth: It will not return to me empty, but will accomplish what I desire and achieve the purpose for which I sent it."

For God has bound all men over to disobedience so that he may have mercy on them all. Oh, the depth of the riches of the wisdom and knowledge of God!

2 PETER 3:8–9. Isa. 55:8–11. Rom. 11:32–33.

EVENING

You were like a burning stick snatched from the fire.

THE SINNERS IN Zion are terrified; trembling grips the godless: "Who of us can dwell with the consuming fire? Who of us can dwell with everlasting burning?" —Indeed, in our hearts we felt the sentence of death. But this happened that we might not rely on ourselves but on God, who raises the dead. He has delivered us from such a deadly peril, and he will deliver us. On him we have set our hope that he will continue to deliver us. —For the wages of sin is death, but the gift of God is eternal life in Christ Jesus our Lord.

For it is a dreadful thing to fall into the hands of the living God. —Since, then, we know what it is to fear the Lord, we try to persuade men.

Be prepared in season and out of season. —Snatch others from the fire and save them.

"Not by might nor by power, but by my Spirit," says the LORD Almighty. —Who wants all men to be saved and to come to a knowledge of the truth.

AMOS 4:11. Isa. 33:14. 2 Cor. 1:9–10. Rom. 6:23. Heb. 10:31. 2 Cor. 5:11. 2 Tim. 4:2. Jude 23. Zech. 4:6. 1 Tim. 2:4.

APRIL 4

MORNING

"Do not be afraid. I am the First and the Last."

YOU HAVE NOT come to a mountain that can be touched and that is burning with fire; to darkness, gloom and storm; ... But you have come to Mount Zion ... to God, the judge of all men, to the spirits of righteous men made perfect, to Jesus the mediator of a new covenant.... Jesus, the author and perfecter of our faith.... For we do not have a high priest who is unable to sympathize with our weaknesses, but we have one who has been tempted in every way, just as we are—yet was without sin. Let us then approach the throne of grace with confidence, so that we may receive mercy and find grace to help us in our time of need.

"This is what the LORD says—Israel's King and Redeemer, the LORD Almighty: I am the first and I am the last; apart from me there is no God." ... Mighty God, Everlasting Father, Prince of Peace.

O LORD, are you not from everlasting? My God, my Holy One.—For who is God besides the LORD? And who is the Rock except our God?

REV. 1:17. Heb. 12:18, 22–24; 12:2; 4:15–16. Isa. 44:6; 9:6. Hab. 1:12. 2 Sam. 22:32.

EVENING

Lead me to the rock that is higher than I.

DO NOT BE anxious about anything, but in everything, by prayer and petition, with thanksgiving, present your requests to God. And the peace of God, which transcends all understanding, will guard your hearts and minds in Christ Jesus. When my spirit grows faint within me, it is you who know my way.—But he knows the way that I take; when he has tested me, I will come forth as gold.—Lord, you have been our dwelling place throughout all generations.—You have been a refuge for the poor, a refuge for the needy in his distress.

And who is the Rock except our God?—"They shall never perish; no one can snatch them out of my hand."—Sustain me according to your promise, and I will live; do not let my hopes be dashed.—We have this hope as an anchor for the soul, firm and secure. It enters the inner sanctuary behind the curtain.

PS. 61:2. Phil. 4:6–7. Ps. 142:3. Job 23:10. Ps. 90:1. Isa. 25:4. Ps. 18:31. John 10:28. Ps. 119:116. Heb. 6:19.

APRIL 5

MORNING

"I will not let you go unless you bless me."

"OR ELSE LET them come to me for refuge; let them make peace with me, yes, let them make peace with me."

Then Jesus answered, "Woman, you have great faith! Your request is granted." ... "According to your faith will it be done to you." — But when he asks, he must believe and not doubt, because he who doubts is like a wave of the sea, blown and tossed by the wind. That man should not think he will receive anything from the Lord.

As they approached the village to which they were going, Jesus acted as if he were going farther. But they urged him strongly, "Stay with us, for it is nearly evening; the day is almost over." So he went in to stay with them.... Then their eyes were opened and they recognized him, and he disappeared from their sight. They asked each other, "Were not our hearts burning within us while he talked with us on the road and opened the Scriptures to us?" — If I have found favor in your eyes, teach me your ways so I may know you and continue to find favor with you. — "My Presence will go with you, and I will give you rest."

GEN. 32:26. Isa. 27:5. Matt. 15:28; 9:29. James 1:6 – 7. Luke 24:28 – 29, 31 – 32. Exod. 33:13 – 14.

EVENING

Jesus, the author and perfecter of our faith.

"I AM THE Alpha and the Omega," says the Lord God, "who is, and who was, and who is to come, the Almighty." — "Who has done this and carried it through, calling forth the generations from the beginning?" — I, the LORD — with the first of them and with the last — I am he." — To those who have been called, who are loved by God the Father and kept by Jesus Christ.

May God himself, the God of peace, sanctify you through and through. May your whole spirit, soul and body be kept blameless at the coming of our Lord Jesus Christ. — He who began a good work in you will carry it on to completion until the day of Christ Jesus. — Are you so foolish? After beginning with the Spirit, are you now trying to attain your goal by human effort? — The LORD will fulfill his purpose for me.

For it is God who works in you to will and to act according to his good purpose.

HEB. 12:2. Rev. 1:8. Isa. 41:4. Jude 1. 1 Thess. 5:23 – 24. Phil. 1:6. Gal. 3:3. Ps. 138:8. Phil. 2:13.

April 6

Morning

He always lives to intercede for them.

WHO IS HE that condemns? Christ Jesus, who died—more than that, who was raised to life—is at the right hand of God and is also interceding for us.—For Christ did not enter a man-made sanctuary that was only a copy of the true one; he entered heaven itself, now to appear for us in God's presence.

But if anybody does sin, we have one who speaks to the Father in our defense—Jesus Christ, the Righteous One.—For there is one God and one mediator between God and men, Christ Jesus.

Therefore, since we have a great high priest who has gone through the heavens, Jesus the Son of God, let us hold firmly to the faith we profess. For we do not have a high priest who is unable to sympathize with our weaknesses, but we have one who has been tempted in every way, just as we are—yet was without sin. Let us then approach the throne of grace with confidence, so that we may receive mercy and find grace to help us in our time of need.—For through him we both have access to the Father by one Spirit.

HEB. 7:25. Rom. 8:34. Heb. 9:24. 1 John 2:1. 1 Tim. 2:5. Heb. 4:14–16. Eph. 2:18.

Evening

Those who know your name will trust in you.

"THIS IS THE name by which he will be called: The LORD Our Righteousness."—I will come and proclaim your mighty acts, O Sovereign LORD; I will proclaim your righteousness, yours alone. And he will be called Wonderful Counselor.—I know, O LORD, that a man's life is not his own; it is not for man to direct his steps.

Mighty God, Everlasting Father.—I know whom I have believed, and am convinced that he is able to guard what I have entrusted to him for that day.

Prince of Peace.—For he himself is our peace.—Therefore, since we have been justified through faith, we have peace with God through our Lord Jesus Christ.

The name of the LORD is a strong tower; the righteous run to it and are safe.—Woe to those who go down to Egypt for help.... "Like birds hovering overhead, the LORD Almighty will shield Jerusalem; he will shield it and deliver it, he will 'pass over' it and will rescue it."

PS. 9:10. Jer. 23:6. Ps. 71:16. Isa. 9:6. Jer. 10:23. Isa. 9:6. 2 Tim. 1:12. Isa. 9:6. Eph. 2:14. Rom. 5:1. Prov. 18:10. Isa. 31:1, 5.

APRIL 7

MORNING

*Sorrowful, yet always rejoicing; poor, yet making many rich;
having nothing, and yet possessing everything.*

AND WE REJOICE in the hope of the glory of God. Not only so, but we also rejoice in our sufferings. — I am greatly encouraged; in all our troubles my joy knows no bounds. — You believe in him and are filled with an inexpressible and glorious joy. Out of the most severe trial, their overflowing joy and their extreme poverty welled up in rich generosity. — Although I am less than the least of all God's people, this grace was given me: to preach to the Gentiles the unsearchable riches of Christ, and to make plain to everyone the administration of this mystery, which for ages past was kept hidden in God, who created all things.

Has not God chosen those who are poor in the eyes of the world to be rich in faith and to inherit the kingdom he promised those who love him? — And God is able to make all grace abound to you, so that in all things at all times, having all that you need, you will abound in every good.

2 COR. 6:10. Rom. 5:2–3. 2 Cor. 7:4. 1 Peter 1:8. 2 Cor. 8:2. Eph. 3:8–9. James 2:5.
2 Cor. 9:8.

EVENING

*The LORD will sustain him on his sickbed and restore him
from his bed of illness.*

IN ALL THEIR distress he too was distressed, and the angel of his presence saved them. In his love and mercy he redeemed them; he lifted them up and carried them. — "Lord, the one you love is sick." — "My grace is sufficient for you, for my power is made perfect in weakness." — Therefore I will boast all the more gladly about my weaknesses, so that Christ's power may rest on me. — I can do everything through him who gives me strength.

Therefore we do not lose heart. Though outwardly we are wasting away, yet inwardly we are being renewed day by day.

"For in him we live and move and have our being." — He gives strength to the weary and increases the power of the weak. Even youths grow tired and weary, and young men stumble and fall; but those who hope in the LORD will renew their strength. — The eternal God is your refuge, and underneath are the everlasting arms.

PS. 41:3. Isa. 63:9. John 11:3. 2 Cor. 12:9. Phil. 4:13. 2 Cor. 4:16. Acts 17:28.
Isa. 40:29–31. Deut. 33:27.

APRIL 8

MORNING

For in him you have been enriched in every way.

WHEN WE WERE still powerless, Christ died for the ungodly. — He who did not spare his own Son, but gave him up for us all — how will he not also, along with him, graciously give us all things?

For in Christ all the fullness of the Deity lives in bodily form. — You have been given fullness in Christ, who is the head over every power and authority.

"Remain in me, and I will remain in you. No branch can bear fruit by itself; it must remain in the vine. Neither can you bear fruit unless you remain in me. I am the vine; you are the branches. If a man remains in me and I in him, he will bear much fruit; apart from me you can do nothing." — For I have the desire to do what is good, but I cannot carry it out. — But to each one of us grace has been given as Christ apportioned it.

"If you remain in me and my words remain in you, ask whatever you wish, and it will be given you." — Let the word of Christ dwell in you richly.

1 COR. 1:5. Rom. 5:6; 8:32. Col. 2:9 – 10. John 15:4 – 5. Rom. 7:18. Eph. 4:7. John 15:7. Col. 3:16.

EVENING

They will see his face.

THEN MOSES SAID, "Now show me your glory." ... "But," he said, "you cannot see my face, for no one may see me and live." — No one has ever seen God, but God the only Son who is at the Father's side, has made him known. Every eye will see him, even those who pierced him; and all the peoples of the earth will mourn because of him. — "I see him, but not now; I behold him, but not near."

I know that my Redeemer lives, and that in the end he will stand upon the earth. And after my skin has been destroyed, yet in my flesh I will see God. — And I — in righteousness I will see your face; when I awake, I will be satisfied with seeing your likeness. — We shall be like him, for we shall see him as he is.

For the Lord himself will come down from heaven, with a loud command, with the voice of the archangel and with the trumpet call of God, and the dead in Christ will rise first. After that, we who are still alive and are left will be caught up with them in the clouds to meet the Lord in the air. And so we will be with the Lord forever.

REV. 22:4. Exod. 33:18, 20. John 1:18. Rev. 1:7. Num. 24:17. Job 19:25 – 26. Ps. 17:15. 1 John 3:2. 1 Thess. 4:16 – 17.

APRIL 9

MORNING

"Fear not, for I have redeemed you."

"Do not be afraid; you will not suffer shame. Do not fear disgrace; you will not be humiliated. You will forget the shame of your youth and remember no more the reproach of your widowhood. For your Maker is your husband—the Lord Almighty is his name—the Holy One of Israel is your Redeemer." ... "I have swept away your offenses like a cloud, your sins like the morning mist. Return to me, for I have redeemed you." —With the precious blood of Christ, a lamb without blemish or defect.

Yet their Redeemer is strong; the Lord Almighty is his name. He will vigorously defend their cause. —"My Father, who has given them to me, is greater than all; no one can snatch them out of my Father's hand."

Grace and peace to you from God our Father and the Lord Jesus Christ, who gave himself for our sins to rescue us from the present evil age, according to the will of our God and Father, to whom be glory for ever and ever. Amen.

ISA. 43:1. Isa. 54:4–5; 44:22. 1 Peter 1:19. Jer. 50:34. John 10:29. Gal. 1:3–5.

EVENING

I will tell of the kindnesses of the Lord, the deeds for which
he is to be praised, according to all the Lord has done for us.

He lifted me out of the slimy pit, out of the mud and mire; he set my feet on a rock and gave me a firm place to stand. —I live by faith in the Son of God, who loved me and gave himself for me. —He who did not spare his own Son, but gave him up for us all—how will he not also, along with him, graciously give us all things?... God demonstrates his own love for us in this: While we were still sinners, Christ died for us.

He anointed us, set his seal of ownership on us, and put his Spirit in our hearts. —Who is a deposit guaranteeing our inheritance until the redemption of those who are God's possession—to the praise of his glory.

God, who is rich in mercy, made us alive with Christ even when we were dead in transgressions—it is by grace you have been saved. And God raised us up with Christ and seated us with him in the heavenly realms in Christ Jesus.

ISA. 63:7. Ps. 40:2. Gal. 2:20. Rom. 8:32; 5:8. 2 Cor. 1:22. Eph. 1:14; 2:4–6.

APRIL 10

MORNING

Dark am I, yet lovely.

Surely I have been a sinner from birth, sinful from the time my mother conceived me. — And your fame spread among the nations on account of your beauty, because the splendor I had given you made your beauty perfect, declares the Sovereign Lord.

"Lord; I am a sinful man!" — How beautiful you are, my darling! Oh, how beautiful! — "Therefore, I despise myself and repent in dust and ashes." — All beautiful you are, my darling; there is no flaw in you.

When I want to do good, evil is right there with me. — "Take heart, son; your sins are forgiven."

But you were washed, you were sanctified, you were justified in the name of the Lord Jesus Christ and by the Spirit of our God. — That you may declare the praises of him who called you out of darkness into his wonderful light.

SONG OF SONGS 1:5. Ps. 51:5. Ezek. 16:14. Luke 5:8. Song of Songs 4:1. Job 42:6. Song of Songs 4:7. Rom. 7:21. Matt. 9:2. 1 Cor. 6:11. 1 Peter 2:9.

EVENING

In fact, everyone who wants to live a godly life in Christ Jesus will be persecuted.

"For I have come to turn 'a man against his father, a daughter against her mother, a daughter-in-law against her mother-in-law — a man's enemies will be the members of his own household.'" — Anyone who chooses to be a friend of the world becomes an enemy of God. — Do not love the world or anything in the world. If anyone loves the world, the love of the Father is not in him. For everything in the world — the cravings of sinful man, the lust of his eyes and the boasting of what he has and does — comes not from the Father but from the world.

"If the world hates you, keep in mind that it hated me first. If you belonged to the world, it would love you as its own. As it is, you do not belong to the world, but I have chosen you out of the world. That is why the world hates you. Remember the words I spoke to you: 'No servant is greater than his master.'" ... "I have given them your word and the world has hated them, for they are not of the world any more than I am of the world."

2 TIM. 3:12. Matt. 10:35 – 36. James 4:4. 1 John 2:15 – 16. John 15:18 – 20; 17:14.

APRIL 11

MORNING

When words are many, sin is not absent, but he who holds his tongue is wise.

MY DEAR BROTHERS, take note of this: Everyone should be quick to listen, slow to speak and slow to become angry. — Better a patient man than a warrior, a man who controls his temper than one who takes a city. — If anyone is never at fault in what he says, he is a perfect man, able to keep his whole body in check. — "For by your words you will be acquitted, and by your words you will be condemned." — Set a guard over my mouth, O LORD, keep watch over the door of my lips.

Christ suffered for you, leaving you an example, that you should follow in his steps. "He committed no sin, and no deceit was found in his mouth." When they hurled their insults at him, he did not retaliate; when he suffered, he made no threats. Instead, he entrusted himself to him who judges justly. — Consider him who endured such opposition from sinful men, so that you will not grow weary and lose heart.

No lie was found in their mouths; they are blameless.

PROV. 10:19. James 1:19. Prov. 16:32. James 3:2. Matt. 12:37. Ps. 141:3. 1 Peter 2:21–23. Heb. 12:3. Rev. 14:5.

EVENING

Teach me your way, O LORD.

I WILL INSTRUCT you and teach you in the way you should go; I will counsel you and watch over you.... Good and upright is the LORD; therefore he instructs sinners in his ways. He guides the humble in what is right and teaches them his way.

"I am the gate; whoever enters through me will be saved. He will come in and go out, and find pasture."

Jesus answered, "I am the way and the truth and the life. No one comes to the Father except through me." — Since we have confidence to enter the Most Holy Place by the blood of Jesus, by a new and living way opened for us through the curtain, that is, his body, and since we have a great priest over the house of God, let us draw near to God with a sincere heart in full assurance of faith.

Let us acknowledge the LORD; let us press on to acknowledge him. — All the ways of the LORD are loving and faithful for those who keep the demands of his covenant.

PS. 27:11. Pss. 32:8; 25:8–9. John 10:9; 14:6. Heb. 10:19–22. Hos. 6:3. Ps. 25:10.

APRIL 12

MORNING

What the law was powerless to do in that it was weakened by the sinful nature, God did by sending his own Son in the likeness of sinful man to be a sin offering. And so he condemned sin in sinful man.

THE LAW IS only a shadow of the good things that are coming — not the realities themselves. For this reason it can never, by the same sacrifices repeated endlessly year after year, make perfect those who draw near to worship. If it could, would they not have stopped being offered? — Through him everyone who believes is justified from everything you could not be justified from by the law of Moses.

Since the children have flesh and blood, he too shared in their humanity so that by his death he might destroy him who holds the power of death — that is, the devil — and free those who all their lives were held in slavery by their fear of death. For surely it is not angels he helps, but Abraham's descendants. For this reason he had to be made like his brothers in every way, in order that he might become a merciful and faithful high priest in service to God, and that he might make atonement for the sins of the people.

ROM. 8:3. Heb. 10:1 – 2. Acts 13:39. Heb. 2:14 – 17.

EVENING

For all have sinned and fall short of the glory of God.

"THERE IS NO one righteous, not even one. — There is not a righteous man on earth who does what is right and never sins. — How can one born of woman be pure?

Therefore, since the promise of entering his rest still stands, let us be careful that none of you be found to have fallen short of it.

For I know my transgressions, and my sin is always before me.... Surely I have been a sinner from birth, sinful from the time my mother conceived me.

"The LORD has taken away your sin. You are not going to die." — Those he called, he also justified; those he justified, he also glorified. — And we, who with unveiled faces all reflect the Lord's glory, are being transformed into his likeness with ever-increasing glory, which comes from the Lord, who is the Spirit. — If you continue in your faith, established and firm, not moved from the hope held out in the gospel.

Live lives worthy of God, who calls you into his kingdom and glory.

ROM. 3:23. Rom. 3:10 – 12. Eccl 7:20. Job 25:4. Heb. 4:1. Ps. 51:3, 5. 2 Sam 12:13. Rom. 8:30. 2 Cor. 3:18. Col. 1:23. 1 Thess. 2:12.

APRIL 13

MORNING

Honor the LORD with your wealth, with the firstfruits of all your crops.

REMEMBER THIS: WHOEVER sows sparingly will also reap sparingly, and whoever sows generously will also reap generously. — On the first day of every week, each one of you should set aside a sum of money in keeping with his income, saving it up. God is not unjust; he will not forget your work and the love you have shown him as you have helped his people and continue to help them.

Therefore, I urge you, brothers, in view of God's mercy, to offer your bodies as living sacrifices, holy and pleasing to God—which is your spiritual worship. — For Christ's love compels us, because we are convinced that one died for all, and therefore all died. And he died for all, that those who live should no longer live for themselves but for him who died for them and was raised again. — So whether you eat or drink or whatever you do, do it all for the glory of God.

PROV. 3:9. 2 Cor. 9:6. 1 Cor. 16:2. Heb. 6:10. Rom. 12:1. 2 Cor. 6:14–15. 1 Cor. 10:31.

EVENING

There will be no night there.

FOR THE LORD will be your everlasting light, and your God will be your glory.

The city does not need the sun or the moon to shine on it, for the glory of God gives it light, and the Lamb is its lamp.... They will not need the light of a lamp or the light of the sun, for the Lord God will give them light.

But you are a chosen people, a royal priesthood, a holy nation, a people belonging to God. — Giving thanks to the Father, who has qualified you to share in the inheritance of the saints in the kingdom of light. For he has rescued us from the dominion of darkness and brought us into the kingdom of the Son he loves. — For you were once darkness, but now you are light in the Lord. Live as children of light.

We do not belong to the night or to the darkness.

The path of the righteous is like the first gleam of dawn, shining ever brighter till the full light of day.

REV. 21:25. Isa. 60:19. Rev. 21:24; 22:5. 1 Peter 2:9. Col. 1:12–13. Eph. 5:8. 1 Thess. 5:5. Prov. 4:18.

APRIL 14

MORNING

My soul will be satisfied as with the richest of foods; with singing lips my mouth will praise you. On my bed I remember you; I think of you through the watches of the night.

HOW PRECIOUS TO me are your thoughts, O God! How vast is the sum of them! Were I to count them, they would outnumber the grains of sand. When I awake, I am still with you.... How sweet are your promises to my taste, sweeter than honey to my mouth! — Thy love is better than wine.

Whom have I in heaven but you? And being with you, I desire nothing on earth. — You are the most excellent of men.

Like an apple tree among the trees of the forest is my lover among the young men. I delight to sit in his shade, and his fruit is sweet to my taste. He has taken me to the banquet hall, and his banner over me is love.... His appearance is like Lebanon, choice as its cedars. His mouth is sweetness itself; he is altogether lovely. This is my lover, this is my friend.

PS. 63:5 – 6. Pss. 139:17 – 18; 119:103. Song of Songs 1:2. Pss. 73:25; 45:2. Song of Songs 2:3 – 4; 5:15 – 16.

EVENING

Restore to me the joy of your salvation.

I HAVE SEEN his ways, but I will heal him; I will guide him and restore comfort to him, creating praise on the lips of the mourners in Israel.

"Come now, let us reason together," says the LORD. "Though your sins are like scarlet, they shall be as white as snow; though they are red as crimson, they shall be like wool." — "Return, faithless people; I will cure you of backsliding." "Yes, we will come to you, for you are the LORD our God." — I will listen to what God the LORD will say; he promises peace to his people, his saints — but let them not return to folly.

Praise the LORD, O my soul, and forget not all his benefits. He forgives all my sins and heals all my diseases.... He restores my soul. — "I will praise you, O LORD. Although you were angry with me, your anger has turned away and you have comforted me."

Uphold me, and I will be delivered.

"I, even I, am he who blots out your transgressions, for my own sake."

PS. 51:12. Isa. 57:18; 1:18. Jer. 3:22. Pss. 85:8; 103:2 – 3; 23:3. Isa. 12:1. Ps. 119:117. Isa. 43:25.

APRIL 15

MORNING

Yet their Redeemer is strong.

For I KNOW how many are your offenses and how great your sins. — "I have bestowed strength on a warrior." — "I, the LORD, am your Savior, your Redeemer, the Mighty One of Jacob." ... "Mighty to save." — To him who is able to keep you from falling. — But where sin increased, grace increased all the more.

"Whoever believes in him is not condemned, but whoever does not believe stands condemned already because he has not believed in the name of God's one and only Son." — Therefore he is able to save completely those who come to God through him.

Was my arm too short to ransom you? ... Who shall separate us from the love of Christ? ... For I am convinced that neither death nor life, neither angels nor demons, neither the present nor the future, nor any powers, neither height nor depth, nor anything else in all creation, will be able to separate us from the love of God that is in Christ Jesus our Lord.

JER. 50:34. Amos 5:12. Ps. 89:19. Isa. 49:26; 63:1. Jude 24. Rom. 5:20. John 3:18. Heb. 7:25. Isa. 50:2. Rom. 8:35, 38–39.

EVENING

Should you then seek great things for yourself? Seek them not.

"TAKE MY YOKE upon you and learn from me, for I am gentle and humble in heart, and you will find rest for your souls." — Your attitude should be the same as that of Christ Jesus: Who, being in very nature God, did not consider equality with God something to be grasped, but made himself nothing, taking the very nature of a servant, being made in human likeness. And being found in appearance as a man, he humbled himself and became obedient to death — even death on a cross!

"Anyone who does not take his cross and follow me is not worthy of me." — Christ suffered for you, leaving you an example, that you should follow in his steps.

But godliness with contentment is great gain. For we brought nothing into the world, and we can take nothing out of it.

I have learned to be content whatever the circumstances.

JER. 45:5. Matt. 11:29. Phil. 2:5–8. Matt. 10:38. 1 Peter 2:21. 1 Tim. 6:6–8. Phil. 4:11.

APRIL 16

MORNING

In my alarm I said, "I am cut off from your sight!" Yet you
heard my cry for mercy when I called to you for help.

I SINK IN the miry depths, where there is no foothold. I have come into the deep waters; the floods engulf me. — The waters closed over my head, and I thought I was about to be cut off. I called on your name, O LORD, from the depths of the pit. You heard my plea: "Do not close your ears to my cry for relief." You came near when I called you, and you said, "Do not fear."

"Will the Lord reject us forever? Will he never show his favor again? Has his unfailing love vanished forever? Has his promise failed for all time? Has God forgotten to be merciful? Has he in anger withheld his compassion?" Then I thought, "To this I will appeal: the years of the right hand of the Most High." I will remember the deeds of the LORD; yes, I will remember your miracles of long ago. . . . I am still confident of this: I will see the goodness of the LORD in the land of the living.

PS. 31:22. Ps. 69:2. Lam. 3:54–57. Pss. 77:7–11; 27:13.

EVENING

He will call upon me, and I will answer him; I will be with
him in trouble, I will deliver him.

JABEZ CRIED OUT to the God of Israel, "Oh that you would bless me and enlarge my territory! Let your hand be with me, and keep me from harm so that I will be free from pain." And God granted his request. — That night God appeared to Solomon and said to him, "Ask for whatever you want me to give you." Solomon answered God, . . . "Give me wisdom and knowledge, that I may lead this people, for who is able to govern this great people of yours?" — God gave Solomon wisdom and very great insight, and a breadth of understanding as measureless as the sand on the seashore.

Then Asa called to the LORD his God and said, "LORD, there is no one like you to help the powerless against the mighty. Help us, O LORD our God, for we rely on you, and in your name we have come against this vast army. O LORD, you are our God; do not let man prevail against you." The LORD struck down the Cushites before Asa and Judah.

O you who hear prayer, to you all men will come.

PS. 91:15. 1 Chron. 4:10. 2 Chron. 1:7–8, 10. 1 Kings 4:29. 2 Chron. 14:11–12. Ps. 65:2.

APRIL 17

MORNING

He who sacrifices thank offerings honors me.

LET THE WORD of Christ dwell in you richly as you teach and admonish one another with all wisdom, and as you sing psalms, hymns and spiritual songs with gratitude in your hearts to God. And whatever you do, whether in word or deed, do it all in the name of the Lord Jesus, giving thanks to God the Father through him. — You were bought at a price. Therefore honor God with your body.

But you are a chosen people, a royal priesthood, a holy nation, a people belonging to God, that you may declare the praises of him who called you out of darkness into his wonderful light.... You also, like living stones, are being built into a spiritual house to be a holy priesthood, offering spiritual sacrifices acceptable to God through Jesus Christ. — Through Jesus, therefore, let us continually offer to God a sacrifice of praise — the fruit of lips that confess his name.

My soul will boast in the LORD; let the afflicted hear and rejoice. Glorify the LORD with me; let us exalt his name together.

PS. 50:23. Col. 3:16–17. 1 Cor. 6:20. 1 Peter 2:9, 5. Heb. 13:15. Ps. 34:2–3.

EVENING

Take me away with you — let us hurry!

"I HAVE LOVED you with an everlasting love; I have drawn you with loving-kindness." — "I led them with cords of human kindness, with ties of love." — "But I, when I am lifted up from the earth, will draw all men to myself." ... "Look, the Lamb of God!" ... "As Moses lifted up the snake in the desert, so the Son of Man must be lifted up, that everyone who believes in him may have eternal life."

Whom have I in heaven but you? And being with you, I desire nothing on earth. — We love because he first loved us.

My lover spoke and said to me, "Arise, my darling, my beautiful one, and come with me. See! The winter is past; the rains are over and gone. Flowers appear on the earth; the season of singing has come, the cooing of doves is heard in our land. The fig tree forms its early fruit; the blossoming vines spread their fragrance. Arise, come, my darling; my beautiful one, come with me."

SONG OF SONGS 1:4. Jer. 31:3. Hos. 11:4. John 12:32; 1:36; 3:14–15. Ps. 73:25.
1 John 4:19. Song of Songs 2:10–13.

APRIL 18

MORNING

"I will raise up for them a prophet like you from among their brothers."

[MOSES] STOOD BETWEEN the LORD and you to declare to you the word of the LORD, because you were afraid. — For there is one God and one mediator between God and men, the man Christ Jesus. Now Moses was a very humble man, more humble than anyone else on the face of the earth. — "Take my yoke upon you and learn from me, for I am gentle and humble in heart, and you will find rest for your souls." — Your attitude should be the same as that of Christ Jesus: Who, being in very nature God, did not consider equality with God something to be grasped, but made himself nothing, taking the very nature of a servant, being made in human likeness.

Moses was faithful as a servant in all God's house, testifying to what would be said in the future. But Christ is faithful as a son over God's house. And we are his house, if we hold on to our courage and the hope of which we boast.

DEUT. 18:18. Deut. 5:5. 1 Tim. 2:5. Num. 12:3. Matt. 11:29. Phil. 2:5–7. Heb. 3:5–6.

EVENING

Eternal encouragement.

"YET I WILL remember the covenant I made with you in the days of your youth, and I will establish an everlasting covenant with you."

Because by one sacrifice he has made perfect forever those who are being made holy.... Therefore he is able to save completely those who come to God through him, because he always lives to intercede for them. — I know whom I have believed, and am convinced that he is able to guard what I have entrusted to him for that day.

For God's gifts and his call are irrevocable.... Who shall separate us from the love of Christ? — "For the Lamb at the center of the throne will be their shepherd; he will lead them to springs of living water. And God will wipe away every tear from their eyes." — And so we will be with the Lord forever. Therefore encourage each other with these words.

For this is not your resting place. — For here we do not have an enduring city, but we are looking for the city that is to come.

2 THESS. 2:16. Ezek. 16:60. Heb. 10:14; 7:25; 2 Tim. 1:12. Rom. 11:29; 8:35. Rev. 7:17. 1 Thess. 4:17–18. Mic. 2:10. Heb. 13:14.

APRIL 19

MORNING

"I tell you the truth, I am the gate for the sheep."

THE CURTAIN OF the temple was torn in two from top to bottom. — For Christ died for sins once for all, the righteous for the unrighteous, to bring you to God. — The Holy Spirit was showing by this that the way into the Most Holy Place had not yet been disclosed as long as the first tabernacle was still standing.

"I am the gate; whoever enters through me will be saved. He will come in and go out, and find pasture." ... "No one comes to the Father except through me." — For through him we both have access to the Father by one Spirit. Consequently, you are no longer foreigners and aliens, but fellow citizens with God's people and members of God's household. — Therefore, brothers, ... we have confidence to enter the Most Holy Place by the blood of Jesus, by a new and living way opened for us through the curtain, that is, his body.

JOHN 10:7. Matt. 27:51. 1 Peter 3:18. Heb. 9:8. John 10:9; 14:6. Eph. 2:18–19. Heb. 10:19–20.

EVENING

His word is in my heart like a burning fire, shut up in my bones. I am weary of holding it in; indeed, I cannot.

YET WHEN I preach the gospel, I cannot boast, for I am compelled to preach. Woe to me if I do not preach the gospel! ... What then is my reward? Just this: that in preaching the gospel I may offer it free of charge, and so not make use of my rights in preaching it. — Then they called them in again and commanded them not to speak or teach at all in the name of Jesus. But Peter and John replied, "Judge for yourselves whether it is right in God's sight to obey you rather than God. For we cannot help speaking about what we have seen and heard." — For Christ's love compels us.

" 'So I was afraid and went out and hid your talent in the ground. See, here is what belongs to you.' His master replied, 'You wicked, lazy servant! So you knew that I harvest where I have not sown and gather where I have not scattered seed? Well then, you should have put my money on deposit with the bankers, so that when I returned I would have received it back with interest.' "

"Go home to your family and tell them how much the Lord has done for you, and how he has had mercy on you."

JER. 20:9. 1 Cor. 9:16, 18. Acts 4:18–20. 2 Cor. 5:14. Matt. 25:25–27. Mark 5:19.

APRIL 20

MORNING

None of those condemned things shall be found in your hands.

"THEREFORE COME OUT from them and be separate, says the Lord. Touch no unclean thing." — Dear friends, I urge you, as aliens and strangers in the world, to abstain from sinful desires, which war against your soul. — Hating even the clothing stained by corrupted flesh.

Dear friends, now we are children of God, and what we will be has not yet been made known. But we know that when he appears, we shall be like him, for we shall see him as he is. Everyone who has this hope in him purifies himself, just as he is pure. — For the grace of God that brings salvation has appeared to all men. It teaches us to say "No" to ungodliness and worldly passions, and to live self-controlled, upright and godly lives in this present age, while we wait for the blessed hope — the glorious appearing of our great God and Savior, Jesus Christ, who gave himself for us to redeem us from all wickedness and to purify for himself a people that are his very own, eager to do what is good.

DEUT. 13:17. 2 Cor. 6:17. 1 Peter 2:11. Jude 23. 1 John 3:2–3. Titus 2:11–14.

EVENING

"Who are you, Lord?" "I am Jesus."

"IT IS I Dont be afraid." — "When you pass through the waters, I will be with you; and when you pass through the rivers, they will not sweep over you. When you walk through the fire, you will not be burned; the flames will not set you ablaze. For I am the LORD, your God, the Holy One of Israel, your Savior."

Even though I walk through the valley of the shadow of death, I will fear no evil, for you are with me; your rod and your staff, they comfort me. — "Immanuel" — which means, "God with us."

"You are to give him the name Jesus, because he will save his people from their sins." — My dear children, I write this to you so that you will not sin. But if anybody does sin, we have one who speaks to the Father in our defense — Jesus Christ, the Righteous One. — Who is he that condemns? Christ Jesus, who died — more than that, who was raised to life — is at the right hand of God and is also interceding for us. Who shall separate us from the love of Christ? Shall trouble or hardship or persecution or famine or nakedness or danger or sword?

ACTS 26:15. Matt. 14:27. Isa. 43:2–3. Ps. 23:4. Matt. 1:23, 21. 1 John 2:1. Rom. 8:34–35.

APRIL 21

MORNING

Stand firm in the Lord.

MY FEET HAVE closely followed his steps; I have kept to his way without turning aside.

For the LORD loves the just and will not forsake his faithful ones. They will be protected forever.... The LORD will keep you from all harm—he will watch over your life.

"But my righteous one will live by faith. And if he shrinks back, I will not be pleased with him." But we are not of those who shrink back and are destroyed, but of those who believe and are saved. — They went out from us, but they did not really belong to us. For if they had belonged to us, they would have remained with us; but their going showed that none of them belonged to us.

"If you hold to my teaching, you are really my disciples." — "But he who stands firm to the end will be saved." — Be on your guard; stand firm in the faith; be men of courage; be strong. — Hold on to what you have, so that no one will take your crown.... "He who overcomes will, like them, be dressed in white. I will never erase his name from the book of life."

PHIL. 4:1. Job 23:11. Pss. 37:28; 121:7. Heb. 10:38–39. 1 John 2:19. John 8:31. Matt. 24:13. 1 Cor. 16:13. Rev. 3:11, 5.

EVENING

Enoch walked with God.

"DO TWO WALK together unless they have agreed to do so?"

By making peace through his blood, shed on the cross. Once you were alienated from God and were enemies in your minds because of your evil behavior. But now he has reconciled you by Christ's physical body through death to present you holy in his sight. — You who once were far away have been brought near through the blood of Christ.

For if, when we were God's enemies, we were reconciled to him through the death of his Son, how much more, having been reconciled, shall we be saved through his life! Not only is this so, but we also rejoice in God through our Lord Jesus Christ, through whom we have now received reconciliation.

And our fellowship is with the Father and with his Son, Jesus Christ.

May the grace of the Lord Jesus Christ, and the love of God, and the fellowship of the Holy Spirit be with you all. Amen.

GEN. 5:22. Amos 3:3. Col. 1:20–22. Eph. 2:13. Rom. 5:10–11. 1 John 1:3. 2 Cor. 13:14.

APRIL 22

MORNING

"If the offering is a burnt offering from the herd, he is to offer a male without defect. He must present it at the entrance to the Tent of Meeting so that it will be acceptable to the LORD. He is to lay his hand on the head of the burnt offering, and it will be accepted on his behalf to make atonement for him."

"GOD HIMSELF WILL provide the lamb for the burnt offering, my son." — "Look, the Lamb of God, who takes away the sin of the world!" — We have been made holy through the sacrifice of the body of Jesus Christ once for all. — "A ransom for many."

"No one takes it from me, but I lay it down of my own accord. I have authority to lay it down and authority to take it up again." — "I will love them freely." — The Son of God ... loved me and gave himself for me.

God made him who had no sin to be sin for us, so that in him we might become the righteousness of God. — To the praise of his glorious grace, which he has freely given us in the One he loves.

LEV. 1:3–4. Gen. 22:8. John 1:29. Heb. 10:10. Matt. 20:28. John 10:18. Hos. 14:4. Gal. 2:20. 2 Cor. 5:21. Eph. 1:6.

EVENING

For great is your love toward me; you have delivered my soul from the depths of the grave.

"BE AFRAID OF the one who can destroy both soul and body in hell."

"Fear not, for I have redeemed you; I have called you by name; you are mine." ... "I, even I, am the LORD, and apart from me there is no savior." ... "I, even I, am he who blots out your transgressions, for my own sake, and makes my way perfect."

Those who trust in their wealth and boast of their great riches? No man can redeem the life of another or give to God a ransom for him — the ransom for a life is costly, no payment is ever enough. — "I have found a ransom for him." — God, who is rich in mercy, made us alive with Christ even when we were dead in transgressions — it is by grace you have been saved.

"Salvation is found in no one else, for there is no other name under heaven given to men by which we must be saved."

PS. 86:13. Matt. 10:28. Isa. 43:1, 11, 25. Ps. 49:6–8. Job 33:24. Eph. 2:4–5. Acts. 4:12.

APRIL 23

MORNING

But the LORD was my support.

SURELY THE IDOLATROUS commotion on the hills and mountains is a deception; surely in the Lord our God is the salvation of Israel. — The LORD is my rock, my fortress and my deliverer; my God is my rock, in whom I take refuge. He is my shield and the horn of my salvation, my stronghold. — "Shout aloud and sing for joy, people of Zion, for great is the Holy One of Israel among you."

The angel of the LORD encamps around those who fear him, and he delivers them. . . . The righteous cry out, and the LORD hears them; he delivers them from all their troubles. — The eternal God is your refuge, and underneath are the everlasting arms. — So we say with confidence, "The Lord is my helper; I will not be afraid. What can man do to me?" — For who is God besides the LORD? And who is the Rock except our God? It is God who arms me with strength.

But by the grace of God I am what I am.

PS. 18:18. Jer. 3:23. Ps. 18:2. Isa. 12:6. Ps. 34:7, 17. Deut. 33:27. Heb. 13:6. Ps. 18:31 – 32. 1 Cor. 15:10.

EVENING

We all, like sheep, have gone astray.

IF WE CLAIM to be without sin, we deceive ourselves and the truth is not in us. — "There is no one righteous, not even one; there is no one who understands, no one who seeks God. All have turned away, they have together become worthless; there is no one who does good, not even one."

For you were like sheep going astray, but now you have returned to the Shepherd and Overseer of your souls. — I have strayed like a lost sheep. Seek your servant, for I have not forgotten your commandments.

He restores my soul. He guides me in paths of righteousness for his name's sake. — "My sheep listen to my voice; I know them, and they follow me. I give them eternal life, and they shall never perish; no one can snatch them out of my hand."

"Suppose one of you has a hundred sheep and loses one of them. Does he not leave the ninety-nine in the open country and go after the lost sheep until he finds it?"

ISA. 53:6. 1 John 1:8. Rom. 3:10 – 12. 1 Peter 2:25. Pss. 119:176; 23:3. John 10:27 – 28. Luke 15:4.

APRIL 24

MORNING

*Now the Lord was gracious to Sarah as he had said, and the
Lord did for Sarah what he had promised.*

TRUST IN HIM at all times, O people; pour out your hearts to him, for God is
our refuge. — But David found strength in the LORD his God. — "But God will
surely come to your aid and take you up out of this land to the land he promised
on oath to Abraham, Isaac and Jacob." — "I have indeed seen the oppression of
my people in Egypt. I have heard their groaning and have come down to set
them free. Now come, I will send you back to Egypt." ... He led them out of
Egypt and did wonders and miraculous signs in Egypt, at the Red Sea and for
forty years in the desert. — Not one of all the LORD's good promises to the house
of Israel failed; every one was fulfilled.

He who promised is faithful. — Does he speak and then not act? Does he
promise and not fulfill? — "Heaven and earth will pass away, but my words will
never pass away." — "The grass withers and the flowers fall, but the word of our
God stands forever."

**GEN. 21:1. Ps. 62:8. 1 Sam. 30:6. Gen. 50:24. Acts 7:34, 36. Josh. 21:45. Heb. 10:23.
Num. 23:19. Matt. 24:35. Isa. 40:8.**

EVENING

The eyes of all look to you.

HE HIMSELF GIVES all men life and breath and everything else. — The LORD is good
to all; he has compassion on all he has made. — "Look at the birds of the air; they
do not sow or reap or store away in barns, and yet your heavenly Father feeds them."

The same Lord is Lord of all and richly blesses all who call on him.

I lift up my eyes to the hills — where does my help come from? ... As the eyes
of slaves look to the hand of their master, as the eyes of a maid look to the hand
of her mistress, so our eyes look to the LORD our God.

For the LORD is a God of justice. Blessed are all who wait for him! ... In
that day they will say, "Surely this is our God; we trusted in him, and he saved
us. This is the LORD, we trusted in him; let us rejoice and be glad in his salvation." — But if we hope for what we do not yet have, we wait for it patiently.

**PS. 145:15. Acts 17:25. Ps. 145:9. Matt. 6:26. Rom. 10:12. Pss. 121:1; 123:2.
Isa. 30:18; 25:9. Rom. 8:25.**

APRIL 25

MORNING

"You are to give him the name Jesus, because he will save his people from their sins."

HE APPEARED SO that he might take away our sins. — That we might die to sins and live for righteousness. — He is able to save completely those who come to God through him.

But he was pierced for our transgressions, he was crushed for our iniquities; the punishment that brought us peace was upon him, and by his wounds we are healed. We all, like sheep have gone astray; ... The LORD has laid on him the iniquity of us all. — "The Christ will suffer, ... and repentance and forgiveness of sins will be preached in his name to all nations." — He has appeared once for all at the end of the ages to do away with sin by the sacrifice of himself.

God exalted him to his own right hand as Prince and Savior that he might give repentance.... "Therefore, my brothers, I want you to know that through Jesus the forgiveness of sins is proclaimed to you. Through him everyone who believes is justified from everything you could not be justified from by the law of Moses." — Your sins have been forgiven on account of his name.

MATT. 1:21. 1 John 3:5. 1 Peter 2:24. Heb. 7:25. Isa. 53:5 – 6. Luke 24:46 – 47. Heb. 9:26. Acts 5:31; 13:38 – 39. 1 John 2:12.

EVENING

Our Lord Jesus Christ, ... that though he was rich, yet for your sakes ... became poor, so that you through his poverty might become rich.

FOR GOD WAS pleased to have all his fullness dwell in him.

The Son is the radiance of God's glory and the exact representation of his being, sustaining all things by his powerful word. After he had provided purification for sins, he sat down at the right hand of the Majesty in heaven. So he became as much superior to the angels as the name he has inherited is superior to theirs. — Who, being in very nature God, did not consider equality with God something to be grasped, but made himself nothing.

"Foxes have holes and birds of the air have nests, but the Son of Man has no place to lay his head."

All things are yours, whether Paul or Apollos or Cephas or the world or life or death or the present or the future — all are yours, and you are of Christ, and Christ is of God.

2 COR. 8:9. Col. 1:19. Heb. 1:3 – 4. Phil. 2:6 – 7. Matt. 8:20. 1 Cor. 3:21 – 23.

APRIL 26

MORNING

His left arm is under my head, and his right arm embraces me.

UNDERNEATH ARE THE everlasting arms. — But when he [Peter] saw the wind, he was afraid and, beginning to sink, cried out, "Lord, save me!" Immediately Jesus reached out his hand and caught him. "You of little faith," he said, "why did you doubt?" — The LORD delights in the way of the man whose steps he has made firm; though he stumble, he will not fall, for the LORD upholds him with his hand.

"Let the beloved of the LORD rest secure in him, for he shields him all day long, and the one the LORD loves rests between his shoulders." — Cast all your anxiety on him because he cares for you. — For whoever touches you touches the apple of his eye.

"They shall never perish; no one can snatch them out of my hand.... My Father, who has given them to me, is greater man all."

SONG OF SONGS 2:6. Deut 33:27. Matt. 14:30 – 31. Ps. 37:23 – 24. Deut. 33:12. 1 Peter 5:7. Zech. 2:8. John 10:28 – 29.

EVENING

Who is this that appears like the dawn, fair as the moon,
bright as the sun, majestic as the stars in procession?

BE SHEPHERDS OF the church of God, which he bought with his own blood.

Christ loved the church and gave himself up for her to make her holy, cleansing her by the washing with water through the word, and to present her to himself as a radiant church, without stain or wrinkle or any other blemish, but holy and blameless.

A great and wondrous sign appeared in heaven: a woman clothed with the sun. — "For the wedding of the Lamb has come, and his bride has made herself ready. Fine linen, bright and clean, was given her to wear." (Fine linen stands for the righteous acts of the saints.) — This righteousness from God comes through faith in Jesus Christ to all who believe.

"I have given them the glory that you gave me."

SONG OF SONGS 6:10. Acts 20:28. Eph. 5:25 – 27. Rev. 12:1; 19:7 – 8. Rom. 3:22. John 17:22.

APRIL 27

MORNING

Brothers, . . . the time is short.

"MAN BORN OF woman is of few days and full of trouble. He springs up like a flower and withers away; like a fleeting shadow, he does not endure." — The world and its desires pass away, but the man who does the will of God lives forever.

For as in Adam all die, so in Christ all will be made alive. . . . "Death has been swallowed up in victory." — If we live, we live to the Lord; and if we die, we die to the Lord. So, whether we live or die, we belong to the Lord. — To live is Christ and to die is gain.

So do not throw away your confidence; it will be richly rewarded. You need to persevere so that when you have done the will of God, you will receive what he has promised. For in just a very little while, "He who is coming will come and will not delay." — The night is nearly over, the day is almost here. So let us put aside the deeds of darkness and put on the armor of light. — The end of all things is near. Therefore be clear minded and self-controlled so that you can pray.

1 COR. 7:29. Job 14:1 – 2. 1 John 2:17. 1 Cor. 15:22, 54. Rom. 14:8. Phil. 1:31. Heb. 10:35 – 37. Rom. 13:12. 1 Peter 4:7.

EVENING

A new name.

THE DISCIPLES WERE first called Christians at Antioch. — "Everyone who confesses the name of the Lord must turn away from wickedness." — Those who belong to Christ Jesus have crucified the sinful nature with its passions and desires. — You were bought at a price. Therefore honor God with your body.

May I never boast except in the cross of our Lord Jesus Christ, through which the world has been crucified to me, and I to the world. Neither circumcision nor uncircumcision means anything; what counts is a new creation.

Be imitators of God, therefore, as dearly loved children and live a life of love, just as Christ loved us and gave himself up for us as a fragrant offering and sacrifice to God. But among you there must not be even a hint of sexual immorality, or of any kind of impurity, or of greed, because these are improper for God's holy people. . . . For you were once darkness, but now you are light in the Lord. Live as children of light.

REV. 2:17. Acts 11:26. 2 Tim. 2:19. Gal. 5:24. 1 Cor. 6:20. Gal. 6:14 – 15. Eph. 5:1 – 3, 8.

MORNING

"Look, the Lamb of God."

IT IS IMPOSSIBLE for the blood of bulls and goats to take away sins. Therefore, when Christ came into the world, he said: "Sacrifice and offering you did not desire, but a body you prepared for me; with burnt offerings and sin offerings you were not pleased. Then I said, 'Here I am—it is written about me in the scroll—I have come to do your will, O God.'"

He was oppressed and afflicted, yet he did not open his mouth; he was led like a lamb to the slaughter, and as a sheep before her shearers is silent, so he did not open his mouth.

For you know that it was hot with perishable things such as silver or gold that you were redeemed from the empty way of life handed down to you from your forefathers, but with the precious blood of Christ, a lamb without blemish or defect.

"Worthy is the Lamb, who was slain, to receive power and wealth and wisdom and strength and honor and glory and praise!"

JOHN 1:29. Heb. 10:4–7. Isa. 53:7. 1 Peter 1:18–19. Rev. 5:12.

EVENING

But as for me, I will always have hope; I will praise you more and more.

NOT THAT I have already obtained all this, or have already been made perfect.—Therefore let us leave the elementary teachings about Christ and go on to maturity, not laying again the foundation of repentance from acts that lead to death, and of faith in God.—The path of the righteous is like the first gleam of dawn, shining ever brighter till the full light of day.

I love the LORD, for he heard my voice; he heard my cry for mercy. Because he turned his ear to me, I will call on him as long as I live.... I will extol the LORD at all times; his praise will always be on my lips.

Praise awaits you, O God, in Zion.—Day and night they never stop saying: "Holy, holy, holy is the Lord God Almighty."—He who sacrifices thank offerings honors me.—Be joyful always; pray continually; give thanks in all circumstances, for this is God's will for you in Christ Jesus.

PS. 71:14. Phil. 3:12. Heb. 6:1. Prov. 4:18. Pss. 116:1–2; 34:1; 65:1. Rev. 4:8. Ps. 50:23. 1 Thess. 5:16–18.

APRIL 29

MORNING

Consider what great things he has done for you.

REMEMBER HOW THE LORD your God led you all the way in the desert these forty years, to humble you and to test you in order to know what was in your heart, whether or not you would keep his commands.... Know then in your heart that as a man disciplines his son, so the LORD your God disciplines you.

I know, O LORD, that your laws are righteous, and in faithfulness you have afflicted me.... It was good for me to be afflicted so that I might learn your decrees.... Before I was afflicted I went astray, but now I obey your word.... The LORD has chastened me severely, but he has not given me over to death.... He does not treat us as our sins deserve or repay us according to our iniquities. For as high as the heavens are above the earth, so great is his love for those who fear him; ... For he knows how we are formed, he remembers that we are dust.

1 SAM. 12:24. Deut. 8:2, 5. Pss. 119:75, 71, 67; 118:18; 103:10 – 11, 14.

EVENING

Blessed hope — the glorious appearing of our great God and Savior, Jesus Christ.

WE HAVE THIS hope as an anchor for the soul, firm and secure. It enters the inner sanctuary behind the curtain, where Jesus, who went before us, has entered on our behalf. — He must remain in heaven until the time comes for God to restore everything. — On the day he comes to be glorified in his holy people and to be marveled at among all those who have believed.

We know that the whole creation has been groaning as in the pains of child-birth right up to the present time. Not only so, but we ourselves, who have the firstfruits of the Spirit, groan inwardly as we wait eagerly for our adoption as sons, the redemption of our bodies. Dear friends, now we are children of God, and what we will be has not yet been made known. But we know that when he appears, we shall be like him, for we shall see him as he is. — When Christ, who is your life, appears, then you also will appear with him in glory.

"Yes, I am coming soon." Amen. Come, Lord Jesus.

TITUS. 2:13. Heb. 6:19 – 20. Acts 3:21. 2 Thess. 1:10. Rom. 8:22 – 23. 1 John 3:2. Col. 3:4. Rev. 22:20.

APRIL 30

MORNING

But if anyone obeys his word, God's love is truly made complete in him.

MAY THE GOD of peace, who through the blood of the eternal covenant brought back from the dead our Lord Jesus, that great Shepherd of the sheep, equip you with everything good for doing his will, and may he work in us what is pleasing to him, through Jesus Christ, to whom be glory for ever and ever. Amen.

We know that we have come to know him if we obey his commands. — "If anyone loves me, he will obey my teaching. My Father will love him, and we will come to him and make our home with him." — No one who lives in him keeps on sinning. No one who continues to sin has either seen him or known him. Dear children, do not let anyone lead you astray. He who does what is right is righteous, just as he is righteous.... Love is made complete among us so that we will have confidence on the day of judgment, because in this world we are like him.

1 JOHN 2:5. Heb. 13:20–21. 1 John 2:3. John 14:23. 1 John 3:6–7; 4:17.

EVENING

A patient man has great understanding.

"THE LORD, THE LORD, the compassionate and gracious God, slow to anger, abounding in love and faithfulness." — The Lord is not slow in keeping his promise, as some understand slowness. He is patient with you, not wanting anyone to perish, but everyone to come to repentance.

Be imitators of God, therefore, as dearly loved children. — But the fruit of the Spirit is love, joy, peace, patience, kindness, goodness, faithfulness, gentleness and self-control. Against such things there is no law. — For it is commendable if a man bears up under the pain of unjust suffering because he is conscious of God. But how is it to your credit if you receive a beating for doing wrong and endure it? But if you suffer for doing good and you endure it, this is commendable before God. To this you were called, because Christ suffered for you, leaving you an example, that you should follow in his steps.... When they hurled their insults at him, he did not retaliate; when he suffered, he made no threats. Instead, he entrusted himself to him who judges justly.

"In your anger do not sin."

PROV. 14:29. Exod. 34:6. 2 Peter 3:9. Eph. 5:1. Gal. 5:22–23. 1 Peter 2:19–21, 23. Eph. 4:26.

MAY 1

MORNING

The fruit of the Spirit is peace.

THE MIND CONTROLLED by the Spirit is life and peace.

God has called us to live in peace. — "Peace I leave with you; my peace I give you. I do not give to you as the world gives. Do not let your heart be troubled, and do not be afraid." — May the God of hope fill you with all joy and peace as you trust in him, so that you may overflow with hope by the power of the Holy Spirit.

I know whom I have believed, and am convinced that he is able to guard what I have entrusted to him for that day. — You will keep in perfect peace him whose mind is steadfast, because he trusts in you.

The fruit of righteousness will be peace; the effect of righteousness will be quietness and confidence forever. My people will live in peaceful dwelling places, in secure homes, in undisturbed places of rest. — "But whoever listens to me will live in safety and be at ease, without fear of harm."

GAL 5:22. Rom. 8:6. 1 Cor. 7:15. John 14:27. Rom. 15:13. 2 Tim. 1:12. Isa. 26:3; 32:17–18. Prov. 1:33.

EVENING

"The LORD is there."

NOW THE DWELLING of God is with men, and he will live with them. They will be his people, and God himself will be with them and be their God.

The Lord God Almighty and the Lamb are its temple. The city does not need the sun or the moon to shine on it, for the glory of God gives it light, and the Lamb is its lamp.

When I awake, I will be satisfied with seeing your likeness.... Whom have I in heaven but you? And being with you, I desire nothing on earth.

"Judah will be inhabited forever and Jerusalem through all generations. Their bloodguilt, which I have not pardoned, I will pardon." The LORD dwells in Zion! — "Shout and be glad, O Daughter of Zion. For I am coming, and I will live among you," declares the LORD. — No longer will there be any curse. The throne of God and of the Lamb will be in the city, and his servants will serve him.

EZEK. 48:35. Rev. 21:3, 22–23. Pss. 17:15; 73:25. Joel 3:20–21. Zech. 2:10. Rev. 22:3.

MAY 2

MORNING

"Surely the LORD is in this place, and I was not aware of it."

"FOR WHERE TWO or three come together in my name, there am I with them." … "I will be with you always, to the very end of the age."

"My Presence will go with you, and I will give you rest." — Where can I go from your Spirit? Where can I flee from your presence? If I go up to the heavens, you are there; if I make my bed in the depths, you are there. — "Am I only a God nearby," declares the LORD, "and not a God far away? Can anyone hide in secret places so that I cannot see him?" declares the LORD. "Do not I fill heaven and earth?" declares the LORD.

"The heavens, even the highest heaven, cannot contain you. How much less this temple I have built!" — For this is what the high and lofty One says — he who lives forever, whose name is holy: "I live in a high and holy place, but also with him who is contrite and lowly in spirit, to revive the spirit of the lowly and to revive the heart of the contrite."

GEN. 28:16. Matt. 18:20; 28:20. Exod. 33:14. Ps. 139:7 – 8. Jer. 23:23 – 24. 1 Kings 8:27. Isa. 57:15.

EVENING

Keep yourselves from idols.

MY SON GIVE me your heart. — Set your minds on things above, not on earthly things. — "Son of man, these men have set up idols in their hearts and put wicked stumbling blocks before their faces. Should I let them inquire of me at all?"

Put to death, therefore, whatever belongs to your earthly nature: sexual immorality, impurity, lust, evil desires and greed, which is idolatry. — People who want to get rich fall into temptation and a trap and into many foolish and harmful desires that plunge men into ruin and destruction. For the love of money is a root of all kinds of evil. Some people, eager for money, have wandered from the faith and pierced themselves with many griefs.

Though your riches increase, do not set your heart on them. — My fruit is better than fine gold; what I yield surpasses choice silver.

"For where your treasure is, there your heart will be also." — "The LORD looks at the heart."

1 JOHN 5:21. Prov. 23:26. Col. 3:2. Ezek. 14:3. Col. 3:5. 1 Tim. 6:9 – 11. Ps. 62:10. Prov. 8:19. Matt. 6:21. 1 Sam. 16:7.

MAY 3

MORNING

"Be perfect, therefore, as your heavenly Father is perfect."

"I AM GOD Almighty; walk before me and be blameless." — "You are to be holy to me because I, the LORD, am holy, and I have set you apart from the nations to be my own."

You were bought at a price. Therefore honor God with your body. — You have been given fullness in Christ, who is the head over every power and authority. — Make every effort to be found spotless, blameless and at peace with him.

Blessed are they whose ways are blameless, who walk according to the law of the LORD. — But the man who looks intently into the perfect law that gives freedom, and continues to do this, not forgetting what he has heard, but doing it — he will be blessed in what he does. — Search me, O God, and know my heart; test me and know my anxious thoughts. See if there is any offensive way in me, and lead me in the way everlasting.

MATT. 5:48. Gen. 17:1. Lev. 20:26. 1 Cor. 6:20. Col. 2:10. Titus 2:14. 2 Peter 3:14. Ps. 119:1. James 1:25. Ps. 139:23–24.

EVENING

Perfecting holiness out of reverence for God.

SINCE WE HAVE these promises, dear friends, let us purify ourselves from everything that contaminates body and spirit. — Surely you desire truth in the inner parts; you teach me wisdom in the inmost place. — It teaches us to say "No" to ungodliness and worldly passions, and to live self-controlled, upright and godly lives in this present age. — "Let your light shine before men, that they may see your good deeds and praise your Father in heaven." — Not that I have already obtained all this, or have already been made perfect.

Everyone who has this hope in him purifies himself, just as he is pure. — Now it is God who has made us for this very purpose and has given us the Spirit. — To prepare God's people for works of service, so that the body of Christ may be built up until we all reach unity in the faith and in the knowledge of the Son of God and become mature, attaining to the whole measure of the fullness of Christ.

2 COR. 7:1. 2 Cor. 7:1. Ps. 51:6. Titus 2:12. Matt. 5:16. Phil. 3:12. 1 John 3:3. 2 Cor. 5:5. Eph. 4:12–13.

MAY 4

MORNING

Surely the arm of the LORD is not too short to save, nor his ear too dull to hear.

WHEN I CALLED, you answered me; you made me bold and stout-hearted. — "While I was still in prayer, Gabriel, the man I had seen in the earlier vision, came to me in swift flight about the time of the evening sacrifice."

Do not hide your face from me, do not turn your servant away in anger; you have been my helper. Do not reject me or forsake me, O God my Savior.... But you, O LORD, be not far off; O my Strength, come quickly to help me.

"Ah, Sovereign LORD, you have made the heavens and the earth by your great power and outstretched arm. Nothing is too hard for you." — He has delivered us from such a deadly peril, and he will deliver us. — And will not God bring about justice for his chosen ones, who cry out to him day and night? Will he keep putting them off? I tell you, he will see that they get justice, and quickly.

ISA. 59:1. Ps. 138:3. Dan. 9:21. Pss. 27:9; 22:19. Jer. 32:17. 2 Cor. 1:10. Luke 18:7 – 8.

EVENING

"I have brought you glory on earth."

"MY FOOD," SAID Jesus, "is to do the will of him who sent me and to finish his work." ... "As long as it is day, we must do the work of him who sent me. Night is coming, when no one can work."

"Didn't you know I had to be in my Father's house?" But they did not understand what he was saying to them. — "This sickness will not end in death. No, it is for God's glory so that God's Son may be glorified through it." ... "Did I not tell you that if you believed, you would see the glory of God?"

And Jesus grew in wisdom and stature, and in favor with God and men.... "You are my Son, whom I love; with you I am well pleased." ... All spoke well of him and were amazed at the gracious words that came from his lips.

"You are worthy to take the scroll and to open its seals, because you were slain, and with your blood you purchased men for God from every tribe and language and people and nation."

JOHN 17:4. John 4:34; 9:4. Luke 2:49 – 50. John 11:4, 40. Luke 2:52; 3:22; 4:22. Rev. 5:9 – 10.

MAY 5

MORNING

"So do not worry, saying, 'What shall we eat?' or 'What shall we drink?' or 'What shall we wear?'... Your heavenly Father knows that you need them."

FEAR THE LORD, you his saints, for those who fear him lack nothing. The lions may grow weak and hungry, but those who seek the LORD lack no good thing.... No good thing does he withhold from those whose walk is blameless. O LORD Almighty, blessed is the man who trusts in you.

I would like you to be free from concern. — Do not be anxious about anything, but in everything, by prayer and petition, with thanksgiving, present your requests to God.

"Are not two sparrows sold for a penny? Yet not one of them will fall to the ground apart from the will of your Father. And even the very hairs of your head are all numbered. So don't be afraid; you are worth more than many sparrows." — "Why are you so afraid? Do you still have no faith?" ... "Have faith in God."

MATT. 6:31 – 32. Pss. 34:9 – 10; 84:11 – 12. 1 Cor. 7:32. Phil. 4:6. Matt. 10:29 – 31. Mark 4:40; 11:22.

EVENING

He spread out a cloud as a covering, and a fire to give light at night.

AS A FATHER has compassion on his children, so the LORD has compassion on those who fear him; for he knows how we are formed, he remembers that we are dust.

The sun will not harm you by day, nor the moon by night. — It will be a shelter and shade from the heat of the day, and a refuge and hiding place from the storm and rain.

The LORD watches over you — the LORD is your shade at your right hand; ... The LORD will watch over your coming and going both now and forevermore. — By day the LORD went ahead of them in a pillar of cloud to guide them on their way and by night in a pillar of fire to give them light, so that they could travel by day or night. Neither the pillar of cloud by day nor the pillar of fire by night left its place in front of the people.

Jesus Christ is the same yesterday and today and forever.

PS. 105:39. Pss. 103:13 – 14; 121:6. Isa. 4:6. Ps. 121:5, 8. Exod. 13:21 – 22. Heb. 13:8.

MAY 6

MORNING

Love and faithfulness meet together; righteousness and peace kiss each other.

A RIGHTEOUS GOD and a Savior.

It pleased the LORD for the sake of his righteousness to make his law great and glorious. — God was reconciling the world to himself in Christ, not counting men's sins against them. — God presented him as a sacrifice of atonement, through faith in his blood. He did this to demonstrate his justice, because in his forbearance he had left the sins committed beforehand unpunished — he did it to demonstrate his justice at the present time, so as to be just and the one who justifies the man who has faith in Jesus.

But he was pierced for our transgressions, he was crushed for our iniquities; the punishment that brought us peace was upon him, and by his wounds we are healed. — Who will bring any charge against those whom God has chosen? It is God who justifies. Who is he that condemns? Christ Jesus.... However, to the man who does not work but trusts God who justifies the wicked, his faith is credited as righteousness.

PS. 85:10. Isa. 45:21; 42:21. 2 Cor. 5:19. Rom. 3:25–26. Isa. 53:5. Rom. 8:33; 4:5.

EVENING

"How are the dead raised? With what kind of body will they come?"

DEAR FRIENDS, NOW we are children of God, and what we will be has not yet been made known. But we know that when he appears, we shall be like him, for we shall see him as he is. — And just as we have borne the likeness of the earthly man, so shall we bear the likeness of the man from heaven.

The Lord Jesus Christ, who, by the power that enables him to bring everything under his control, will transform our lowly bodies so that they will be like his glorious body.

Jesus himself stood among them and said to them, "Peace be with you." They were startled and frightened, thinking they saw a ghost. — He appeared to Peter, and then to the Twelve. After that, he appeared to more than five hundred of the brothers at the same time.

And if the Spirit of him who raised Jesus from the dead is living in you, he who raised Christ from the dead will also give life to your mortal bodies through his Spirit, who lives in you.

1 COR. 15:35. 1 John 3:2. 1 Cor. 15:49. Phil. 3:20–21. Luke 24:36–37. 1 Cor. 15:5–6. Rom 8:11.

May 7

Morning

"You will hear of wars and rumors of wars, but see to it that you are not alarmed."

GOD IS OUR refuge and strength, an ever present help in trouble. Therefore we will not fear, though the earth give way and the mountains fall into the heart of the sea, though its waters roar and foam and the mountains quake with their surging. — Go, my people, enter your rooms and shut the doors behind you; hide yourselves for a little while until his wrath has passed by. See, the LORD is coming out of his dwelling to punish the people of the earth for their sins. — I will take refuge in the shadow of your wings until the disaster has passed.

Your life is now hidden with Christ in God. — He will have no fear of bad news; his heart is steadfast, trusting in the LORD.

"I have told you these things, so that in me you may have peace. In this world you will have trouble. But take heart! I have overcome the world."

MATT. 24:6. Ps. 46:1–3. Isa. 26:20–21. Ps. 57:1. Col. 3:3. Ps. 112:7. John 16:33.

Evening

For they persecute those you wound.

"THINGS THAT CAUSE people to sin are bound to come, but woe to that person through whom they come." — "This man was handed over to you by God's set purpose and foreknowledge; and you, with the help of wicked men, put him to death by nailing him to the cross." — Then they spit in his face and struck him with their fists. Others slapped him and said, "Prophesy to us, Christ. Who hit you?"

In the same way the chief priests, the teachers of the law and the elders mocked him. "He saved others," they said, "but he can't save himself! He's the king of Israel! Let him come down now from the cross, and we will believe in him." — "Indeed Herod and Pontius Pilate met together with the Gentiles and the people of Israel in this city to conspire against your holy servant Jesus, whom you anointed. They did what your power and will had decided beforehand should happen."

Surely he took up our infirmities and carried our sorrows, yet we considered him stricken by God, smitten by him, and afflicted.

PS. 69:26. Luke 17:1. Acts 2:23. Matt. 26:67–68; 27:41–42. Acts 4:27–28. Isa. 53:4.

MAY 8

MORNING

Yet it was the LORD'S will to crush him and cause him to suffer.

"Now my heart is troubled, and what shall I say? 'Father, save me from this hour'? No, it was for this very reason I came to this hour. Father, glorify your name!" Then a voice came from heaven, "I have glorified it, and will glorify it again." — "Father, if you are willing, take this cup from me; yet not my will, but yours be done." An angel from heaven appeared to him and strengthened him.

And being found in appearance as a man, he humbled himself and became obedient to death — even the death on a cross! — "The reason my Father loves me is that I lay down my life — only to take it up again." . . . "For I have come down from heaven not to do my will but to do the will of him who sent me." . . . "Shall I not drink the cup the Father has given me?"

"The one who sent me is with me; he has not left me alone, for I always do what pleases him." — "This is my Son, whom I love; with him I am well pleased." — "My chosen one in whom I delight."

ISA. 53:10. John 12:27–28. Luke 22:42–43. Phil. 2:8. John 10:17; 6:38; 18:11; 8:29. Matt. 3:17. Isa. 42:1.

EVENING

You who call on the LORD, give yourselves no rest

"You have made them to be a kingdom and priests to serve our God." — "The sons of Aaron, the priests, are to blow the trumpets. This is to be a lasting ordinance for you and the generations to come. When you go into battle in your own land against an enemy who is oppressing you, sound a blast on the trumpets. Then you will be remembered by the LORD your God and rescued from your enemies."

"I have not said to Jacob's descendants, 'Seek me in vain.'" — God heard them, for their prayer reached heaven, his holy dwelling place. — The eyes of the LORD are on the righteous and his ears are attentive to their cry. — Pray for each other so that you may be healed. The prayer of a righteous man is powerful and effective.

Come, Lord Jesus. — O my God, do not delay. — We are looking forward to a new heaven and a new earth, the home of righteousness.

ISA. 62:6. Rev. 5:10. Num. 10:8–9. Isa. 45:19. 2 Chron. 30:27. Ps. 34:15. James 5:16. Rev. 22:20. Ps. 40:17. 2 Peter 3:12.

MAY 9

MORNING

Now faith is being sure of what we hope for and certain of what we do not see.

IF ONLY FOR this life we have hope in Christ, we are to be pitied more than all men.

"No eye has seen, no ear has heard, no mind has conceived what God has prepared for those who love him"—but God has revealed it to us by his Spirit.—Having believed, you were marked in him with a seal, the promised Holy Spirit, who is a deposit guaranteeing our inheritance until the redemption of those who are God's possession.

Then Jesus told him, "Because you have seen me, you have believed; blessed are those who have not seen and yet have believed."—Though you have not seen him, you love him; and even though you do not see him now, you believe in him and are filled with an inexpressible and glorious joy, for you are receiving the goal of your faith, the salvation of your souls.

We live by faith, not by sight.—So do not throw away your confidence; it will be richly rewarded.

HEB. 11:1. 1 Cor. 15:19; 2:9–10. Eph. 1:13–14. John 20:29. 1 Peter 1:8–9. 2 Cor. 5:7. Heb. 10:35.

EVENING

"It is I; don't be afraid."

WHEN I SAW him, I fell at his feet as though dead. Then he placed his right hand on me and said: "Do not be afraid. I am the First and the Last. I am the Living One; I was dead, and behold I am alive for ever and ever! And I hold the keys of death and Hades."—"I, even I, am he who blots out your transgressions, for my own sake, and remembers your sins no more."

"Woe to me!" I cried. "I am ruined! For I am a man of unclean lips, and I live among a people of unclean lips, and my eyes have seen the King, the LORD Almighty." Then one of the seraphs flew to me with a live coal in his hand, which he had taken with tongs from the altar. With it he touched my mouth and said, "See, this has touched your lips; your guilt is taken away and your sin atoned for." ... "I have swept away your offenses like a cloud, your sins like the morning mist. Return to me, for I have redeemed you."

But if anybody does sin, we have one who speaks to the Father in our defense—Jesus Christ, the Righteous One.

JOHN 6:20. Rev. 1:17–18. Isa. 43:25; 6:5–7; 44:22. 1 John 2:1.

MAY 10

MORNING

The reason the Son of God appeared was to destroy the devil's work.

FOR OUR STRUGGLE is not against flesh and blood, but against the rulers, against the authorities, against the powers of this dark world and against the spiritual forces of evil in the heavenly realms. — Since the children have flesh and blood, he too shared in their humanity so that by his death he might destroy him who holds the power of death — that is, the devil. — And having disarmed the powers and authorities, he made a public spectacle of them, triumphing over them by the cross. — Then I heard a loud voice in heaven say: "Now have come the salvation and the power and the kingdom of our God, and the authority of his Christ. For the accuser of our brothers, who accuses them before our God day and night, has been hurled down. They overcame him by the blood of the Lamb and by the word of their testimony; they did not love their lives so much as to shrink from death."

But thanks be to God! He gives us the victory through our Lord Jesus Christ.

1 JOHN 3:8. Eph. 6:12. Heb. 2:14. Col. 2:15. Rev. 12:10–11. 1 Cor. 15:57.

EVENING

"Meaningless! Meaningless!" Everything is meaningless.

ALL OUR DAYS pass away under your wrath; we finish our years with a moan. The length of our days is seventy years — or eighty, if we have the strength; yet their span is but trouble and sorrow, for they quickly pass, and we fly away. — If only for this life we have hope in Christ, we are to be pitied more than all men.

For here we do not have an enduring city, but we are looking for the city that is to come. — I the LORD do not change. — But our citizenship is in heaven. And we eagerly await a Savior from there, the Lord Jesus Christ, who, by the power that enables him to bring everything under his control, will transform our lowly bodies so that they will be like his glorious body. — For the creation was subjected to frustration, not by its own choice, but by the will of the one who subjected it, in hope.

Jesus Christ is the same yesterday and today and forever. — "Holy, holy, holy is the Lord God Almighty, who was, and is, and is to come."

ECCL. 1:2. Ps. 90:9–10. 1 Cor. 15:19. Heb. 13:14. Mal. 3:6. Phil. 3:20–21. Rom. 8:20. Heb. 13:8. Rev. 4:8.

MAY 11

MORNING

Come back to your senses as you ought, and stop sinning.

YOU ARE ALL sons of light and sons of the day. We do not belong to the night or to the darkness. So then, let us not be like others, who are asleep, but let us be alert and self-controlled.

The hour has come for you to wake up from your slumber, because our salvation is nearer now than when we first believed. The night is nearly over; the day is almost here. So let us put aside the deeds of darkness and put on the armor of light. — Therefore put on the full armor of God, so that when the day of evil comes, you may be able to stand your ground, and after you have done everything, to stand. — Rid yourselves of all the offenses you have committed, and get a new heart and a new spirit. — Therefore, get rid of all moral filth and the evil that is so prevalent, and humbly accept the word planted in you, which can save you.

And now, dear children, continue in him, so that when he appears we may be confident and unashamed before him at his coming. If you know that he is righteous, you know that everyone who does what is right has been born of him.

1 COR. 15:34. 1 Thess. 5:5 – 6. Rom. 13:11 – 12. Eph. 6:13. Ezek. 18:31. James 1:21.
   1 John 2:28 – 29.

EVENING

"My sheep listen to my voice."

"HERE I AM! I stand at the door and knock. If anyone hears my voice and opens the door, I will go in and eat with him, and he with me."

I slept but my heart was awake. Listen! My lover is knocking: "Open to me, my sister, my darling, my dove, my flawless one. My head is drenched with dew, my hair with the dampness of the night." . . . I opened for my lover, but my lover had left, he was gone. My heart had gone out to him when he spoke. I looked for him but did not find him. I called him but he did not answer.

"Speak, for your servant is listening." — When Jesus reached the spot, he looked up and said to him, "Zacchaeus, come down immediately. I must stay at your house today." So he came down at once and welcomed him gladly. — I will listen to what God the LORD will say; he promises peace to his people, his saints — but let them not return to folly.

JOHN 10:27. Rev. 3:20. Song of Songs 5:2, 6. 1 Sam. 3:10. Luke 19:5 – 6. Ps. 85:8.

May 12

Morning

Dear friends, let us love one another, for love comes from God. Everyone who loves has been born of God and knows God.

GOD HAS POURED out his love into our hearts by the Holy Spirit, whom he has given us.... For you did not receive a spirit that makes you a slave again to fear, but you received the Spirit of sonship. And by him we cry, *"Abba,* Father." The Spirit himself testifies with our spirit that we are God's children.

This is how God showed his love among us: He sent his one and only Son into the world that we might live through him. — In him we have redemption through his blood, the forgiveness of sins, in accordance with the riches of God's grace.... In order that in the coming ages he might show the incomparable riches of his grace, expressed in his kindness to us in Christ Jesus.

1 JOHN 4:7. Rom. 5:5; 8:15 – 16. 1 John 4:9. Eph. 1:7; 2:7.

Evening

Scorn has broken my heart.

"ISN'T THIS THE carpenter's son?" — "Nazareth! Can anything good come from there?" ... "Aren't we right in saying that you are a Samaritan and demon-possessed?" — "It is by the prince of demons that he drives out demons." — "We know this man is a sinner." ... "No, he deceives the people." — "This fellow is blaspheming!" ... "Here is a glutton and a drunkard, a friend of tax collectors and 'sinners.' ..."

"It is enough for the student to be like his teacher, and the servant like his master." — For it is commendable if a man bears up under the pain of unjust suffering because he is conscious of God. But how is it to your credit if you receive a beating for doing wrong and endure it? But if you suffer for doing good and you endure it, this is commendable before God. To this you were called, because Christ suffered for you, leaving you an example, that you should follow in his steps. "He committed no sin, and no deceit was found in his mouth." When they hurled their insults at him, he did not retaliate; when he suffered, he made no threats. Instead, he entrusted himself to him who judges justly.... If you are insulted because of the name of Christ, you are blessed, for the Spirit of glory and of God rests on you.

PS. 69:20. Matt. 13:55. John 1:46; 8:48. Matt. 9:34. John 9:24; 7:12. Matt. 9:3; 11:19; 10:25. 1 Peter 2:19 – 23; 4:14.

MAY 13

MORNING

I want men everywhere to lift up holy hands in prayer,
without anger or disputing.

"YET A TIME is coming and has now come when the true worshipers will worship the Father in spirit and truth, for they are the kind of worshipers the Father seeks. God is spirit, and his worshipers must worship in spirit and in truth." — Then you will call, and the LORD will answer; you will cry for help, and he will say: Here am I. — "And when you stand praying, if you hold anything against anyone, forgive."

Without faith it is impossible to please God, because anyone who comes to him must believe that he exists and that he rewards those who earnestly seek him. — But when he asks, he must believe and not doubt, because he who doubts is like a wave of the sea, blown and tossed by the wind. That man should not think he will receive anything from the Lord.

If I had cherished sin in my heart, the Lord would not have listened. — My dear children, I write this to you so that you will not sin. But if anybody does sin, we have one who speaks to the Father in our defense — Jesus Christ, the Righteous One. He is the atoning sacrifice for our sins.

1 TIM. 2:8. John 4:23 – 24. Isa. 58:9. Mark 11:25. Heb. 11:6. James 1:6 – 7. Ps. 66:18. 1 John 2:1 – 2.

EVENING

My heart pounds, my strength fails me.

HEAR MY CRY, O God; listen to my prayer. From the ends of the earth I call to you.

But he said to me, "My grace is sufficient for you, for my power is made perfect in weakness." — Therefore I will boast all the more gladly about my weaknesses, so that Christ's power may rest on me. That is why, for Christ's sake, I delight in weaknesses, in insults, in hardships, in persecutions, in difficulties. For when I am weak, then I am strong.

But when he saw the wind, he was afraid and, beginning to sink, cried out, "Lord, save me!" Immediately Jesus reached out his hand and caught him. "You of little faith," he said, "why did you doubt?" — If you falter in times of trouble, how small is your strength! — He gives strength to the weary and increases the power of the weak. — The eternal God is your refuge, and underneath are the everlasting arms. — Being strengthened with all power according to his glorious might.

PS. 38:10. Ps. 61:1 – 2. 2 Cor. 12:9 – 10. Matt. 14:30 – 31. Prov. 24:10. Isa. 40:29. Deut. 33:27. Col. 1:11.

MAY 14

MORNING

The fellowship of sharing in his sufferings.

IT IS ENOUGH for the student to be like his teacher, and the servant like his master.

He was despised and rejected by men, a man of sorrows, and familiar with suffering. Like one from whom men hide their faces he was despised, and we esteemed him not. — "In this world you will have trouble.... As it is, you do not belong to the world, but I have chosen you out of the world. That is why the world hates you."

I looked for sympathy, but there was none. — At my first defense, no one came to my support, but everyone deserted me.

"Foxes have holes and birds of the air have nests, but the Son of Man has no place to lay his head." For here we do not have an enduring city, but we are looking for the city that is to come.... Let us run with perseverance the race marked out for us. Let us fix our eyes on Jesus, the author and perfecter of our faith, who for the joy set before him endured the cross, scorning its shame, and sat down at the right hand of the throne of God.

PHIL. 3:10. Matt. 10:25. Isa. 53:3. John 16:33; 15:19. Ps. 69:20. 2 Tim. 4:16. Matt. 8:20. Heb. 13:14; 12:1 – 2.

EVENING

They overcame him by the blood of the Lamb.

WHO WILL BRING any charge against those whom God has chosen? It is God who justifies. Who is he that condemns? Christ Jesus, who died — It is the blood that makes atonement for one's life. — "I am the LORD. The blood will be a sign for you on the houses where you are; and when I see the blood, I will pass over you."

Therefore, there is now no condemnation for those who are in Christ Jesus. — "These in white robes — who are they, and where did they come from?" I answered, "Sir, you know." And he said, "These are they who have come out of the great tribulation; they have washed their robes and made them white in the blood of the Lamb."

To him who loves us and has freed us from our sins by his blood, and has made us to be a kingdom and priests to serve his God and Father — to him be glory and power for ever and ever! Amen.

REV. 12:11. Rom. 8:33 – 34. Lev. 17:11. Exod. 12:12 – 13. Rom. 8:1. Rev. 7:13 – 14; 1:5 – 6.

MAY 15

MORNING

"He will wipe every tear from their eyes. There will be no more death or mourning or crying or pain, for the old order of things has passed away."

HE WILL SWALLOW up death forever.—The Sovereign LORD will wipe away the tears from all faces; he will remove the disgrace of his people from all the earth. The LORD has spoken.... No one living in Zion will say, "I am ill"; and the sins of those who dwell there will be forgiven.... The sound of weeping and of crying will be heard in it no more.... Sorrow and sighing will flee away.

"I will ransom them from the power of the grave; I will redeem them from death. Where, O death, are your plagues? Where, O grave, is your destruction?"—The last enemy to be destroyed is death.... Then the saying that is written will come true: "Death has been swallowed up in victory."

What is unseen is eternal.

REV. 21:4. Isa. 25:8; 60:20; 33:24; 65:19; 35:10. Hos. 13:14. 1 Cor. 15:26, 54. 2 Cor. 4:18.

EVENING

God raised us up with Christ.

"DO NOT BE afraid.... I am the Living One."—"Father, I want those you have given me to be with me where I am."

For we are members of his body.—And he is the head of the body, the church; he is the beginning and the firstborn from among the dead.... You have been given fullness in Christ, who is the head over every power and authority.

Since the children have flesh and blood, he too shared in their humanity so that by his death he might destroy him who holds the power of death—that is, the devil—and free those who all their lives were held in slavery by their fear of death.

For the perishable must clothe itself with the imperishable, and the mortal with immortality. When the perishable has been clothed with the imperishable, and the mortal with immortality, then the saying that is written will come true: "Death has been swallowed up in victory."

EPH. 2:6. Rev. 1:17–18. John 17:24. Eph. 5:30. Col. 1:18; 2:10. Heb. 2:14–15. 1 Cor. 15:53–54.

MAY 16

MORNING

A servant of Christ Jesus.

"You CALL ME 'Teacher' and 'Lord,' and rightly so, for that is what I am." ... "Whoever serves me must follow me; and where I am, my servant also will be. My Father will honor the one who serves me." — "Take my yoke upon you and learn from me, for I am gentle and humble in heart, and you will find rest for your souls. For my yoke is easy and my burden is light."

But whatever was to my profit I now consider loss for the sake of Christ. — But now that you have been set free from sin and have become slaves to God, the benefit you reap leads to holiness, and the result is eternal life.

"I no longer call you servants, because a servant does not know his master's business. Instead, I have called you friends, for everything that I learned from my Father I have made known to you." — So you are no longer a slave, but a son.

Stand firm, then, and do not let yourselves be burdened again by a yoke of slavery.... You, my brothers, were called to be free. But do not use your freedom to indulge the sinful nature.

ROM. 1:1. John 13:13; 12:26. Matt. 11:29 – 30. Phil. 3:7. Rom. 6:22. John 15:15. Gal. 4:7; 5:1, 13.

EVENING

I will praise the LORD, who counsels me.

AND HE WILL be called Wonderful Counselor, Mighty God. — "Counsel and sound judgment are mine; I have understanding and power." — Your word is a lamp to my feet and a light for my path. — Trust in the LORD with all your heart and lean not on your own understanding; in all your ways acknowledge him, and he will make your paths straight.

I know, O LORD, that a man's life is not his own; it is not for man to direct his steps. — Whether you turn to the right or to the left, your ears will hear a voice behind you, saying, "This is the way; walk in it." — Commit to the LORD whatever you do, and your plans will succeed. — But he knows the way that I take. — A man's steps are directed by the LORD. How then can anyone understand his own way?

You guide me with your counsel, and afterward you will take me into glory.... For this God is our God for ever and ever; he will be our guide even to the end.

PS. 16:7. Isa. 9:6. Prov. 8:14. Ps. 119:105. Prov. 3:5 – 6. Jer. 10:23. Isa. 30:21. Prov. 16:3. Job 23:10. Prov. 20:24. Pss. 73:24; 48:14.

MAY 17

MORNING

I am the LORD your God; follow my decrees and be careful to keep my laws.

BUT JUST AS he who called you is holy, so be holy in all you do. — Whoever claims to live in him must walk as Jesus did.... If you know that he is righteous, you know that everyone who does what is right has been born of him. — Circumcision is nothing and uncircumcision is nothing. Keeping God's commands is what counts. — For whoever keeps the whole law and yet stumbles at just one point is guilty of breaking all of it.

Not that we are competent to claim anything for ourselves, but our competence comes from God: — Teach me, O LORD, to follow your decrees.

Continue to work out your salvation with fear and trembling, for it is God who works in you to will and to act according to his good purpose. — May the God of peace, who through the blood of the eternal covenant brought back from the dead our Lord Jesus, that great Shepherd of the sheep, equip you with everything good for doing his will, and may he work in us what is pleasing to him, through Jesus Christ.

EZEK. 20:19. 1 Peter 1:15. 1 John 2:6, 29. 1 Cor. 7:19. James 2:10. 2 Cor. 3:5. Ps. 119:33. Phil. 2:12 – 13. Heb. 13:20 – 21.

EVENING

I have exalted a young man from among the people.

FOR SURELY IT is not angels he helps, but Abraham's descendants. For this reason he had to be made like his brothers. — High above on the throne was a figure like that of a man. — "The one who came from heaven — the Son of Man." — "Look at my hands and my feet. It is I myself! Touch me and see; a ghost does not have flesh and bones, as you see I have."

But made himself nothing, taking the very nature of a servant, being made in human likeness. And being found in appearance as a man, he humbled himself and became obedient to death — even death on a cross! Therefore God exalted him to the highest place and gave him the name that is above every name, that at the name of Jesus every knee should bow. — "Wake up! Strengthen what remains and is about to die, for I have not found your deeds complete in the sight of my God."

PS. 89:19. Heb. 2:16 – 17. Ezek. 1:26. John 3:13. Luke 24:39. Phil. 2:7 – 10. Rev. 3:2.

MAY 18

MORNING

*"For as the Father has life in himself, so he has granted the
Son to have life in himself."*

OUR SAVIOR, CHRIST Jesus, who has destroyed death and has brought life and
immortality to light through the gospel. — "I am the resurrection and the life."
... "Because I live, you also will live." — We have come to share in Christ....
Participate in the Holy Spirit. — Shared in the divine nature. — "The first man
Adam became a living being"; the last Adam, a life-giving spirit.... Listen, I tell
you a mystery: We will not all sleep, but we will all be changed — in a flash, in
the twinkling of an eye, at the last trumpet. For the trumpet will sound, the
dead will be raised imperishable, and we will be changed.

"Holy, holy, holy is the Lord God Almighty, who was, and is, and is to come."
... Who lives for ever and ever. — The blessed and only Ruler, the King of kings
and Lord of lords, who alone is immortal and who lives in unapproachable light,
whom no one has seen or can see. To him be honor and might forever. Amen....
Now to the King eternal, immortal, invisible, the only God, be honor and glory
for ever and ever. Amen.

**JOHN 5:26. 2 Tim. 1:10. John 11:25; 14:19. Heb. 3:14; 6:4. 2 Peter 1:4.
1 Cor. 15:45, 51 – 52. Rev. 4:8 – 9. 1 Tim. 6:15 – 16; 1:17.**

EVENING

Let us not become conceited, provoking and envying each other.

AND HE [GIDEON] said, "I do have one request, that each of you give me an earring from your share of the plunder." (It was the custom of the Ishmaelites to wear
gold earrings.) They answered, "We'll be glad to give them." So they spread out a
garment, and each man threw a ring from his plunder onto it.... Gideon made the
gold into an ephod, which he placed in Ophrah, his town. All Israel prostituted
themselves by worshiping it there, and it became a snare to Gideon and his family.

Do nothing out of selfish ambition or vain conceit, but in humility consider
others better than yourselves. — Love is patient, love is kind. It does not envy, it
does not boast, it is not proud. It is not rude, it is not self-seeking.

"Take my yoke upon you and learn from me."

GAL. 5:26. Judg. 8:24 – 25, 27. Phil. 2:3. 1 Cor. 13:4 – 5. Matt. 11:29.

MAY 19

MORNING

Wash away all my iniquity and cleanse me from my sin.

"I WILL CLEANSE them from all the sin they have committed against me and will forgive all their sins of rebellion against me." — "I will sprinkle clean water on you, and you will be clean; I will cleanse you from all your impurities and from all your idols."

"Unless a man is born of water and the Spirit, he cannot enter the kingdom of God." — The blood of goats and bulls and the ashes of a heifer sprinkled on those who are ceremonially unclean sanctify them so that they are outwardly clean. How much more, then, will the blood of Christ, who through the eternal Spirit offered himself unblemished to God, cleanse our consciences from acts that lead to death, so that we may serve the living God!

Yet he saved them for his name's sake, to make his mighty power known.... Not to us, O LORD, not to us but to your name be the glory, because of your love and faithfulness.

PS. 51:2. Jer. 33:8. Ezek. 36:25. John 3:5. Heb. 9:13–14. Pss. 106:8; 115:1.

EVENING

Partnership in the gospel.

THE BODY IS a unit, though it is made up of many parts; and though all its parts are many, they form one body. So it is with Christ. For we were all baptized by one Spirit into one body — whether Jews or Greeks, slave or free — and we were all given the one Spirit to drink.

God, who has called you into fellowship with his Son Jesus Christ our Lord, is faithful. — We proclaim to you what we have seen and heard, so that you also may have fellowship with us. And our fellowship is with the Father and with his Son, Jesus Christ.

But if we walk in the light, as he is in the light, we have fellowship with one another, and the blood of Jesus, his Son, purifies us from every sin. — After Jesus said this,... "My prayer is not for them alone. I pray also for those who will believe in me through their message, that all of them may be one, Father, just as you are in me and I am in you. May they also be in us so that the world may believe that you have sent me."

PHIL. 1:5. 1 Cor. 12:12–13; 1:9. 1 John 1:3, 7. John 17:1, 20–21.

MAY 20

MORNING

You too should be on your guard.

EVERYONE WHO COMPETES in the games goes into strict training. They do it to get a crown that will not last; but we do it to get a crown that will last forever. Therefore I do not run like a man running aimlessly; I do not fight like a man beating the air. No, I beat my body and make it my slave so that after I have preached to others, I myself will not be disqualified for the prize. — Put on the full armor of God so that you can take your stand against the devil's schemes. For our struggle is not against flesh and blood, but against the rulers, against the authorities, against the powers of this dark world and against the spiritual forces of evil in the heavenly realms.

Those who belong to Christ Jesus have crucified the sinful nature with its passions and desires. Since we live by the Spirit, let us keep in step with the Spirit. — Because those who are led by the Spirit of God are sons of God. — Be diligent in these matters; give yourself wholly to them, so that everyone may see your progress.

1 TIM. 4:16. 1 Cor. 9:25 – 27. Eph. 6:11 – 12. Gal. 5:24 – 25. Rom. 8:14. 1 Tim. 4:15.

EVENING

Jesus said to her, "Mary."

"FEAR NOT, FOR I have redeemed you; I have called you by name; you are mine." — "The sheep listen to his voice. He calls his own sheep by name and leads them out."

"See, I have engraved you on the palms of my hands; your walls are ever before me."

God's solid foundation stands firm, sealed with this inscription: "The Lord knows those who are his." — We have a great high priest who has gone through the heavens, Jesus the Son of God.

"Take two onyx stones and engrave on them the names of the sons of Israel. . . . And fasten them on the shoulder pieces of the ephod as memorial stones for the sons of Israel. Aaron is to bear the names on his shoulders as a memorial before the LORD. . . . Fashion a breastpiece for making decisions. . . . Then mount four rows of precious stones on it. . . . There are to be twelve stones, one for each of the names of the sons of Israel. . . . So they may be over Aaron's heart whenever he enters the presence of the LORD."

JOHN 20:16. Isa. 43:1. John 10:3 – 4. Isa. 49:16. 2 Tim. 2:19. Heb. 4:14.
Exod. 28:9, 12, 15, 17, 21, 30.

MAY 21

MORNING

Finally, be strong in the Lord and in his mighty power.

"MY GRACE IS sufficient for you, for my power is made perfect in weakness." Therefore I will boast all the more gladly about my weaknesses, so that Christ's power may rest on me. That is why, for Christ's sake, I delight in weaknesses, in insults, in hardships, in persecutions, in difficulties. For when I am weak, then I am strong. — I will come and proclaim your mighty acts, O Sovereign LORD; I will proclaim your righteousness, yours alone. — The gospel ... is the power of God for the salvation.

I can do everything through him who gives me strength. — I labor, struggling with all his energy, which so powerfully works in me. — But we have this treasure in jars of clay to show that this all-surpassing power is from God and not from us.

"The joy of the LORD is your strength." — Being strengthened with all power according to his glorious might so that you may have great endurance and patience, and joyfully giving thanks to the Father.

EPH. 6:10. 2 Cor. 12:9 – 10. Ps. 71:16. Rom. 1:16. Phil. 4:13. Col. 1:29. 2 Cor. 4:7. Neh. 8:10. Col. 1:11 – 12.

EVENING

Jesus Christ our Lord.

"JESUS, BECAUSE HE will save his people from their sins." — He humbled himself and became obedient to death — even death on a cross! Therefore God exalted him to the highest place and gave him the name that is above every name, that at the name of Jesus every knee should bow, in heaven and on earth and under the earth.

"The Messiah" (called Christ). — "Because the LORD has anointed me to preach good news to the poor. He has sent me to bind up the brokenhearted, to proclaim freedom for the captives." — The last Adam, a life-giving spirit.... The first man was of the dust of the earth, the second man from heaven. — "My Lord and my God!" ... "You call me 'Teacher' and 'Lord,' and rightly so, for that is what I am. Now that I, your Lord and Teacher, have washed your feet, you also should wash one another's feet. I have set you an example that you should do as I have done for you."

1 COR. 1:9. Matt. 1:21. Phil. 2:8 – 10. John 4:25. Isa. 61:1. 1 Cor. 15:45, 47. John 20:28; 13:13 – 15.

MAY 22

MORNING

"Peace I leave with you; my peace I give you. I do not give to you as the world gives."

THE WORLD AND its desires pass away. — Man is a mere phantom as he goes to and fro: He bustles about, but only in vain; he heaps up wealth, not knowing who will get it. — What benefit did you reap at that time from the things you are now ashamed of? Those things result in death! — "Martha, Martha," the Lord answered, "you are worried and upset about many things, but only one thing is needed. Mary has chosen what is better, and it will not be taken away from her." — I would like you to be free from concern.

"I have told you these things, so that in me you may have peace. In this world you will have trouble. But take heart! I have overcome the world." — Now may the Lord of peace himself give you peace at all times and in every way. — "The LORD bless you and keep you; the LORD make his face shine upon you and be gracious to you; the LORD turn his face toward you and give you peace."

JOHN 14:27. 1 John 2:17. Ps. 39:6. Rom. 6:21. Luke 10:41–42. 1 Cor. 7:32. John 16:33. 2 Thess. 3:16. Num. 6:24–26.

EVENING

The Spirit helps us in our weakness.

"THE COUNSELOR, THE Holy Spirit." — Do you not know that your body is a temple of the Holy Spirit, who is in you, whom you have received from God? You are not your own. — For it is God who works in you to will and to act according to his good purpose.

We do not know what we ought to pray, but the Spirit himself intercedes for us with groans that words cannot express. And he who searches our hearts knows the mind of the Spirit, because the Spirit intercedes for the saints in accordance with God's will.

For he knows how we are formed, he remembers that we are dust. — A bruised reed he will not break, and a smoldering wick he will not snuff out.

"The spirit is willing, but the body is weak."

The LORD is my shepherd, I shall lack nothing. He makes me lie down in green pastures, he leads me beside quiet waters.

ROM. 8:26. John 14:26. 1 Cor. 6:19. Phil. 2:13. Rom. 8:26–27. Ps. 103:14. Isa. 42:3. Matt. 26:41. Ps. 23:1–2.

MAY 23

MORNING

Fasten them on the shoulder pieces of the ephod as memorial stones for the sons of Israel. Aaron is to bear the names on his shoulders as a memorial before the LORD.

BUT BECAUSE JESUS lives forever, he has a permanent priesthood. Therefore he is able to save completely those who come to God through him, because he always lives to intercede for them. — To him who is able to keep you from falling and to present you before his glorious presence without fault and with great joy.

Therefore, since we have a great high priest who has gone through the heavens, Jesus the Son of God, let us hold firmly to the faith we profess. For we do not have a high priest who is unable to sympathize with our weaknesses, but we have one who has been tempted in every way, just as we are — yet was without sin. Let us then approach the throne of grace with confidence.

"Let the beloved of the LORD rest secure in him, for he shields him all day long, and the one the LORD loves rests between his shoulders."

EXOD. 28:12. Heb. 7:24 – 25. Jude 24. Heb. 4:14 – 16. Deut. 33:12.

EVENING

That night the king could not sleep.

YOU KEPT MY eyes from closing. . . . Who is like the LORD our God, the One who sits enthroned on high, who stoops down to look on the heavens and the earth?

He does as he pleases with the powers of heaven and the peoples of the earth. — Your path led through the sea, your way through the mighty waters, though your footprints were not seen.

For the eyes of the LORD range throughout the earth to strengthen those whose hearts are fully committed to him. — We know that in all things God works for the good of those who love him.

"Are not two sparrows sold for a penny? Yet not one of them will fall to the ground apart from the will of your Father. And even the very hairs of your head are all numbered."

ESTH. 6:1. Pss. 77:4; 113:5 – 6. Dan. 4:35. Pss. 77:19; 76:10. 2 Chron. 16:9. Rom. 8:28. Matt. 10:29 – 30.

MAY 24

MORNING

Do not grieve the Holy Spirit of God, with whom you were
sealed for the day of redemption.

THE LOVE OF the Spirit. — The Counselor, the Holy Spirit. — In all their distress he too was distressed, and the angel of his presence saved them. In his love and mercy he redeemed them; he lifted them up and carried them all the days of old. Yet they rebelled and grieved his Holy Spirit. So he turned and became their enemy and he himself fought against them. — And you also were included in Christ when you heard the word of truth, the gospel of your salvation.

We know that we live in him and he in us, because he has given us of his Spirit. — Having believed, you were marked in him with a seal, the promised Holy Spirit, who is a deposit guaranteeing our inheritance with the redemption of those who are God's possession. — So I say, live by the Spirit, and you will not gratify the desires of the sinful nature. For the sinful nature desires what is contrary to the Spirit, and the Spirit what is contrary to the sinful nature. They are in conflict with each other, so that you do not do what you want.

The Spirit helps us in our weakness.

EPH. 4:30. Rom. 15:30. John 14:26. Isa. 63:9 – 10. 1 John 4:13. Eph. 1:13 – 14.
Gal. 5:16 – 17. Rom. 8:26.

EVENING

Then I will go back to my place until they admit their guilt.
And they will seek my face.

BUT YOUR INIQUITIES have separated you from your God; your sins have hidden his face from you. — I looked for him but did not find him. I called him but he did not answer. — "I punished him, and hid my face in anger, yet he kept on in his willful ways. I have seen his ways, but I will heal him." — Have you not brought this on yourselves by forsaking the LORD your God when he led you in the way?

"So he got up and went to his father. But while he was still a long way off, his father saw him and was filled with compassion for him; he ran to his son, threw his arms around him and kissed him." — "I will heal their waywardness and love them freely, for my anger has turned away from them."

If we confess our sins, he is faithful and just and will forgive us our sins and purify us from all unrighteousness.

HOS. 5:15. Isa. 59:2. Song of Songs 5:6. Isa. 57:17 – 18. Jer. 2:17. Luke 15:20. Hos. 14:4.
1 John 1:9.

MAY 25

MORNING

How great is your goodness, which you have stored up for those who fear you.

SINCE ANCIENT TIMES no one has heard, no ear has perceived, no eye has seen any God besides you, who acts on behalf of those who wait for him. — "No eye has seen, no ear has heard, no mind has conceived what God has prepared for those who love him" — but God has revealed it to us by his Spirit. — You have made known to me the path of life; you will fill me with joy in your presence, with eternal pleasures at your right hand.

How priceless is your unfailing love! Both high and low among men find refuge in the shadow of your wings. They feast on the abundance of your house; you give them drink from your river of delights. For with you is the fountain of life; in your light we see light.

Godliness has value for all things, holding promise for both the present life and the life to come.

PS. 31:19. Isa. 64:4. 1 Cor. 2:9 – 10. Pss. 16:11; 36:7 – 9. 1 Tim. 4:8.

EVENING

"The Son of God, whose eyes are like blazing fire."

THE HEART IS deceitful above all things and beyond cure. Who can understand it? "I the LORD search the heart and examine the mind, to reward a man according to his conduct, according to what his deeds deserve." — You have set our iniquities before you, our secret sins in the light of your presence. — The Lord turned and looked straight at Peter.... And he went outside and wept bitterly.

But Jesus would not entrust himself to them, for he knew all men. He did not need man's testimony about man, for he knew what was in a man. — For he knows how we are formed, he remembers that we are dust. — A bruised reed he will not break, and a smoldering wick he will not snuff out. — The Lord knows those who are his.

"I am the good shepherd; I know my sheep and my sheep know me." ... "My sheep listen to my voice; I know them, and they follow me. I give them eternal life, and they shall never perish; no one can snatch them out of my hand."

REV. 2:18. Jer. 17:9 – 10. Ps. 90:8. Luke 22:61 – 62. John 2:24 – 25. Ps. 103:14. Isa. 42:3. 2 Tim. 2:19. John 10:14, 27 – 28.

MAY 26

MORNING

Our Lord Jesus, that great Shepherd of the sheep.

THE CHIEF SHEPHERD. — "I am the good shepherd; I know my sheep and my sheep know me." ... "My sheep listen to my voice; I know them, and they follow me. I give them eternal life, and they shall never perish; no one can snatch them out of my hand."

The LORD is my shepherd, I shall lack nothing. He makes me lie down in green pastures, he leads me beside quiet waters, he restores my soul. He guides me in paths of righteousness for his name's sake.

We all, like sheep, have gone astray, each of us has turned to his own way; and the LORD has laid on him the iniquity of us all. — "I am the good shepherd. The good shepherd lays down his life for the sheep." — "I will search for the lost and bring back the strays. I will bind up the injured and strengthen the weak." — For you were like sheep going astray, but now you have returned to the Shepherd and Overseer of your souls.

HEB. 13:20. 1 Peter 5:4. John 10:14, 27 – 28. Ps. 23:1 – 3. Isa. 53:6. John 10:11. Ezek. 34:16. 1 Peter 2:25.

EVENING

The city does not need the sun or the moon to shine on it, for the glory of God gives it light, and the Lamb is its lamp.

"I SAW A light from heaven, brighter than the sun, blazing around me and my companions.... Then I asked, 'Who are you, Lord?' 'I am Jesus, whom you are persecuting,' the Lord replied." — Jesus took with him Peter, James and John the brother of James, and led them up a high mountain by themselves. There he was transfigured before them. His face shone like the sun, and his clothes became as white as the light.

The sun will no more be your light by day, nor will the brightness of the moon shine on you, for the LORD will be your everlasting light, and your God will be your glory. Your sun will never set again, and your moon will wane no more; the LORD will be your everlasting light, and your days of sorrow will end.

And the God of all grace ... called you to his eternal glory in Christ.

REV. 21:23. Acts 26:13, 15. Matt. 17:1 – 2. Isa. 60:19 – 20. 1 Peter 5:10.

MAY 27

MORNING

The LORD is good, a refuge in times of trouble. He cares for those who trust in him.

"GIVE THANKS TO the LORD Almighty, for the LORD is good; his love endures forever." — God is our refuge and strength, an ever present help in trouble.... I will say of the LORD, "He is my refuge and my fortress, my God, in whom I trust." — Who is like you, a people saved by the LORD? He is your shield and helper and your glorious sword. — "As for God, his way is perfect; the word of the LORD is flawless. He is a shield for all who take refuge in him. For who is God besides the LORD? And who is the Rock except our God?"

But the man who loves God is known by God. — God's solid foundation stands firm, sealed with this inscription: "The Lord knows those who are his," and, "Everyone who confesses the name of the Lord must turn away from wickedness." — For the LORD watches over the way of the righteous, but the way of the wicked will perish. — "I am pleased with you and I know you by name."

NAH. 1:7. Jer. 33:11. Pss. 46:1; 91:2. Deut. 33:29. 2 Sam. 22:31 – 32. 1 Cor. 8:3. 2 Tim. 2:19. Ps. 1:6. Exod. 33:17.

EVENING

I would like you to be free from concern.

HE CARES FOR you. — For the eyes of the LORD range throughout the earth to strengthen those whose hearts are fully committed to him.

Taste and see that the LORD is good; blessed is the man who takes refuge in him.... The lions may grow weak and hungry, but those who seek the LORD lack no good thing. — "Therefore I tell you, do not worry about your life, what you will eat or drink; or about your body, what you will wear. Is not life more important than food, and the body more important than clothes? Look at the birds of the air; they do not sow or reap or store away in barns, and yet your heavenly Father feeds them. Are you not much more vaulable than they?" — Do not be anxious about anything, but in everything, by prayer and petition, with thanksgiving, present your requests to God. And the peace of God, which transcends all understanding, will guard your hearts and your minds in Christ Jesus.

1 COR. 7:32. 1 Peter. 5:7. 2 Chron. 16:9. Ps. 34:8, 10. Matt. 6:25 – 26. Phil. 4:6 – 7.

MAY 28

MORNING

We eagerly await a Savior.

FOR THE GRACE of God that brings salvation has appeared to all men. It teaches us to say "No" to ungodliness and worldly passions, and to live self-controlled, upright and godly lives in this present age, while we wait for the blessed hope—the glorious appearing of our great God and Savior, Jesus Christ, who gave himself for us to redeem us from all wickedness and to purify for himself a people that are his very own, eager to do what is good.—But in keeping with his promise we are looking forward to a new heaven and a new earth, the home of righteousness. So then, dear friends, since you are looking forward to this, make every effort to be found spotless, blameless and at peace with him.

So Christ was sacrificed once to take away the sins of many people; and he will appear a second time, not to bear sin, but to bring salvation to those who are waiting for him.—In that day they will say, "Surely this is our God; we trusted in him, and he saved us. This is the LORD, we trusted in him; let us rejoice and be glad in his salvation."

PHIL. 3:20. Titus 2:11–14. 2 Peter 3:13–14. Heb. 9:28. Isa. 25:9.

EVENING

Run in such a way as to get the prize.

THE SLUGGARD SAYS, "There is a lion outside!"—Let us throw off everything that hinders and the sin that so easily entangles, and let us run with perseverance the race marked out for us. Let us fix our eyes on Jesus, the author and perfecter of our faith.... Let us purify ourselves from everything that contaminates body and spirit, perfecting holiness out of reverence for God.

I press on toward the goal.—Therefore I do not run like a man running aimlessly; I do not fight like a man beating the air. No, I beat my body and make it my slave so that after I have preached to others, I myself will not be disqualified for the prize.

For this world in its present form is passing away.

But in keeping with his promise we are looking forward to a new heaven and a new earth, the home of righteousness. So then, dear friends, since you are looking forward to this, make every effort to be found spotless, blameless and at peace with him.

1 COR. 9:24. Prov. 22:13. Heb. 12:1–2. 2 Cor. 7:1. Phil. 3:14. 1 Cor. 9:26–27; 7:31. 2 Peter 3:13–14.

MAY 29

MORNING

*For the life of a creature is in the blood, and I have given it
to you to make atonement for yourselves on the altar; it is the
blood that makes atonement for one's life.*

"Look, the Lamb of God, who takes away the sin of the world!" — The blood of the Lamb. — The precious blood of Christ, a lamb without blemish or defect. — Without the shedding of blood there is no forgiveness. — The blood of Jesus, his Son, purifies us from every sin.

He entered the Most Holy Place once for all by his own blood, having obtained eternal redemption.... Therefore, brothers, since we have confidence to enter the Most Holy Place by the blood of Jesus, by a new and living way opened for us through the curtain, that is, his body, and since we have a great priest over the house of God, let us draw near to God with a sincere heart in full assurance of faith.

You were bought at a price. Therefore honor God with your body.

**LEV. 17:11. John 1:29. Rev. 7:14. 1 Peter 1:19. Heb. 9:22. 1 John 1:7. Heb. 9:12;
10:19–22. 1 Cor. 6:20.**

EVENING

"Oh that I had the wings of a dove! I would fly away and be at rest."

When the sun rose, God provided a scorching east wind, and the sun blazed on Jonah's head so that he grew faint. He wanted to die, and said, "It would be better for me to die than to live."

Job opened his mouth and ... said: "May the day of my birth perish, and the night it was said, 'A boy is born!' ... Why is light given to those in misery, and life to the bitter of soul, to those who long for death that does not come, who search for it more than for hidden treasure?" — A righteous man may have many troubles, but the Lord delivers him from them all.

"Now my heart is troubled, and what shall I say? 'Father, save me from this hour'?" — For this reason he had to be made like his brothers in every way, in order that he might become a merciful and faithful high priest in service to God, and that he might make atonement for the sins of the people. Because he himself suffered when he was tempted, he is able to help those who are being tempted.

PS. 55:6. Jonah 4:8. Job 3:1–3, 20–21. Ps. 34:19. John 12:27. Heb. 2:17–18.

MAY 30

MORNING

Let us, therefore, make every effort to enter that rest.

"ENTER THROUGH THE narrow gate. For wide is the gate and broad is the road that leads to destruction, and many enter through it. But small is the gate and narrow the road that leads to life, and only a few find it." ... "The kingdom of heaven has been forcefully advancing, and forceful men lay hold of it." — "Do not work for food that spoils, but for food that endures to eternal life, which the Son of Man will give you."

Therefore, my brothers, be all the more eager to make your calling and election sure. For if you do these things, you will never fall, and you will receive a rich welcome into the eternal kingdom of our Lord and Savior Jesus Christ. — Run in such a way as to get the prize. Everyone who competes in the games goes into strict training. They do it to get a crown that will not last; but we do it to get a crown that will last forever.

For anyone who enters God's rest also rests from his own work, just as God did from his. — For the LORD will be your everlasting light, and your God will be your glory.

HEB. 4:11. Matt. 7:13–14; 11:12. John 6:27. 2 Peter 1:10–11. 1 Cor. 9:24–25. Heb. 4:10. Isa. 60:19.

EVENING

"You always hear me."

THEN JESUS LOOKED up and said, "Father, I thank you that you have heard me." ... "Father, glorify your name!" Then a voice came from heaven, "I have glorified it, and will glorify it again." — "I have come to do your will, O God." — "Yet not my will, but yours be done."

In this world we are like him.... This is the assurance we have in approaching God: that if we ask anything according to his will, he hears us.... And receive from him anything we ask, because we obey his commands and do what pleases him.

And without faith it is impossible to please God, because anyone who comes to him must believe that he exists and that he rewards those who earnestly seek him.... He always lives to intercede for them. — We have one who speaks to the Father in our defense — Jesus Christ, the Righteous One.

JOHN 11:42. John 11:41; 12:28. Heb. 10:7. Luke 22:42. 1 John 4:17; 5:14; 3:22. Heb. 11:6; 7:25. 1 John 2:1.

MAY 31

MORNING

*"Your name will no longer be Jacob, but Israel, because you
have struggled with God and with men and have overcome."*

As a man he struggled with God. He struggled with the angel and overcame
him; he wept and begged for his favor. — Yet he [Abraham] did not waver
through unbelief regarding the promise of God, but was strengthened in his
faith and gave glory to God.

"Have faith in God," Jesus answered. "I tell you the truth, if anyone says to
this mountain, 'Go, throw yourself into the sea,' and does not doubt in his heart
but believes that what he says will happen, it will be done for him. Therefore I
tell you, whatever you ask for in prayer, believe that you have received it, and it
will be yours." ... "'If you can'?" said Jesus. "Everything is possible for him who
believes." — "Blessed is she who has believed that what the Lord has said to her
will be accomplished!"

Increase our faith.

GEN. 32:29. Hos. 12:3–4. Rom. 4:20. Mark 11:22–24; 9:23. Luke 1:45; 17:5.

EVENING

Dear children, continue in him.

He who doubts is like a wave of the sea, blown and tossed by the wind. That
man should not think he will receive anything from the Lord; he is a double-
minded man, unstable in all he does.

I am astonished that you are so quickly deserting the one who called you by the
grace of Christ and are turning to a different gospel — which is really no gospel
at all. Evidently some people are throwing you into confusion and are trying to
pervert the gospel of Christ. But even if we or an angel from heaven should preach
a gospel other than the one we preached to you, let him be eternally condemned!

You who are trying to be justified by law have been alienated from Christ;
you have fallen away from grace.... You were running a good race. Who cut in
on you and kept you from obeying the truth?

"No branch can bear fruit by itself; it must remain in the vine.... If you
remain in me and my words remain in you, ask whatever you wish, and it will be
given you." — For no matter how many promises God has made, they are "Yes"
in Christ. And so through him the "Amen" is spoken by us to the glory of God.

1 JOHN 2:28. James 1:6–8. Gal 1:6–8; 5:4, 7. John 15:4, 7. 2 Cor. 1:20.

JUNE 1

MORNING

The fruit of the Spirit is faithfulness, gentleness.

THE LORD, THE LORD, the compassionate and gracious God, slow to anger, abounding in love and faithfulness.

Live a life worthy of the calling you have received. Be completely humble and gentle; be patient, bearing with one another in love.... Be kind and compassionate to one another, forgiving each other, just as in Christ God forgave you. — The wisdom that comes from heaven is first of all pure; then peace loving, considerate, submissive, full of mercy and good fruit, impartial and sincere. — Love is patient, love is kind.

For in the proper time we will reap a harvest if we do not give up. — Be patient, then, brothers, until the Lord's coming. See how the farmer waits for the land to yield its valuable crop and how patient he is for the fall and spring rains. You too, be patient and stand firm, because the Lord's coming is near.

GAL. 5:22. Exod. 34:6. Eph. 4:1–2, 32. James 3:17. 1 Cor. 13:4. Gal. 6:9. James 5:7–8.

EVENING

"Immanuel"... "God with us."

"BUT WILL GOD really dwell on earth with men? The heavens, even the highest heavens, cannot contain you." — The Word became flesh and lived for a while among us. We have seen his glory, the glory of the one and only Son, who came from the Father, full of grace and truth. — Beyond all question, the mystery of godliness is great.

But in these last days he has spoken to us by his Son, whom he appointed heir of all things, and through whom he made the universe.

On the evening of that first day of the week, when the disciples were together, ... Jesus came and stood among them.... The disciples were overjoyed when they saw the Lord.... A week later his disciples were in the house again, and Thomas was with them.... Then he [Jesus] said to Thomas, "Put your finger here; see my hands. Reach out your hand and put it into my side. Stop doubting and believe." Thomas said to him, "My Lord and my God!" — To us a son is given ... Mighty God.

MATT. 1:23. 2 Chron. 6:18. John 1:14. 1 Tim. 3:16. Heb. 1:2. John 20:19–20, 26–28. Isa. 9:6.

JUNE 2

MORNING

"This is how you are to eat it: with your cloak tucked into your belt, your sandals on your feet and your staff in your hand. Eat it in haste; it is the LORD's Passover."

GET UP, GO away! For this is not your resting place. — For here we do not have an enduring city, but we are looking for the city that is to come.... There remains, then, a Sabbath-rest for the people of God.

"Be dressed ready for service and keep your lamps burning, like men waiting for their master to return from a wedding banquet, so that when he comes and knocks they can immediately open the door for him. It will be good for those servants whose master finds them watching when he comes." — Therefore, prepare your minds for action; be self-controlled; set your hope fully on the grace to be given you when Jesus Christ is revealed. — But one thing I do: Forgetting what is behind, ... I press on toward the goal to win the prize for which God has called me heavenward in Christ Jesus.

EXOD. 12:11. Mic. 2:10. Heb. 13:14; 4:9. Luke 12:35 – 37. 1 Peter 1:13. Phil. 3:13 – 15.

EVENING

Lord, you have assigned me my portion and my cup.

HEIRS OF GOD and co-heirs with Christ. — All things are yours. — My lover is mine. — The Son of God ... loved me and gave himself for me.

The LORD said to Aaron, "You will have no inheritance in their land, nor will you have any share among them; I am your share and your inheritance among the Israelites."

Whom have I in heaven but you? And being with you, I desire nothing on earth. My flesh and my heart may fail, but God is the strength of my heart and my portion forever.

Even though I walk through the valley of the shadow of death, I will fear no evil, for you are with me; your rod and your staff, they comfort me. — I know whom I have believed, and am convinced that he is able to guard what I have entrusted to him for that day.

O God, you are my God, earnestly I seek you; my soul thirsts for you, my body longs for you, in a dry and weary land where there is no water.

PS. 16:5. Rom. 8:17. 1 Cor. 3:21. Song of Songs 2:16. Gal. 2:20. Num. 18:20.
Pss. 73:25 – 26; 23:4. 2 Tim. 1:12. Ps. 63:1.

JUNE 3

MORNING

"Therefore keep watch, because you do not know the day or the hour."

"BE CAREFUL, OR your hearts will be weighed down with dissipation, drunkenness and the anxieties of life, and that day will close on you unexpectedly like a trap. For it will come upon all those who live on the face of the whole earth. Be always on the watch, and pray that you may be able to escape all that is about to happen, and that you may be able to stand before the Son of Man."

The day of the Lord will come like a thief in the night. While people are saying, "Peace and safety," destruction will come on them suddenly, as labor pains on a pregnant woman, and they will not escape. But you, brothers, are not in darkness so that this day should surprise you like a thief. You are all sons of the light and sons of the day. We do not belong to the night or to the darkness. So then, let us not be like others, who are asleep, but let us be alert and self-controlled.

MATT. 25:13. Luke 21:34–36. 1 Thess. 5:2–6.

EVENING

"I am God Almighty; walk before me and be blameless."

NOT THAT I have already obtained all this, or have already been made perfect, but I press on to take hold of that for which Christ Jesus took hold of me. Brothers, I do not consider myself yet to have taken hold of it. But one thing I do: Forgetting what is behind and straining toward what is ahead, I press on toward the goal to win the prize for which God has called me heavenward in Christ Jesus.

Enoch walked with God; then he was no more, because God took him away.

Grow in the grace and knowledge of our Lord and Savior Jesus Christ.—We, who with unveiled faces all reflect the Lord's glory, are being transformed into his likeness with ever-increasing glory, which comes from the Lord, who is the Spirit.

After Jesus said this, he looked toward heaven and prayed: ... "My prayer is not that you take them out of the world but that you protect them from the evil one.... I in them and you in me. May they be brought to complete unity to let the world know that you sent me and have loved them even as you have loved me."

GEN. 17:1. Phil. 3:12–14. Gen. 5:24. 2 Peter 3:18. 2 Cor. 3:18. John 17:1, 15, 23.

JUNE 4

MORNING

"The glory of this present house will be greater than the glory of the former house, ... And in this place I will grant peace."

"THE HOUSE TO be built for the LORD should be of great magnificence and fame and splendor in the sight of all the nations." — The glory of the LORD filled it [the Lord's house].

"Destroy this temple, and I will raise it again in three days." — For what was glorious has no glory now in comparison with the surpassing glory. — The Word became flesh and lived for a while among us. We have seen his glory, the glory of the one and only Son, who came from the Father, full of grace and truth. — God ... in these last days has spoken to us by his Son, whom he appointed heir of all things and through whom he made the universe.

"Glory to God in the highest, and on earth peace to men on whom his favor rests." — The Prince of Peace. — For he himself is our peace. — The peace of God, which transcends all understanding, will guard your hearts and your minds in Christ Jesus.

HAG. 2:9. 1 Chron. 22:5. 2 Chron. 7:2. John 2:19, 21. 2 Cor. 3:10. John 1:14. Heb. 1:1–2. Luke 2:14. Isa. 9:6. Eph. 2:14. Phil. 4:7.

EVENING

Put on the armor of light.

RATHER, CLOTHE YOURSELVES with the Lord Jesus Christ. — That I may gain Christ and be found in him, not having a righteousness of my own that comes from the law, but that which is through faith in Christ — the righteousness that comes from God and is by faith. — This righteousness from God comes through faith in Jesus Christ to all who believe.

For he ... arrayed me in a robe of righteousness. — I will come and proclaim your mighty acts, O Sovereign LORD; I will proclaim your righteousness, yours alone.

For you were once darkness, but you are light in the Lord. Live as children of light.... Have nothing to do with the fruitless deeds of darkness, but rather expose them.... But everything exposed by the light becomes visible, for it is light that makes everything visible.... "Wake up, O sleeper, rise from the dead, and Christ will shine on you." Be very careful, then, how you live.

ROM. 13:12. Rom. 13:14. Phil. 3:8–9. Rom. 3:22. Isa. 61:10. Ps. 71:16. Eph. 5:8, 11, 13–15.

JUNE 5

MORNING

"So you also, when you have done everything you were told to do, should say, 'We are unworthy servants.'"

WHERE, THEN, IS boasting? It is excluded. On what principle? On that of observing the law? No, but on that of faith.—What do you have that you did not receive? And if you did receive it, why do you boast as though you did not?—For it is by grace you have been saved, through faith—and this not from yourselves, it is the gift of God—not by works, so that no one can boast. For we are God's workmanship, created in Christ Jesus to do good works, which God prepared in advance for us to do.

But by the grace of God I am what I am, and his grace to me was not without effect. No, I worked harder than all of them—yet not I, but the grace of God that was with me.—For from him and through him and to him are all things.—Everything comes from you, and we have given you only what comes from your hand.

LUKE 17:10. Rom. 3:27. 1 Cor. 4:7. Eph. 2:8–10. 1 Cor. 15:10. Rom. 11:36. 1 Chron. 29:14.

EVENING

For he knows how we are formed, he remembers that we are dust.

THE LORD GOD formed man from the dust of the ground and breathed into his nostrils the breath of life, and man became a living being.

I praise you because I am fearfully and wonderfully made; your works are wonderful, I know that full well. My frame was not hidden from you when I was made in the secret place. When I was woven together in the depths of the earth, your eyes saw my unformed body. All the days ordained for me were written in your book before one of them came to be.

Have we not all one Father? Did not one God create us?—For in him we live and move and have our being.—As a father has compassion on his children, so the LORD has compassion on those who fear him.

Yet he was merciful, he atoned for their iniquities and did not destroy them. Time after time he restrained his anger and did not stir up his full wrath. He remembered that they were but flesh, a passing breeze that does not return.

PS. 103:14. Gen. 2:7. Ps. 139:14–16. Mal. 2:10. Acts 17:28. Pss. 103:13; 78:38–39.

JUNE 6

MORNING

He will quiet you with his love.

THE LORD DID not set his affection on you and choose you because you were more numerous than other peoples, for you were the fewest of all peoples. But it was because the LORD loved you. — We love him because he first loved us.

He has reconciled you by Christ's physical body through death to present you holy in his sight. — This is love: not that we loved God, but that he loved us and sent his Son as an atoning sacrifice for our sins. — But God demonstrates his own love for us in this: While we were still sinners, Christ died for us.

And a voice from heaven said, "This is my Son, whom I love; with him I am well pleased." — "The reason my Father loves me is that I lay down my life — only to take it up again." — The Son is the radiance of God's glory and the exact representation of his being, sustaining all things by his powerful word. After he had provided purification for sins, he sat down at the right hand of the Majesty in heaven.

ZEPH. 3:17. Deut. 7:7–8. 1 John 4:19. Col. 1:22. 1 John 4:10. Rom. 5:8. Matt. 3:17. John 10:17. Heb. 1:3.

EVENING

A new and living way.

SO CAIN WENT out from the LORD's presence. — But your iniquities have separated you from your God; your sins have hidden his face from you. — Without holiness no one will see the Lord.

"I am the way and the truth and the life. No one comes to the Father except through me." — Our Savior, Christ Jesus, who has destroyed death and has brought life and immortality to light through the gospel.

The way into the Most Holy Place had not yet been disclosed as long as the first tabernacle was still standing. — For he himself is our peace, who has made the two one and has destroyed the barrier, the dividing wall of hostility. — The curtain of the temple was torn in two from top to bottom.

"Small is the gate and narrow the road that leads to life, and only a few find it." — You have made known to me the path of life; you will fill me with joy in your presence, with eternal pleasures at your right hand.

HEB. 10:20. Gen. 4:16. Isa. 59:2. Heb. 12:14. John 14:6. 2 Tim. 1:10. Heb. 9:8. Eph. 2:14. Matt. 27:51; 7:14. Ps. 16:11.

JUNE 7

MORNING

They should always pray and not give up.

"SUPPOSE ONE OF you has a friend, and he goes to him at midnight and says, 'Friend, lend me three loaves of bread, because a friend of mine on a journey has come to me, and I have nothing to set before him.' Then the one inside answers, 'Don't bother me. The door is already locked, and my children are with me in bed. I can't get up and give you anything.' I tell you, though he will not get up and give him the bread because he is his friend, yet because of the man's persistence he will get up and give him as much as he needs." — Pray in the Spirit on all occasions with all kinds of prayers and requests. With this in mind, be alert and always keep on praying for all the saints.

"I will not let you go unless you bless me." ... "Because you have struggled with God and with men and have overcome." — Devote yourselves to prayer, being watchful and thankful.

Jesus went out into the hills to pray, and spent the night praying to God.

LUKE 18:1. Luke 11:5–8. Eph. 6:18. Gen. 32:26, 28. Col. 4:2. Luke 6:12.

EVENING

Take away all my sins.

"COME NOW, LET us reason together," says the LORD. "Though your sins are like scarlet, they shall be as white as snow; though they are red as crimson, they shall be like wool."

"Take heart, son; your sins are forgiven." — "I, even I, am he who blots out your transgressions, for my own sake, and remembers your sins no more."

"The Son of Man has authority on earth to forgive sins." — In him we have redemption through his blood, the forgiveness of sins, in accordance with the riches of God's grace. — He saved us, not because of righteous things we had done, but because of his mercy. He saved us through the washing of rebirth and renewal by the Holy Spirit, whom he poured out on us generously through Jesus Christ our Savior. — Having canceled the written code, with its regulations, that was against us and that stood opposed to us; he took it away, nailing it to the cross.

Praise the LORD, O my soul.... He forgives all my sins.

PS. 25:18. Isa. 1:18. Matt. 9:2. Isa. 43:25. Matt. 9:6. Eph. 1:7. Titus 3:5–6. Col. 2:13–14. Ps. 103:2–3.

JUNE 8

MORNING

The LORD gave him success in everything he did.

BLESSED ARE ALL who fear the LORD, who walk in his ways. You will eat the fruit of your labor; blessings and prosperity will be yours.... Trust in the LORD and do good; dwell in the land and enjoy safe pasture. Delight yourself in the LORD and he will give you the desires of your heart. — "Do not be terrified; do not be discouraged, for the LORD your God will be with you wherever you go."

"But seek first his kingdom and his righteousness, and all these things will be given to you as well."

As long as he sought the LORD, God gave him success. — Be careful that you do not forget the LORD your God, failing to observe his commands, his laws and his decrees that I am giving you this day.... "My power and the strength of my hands have produced this wealth for me."

"Is not the LORD your God with you? And has he not granted you rest on every side?"

GEN. 39:3. Pss. 128:1–2; 37:3–4. Josh. 1:9. Matt. 6:33. 2 Chron. 26:5. Deut. 8:11, 17. 1 Chron. 22:18.

EVENING

Why are you thinking these things?

WITHOUT WEAKENING IN his faith, he [Abraham] faced the fact that his body was as good as dead — since he was about a hundred years old — and that Sarah's womb was also dead. Yet he did not waver through unbelief regarding the promise of God, but was strengthened in his faith and gave glory to God.

"Which is easier: to say to the paralytic, 'Your sins are forgiven,' or to say, 'Get up, take your mat and walk'?" ... "'If you can'?" ... "Everything is possible for him who believes."

"All authority in heaven and on earth has been given to me." — "Why are you so afraid? Do you still have no faith?" — "Look at the birds of the air ... your heavenly Father feeds them. Are you not much more valuable than they?" ... "Why are you talking among yourselves about having no bread?... Don't you remember the five loaves for the five thousand?"

And my God will meet all your needs according to his glorious riches in Christ Jesus.

MARK 2:8. Rom. 4:19–20. Mark 2:9; 9:23. Matt. 28:18. Mark 4:40. Matt. 6:26; 16:8–9. Phil. 4:19.

JUNE 9

MORNING

No one ever spoke the way this man does.

YOU ARE THE most excellent of men and your lips have been anointed with grace, since God has blessed you forever. — The Sovereign LORD has given me an instructed tongue, to know the word that sustains the weary. — His mouth is sweetness itself; he is altogether lovely. This is my lover, this my friend.

All spoke well of him and were amazed at the gracious words that came from his lips. — He taught as one who had authority, and not as their teachers of the law.

Let the word of Christ dwell in you richly. — The sword of the Spirit ... is the word of God. — The word of God is living and active. Sharper than any double-edged sword. — The weapons we fight with are not the weapons of the world. On the contrary, they have divine power to demolish strongholds. We demolish arguments and every pretension that sets itself up against the knowledge of God, and we take captive every thought to make it obedient to Christ.

JOHN 7:46. Ps. 45:2. Isa. 50:4. Song of Songs 5:16. Luke 4:22. Matt 7:29. Col. 3:16. Eph. 6:17. Heb. 4:12. 2 Cor. 10:4–5.

EVENING

The mirth of the wicked is brief.

"YOU WILL STRIKE his heel." — "But this is your hour — when darkness reigns." — Since the children have flesh and blood, he too shared in their humanity so that by his death he might destroy him who holds the power of death — that is, the devil. — Having disarmed the powers and authorities, he made a public spectacle of them, triumphing over them by the cross. — Be self-controlled and alert. Your enemy the devil prowls around like a roaring lion looking for someone to devour. Resist him, standing firm in the faith. — Resist the devil and he will flee from you.

The wicked plot against the righteous and gnash their teeth at them; but the Lord laughs at the wicked, for he knows their day is coming. — The God of peace will soon crush Satan under your feet. — The devil, who deceived them, was thrown into the lake of burning sulfur.... They will be tormented day and night for ever and ever.

JOB 20:5. Gen. 3:15. Luke 22:53. Heb. 2:14. Col. 2:15. 1 Peter 5:8–9. James 4:7. Ps. 37:12–13. Rom. 16:20. Rev. 20:10.

JUNE 10

MORNING

"The younger son got together all he had, set off for a distant country and there squandered his wealth in wild living."

THAT IS WHAT some of you were. But you were washed, you were sanctified, you were justified in the name of the Lord Jesus Christ and by the Spirit of our God. — We were by nature objects of wrath. But because of his great love for us, God, who is rich in mercy, made us alive with Christ even when we were dead in transgressions — it is by grace you have been saved. And God raised us up with Christ and seated us with him in the heavenly realms in Christ Jesus.

This is love: not that we loved God, but that he loved us and sent his Son as an atoning sacrifice for our sins.

But God demonstrates his own love for us in this: While we were still sinners, Christ died for us.... For if, when we were God's enemies, we were reconciled to him through the death of his Son, how much more, having been reconciled, shall we be saved through his life!

LUKE 15:13. 1 Cor. 6:11. Eph. 2:3–6. 1 John 4:10. Rom. 5:8, 10.

EVENING

Forgive as the Lord forgave you.

"TWO MEN OWED money to a certain moneylender. One owed him five hundred denarii, and the other fifty. Neither of them had the money to pay him back, so he canceled the debts of both." — " 'I canceled all that debt of yours because you begged me to. Shouldn't you have had mercy on your fellow servant just as I had on you?' "

"When you stand praying, if you hold anything against anyone, forgive him, so that your Father in heaven may forgive you your sins." — God's chosen people, holy and dearly loved, clothe yourselves with compassion, kindness, humility, gentleness and patience. Bear with each other and forgive whatever grievances you may have against one another. Forgive as the Lord forgave you.

"Lord, how many times shall I forgive my brother when he sins against me? Up to seven times?" Jesus answered, "I tell you, not seven times, but seventy-seven times."

Love ... binds them all together in perfect unity.

COL. 3:13. Luke 7:41–42. Matt. 18:32–33. Mark 11:25–26. Col. 3:12–13. Matt. 18:21–22. Col. 3:14.

JUNE 11

MORNING

So he got up and went to his father. But while he was still
a long way off, his father saw him and was filled with
compassion for him; he ran to his son, threw his arms around
him and kissed him.

THE LORD IS compassionate and gracious, slow to anger, abounding in love. He
will not always accuse, nor will he harbor his anger forever; he does not treat us as
our sins deserve or repay us according to our iniquities. For as high as the heavens
are above the earth, so great is his love for those who fear him; as far as the east is
from the west, so far has he removed our transgressions from us. As a father has
compassion on his children, so the LORD has compassion on those who fear him.

You received the Spirit of sonship. And by him we cry, *"Abba,* Father." The
Spirit himself testifies with our spirit that we are God's children. — You who
once were far away have been brought near through the blood of Christ.... You
are no longer foreigners and aliens but fellow citizens with God's people and
members of God's household.

LUKE 15:20. Ps. 103:8 – 13. Rom. 8:15 – 16. Eph. 2:13, 19.

EVENING

I am making everything new.

"UNLESS A MAN is born again, he cannot see the kingdom of God." — If anyone
is in Christ, he is a new creation; the old has gone, the new has come!

"I will give you a new heart and put a new spirit in you; I will remove from
you your heart of stone and give you a heart of flesh." — Get rid of the old yeast
that you may be a new batch. — The new self, created to be like God in true
righteousness and holiness.

You will be called by a new name that the mouth of the LORD will bestow.

"Behold, I will create new heavens and a new earth. The former things will
not be remembered, nor will they come to mind." — Since everything will be
destroyed in this way, what kind of people ought you to be? You ought to live
holy and godly lives.

REV. 21:5. John 3:3. 2 Cor. 5:17. Ezek. 36:26. 1 Cor. 5:7. Eph. 4:24. Isa. 62:2; 65:17.
2 Peter 3:11.

JUNE 12

MORNING

Anything else that can withstand fire must be put through the fire, and then it will be clean.

THE LORD YOUR God is testing you to find out whether you love him with all your heart and with all your soul. — He will sit as a refiner and purifier of silver; he will purify the Levites and refine them like gold and silver. Then the LORD will have men who will bring offerings in righteousness. — [Men's] work will be shown for what it is, because the Day will bring it to light. It will be revealed with fire, and the fire will test the quality of each man's work.

I will turn my hand against you; I will thoroughly purge away your dross and remove your impurities. — I will refine and test them.

For you, O God, tested us; you refined us like silver.... We went through fire and water, but you brought us to a place of abundance.

When you walk through the fire, you will not be burned; the flames will not set you ablaze.

NUM. 31:23. Deut. 13:3. Mal. 3:3. 1 Cor. 3:13. Isa. 1:25. Jer. 9:7. Ps. 66:10, 12. Isa. 43:2.

EVENING

We might die to sins and live for righteousness.

PUT OFF YOUR old self, which is being corrupted by its deceitful desires; to be made new in the attitude of your minds; and to put on the new self, created to be like God in true righteousness and holiness.

For you died and your life is now hidden with Christ in God. — Just as Christ was raised from the dead through the glory of the Father, we too may live a new life.... For we know that our old self was crucified with him so that the body of sin might be rendered powerless, that we should no longer be slaves to sin.... In the same way, count yourselves dead to sin but alive to God in Christ Jesus. Therefore do not let sin reign in your mortal body so that you obey its evil desires. Do not offer the parts of your body to sin, as instruments of wickedness, but rather offer yourselves to God, as those who have been brought from death to life; and offer the parts of your body to him as instruments of righteousness.

1 PETER 2:24. Eph. 4:22 – 24. Col. 3:3. Rom. 6:4, 6 – 7, 11 – 13.

J U N E   1 3

MORNING

"Remain in me, and I will remain in you."

I HAVE BEEN crucified with Christ and I no longer live, but Christ lives in me. The life I live in the body, I live by faith in the Son of God, who loved me and gave himself for me.

I know that nothing good lives in me, that is, in my sinful nature. For I have the desire to do what is good, but I cannot carry it out.... What a wretched man I am! Who will rescue me from this body of death? Thanks be to God — through Jesus Christ our Lord!... But if Christ is in you, your body is dead because of sin, yet your spirit is alive because of righteousness. — If you continue in your faith, established and firm, not moved from the hope held out in the gospel. This is the gospel that you heard.

Dear children, continue in him, so that when he appears we may be confident and unashamed before him at his coming.... Whoever claims to live in him must walk as Jesus did.

JOHN 15:4. Gal. 2:20. Rom. 7:18, 24–25; 8:10. Col. 1:23. 1 John 2:28, 6.

EVENING

"Do you believe in the Son of Man?"

"WHO IS HE, sir?" the man asked. "Tell me so that I may believe in him."

The Son is the radiance of God's glory and the exact representation of his being. — God, the blessed and only Ruler, the King of kings and Lord of lords, who alone is immortal and who lives in unapproachable light, whom no one has seen or can see. To him be honor and might forever. Amen. — "I am the Alpha and the Omega," says the Lord God, "who is, and who was, and who is to come, the Almighty."

"Lord, I believe." — I know whom I have believed and am convinced that he is able to guard what I have entrusted to him for that day.

"See, I lay a stone in Zion, a chosen and precious cornerstone, and the one who trusts in him will never be put to shame." Now to you who believe, this stone is precious.

JOHN 9:35. John 9:36. Heb. 1:3. 1 Tim. 6:15–16. Rev. 1:8. John 9:38. 2 Tim. 1:12. 1 Peter 2:6–7.

JUNE 14

MORNING

For just as the sufferings of Christ flow over into our lives, so also through Christ our comfort overflows.

SHARING IN HIS sufferings. — Rejoice that you participate in the sufferings of Christ, so that you may be overjoyed when his glory is revealed. — If we died with him, we will also live with him. — Now if we are children, then we are heirs — heirs of God and co-heirs with Christ, if indeed we share in his sufferings in order that we may also share in his glory.

Because God wanted to make the unchanging nature of his purpose very clear to the heirs of what was promised, he confirmed it with an oath. God did this so that, by two unchangeable things in which it is impossible for God to lie, we who have fled to take hold of the hope offered to us may be greatly encouraged. — Our Lord Jesus Christ himself and God our Father, who loved us and by his grace gave us eternal encouragement and good hope, encourage your hearts and strengthen you in every good deed and word.

2 COR. 1:5. Phil. 3:10. 1 Peter 4:13. 2 Tim. 2:11. Rom. 8:17. Heb. 6:17 – 18. 2 Thess. 2:16 – 17.

EVENING

"Martha, Martha," the Lord answered, "you are worried and upset about many things."

"CONSIDER THE RAVENS: They do not sow or reap.... Consider how the lilies grow. They do not labor or spin.... And do not set your heart on what you will eat or drink; do not worry about it. For the pagan world runs after all such things, and your Father knows that you need them."

But if we have food and clothing, we will be content with that. People who want to get rich fall into temptation and a trap and into many foolish and harmful desires that plunge men into ruin and destruction. For the love of money is a root of all kinds of evil. Some people, eager for money, have wandered from the faith and pierced themselves with many griefs.

"The worries of this life, the deceitfulness of wealth and the desires for other things come in and choke the word, making it unfruitful."

Let us throw off everything that hinders and the sin that so easily entangles, and let us run with perseverance the race marked out for us.

LUKE 10:41. Luke 12:24, 27, 29 – 30. 1 Tim. 6:8 – 10. Mark 4:19. Heb. 12:1.

JUNE 15

MORNING

The secret things belong to the LORD our God, but the things revealed belong to us.

MY HEART IS not proud, O LORD, my eyes are not haughty; I do not concern myself with great matters or things too wonderful for me. But I have stilled and quieted my soul; like a weaned child with its mother, like a weaned child is my soul within me.

The LORD confides in those who fear him; he makes his covenant known to them. — But there is a God in heaven who reveals mysteries. — And these are but the outer fringe of his works; how faint the whisper we hear of him! — "I no longer call you servants, because a servant does not know his master's business. Instead, I have called you friends, for everything that I learned from my Father I have made known to you." ... "If you love me, you will obey what I command. And I will ask the Father, and he will give you another Counselor to be with you forever — the Spirit of truth."

DEUT. 29:29. Pss. 131:1 – 2; 25:14. Dan. 2:28. Job 26:14. John 15:15; 14:15 – 17.

EVENING

The Spirit intercedes for the saints in accordance with God's will.

"I TELL YOU the truth, my Father will give you whatever you ask in my name. Until now you have not asked for anything in my name. Ask and you will receive, and your joy will be complete." — And pray in the Spirit on all occasions with all kinds of prayers and requests.

This is the assurance we have in approaching God: that if we ask anything according to his will, he hears us. And if we know that he hears us — whatever we ask — we know that we have what we asked of him. — It is God's will that you should be holy.... For God did not call us to be impure, but to live a holy life.... God, who gives you his Holy Spirit.

Be joyful always; pray continually; give thanks in all circumstances, for this is God's will for you in Christ Jesus. Do not put out the Spirit's fire.

ROM. 8:27. John 16:23 – 24. Eph. 6:18. 1 John 5:14 – 15. 1 Thess. 4:3, 7 – 8; 5:16 – 19.

JUNE 16

MORNING

Be very careful, then, how you live—not as unwise but as wise, making the most of every opportunity, because the days are evil.

"BUT BE VERY careful to keep the commandment and the law ... to love the LORD your God, to walk in all his ways, to obey his commands, to hold fast to him and to serve him with all your heart and all your soul."—Be wise in the way you act toward outsiders; make the most of every opportunity. Let your conversation be always full of grace, seasoned with salt, so that you may know how to answer everyone.—Avoid every kind of evil.

"The bridegroom was a long time in coming, and they all became drowsy and fell asleep. At midnight the cry rang out: 'Here's the bridegroom! Come out to meet him!' ... Therefore keep watch, because you do not know the day or the hour."

My brothers, be all the more eager to make your calling and election sure. For if you do these things, you will never fall.—It will be good for those servants whose master finds them watching when he comes.

EPH. 5:15–16. Josh. 22:5. Col. 4:5–6. 1 Thess. 5:22. Matt. 25:5–6, 13. 2 Peter 1:10. Luke 12:37.

EVENING

Hold on to what you have, so that no one will take your crown.

"IF I ONLY touch his cloak, I will be healed." ... "Lord, if you are willing, you can make me clean." ... "Faith as small as a mustard seed."

So do not throw away your confidence; it will be richly rewarded.—Work out your salvation with fear and trembling, for it is God who works in you to will and to act according to his good purpose.

"First the stalk, then the head, then the full kernel in the head."—Let us acknowledge the LORD; let us press on to acknowledge him.—"The kingdom of heaven has been forcefully advancing, and forceful men lay hold of it."—Run in such a way as to get the prize.

I have fought the good fight, I have finished the race, I have kept the faith. Now there is in store for me the crown of righteousness, which the Lord, the righteous Judge, will award to me on that day.

REV. 3:11. Matt. 9:21; 8:2–3; 17:20. Heb. 10:35. Phil. 2:12–13. Mark 4:28. Hos. 6:3. Matt. 11:12. 1 Cor. 9:24. 2 Tim. 4:7–8.

JUNE 17

MORNING

*In everything, by prayer and petition, with thanksgiving,
present your requests to God.*

I LOVE THE LORD, for he heard my voice; he heard my cry for mercy. Because he turned his ear to me, I will call on him as long as I live.

"And when you pray, do not keep on babbling like pagans, for they think they will be heard because of their many words." — The Spirit himself intercedes for us with groans that words cannot express.

I want men everywhere to lift up holy hands in prayer, without anger or disputing. — Pray in the Spirit on all occasions with all kinds of prayers and requests. With this in mind, be alert and always keep on praying for all the saints.

"If two of you on earth agree about anything you ask for, it will be done for you by my Father in heaven."

PHIL. 4:6. Ps. 116:1 – 2. Matt. 6:7. Rom. 8:26. 1 Tim. 2:8. Eph. 6:18. Matt. 18:19.

EVENING

All you have made will praise you, O LORD; your saints will extol you.

PRAISE THE LORD, O my soul; all my inmost being, praise his holy name. Praise the LORD, O my soul, and forget not all his benefits.... I will extol the LORD at all times; his praise will always be on my lips.... Every day I will praise you and extol your name for ever and ever.

Because your love is better than life, my lips will glorify you. I will praise you as long as I live, and in your name I will lift up my hands. My soul will be satisfied as with the richest of foods; with singing lips my mouth will praise you.

"My soul praises the Lord and my spirit rejoices in God my Savior."

"You are worthy, our Lord and God, to receive glory and honor and power, for you created all things, and by your will they were created and have their being."

PS. 145:10. Pss. 103:1 – 2; 34:1; 145:2; 63:3 – 5. Luke 1:46 – 47. Rev. 4:11.

JUNE 18

MORNING

"Place the cover on top of the ark and put in the ark."...
There ... I will meet with you."

THE WAY INTO the Most Holy Place had not yet been disclosed. — When Jesus had cried out again in a loud voice, he gave up his spirit. At that moment the curtain of the temple was torn in two from top to bottom. Therefore, brothers, since we have confidence to enter the Most Holy Place by the blood of Jesus, by a new and living way opened for us through the curtain, that is, his body, ... let us draw near to God with a sincere heart in full assurance of faith, having our hearts sprinkled to cleanse us from a guilty conscience and having our bodies washed with pure water. ... Let us then approach the throne of grace with confidence, so that we may receive mercy and find grace to help us in our time of need.

Christ Jesus. God presented him as a sacrifice of atonement, through faith in his blood. He did this to demonstrate his justice, because in his forbearance he had left the sins committed beforehand unpunished. — Through him we both have access to the Father by one Spirit.

EXOD. 25:21–22. Heb. 9:8. Matt. 27:50–51. Heb. 10:19–20, 22; 4:16. Rom. 3:24–25. Eph. 2:18.

EVENING

"Faith as small as a mustard seed."

BARAK SAID TO her [Deborah], "If you go with me, I will go; but if you don't go with me, I won't go." ... God subdued Jabin, the Canaanite king, before the Israelites. ... Because he [Gideon] was afraid of his family and the men of the town, he did it at night rather than in the daytime. ... Gideon said to God, "If you will save Israel by my hand as you have promised." ... "Let me make just one more request." ... That night God did so.

You have little strength, yet you have kept my word and have not denied my name. — Who despises the day of small things?

We ought always to thank God for you, brothers, and rightly so, because your faith is growing more and more. — "Lord, increase our faith." — I will be like the dew to Israel; he will blossom like a lily. Like a cedar of Lebanon he will send down his roots; his young shoots will grow. His splendor will be like an olive tree, his fragrance like a cedar of Lebanon.

MATT. 17:20. Judg. 4:8, 23; 6:27, 36, 39–40. Rev. 3:8. Zech. 4:10. 2 Thess. 1:3. Luke 17:5. Hos. 14:5–6.

JUNE 19

MORNING

Without holiness no one will see the Lord.

UNLESS A MAN is born again, he cannot see the kingdom of God. — Nothing impure will ever enter it. — There is no flaw in you.

Be holy because I, the LORD your God, am holy. — As obedient children, do not conform to the evil desires you had when you lived in ignorance. But just as he who called you is holy, so be holy in all you do; for it is written: "Be holy, because I am holy." Since you call on a Father who judges each man's work impartially, live your lives as strangers here in reverent fear. — Put off your old self, which is being corrupted by its deceitful desires; to be made new in the attitude of your minds; and to put on the new self, created to be like God in true righteousness and holiness.... For he chose us in him before the creation of the world to be holy and blameless in his sight.

HEB. 12:14. John 3:3. Rev. 21:27. Song of Songs 4:7. Lev. 19:2. 1 Peter 1:14 – 17. Eph. 4:22 – 24; 1:4.

EVENING

Gold refined in the fire.

"NO ONE WHO has left home or brothers or sisters or mother or father or children or fields for me and the gospel will fail to receive a hundred times as much in this present age (homes, brothers, sisters, mothers, children and fields — and with them, persecutions) and in the age to come, eternal life."

Dear friends, do not be surprised at the painful trial you are suffering, as though something strange were happening to you.... In this you greatly rejoice, though now for a little while you may have had to suffer grief in all kinds of trials. These have come so that your faith — of greater worth than gold, which perishes even though refined by fire — may proved genuine and may result in praise, glory and honor when Jesus Christ is revealed.

And the God of all grace, who called you to his eternal glory in Christ, after you have suffered a little while, will himself restore you and make you strong, firm and steadfast. — "In this world you will have trouble. But take heart! I have overcome the world."

REV. 3:18. Mark 10:29 – 30. 1 Peter 4:12; 1:6 – 7; 5:10. John 16:33.

JUNE 20

MORNING

"Take this baby and nurse him for me, and I will pay you."

"You ALSO GO and work in my vineyard, and I will pay you whatever is right." — "I tell you the truth, anyone who gives you a cup of water in my name because you belong to Christ will certainly not lose his reward." — A generous man will prosper; he who refreshes others will himself be refreshed. — God is not unjust; he will not forget your work and the love you have shown him as you have helped his people and continue to help them.

Each will be rewarded according to his own labor.

"Lord, when did we see you hungry and feed you, or thirsty and give you something to drink? When did we see you a stranger and invite you in, or needing clothes and clothe you?" ... "The King will reply, 'I tell you the truth, whatever you did for one of the least of these brothers of mine, you did for me.'" ... "Come, you who are blessed by my Father, take your inheritance, the kingdom prepared for you since the creation of the world."

EXOD. 2:9. Matt. 20:4. Mark. 9:41. Prov. 11:25. Heb. 6:10. 1 Cor. 3:8.
    Matt. 25:37 – 38, 40, 34.

EVENING

You discern my going out and my lying down.

WHEN JACOB AWOKE from his sleep, he thought, "Surely the LORD is in this place, and I was not aware of it." ... "How awesome is this place! This is none other than the house of God; this is the gate of heaven."

The eyes of the LORD range throughout the earth to strengthen those whose hearts are fully committed to him. — I will lie down and sleep in peace, for you alone, O LORD, make me dwell in safety.

If you make the Most High your dwelling — even the LORD, who is my refuge — then no harm will befall you, no disaster will come near your tent. For he will command his angels concerning you to guard you in all your ways. — When you lie down, you will not be afraid; when you lie down, your sleep will be sweet. — For he grants sleep to those he loves.

PS. 139:3. Gen. 28:16 – 17. 2 Chron. 16:9. Pss. 4:8; 91:9 – 11. Prov. 3:24. Ps. 127:2.

JUNE 21

MORNING

Christ suffered for you, leaving you an example, that you should follow in his steps.

"EVEN THE SON of Man did not come to be served, but to serve." ... "Whoever wants to be first must be slave of all."

Jesus of Nazareth ... went around doing good. — Carry each other's burdens, and in this way you will fulfill the law of Christ.

The meekness and gentleness of Christ. — But in humility consider others better than yourselves.

"Father, forgive them, for they do not know what they are doing." — Be kind and compassionate to one another, forgiving each other just as in Christ God forgave you.

Whoever claims to live in him must walk as Jesus did. — Let us fix our eyes on Jesus, the author and perfecter of our faith, who for the joy set before him endured the cross, scorning its shame, and sat down at the right hand of the throne of God.

1 PETER 2:21. Mark 10:45, 44. Acts 10:38. Gal. 6:2. 2 Cor. 10:1. Phil. 2:3. Luke 23:34. Eph. 4:32. 1 John 2:6. Heb. 12:2.

EVENING

I sought him, but I could not find him; I called him, but he gave me no answer.

"O LORD, WHAT can I say, now that Israel has been routed by its enemies?" ... The LORD said to Joshua, "Stand up! What are you doing down on your face? Israel has sinned; ... They have taken some of the devoted things; ... they have put them with their own possessions."

Surely the arm of the LORD is not too short to save, nor his ear too dull to hear. But your iniquities have separated you from your God; your sins have hidden his face from you, so that he will not hear.

If I had cherished sin in my heart, the Lord would not have listened.

Dear friends, if our hearts do not condemn us, we have confidence before God and receive from him anything we ask, because we obey his commands and do what pleases him.

SONG OF SONGS 5:6. Josh. 7:8, 10 – 11. Isa. 59:1 – 2. Ps. 66:18. 1 John 3:21 – 22.

JUNE 22

MORNING

For you died, and your new life is now hidden with Christ in God.

WE DIED TO sin; how can we live in it any longer? — I have been crucified with Christ and I no longer live, but Christ lives in me. The life I live in the body, I live by faith in the Son of God, who loved me and gave himself for me. — He died for all that those who live should no longer live for themselves but for him who died for them and was raised again.... Therefore, if anyone is in Christ, he is a new creation; the old has gone, the new has come!

We are in him who is true — even his Son Jesus Christ. — "That all of them may be one, Father, just as you are in me and I am in you." — Now you are the body of Christ, and each one of you is a part of it. — "Because I live, you also will live."

"To him who overcomes, I will give some of the hidden manna. I will also give him a white stone with a new name written on it, known only to him who receives it."

COL. 3:3. Rom. 6:2. Gal. 2:20. 2 Cor. 5:15, 17. 1 John 5:20. John 17:21. 1 Cor. 12:27. John 14:19. Rev. 2:17.

EVENING

See how he loved him!

HE DIED FOR all. — "Greater love has no one than this, that one lay down his life for his friends."

Therefore he ... always lives to intercede for them. — "I am going to prepare a place for you.... I will come back and take you to be with me that you also may be where I am."

"Father, I want those you have given me to be with me where I am." — Having loved his own who were in the world, he now showed them the full extent of his love.

We love because he first loved us. — Christ's love compels us, because we are convinced that one died for all, and therefore all died. And he died for all, that those who live should no longer live for themselves but for him who died for them and was raised again.

"If you obey my commands, you will remain in my love, just as I have obeyed my Father's commands and remain in his love."

JOHN 11:36. 2 Cor. 5:15. John 15:13. Heb. 7:25. John 14:2–3; 17:24; 13:1. 1 John 4:19. 2 Cor. 5:14–15. John 15:10.

JUNE 23

MORNING

*"I will ask the Father, and he will give you another Counselor
to be with you forever—the spirit of truth."*

"IT IS FOR your good that I am going away. Unless I go away, the Counselor will not come to you; but if I go, I will send him to you."—The Spirit himself testifies with our spirit that we are God's children.

For you did not receive a spirit that makes you a slave.... The Spirit helps us in our weakness. We do not know what we ought to pray, but the Spirit himself intercedes for us with groans that words cannot express.

May the God of hope fill you with all joy and peace as you trust in him, so that you may overflow with hope by the power of the Holy Spirit.... Hope does not disappoint us, because God has poured out his love into our hearts by the Holy Spirit, whom he has given us.

We know that we live in him and he in us, because he has given us of his Spirit.

JOHN 14:16–17. John 16:7. Rom. 8:16, 15, 26; 15:13; 5:5. 1 John 4:13.

EVENING

*"Should I not try to find a home for you, where you will be
well provided for?"*

THERE REMAINS, THEN, a Sabbath-rest for the people of God.—My people will live in peaceful dwelling places, in secure homes, in undisturbed places of rest.—There the wicked cease from turmoil, and there the weary are at rest.—They will rest from their labors.

Where Jesus, who went before us, has entered on our behalf. He has become a high priest forever, in the order of Melchizedek.

"Come to me, all you who are weary and burdened, and I will give you rest. Take my yoke upon you and learn from me, for I am gentle and humble in heart, and you will find rest for your souls. For my yoke is easy and my burden is light."—"In repentance and rest is your salvation, in quietness and trust is your strength."

The LORD is my shepherd, I shall lack nothing. He makes me lie down in green pastures, he leads me beside quiet waters.

RUTH 3:1. Heb. 4:9. Isa. 32:18. Job 3:17. Rev. 14:13. Heb. 6:20. Matt. 11:28–30.
Isa. 30:15. Ps. 23:1–2.

JUNE 24

MORNING

*The ark of the covenant of the LORD went before them during
those three days to find them a place to rest.*

MY TIMES ARE in your hands.... He chose our inheritance for us.... Lead me, O
LORD, in your righteousness.... Make straight your way before me.

Commit your way to the LORD; trust in him and he will do this. — In all your
ways acknowledge him, and he will make your paths straight. — Whether you
turn to the right or to the left, your ears will hear a voice behind you, saying,
"This is the way; walk in it."

The LORD is my shepherd, I shall lack nothing. He makes me lie down in green
pastures, he leads me beside quiet waters.... "As a father has compassion on his
children, so the LORD has compassion on those who fear him; for he knows how
we are formed, he remembers that we are dust." — "Your heavenly Father knows
that you need them." — Cast all your anxiety on him because he cares for you.

**NUM. 10:33. Pss. 31:15; 47:4; 5:8; 37:5. Prov. 3:6. Isa. 30:21. Pss. 23:1–2; 103:13–14.
Matt. 6:32. 1 Peter 5:7.**

EVENING

*"Rabbi" (which means Teacher), "where are you staying?"
"Come," he replied, "and you will see."*

"IN MY FATHERS house are many rooms; if it were not so, I would have told you.
I am going there to prepare a place for you. And if I go and prepare a place for
you, I will come back and take you to be with me that you also may be where I
am." — "To him who overcomes, I will give the right to sit with me on my throne."

For this is what the high and lofty One says — he who lives forever, whose name
is holy: "I live in a high and holy place, but also with him who is contrite and lowly
in spirit, to revive the spirit of the lowly and to revive the heart of the contrite."

"Here I am! I stand at the door and knock. If anyone hears my voice and
opens the door, I will go in and eat with him, and he with me."

"I will be with you always, to the very end of the age." — How priceless is
your unfailing love! Both high and low among men find refuge in the shadow
of your wings.

JOHN 1:38–39. John 14:2–3. Rev. 3:21. Isa. 57:15. Rev. 3:20. Matt. 28:20. Ps. 36:7.

J U N E 25

Morning

But we know that when he appears we shall be like him, for
we shall see him as he is.

Yet to all who received him, to those who believed in his name, he gave the right to become children of God. — Through these he has given us his very great and precious promises, so that through them you may participate in the divine nature and escape the corruption in the world caused by evil desires.

Since ancient times no one has heard, no ear has perceived, no eye has seen any God besides you, who acts on behalf of those who wait for him.

Now we see but a poor reflection; then we shall see face to face. Now I know in part; then I shall know fully, even as I am fully known. — The Lord Jesus Christ, who, by the power that enables him to bring everything under his control, will transform our lowly bodies so that they will be like his glorious body. — And I — in righteousness I will see your face; when I awake, I will be satisfied with seeing your likeness.

1 JOHN 3:2. John 1:12. 2 Peter 1:4. Isa. 64:4. 1 Cor. 13:12. Phil. 3:20–21. Ps. 17:15.

Evening

"The man who is close to me!" declares the LORD Almighty.

For in Christ all the fullness of the Deity lives in bodily form. — "I have bestowed strength on a warrior; I have exalted a young man from among the people." — "I have trodden the winepress alone; from the nations no one was with me."

Beyond all question, the mystery of godliness is great. — For to us a child is born, to us a son is given, and the government will be on his shoulders. And he will be called Wonderful Counselor, Mighty God, Everlasting Father, Prince of Peace.

The Son is the radiance of God's glory and the exact representation of his being, sustaining all things by his powerful word. After he had provided purification for sins, he sat down at the right hand of the Majesty in heaven.... But about the Son he says, "Your throne, O God, will last for ever and ever."

"Let all God's angels worship him. — "king of kings and lord of lords."

ZECH. 13:7. Col. 2:9. Ps. 89:19. Isa. 63:3. 1 Tim. 3:16. Isa. 9:6. Heb. 1:3, 8, 6.
Rev. 19:16.

JUNE 26

MORNING

"Oh that you would bless me and enlarge my territory! Let your hand be with me, and keep me from harm so that I will be free from pain." And God granted his request.

THE BLESSING OF the LORD brings wealth, and he adds no trouble to it. — But if he remains silent, who can condemn him? If he hides his face, who can see him?

From the LORD comes deliverance. May your blessing be on your people.... How great is your goodness, which you have stored up for those who fear you, which you bestow in the sight of men on those who take refuge in you. — "My prayer is not that you take them out of the world but that you protect them from the evil one."

"Ask and it will be given to you; seek and you will find; knock and the door will be opened to you. For everyone who asks receives; he who seeks finds; and to him who knocks, the door will be opened." — The LORD redeems his servants; no one who takes refuge in him will be condemned.

1 CHRON. 4:10. Prov. 10:22. Job 34:29. Pss. 3:8; 31:19. John 17:15. Matt. 7:7 – 8. Ps. 34:22.

EVENING

Because the LORD kept vigil that night to bring them out of Egypt.

THE LORD JESUS, on the night he was betrayed, took bread, and when he had given thanks, he broke it and said, "This is my body, which is for you; do this in remembrance of me." In the same way, after supper he took the cup, saying, "This cup is the new covenant in my blood; do this, whenever you drink it, in remembrance of me."

He knelt down and prayed.... And being in anguish, he prayed more earnestly, and his sweat was like drops of blood falling to the ground.

It was the day of Preparation of Passover Week, about the sixth hour.... So the soldiers took charge of Jesus. Carrying his own cross, he went out to The Place of the Skull (which in Aramaic is called Golgotha). Here they crucified him.

For Christ, our Passover lamb, has been sacrificed. Therefore let us keep the Festival.

EXOD. 12:42. 1 Cor. 11:23 – 25. Luke 22:41, 44. John 19:14, 16 – 18. 1 Cor. 5:7 – 8.

MORNING

Who can stand?

BUT WHO CAN endure the day of his coming? Who can stand when he appears? For he will be like a refiner's fire or a laundered's soap.

After this I looked and there before me was a great multitude that no one could count, from every nation, tribe, people and language, standing before the throne and in front of the Lamb. They were wearing white robes and were holding palm branches in their hands.... "These are they who have come out of the great tribulation; they have washed their robes and made them white in the blood of the Lamb. Therefore, they are before the throne of God and serve him day and night in his temple; and he who sits on the throne will spread his tent over them. Never again will they hunger; never again will they thirst. The sun will not beat upon them, nor any scorching heat. For the Lamb at the center of the throne will be their shepherd; he will lead them to springs of living water. And God will wipe away every tear from their eyes."

Therefore, there is now no condemnation for those who are in Christ Jesus. — Stand firm, then, and do not let yourselves be burdened again by a yoke of slavery.

REV. 6:17. Mal. 3:2. Rev. 7:9, 14 – 17. Rom. 8:1. Gal. 5:1.

EVENING

Do not bring your servant into judgment, for no one living is righteous before you.

"COME NOW, LET us reason together," says the LORD. "Though your sins are like scarlet, they shall be as white as snow; though they are red as crimson, they shall be like wool."

Or else let them come to me for refuge; let them make peace with me, yes, let them make peace with me. — "Submit to God and be at peace with him."

Since we have been justified through faith, we have peace with God through our Lord Jesus Christ. — A man is not justified by observing the law, but by faith in Jesus Christ. — Therefore no one will be declared righteous in his sight by observing the law.

Through him everyone who believes is justified from everything you could not be justified from by the law of Moses. — But thanks be to God. He gives us the victory through our Lord Jesus Christ.

PS. 143:2. Isa. 1:18; 27:5. Job 22:21. Rom. 5:1. Gal. 2:16. Rom. 3:20. Acts 13:39.
1 Cor. 15:57.

JUNE 28

MORNING

"I know that my Redeemer lives."

FOR IF, WHEN we were God's enemies, we were reconciled to him through the death of his Son, how much more, having been reconciled, shall we be saved through his life! — But because Jesus lives forever, he has a permanent priesthood. Therefore he is able to save completely those who come to God through him, because he always lives to intercede for them.

"Because I live, you also will live." — If only for this life we have hope in Christ, we are to be pitied more than all men. But Christ has indeed been raised from the dead, the firstfruits of those who have fallen asleep.

"The Redeemer will come to Zion, to those in Jacob who repent of their sins," declares the LORD — We have redemption through his blood, the forgiveness of sins, in accordance with the riches of God's grace. — For you know that it was not with perishable things such as silver or gold that you were redeemed from the empty way of life handed down to you from your forefathers, but with the precious blood of Christ, a lamb without blemish or defect.

JOB 19:25. Rom. 5:10. Heb. 7:24 – 25. John 14:19. 1 Cor. 15:19 – 20. Isa. 59:20. Eph. 1:7. 1 Peter 1:18 – 19.

EVENING

The Spirit clearly says that in later times some will abandon the faith and follow deceiving spirits and things taught by demons.

CONSIDER CAREFULLY HOW you listen. — Let the word of Christ dwell in you richly as you teach and admonish one another with all wisdom. — In addition to all this, take up the shield of faith, with which you can extinguish all the flaming arrows of the evil one.

Great peace have they who love your law, and nothing can make them stumble.... How sweet are your promises to my taste, sweeter than honey to my mouth! I gain understanding from your precepts; therefore I hate every wrong path.

Your word is a lamp to my feet and a light for my path.... I have more insight than all my teachers, for I meditate on your statutes.

For Satan himself masquerades as an angel of light. — Even if we or an angel from heaven should preach a gospel other than the one we preached to you, let him be eternally condemned!

1 TIM. 4:1. Luke 8:18. Col. 3:16. Eph. 6:16. Pss. 119:165, 103 – 104; 119:105, 99. 2 Cor. 11:14. Gal. 1:8.

JUNE 29

MORNING

His commandments are not burdensome.

"FOR MY FATHER'S will is that everyone who looks to the Son and believes in him shall have eternal life." — And receive from him anything we ask, because we obey his commands and do what pleases him.

"For my yoke is easy and my burden is light." — "If you love me, you will obey what I command.... Whoever has my commands and obeys them, he is the one who loves me. He who loves me will be loved by my Father, and I too will love him and show myself to him."

Blessed is the man who finds wisdom, the man who gains understanding. — Her ways are pleasant ways, and all her paths are peace. — Great peace have they who love your law, and nothing can make them stumble — For in my inner being I delight in God's law.

This is his command: to believe in the name of his Son, Jesus Christ, and to love one another as he commanded us. — Love does no harm to its neighbor. Therefore love is the fulfillment of the law.

1 JOHN 5:3. John 6:40. 1 John 3:22. Matt. 11:30. John 14:15, 21. Prov. 3:13, 17. Ps. 119:165. Rom. 7:22. 1 John 3:23. Rom. 13:10.

EVENING

Remember not the sins of my youth and my rebellious ways.

"I HAVE SWEPT away your offenses like a cloud, your sins like the morning mist." ... "I, even I, am he who blots out your transgressions, for my own sake, and remembers your sins no more." ... "Come now, let us reason together," says the LORD. "Though your sins are like scarlet, they shall be as white as snow; though they are red as crimson, they shall be like wool." — "For I will forgive their wickedness and will remember their sins no more." — You will hurl all our iniquities into the depths of the sea.

In your love you kept me from the pit of destruction; you have put all my sins behind your back. — Who is a God like you, who pardons sin and forgives the transgression? ... You do not stay angry forever but delight to show mercy. — To him who loves us and has freed us from our sins by his blood, and has made us to be a kingdom and priests to serve his God and Father — to him be glory and power for ever and ever! Amen.

PS. 25:7. Isa. 44:22; 43:25; 1:18. Jer. 31:34. Mic. 7:19. Isa. 38:17. Mic. 7:18. Rev. 1:5.

JUNE 30

MORNING

"Those whom I love I rebuke and discipline."

"MY SON, DO not make light of the Lord's discipline, and do not lose heart when he rebukes you, because the Lord disciplines those he loves, and he punishes everyone he accepts as a son." — Because the LORD disciplines those he loves, as a father the son he delights in. — For he wounds, but he also binds up, he injures, but his hands also heal. — Humble yourselves, therefore, under God's mighty hand, that he may lift you up in due time. — I have tested you in the furnace of affliction.

For he does not willingly bring affliction or grief to the children of men. — He does not treat us as our sins deserve or repay us according to our iniquities. For as high as the heavens are above the earth, so great is his love for those who fear him; as far as the east is from the west, so far has he removed our transgressions from us. As a father has compassion on his children, so the LORD has compassion on those who fear him; for he knows how we are formed, he remembers that we are dust.

REV. 3:19. Heb. 12:5–6. Prov. 3:12. Job 5:18. 1 Peter 5:6. Isa. 48:10. Lam. 3:33. Ps. 103:10–14.

EVENING

Do not be quick with your mouth, do not be hasty in your heart to utter anything before God.

"WHEN YOU PRAY, do not keep on babbling like pagans, for they think they will be heard because of their many words. Do not be like them, for your Father knows what you need before you ask him."

Then they called on the name of Baal from morning till noon. "O Baal, answer us!"

"Two men went up to the temple to pray, one a Pharisee and the other a tax collector. The Pharisee stood up and prayed about himself; 'God, I thank you that I am not like all other men — robbers, evildoers, adulterers — or even like this tax collector.' ... But the tax collector stood at a distance. He would not even look up to heaven, but beat his breast and said, 'God, have mercy on me, a sinner.' I tell you that this man, rather than the other, went home justified before God."

"Lord, teach us to pray."

ECCL. 5:2. Matt. 6:7–8. 1 Kings 18:26. Luke 18:10–11, 13–14; 11:1.

JULY 1

MORNING

The fruit of the Spirit is goodness.

BE IMITATORS OF God, therefore, as dearly loved children. — "Love your enemies and pray for those who persecute you, that you may be sons of your Father in heaven. He causes his sun to rise on the evil and the good, and sends rain on the righteous and the unrighteous." — "Be merciful, just as your Father is merciful."

For the fruit of the light consists in all goodness, righteousness and truth.

But when the kindness and love of God our Savior appeared, he saved us, not because of righteous things we had done, but because of his mercy. He saved us through the washing of rebirth and renewal by the Holy Spirit, whom he poured out on us generously through Jesus Christ our Savior. — The LORD is good to all; he has compassion on all he has made. — He who did not spare his own Son, but gave him up for us all — how will he not also, along with him, graciously give us all things?

GAL. 5:22. Eph. 5:1. Matt. 5:44–45. Luke 6:36. Eph. 5:9. Titus 3:4–6. Ps. 145:9. Rom. 8:32.

EVENING

Ebenezer . . . "Thus far has the LORD helped us."

WHEN I WAS in great need, he saved me. . . . Praise be to the LORD, for he has heard my cry for mercy. The LORD is my strength and my shield; my heart trusts in him, and I am helped. My heart leaps for joy and I will give thanks to him in song.

It is better to take refuge in the LORD than to trust in man. It is better to take refuge in the LORD than to trust in princes. . . . Blessed is he whose help is the God of Jacob, whose hope is in the LORD his God. . . . He led them by a straight way to a city where they could settle. — Not one of all the LORD's good promises to the house of Israel failed; every one was fulfilled.

"When I sent you without purse, bag or sandals, did you lack anything?" "Nothing," they answered. — Because you are my help, I sing in the shadow of your wings.

1 SAM. 7:12. Pss. 116:6; 28:6–7; 118:8–9; 146:5; 107:7. Josh. 21:45. Luke 22:35. Ps. 63:7.

JULY 2

MORNING

"These are the regulations for the Passover: No foreigner is to eat of it."

WE HAVE AN altar from which those who minister at the tabernacle have no right to eat. — "Unless a man is born again, he cannot see the kingdom of God." — At that time you were separate from Christ, excluded from citizenship in Israel and foreigners to the covenants of the promise.... But now in Christ Jesus you who were once far away have been brought near through the blood of Christ.

For he himself is our peace, who has made the two one ... by abolishing in his flesh the law with its commandments and regulations. His purpose was to create in himself one new man out of the two, thus making peace.

You are no longer foreigners and aliens, but fellow citizens with God's people and members of God's household.

"If anyone hears my voice and opens the door, I will go in and eat with him and he with me."

EXOD. 12:43. Heb. 13:10. John 3:3. Eph. 2:12–15, 19. Rom. 3:20.

EVENING

[Jesus] prayed the third time, saying the same thing.

DURING THE DAYS of Jesus' life on earth, he offered up prayers and petitions with loud cries and tears to the one who could save him from death.

Let us acknowledge the LORD. — Be ... faithful in prayer. — Pray in the Spirit on all occasions with all kinds of prayers and requests. With this in mind, be alert and always keep on praying. — But in everything, by prayer and petition, with thanksgiving, present your requests to God. And the peace of God, which transcends all understanding, will guard your hearts and your minds in Christ Jesus.

"Yet not as I will, but as you will." — This is the assurance we have in approaching God: that if we ask anything according to his will, he hears us.

Delight yourself in the LORD and he will give you the desires of your heart. Commit your way to the LORD; trust in him and he will do this.

MATT. 26:44. Heb. 5:7. Hos. 6:3. Rom. 12:12. Eph. 6:18. Phil. 4:6–7. Matt. 26:39.
1 John 5:14. Ps. 37:4–5.

July 3

Morning

If we are children, then we are heirs—heirs of God and
co-heirs with Christ.

IF YOU BELONG to Christ, then you are Abraham's seed, and heirs according to the promise.

How great is the love the Father has lavished on us, that we should be called children of God.—So you are no longer a slave, but a son; and since you are a son, God has made you also an heir.—He predestined us to be adopted as his sons through Jesus Christ, in accordance with his pleasure and will.

"Father, I want those you have given me to be with me where I am, and to see my glory, the glory you have given me."

"To him who overcomes and does my will to the end, I will give authority over the nations." ... "To him who overcomes, I will give the right to sit with me on my throne, just as I overcame and sat down with my Father on his throne."

ROM. 8:17. Gal. 3:29. 1 John 3:1. Gal. 4:7. Eph. 1:5. John 17:24. Rev. 2:26; 3:21.

Evening

[God] chose the lowly things of this world and the despised things.

"ARE NOT ALL these men who are speaking Galileans?"

Jesus ... saw two brothers ... casting a net into the lake, for they were fishermen. "Come, follow me," Jesus said.—When they saw the courage of Peter and John and realized that they were unschooled, ordinary men, they were astonished and they took note that these men had been with Jesus.

My message and my preaching were not with wise and persuasive words, but with a demonstration of the Spirit's power, so that your faith might not rest on men's wisdom, but on God's power.

"You did not choose me, but I chose you to go and bear fruit." ... "If a man remains in me and I in him, he will bear much fruit; apart from me you can do nothing."—We have this treasure in jars of clay to show that this all-surpassing power is from God.

1 COR. 1:28. Acts 2:7. Matt. 4:18–19. Acts 4:13. 1 Cor. 2:4–5. John 15:16, 5. 2 Cor. 4:7.

JULY 4

MORNING

Reclining next to him.

"As a mother comforts her child, so will I comfort you." — People were bringing little children to Jesus to have him touch them.... And he took the children in his arms, put his hands on them and blessed them. — Jesus called his disciples to him and said, "I have compassion for these people; they have already been with me three days and have nothing to eat. I do not want to send them away hungry, or they may collapse on the way." — A high priest ... tempted in every way, just as we are. — In his love and mercy he redeemed them.

"I will not leave you as orphans; I will come to you." — "Can a mother forget the baby at her breast and have no compassion on the child she has borne? Though she may forget, I will not forget you!"

"For the Lamb at the center of the throne will be their shepherd; he will lead them to springs of living water. And God will wipe away every tear from their eyes."

JOHN 13:23. Isa. 66:13. Mark 10:13, 16. Matt. 15:32. Heb. 4:15. Isa. 63:9. John 14:18. Isa. 49:15. Rev. 7:17.

EVENING

[Jesus] is the atoning sacrifice for our sins.

"The cherubim are to face each other, looking toward the cover. Place the cover on top of the ark and put in the ark the Testimony, which I will give you.... I will meet with you."

Surely his salvation is near those who fear him. Love and faithfulness meet together; righteousness and peace kiss each other.

If you, O Lord, kept a record of sins, O Lord, who could stand? But with you there is forgiveness, therefore you are feared.... O Israel, put your hope in the Lord, for with the Lord is unfailing love and with him is full redemption. He himself will redeem Israel from all their sins. — All have sinned and fall short of the glory of God, and are justified freely by his grace through the redemption that came by Christ Jesus. God presented him as a sacrifice of atonement, through faith in his blood. He did this to demonstrate his justice, because in his forbearance he had left the sins committed beforehand unpunished — he did it to demonstrate his justice at the present time, so as to be just and the one who justifies the man who has faith in Jesus.

1 JOHN 2:1 – 2. Exod. 25:20 – 22. Pss. 85:9 – 10; 130:3 – 4, 7 – 8. Rom. 3:23 – 25.

JULY 5

MORNING

So we know and rely on the love God has for us.

GOD, WHO IS rich in mercy, made us alive with Christ even when we were dead in transgressions—it is by grace you have been saved.

And God raised us up with Christ and seated us with him in the heavenly realms in Christ Jesus, in order that in the coming ages he might show the incomparable riches of his grace, expressed in his kindness to us in Christ Jesus.

"God so loved the world that he gave his one and only Son, that whoever believes in him shall not perish but have eternal life."—He who did not spare his own Son, but gave him up for us all—how will he not also, along with him, graciously give us all things?—The LORD is good to all; he has compassion on all he has made.

We love him because he first loved us.

"Blessed is she who has believed that what the Lord has said to her will be accomplished!"

1 JOHN 4:16. Eph. 2:4–7. John 3:16. Rom. 8:32. Ps. 145:9. 1 John 4:19. Luke 1:45.

EVENING

Do not be proud, but be willing to associate with people of
low position. Do not be conceited.

MY BROTHERS, AS believers in our glorious Lord Jesus Christ, don't show favoritism.... Has not God chosen those who are poor in the eyes of the world to be rich in faith and to inherit the kingdom he promised those who love him?

Nobody should seek his own good, but the good of others.—But if we have food and clothing, we will be content with that. People who want to get rich fall into temptation and a trap and into many foolish and harmful desires that plunge men into ruin and destruction.

But God chose the foolish things of the world to shame the wise; God chose the weak things of the world to shame the strong. He chose the lowly things of this world and the despised things—and the things that are not—to nullify the things that are, so that no one may boast before him.

My heart is not proud, O LORD, my eyes are not haughty.

ROM. 12:16. James 2:1, 5. 1 Cor. 10:24. 1 Tim. 6:8–9. 1 Cor. 1:27–29. Ps. 131:1.

JULY 6

MORNING

Let your conversation be always full of grace.

A WORD APTLY spoken is like apples of gold in settings of silver. Like an earring of gold or an ornament of fine gold is a wise man's rebuke to a listening ear. — "Do not let any unwholesome talk come out of your mouths, . . . but only what is helpful for building others up according to their needs." — "The good man brings good things out of the good stored up in him, and the evil man brings evil things out of the evil stored up in him." . . . "By your words you will be acquitted." — The tongue of the wise brings healing.

Then those who feared the LORD talked with each other, and the LORD listened and heard. A scroll of remembrance was written in his presence concerning those who feared the LORD and honored his name.

"If you utter worthy, not worthless, words, you will be my spokesman." — But just as you excel in everything — in faith, in speech, in knowledge, in complete earnestness, . . . see that you also excel in this grace of giving.

COL. 4:6. Prov. 25:11–12. Eph. 4:29. Matt. 12:35, 37. Prov. 12:18. Matt. 3:16. Jer. 15:19. 2 Cor. 8:7.

EVENING

For your life is ever before me.

THE LORD IS gracious and compassionate, slow to anger and rich in love. — Your Father in heaven . . . causes his sun to rise on the evil and the good, and sends rain on the righteous and the unrighteous. Be imitators of God, therefore, as dearly loved children and live a life of love, just as Christ loved us and gave himself up for us as a fragrant offering and sacrifice to God. . . . Be kind and compassionate to one another, forgiving each other, just as in Christ God forgave you. — Now that you have purified yourselves by obeying the truth so that you have sincere love for your brothers, love one another deeply, from the heart. — For Christ's love compels us.

"But love your enemies, do good to them, and lend to them without expecting to get anything back. Then your reward will be great, and you will be sons of the Most High, because he is kind to the ungrateful and wicked. Be merciful just as your Father is merciful."

PS. 26:3. Ps. 145:8. Matt. 5:45. Eph. 5:1–2; 4:32. 1 Peter 1:22. 2 Cor. 5:14. Luke 6:35–36.

July 7

Morning

Then Jesus was led by the Spirit into the desert to be tempted by the devil.

During the days of Jesus' life on earth, he offered up prayers and petitions with loud cries and tears to the one who could save him from death, and he was heard because of his reverent submission. Although he was a son, he learned obedience from what he suffered and, once made perfect, he became the source of eternal salvation for all who obey him. . . . We do not have a high priest who is unable to sympathize with our weaknesses, but we have one who has been tempted in every way, just as we are—yet was without sin.

No temptation has seized you except what is common to man. And God is faithful; he will not let you be tempted beyond what you can bear. But when you are tempted, he will also provide a way out so that you can stand up under it. — "My grace is sufficient for you, for my power is made perfect in weakness."

MATT. 4:1. Heb. 5:7–9; 4:15. 1 Cor. 10:13. 2 Cor. 12:9.

Evening

"The Son of Man . . . [came] to give his life as a ransom for many."

The blood of goats and bulls and the ashes of a heifer sprinkled on those who are ceremonially unclean sanctify them so that they are outwardly clean. How much more, then, will the blood of Christ, who through the eternal Spirit offered himself unblemished to God, cleanse our consciences from acts that lead to death, so that we may serve the living God!

He was led like a lamb to the slaughter. — "I lay down my life for the sheep. . . . No one takes it from me, but I lay it down of my own accord. I have authority to lay it down and authority to take it up again."

"For the life of a creature is in the blood, and I have given it to you to make atonement for yourselves on the altar; it is the blood that makes atonement for one's life." — Without the shedding of blood there is no forgiveness.

While we were still sinners, Christ died for us. Since we now have been justified by his blood, how much more shall we be saved from God's wrath through him!

MATT. 20:28. Heb. 9:13–14. Isa. 53:7. John 10:15, 18. Lev. 17:11. Heb. 9:22. Rom. 5:8–9.

July 8

Morning

*If we confess our sins, he is faithful and just and will forgive
us our sins and purify us from all unrighteousness.*

FOR I KNOW my transgressions, and my sin is always before me. Against you,
you only, have I sinned and done what is evil in your sight. — "So he got up and
went to his father. But while he was still a long way off, his father saw him and
was filled with compassion for him; he ran to his son, threw his arms around
him and kissed him." — "I have swept away your offenses like a cloud, your sins
like the morning mist. Return to me, for I have redeemed you." — Your sins have
been forgiven on account of his name. — Just as in Christ God forgave you. — So
as to be just and the one who justifies the man who has faith in Jesus.

"I will sprinkle clean water on you, and you will be clean." — "They will walk
with me, dressed in white, for they are worthy."

This is the one who came by water and blood — Jesus Christ. He did not
come by water only, but by water and blood.

1 JOHN 1:9. Ps. 51:3–4. Luke 15:20. Isa. 44:22. 1 John 2:12. Eph. 4:32. Rom. 3:26.
Ezek. 36:25. Rev. 3:4. 1 John 5:6.

Evening

Can a corrupt throne be allied with you?

OUR FELLOWSHIP IS with the Father and with his Son, Jesus Christ.... Dear
friends, now we are children of God, and what we will be has not yet been made
known. But we know that when he appears, we shall be like him, for we shall see
him as he is. Everyone who has this hope in him purifies himself, just as he is pure.

"The prince of the world is coming. He has no hold on me." — A high priest
... holy, blameless, pure.

For our struggle is not against flesh and blood, but against the rulers, against
the authorities, against the powers of this dark world and against the spiritual
forces of evil in the heavenly realms.... The ruler of the kingdom of the air, the
spirit who is now at work in those who are disobedient.

Anyone born of God does not continue to sin; the one who was born of
God keeps him safe, and the evil one does not touch him. We know that we are
children of God, and that the whole world is under the control of the evil one.

PS. 94:20. 1 John 1:3; 3:2–3. John 14:30. Heb. 7:26. Eph. 6:12; 2:2. 1 John 5:18–19.

JULY 9

MORNING

"I have taken away your sin, and I will put rich garments on you."

BLESSED IS HE whose transgressions are forgiven, whose sins are covered. — All of us have become like one who is unclean. — I know that nothing good lives in me, that is, in my sinful nature. For I have the desire to do what is good, but I cannot carry it out.

For all of you who were baptized into Christ have been clothed with Christ. — You have taken off your old self with its practices and have put on the new self, which is being renewed in knowledge in the image of its Creator. — Not having a righteousness of my own that comes from the law, but . . . the righteousness that comes from God and is by faith.

"Bring forth the best robe and put it on him." — Fine linen stands for the righteous acts of the saints. — I delight greatly in the LORD; my soul rejoices in my God. For he has clothed me with garments of salvation and arrayed me in a robe of righteousness.

ZECH. 3:4. Ps. 32:1. Isa. 64:6. Rom. 7:18. Gal. 3:27. Col. 3:9–10. Phil. 3:9. Luke 15:22. Rev. 19:8. Isa. 61:10.

EVENING

Day will bring it to light.

YOU, THEN, WHY do you judge your brother? Or why do you look down on your brother? For we will all stand before God's judgment seat. . . . So then, each of us will give an account of himself to God. Therefore let us stop passing judgment on one another.

Therefore judge nothing before the appointed time; wait till the Lord comes. He will bring to light what is hidden in darkness and will expose the motives of men's hearts. At that time each will receive his praise from God. — God will judge men's secrets through Jesus Christ. — The Father judges no one, but has entrusted all judgment to the Son. . . . And he has given him authority to judge because he is the Son of Man.

O great and powerful God, whose name is the LORD Almighty, great are your purposes and mighty are your deeds. Your eyes are open to all the ways of men; you reward everyone according to his conduct and as his deeds deserve.

1 COR. 3:13. Rom. 14:10, 12–13. 1 Cor. 4:5. Rom. 2:16. John 5:22, 27. Jer. 32:18–19.

JULY 10

MORNING

"A servant [is not] above his master."

"YOU CALL ME 'Teacher' and 'Lord' and rightly so, for that is what I am."

"It is enough for the student to be like his teacher, and the servant like his master." — "If they persecuted me, they will persecute you also. If they obeyed my teaching, they will obey yours also." ... "I have given them your word and the world has hated them, for they are not of the world any more than I am of the world."

Consider him who endured such opposition from sinful men, so that you will not grow weary and lose heart. In your struggle against sin, you have not yet resisted to the point of shedding your blood.

Let us run with perseverance the race marked out for us. Let us fix our eyes on Jesus, the author and perfecter of our faith, who for the joy set before him endured the cross, scorning its shame, and sat down at the right hand of the throne of God. — Since Christ suffered in his body, arm yourselves also with the same attitude.

MATT. 10:24. John 13:13. Matt. 10:25. John 15:20; 17:14. Heb. 12:3–4, 1–2. 1 Peter 4:1.

EVENING

My son, give me your heart.

"OH, THAT THEIR hearts would be inclined to fear me and keep all my commands always, so that it might go well with them and their children forever!"

Your heart is not right before God. — The sinful mind is hostile to God. It does not submit to God's law, nor can it do so. Those controlled by the sinful nature cannot please God.

But they gave themselves first to the Lord. — In everything that he [Hezekiah] undertook ... he sought his God and worked wholeheartedly. And so he prospered.

Guard your heart, for it is the wellspring of life.

Whatever you do, work at it with all your heart, as working for the Lord. — Like slaves of Christ, doing the will of God from your heart. Serve wholeheartedly, as if you were serving the Lord, not men.

I run in the path of your commands, for you have set my heart free.

PROV. 23:26. Deut. 5:29. Acts 8:21. Rom. 8:7–8. 2 Cor. 8:5. 2 Chron. 31:21. Prov. 4:23. Col. 3:23. Eph. 6:6–7. Ps. 119:32.

JULY 11

MORNING

"I am with you to rescue and save you."

CAN PLUNDER BE taken from warriors, or captives rescued from the fierce? But this is what the LORD says: "Yes, captives will be taken from warriors, and plunder retrieved from the fierce; I will contend with those who contend with you, and your children I will save. I will make your oppressors eat their own flesh; they will be drunk on their own blood, as with wine. Then all mankind will know that I, the LORD, am your Savior, your Redeemer, the Mighty One of Jacob." ... "So do not fear, for I am with you; do not be dismayed, for I am your God. I will strengthen you and help you; I will uphold you with my righteous right hand."

We do not have a high priest who is unable to sympathize with our weaknesses, but we have one who has been tempted in every way, just as we are — yet was without sin.... Because he himself suffered when he was tempted; he is able to help those who are being tempted. — The LORD delights in the way of the man whose steps he has made firm; though he stumble, he will not fall, for the LORD upholds him with his hand.

JER. 15:20. Isa. 49:24 – 26; 41:10. Heb. 4:15; 2:18. Ps. 37:23 – 24.

EVENING

For he satisfies the thirsty and fills the hungry with good things.

YOU HAVE TASTED that the Lord is good. — O God, you are my God, earnestly I seek you; my soul thirsts for you, my body longs for you, in a dry and weary land where there is no water. I have seen you in the sanctuary and beheld your power and your glory.

My soul yearns, even faints for the courts of the LORD; my heart and my flesh cry out for the living God. — I desire to depart and be with Christ, which is better by far.

When I awake, I will be satisfied with seeing your likeness.

"Never again will they hunger; never again will they thirst. The sun will not beat upon them, for the Lamb at the center of the throne will be their shepherd; he will lead them to springs of living water. And God will wipe away every tear from their eyes." — They feast on the abundance of your house; you give them drink from your river of delights. — "My people will be filled with my bounty," declares the LORD.

PS. 107:9. 1 Peter 2:3. Pss. 63:1 – 2; 84:2. Phil. 1:23. Ps. 17:15. Rev. 7:16 – 17. Ps. 36:8. Jer. 31:14.

July 12

MORNING

"My Presence will go with you, and I will give you rest."

"BE STRONG AND courageous. Do not be afraid or terrified because of them, for the LORD your God goes with you; he will never leave you nor forsake you." ... "The LORD himself goes before you and will be with you; he will never leave you nor forsake you. Do not be afraid; do not be discouraged." — "Have I not commanded you? Be strong and courageous. Do not be terrified; do not be discouraged, for the LORD your God will be with you wherever you go."

In all your ways acknowledge him, and he will make your paths straight. — "The Lord is my helper; I will not be afraid. What can man do to me?" — Our competence comes from God.

"Lead us not into temptation." — I know, O LORD, that a man's life is not his own; it is not for man to direct his steps. — My times are in your hands.

EXOD. 33:14. Deut. 31:6, 8. Josh. 1:9. Prov. 3:6. Heb. 13:5–6. 2 Cor. 3:5. Matt. 6:13. Jer. 10:23. Ps. 31:15.

EVENING

Let us consider how we may spur one another on toward love and good deeds.

"How PAINFUL ARE honest words." — As reminders to stimulate you to wholesome thinking.

Then those who feared the LORD talked with each other, and the LORD listened and heard. A scroll of remembrance was written in his presence concerning those who feared the LORD and honored his name. — "If two of you on earth agree about anything you ask for, it will be done for you by my Father in heaven."

The LORD God said, "It is not good for the man to be alone." — Two are better than one, because they have a good return for their work: if one falls down, his friend can help him up. But pity the man who falls and has no one to help him up!

Make up your mind not to put any stumbling block or obstacle in your brother's way. — Carry each other's burdens, and in this way you will fulfill the law of Christ.... But watch yourself, or you also may be tempted.

HEB. 10:24. Job 6:25. 2 Peter 3:1. Mal. 3:16. Matt. 18:19. Gen. 2:18. Eccl. 4:9–10. Rom. 14:13. Gal. 6:2, 1.

JULY 13

MORNING

I belong to my lover, and his desire is for me.

I KNOW WHOM I have believed, and am convinced that he is able to guard what I have entrusted to him for that day. For I am convinced that neither death nor life, neither angels nor demons, neither the present nor the future, nor any powers, neither height nor depth, nor anything else in all creation, will be able to separate us from the love of God that is in Christ Jesus our Lord. — "I protected them and kept them safe by that name you gave me. None has been lost."

For the LORD takes delight in his people. — Delighting in mankind. — But because of his great love for us, God. — "Greater love has no one than this, that one lay down his life for his friends."

You were bought with a price. Therefore honor God with your body. — If we live, we live to the Lord; and if we die, we die to the Lord. So, whether we live or die, we belong to the Lord.

SONG OF SONGS 7:10. 2 Tim. 1:12. Rom. 8:38–39. John 17:12. Ps. 149:4. Prov. 8:31. Eph. 2:4. John 15:13. 1 Cor. 6:20. Rom. 14:8.

EVENING

Look in the scroll of the Lord and read.

"FIX THESE WORDS of mine in your hearts and minds; tie them as symbols on your hands and bind them on your foreheads." — "Do not let this Book of the Law depart from your mouth; meditate on it day and night, so that you may be careful to do everything written in it. Then you will be prosperous and successful."

The law of his God is in his heart; his feet do not slip. . . . By the word of your lips I have kept myself from the ways of the violent. . . . I have hidden your word in my heart that I might not sin against you.

We have the word of the prophets made more certain, and you will do well to pay attention to it, as to a light shining in a dark place, until the day dawns and the morning star rises in your hearts. — That through endurance and the encouragement of the Scriptures we might have hope.

ISA. 34:16. Deut. 11:18. Josh. 1:8. Pss. 37:31; 17:4; 119:11. 2 Peter 1:19. Rom. 15:4.

JULY 14

MORNING

For out of the overflow of the heart the mouth speaks.

LET THE WORD of Christ dwell in you richly as you teach and admonish one another with all wisdom.

Guard your heart, for it is the wellspring of life.... The tongue has the power of life and death.—The mouth of the righteous man utters wisdom, and his tongue speaks what is just. The law of his God is in his heart; his feet do not slip.—Do not let any unwholesome talk come out of your mouths, but only what is helpful for building others up according to their needs, that it may benefit those who listen.

"For we cannot help speaking about what we have seen and heard."—I believed; therefore I said.

"Whoever acknowledges me before men, I will also acknowledge him before my Father in heaven."—For it is with your heart that you believe and are justified, and it is with your mouth that you confess and are saved.

MATT. 12:34. Col. 3:16. Prov. 4:23; 18:21. Ps. 37:30–31. Eph. 4:29. Acts 4:20. Ps. 116:10. Matt. 10:32. Rom. 10:10.

EVENING

I hope to see you soon, and we will talk face to face.

OH, THAT YOU would rend the heavens and come down.—As the deer pants for streams of water, so my soul pants for you, O God. My soul thirsts for God, for the living God. When can I go and meet with God?—Come away, my lover, and be like a gazelle or like a young stag on the spice-laden mountains.

Our citizenship is in heaven. And we eagerly await a Savior from there, the Lord Jesus Christ.—We wait for the blessed hope—the glorious appearing of our great God and Savior, Jesus Christ.—God our Savior and ... Christ Jesus our hope.—Though you have not seen him, you love him.

He who testifies to these things says, "Yes, I am coming soon." Amen. Come, Lord Jesus.—In that day they will say, "Surely this is our God; we trusted in him, and he saved us. This is the LORD, we trusted in him; let us rejoice and be glad in his salvation."

3 JOHN 14. Isa. 64:1. Ps. 42:1–2. Song of Songs 8:14. Phil. 3:20. Titus 2:13. 1 Tim. 1:1. 1 Peter 1:8. Rev. 22:20. Isa. 25:9.

JULY 15

MORNING

"Your will be done on earth as it is in heaven."

PRAISE THE LORD, you his angels, you mighty ones who do his bidding, who obey his word. Praise the LORD, all his heavenly hosts, you his servants who do his will.

"For I have come down from heaven not to do my will but to do the will of him who sent me." — "To do your will, O my God, is my desire; your law is within my heart." — "My Father, if it is not possible for this cup to be taken away unless I drink it, may your will be done."

"Not everyone who says to me, 'Lord, Lord,' will enter the kingdom of heaven, but only he who does the will of my Father who is in heaven." — For it is not those who hear the law who are righteous in God's sight, but it is those who obey the law who will be declared righteous. — "Now that you know these things, you will be blessed if you do them." — Anyone, then, who knows the good he ought to do and doesn't do it, sins.

MATT. 6:10. Ps. 103:20–21. John 6:38. Ps. 40:8. Matt. 26:42; 7:21. Rom. 2:13. John 13:17. James 4:17.

EVENING

For the ear tests words as the tongue tastes food.

DEAR FRIENDS, DO not believe every spirit, but test the spirits to see whether they are from God, because many false prophets have gone out into the world. — "Stop judging by mere appearances, and make a right judgment." — I speak to sensible people; judge for yourselves what I say. — Let the word of Christ dwell in you richly as you teach and admonish one another with all wisdom.

"He who has an ear, let him hear what the Spirit says." — The spiritual man makes judgments about all things. — "Consider carefully what you hear."

"I know your deeds, your hard work ... that you have tested those who claim to be apostles but are not, and have found them false." — Test everything. Hold on to the good.

"He calls his own sheep by name and leads them out. When he has brought out all his own, he goes on ahead of them, and his sheep follow him because they know his voice. But they will never follow a stranger, in fact, they will run away from him because they do not recognize a stranger's voice."

JOB 34:3. 1 John 4:1. John 7:24. 1 Cor. 10:15. Col. 3:16. Rev. 2:29. 1 Cor. 2:15. Mark 4:24. Rev. 2:2. 1 Thess. 5:21. John 10:3–5.

JULY 16

MORNING

"You will be for me a kingdom of priests and a holy nation."

YOU WERE SLAIN, and with your blood you purchased men for God from every tribe and language and people and nation. You have made them to be a kingdom and priests to serve our God. — You are a chosen people, a royal priesthood, a holy nation, a people belonging to God, that you may declare the praises of him who called you out of darkness into his wonderful light.

And you will be called priests of the LORD, you will be named ministers of our God. — Priests of God and of Christ.

Therefore, holy brothers, who share in the heavenly calling, fix your thoughts on Jesus, the apostle and high priest whom we confess. . . . Through Jesus, therefore, let us continually offer to God a sacrifice of praise — the fruit of lips that confess his name.

For we are God's workmanship, created in Christ Jesus to do good works, which God prepared in advance for us to do. — God's temple is sacred, and you are that temple.

EXOD. 19:6. Rev. 5:9 – 10. 1 Peter 2:9. Isa. 61:6. Rev. 20:6. Heb. 3:1; 13:15. Eph. 2:10. 1 Cor. 3:17.

EVENING

But we prayed to our God and posted a guard day and night to meet this threat.

"WATCH AND PRAY so that you will not fall into temptation." — Devote yourself to prayer, being watchful and thankful. — Cast all your anxiety on him because he cares for you. Be self-controlled and alert. Your enemy the devil prowls around like a roaring lion looking for someone to devour. Resist him, standing firm in the faith.

"Why do you call me, 'Lord, Lord,' and do not do what I say?" — Do not merely listen to the word, and so deceive yourselves. Do what it says.

"Why are you crying out to me? Tell the Israelites to move on." — Do not be anxious about anything, but in everything, by prayer and petition, with thanksgiving, present your requests to God. And the peace of God, which transcends all understanding, will guard your hearts and your minds in Christ Jesus.

NEH. 4:9. Matt. 26:41. Col. 4:2. 1 Peter 5:7 – 9. Luke 6:46. James 1:22. Exod. 14:15. Phil. 4:6 – 7.

JULY 17

MORNING

You are a gracious and compassionate God, slow to anger and abounding in love, a God who relents from sending calamity.

"Now may the Lord's strength be displayed, just as you have declared: 'The LORD is slow to anger, abounding in love and forgiving sin and rebellion. Yet he does not leave the guilty unpunished; he punishes the children for the sin of the fathers to the third and fourth generation.'"

Do not hold against us the sins of the fathers; may your mercy come quickly to meet us, for we are in desperate need. Help us, O God our Savior, for the glory of your name; deliver us and atone for our sins for your name's sake. — Although our sins testify against us, O LORD, do something for the sake of your name. For our backsliding is great; we have sinned against you. . . . O LORD, we acknowledge our wickedness and the guilt of our fathers; we have indeed sinned against you.

If you, O LORD, kept a record of sins, O Lord, who could stand? But with you there is forgiveness; therefore you are feared.

JONAH 4:2. Num. 14:17–18. Ps. 79:8–9. Jer. 14:7, 20. Ps. 130:3–4.

EVENING

Sanctifying work of the Spirit.

AWAKE, O NORTH wind; and come, thou south; blow upon my garden, that the spices thereof may flow out.

See what this godly sorrow has produced in you: what earnestness, what eagerness to clear yourselves, what indignation, what alarm, what longing, what concern, what readiness to see justice done. — (For the fruit of the light consists in all goodness, righteousness and truth.) And find out what pleases the Lord.

"Another Counselor." — God has poured out his love into our hearts by the Holy Spirit, whom he has given us.

The fruit of the Spirit is love, joy, peace. — Out of the most severe trial, their overflowing joy and their extreme poverty welled up in rich generosity.

All these are the work of one and the same Spirit, and he gives them to each man, just as he determines.

2 THESS. 2:13. Song of Songs 4:16. 2 Cor. 7:11. Eph. 5:9–10. John 14:16. Rom. 5:5. Gal. 5:22. 2 Cor. 8:2. 1 Cor. 12:11.

JULY 18

MORNING

"He calls his own sheep by name and leads them out."

GOD'S SOLID FOUNDATION stands firm, sealed with this inscription: "The Lord knows those who are his," and, "Everyone who confesses the name of the Lord must turn away from wickedness." — "Many will say to me on that day, 'Lord, Lord, did we not prophesy in your name, and in your name drive out demons and perform many miracles?' Then I will tell them plainly, 'I never knew you. Away from me, you evildoers!'" — The LORD watches over the way of the righteous, but the way of the wicked will perish.

See, I have engraved you on the palms of my hands; your walls are ever before me. — Place me like a seal over your heart, like a seal over your arm. — The LORD is good, a refuge in times of trouble. He cares for those who trust in him.

"I am going there to prepare a place for you. And if I go and prepare a place for you, I will come back and take you to be with me that you also may be where I am."

JOHN 10:3. 2 Tim. 2:19. Matt. 7:22–23. Ps. 1:6. Isa. 49:16. Song of Songs 8:6. Nah. 1:7. John 14:2–3.

EVENING

"She did what she could."

"THIS POOR WIDOW has put in more than all the others." — "Anyone who gives you a cup of water in my name because you belong to Christ will certainly not lose his reward." — For if the willingness is there, the gift is acceptable according to what one has, not according to what he does not have. — Let us not love with words or tongue but with actions and in truth.

Suppose a brother or sister is without clothes and daily food. If one of you says to him, "Go, I wish you well; keep warm and well fed," but does nothing about his physical needs, what good is it? — Whoever sows sparingly will also reap sparingly, and whoever sows generously will also reap generously. Each man should give what he has decided in his heart to give, not reluctantly or under compulsion, for God loves a cheerful giver.

"So you also, when you have done everything you were told to do, should say, 'We are unworthy servants; we have only done our duty.'"

MARK 14:8. Luke 21:3. Mark 9:41. 2 Cor. 8:12. 1 John 3:18. James 2:15–16. 2 Cor. 9:6–7. Luke 17:10.

JULY 19

MORNING

For the Mighty One has done great things for me — holy is his name.

"WHO AMONG THE gods is like you, O LORD? Who is like you — majestic in holiness, awesome in glory, working wonders?"

Among the gods there is none like you, O Lord; no deeds can compare with yours. — "Who will not fear you, O Lord, and bring glory to your name? For you alone are holy." — "Hallowed be your name."

"Praise be to the Lord, the God of Israel, because he has come and has redeemed his people."

Who is this coming from Edom, from Bozrah, with his garments Stained crimson? Who is this, robed in splendor, striding forward in the greatness of his strength? "It is I, speaking in righteousness, mighty to save."

"I have bestowed strength on a warrior; I have exalted a young man from among the people. — Now to him who is able to do immeasurably more than all we ask or imagine, according to his power that is at work within us, to him be glory.

LUKE 1:49. Exod. 15:11. Ps. 86:8. Rev. 15:4. Matt. 6:9. Luke 1:68. Isa. 63:1. Ps. 89:19. Eph. 3:20–21.

EVENING

The dew of Hermon.

FOR THERE THE LORD bestows his blessing, even life forevermore. — "I will be like the dew to Israel; he will blossom like a lily. Like a cedar of Lebanon he will send down his roots."

Let my teaching fall like rain and my words descend like dew, like showers on new grass. — "As the rain and the snow come down from heaven, and do not return to it without watering the earth and making it bud and flourish, so that it yields seed for the sower and bread for the eater: so is my word that goes out from my mouth: It will not return to me empty, but will accomplish what I desire and achieve the purpose for which I sent it."

"To him God gives the Spirit without limit." ... From the fullness of his grace we have all received one blessing after another. — It is like precious oil poured on the head, running down on the beard, running down on Aaron's beard, down upon the collar of his robes.

PS. 133:3. Ps. 133:3. Hos. 14:5. Deut. 32:2. Isa. 55:10–11. John 3:34; 1:16. Ps. 133:2.

JULY 20

MORNING

"They are not of the world, even as I am not of it."

HE WAS DESPISED and rejected by men, a man of sorrows, and familiar with suffering. — "In this world you will have trouble. But take heart! I have overcome the world."

Such a high priest meets our need — one who is holy, blameless, pure, set apart from sinners. — So that you may become blameless and pure, children of God without fault in a crooked and depraved generation.

Jesus of Nazareth ... went around doing good and healing all who were under the power of the devil, because God was with him. — As we have opportunity, let us do good to all people, especially to those who belong to the family of believers.

The true light that gives light to every man was coming into the world. — "You are the light of the world. A city on a hill cannot be hidden." ... "Let your light shine before men, that they may see your good deeds and praise your Father in heaven."

JOHN 17:16. Isa. 53:3. John 16:33. Heb. 7:26. Phil. 2:15. Acts 10:38. Gal. 6:10. John 1:9. Matt. 5:14, 16.

EVENING

But the cheerful heart has a continual feast.

THE JOY OF the Lord is your strength. — For the kingdom of God is not a matter of eating and drinking, but of righteousness, peace and joy in the Holy Spirit. — Instead, be filled with the Spirit. Speak to one another with psalms, hymns and spiritual songs. Sing and make music in your heart to the Lord, always giving thanks to God the Father for everything, in the name of our Lord Jesus Christ.

Through Jesus, therefore, let us continually offer to God a sacrifice of praise — the fruit of lips that confess his name.

Though the fig tree does not bud and there are no grapes on the vines, though the olive crop fails and the fields produce no food, though there are no sheep in the pen and no cattle in the stalls, yet I will rejoice in the LORD, I will be joyful in God my Savior. — Sorrowful, yet always rejoicing. — We also rejoice in our sufferings.

PROV. 15:15. Neh. 8:10. Rom. 14:17. Eph. 5:18–20. Heb. 13:15. Hab. 3:17–18. 2 Cor. 6:10. Rom. 5:3.

July 21

Morning

What value is there in circumcision?

MUCH IN EVERY way!—Circumcise yourselves to the LORD, circumcise your hearts.—Then when their uncircumcised hearts are humbled and they pay for their sin, I will remember my covenant with Jacob and my covenant with Isaac and my covenant with Abraham, and I will remember the land. Christ has become a servant of the Jews on behalf of God's truth, to confirm the promises made to the patriarchs.

In him you were also circumcised, in the putting off of the sinful nature, not with a circumcision done by the hands of men but with the circumcision done by Christ.... When you were dead in your sins and in the uncircumcision of your sinful nature, God made you alive with Christ. He forgave us all our sins.

Put off your old self, which is being corrupted by its deceitful desires; to be made new in the attitude of your minds; and to put on the new self, created to be like God in true righteousness and holiness.

ROM. 3:1. Rom. 3:2. Jer. 4:4. Lev. 26:41–42. Rom. 15:8. Col 2:11, 13. Eph. 4:22–24.

Evening

The curtain of the temple was torn in two from top to bottom.

THE LORD JESUS, on the night he was betrayed, took bread, and when he had given thanks, he broke it and said, "This is my body, which is for you; do this in remembrance of me."—"This bread is my flesh, which I will give for the life of the world."

"Unless you eat the flesh of the Son of Man and drink his blood, you have no life in you. Whoever eats my flesh and drinks my blood has eternal life.... Whoever eats my flesh and drinks my blood remains in me, and I in him. Just as the living Father sent me and I live because of the Father, so the one who feeds on me will live because of me." ... "Does this offend you? What if you see the Son of Man ascend to where he was before! The Spirit gives life; the flesh counts for nothing."

A new and living way opened for us through the curtain, that is, his body.... Let us draw near to God.

MATT. 27:51. 1 Cor. 11:23–24. John 6:51, 53–54, 56–57, 61–63. Heb. 10:20, 22.

July 22

Morning

The death he died, he died to sin once for all; but the life he lives, he lives to God.

HE WAS NUMBERED with the transgressors. — Christ was sacrificed once to take away the sins of many people. — He himself bore our sins in his body on the tree, so that we might die to sins and live for righteousness; by his wounds you have been healed. — Because by one sacrifice he has made perfect forever those who are being made holy.

Because Jesus lives forever, he has a permanent priesthood. Therefore he is able to save completely those who come to God through him, because he always lives to intercede for them. — While we were still sinners, Christ died for us. Since we have now been justified by his blood, how much more shall we be saved from God's wrath through him!

Therefore, since Christ suffered in his body, arm yourselves also with the same attitude, because he who has suffered in his body is done with sin. As a result, he does not live the rest of his earthly life for evil human desires but rather for the will of God.

ROM. 6:10. Isa. 53:12. Heb. 9:28. 1 Peter 2:24. Heb. 10:14; 7:24–25. Rom. 5:8–9. 1 Peter 4:1–2.

Evening

Keep yourselves in God's love.

"REMAIN IN ME, and I will remain in you. No branch can bear fruit by itself, it must remain in the vine. Neither can you bear fruit unless you remain in me. I am the vine; you are the branches. If a man remains in me and I in him, he will bear much fruit; apart from me you can do nothing."

The fruit of the Spirit is love.

"This is to my Father's glory, that you bear much fruit, showing yourselves to be my disciples. As the Father has loved me, so have I loved you. Now remain in my love. If you obey my commands, you will remain in my love." — But if anyone obeys his word, God's love is truly made complete in him.

"My command is this: Love each other as I have loved you." — But God demonstrates his own love for us in this: While we were still sinners, Christ died for us. — God is love. Whoever lives in love lives in God, and God in him.

JUDE 21. John 15:4–5. Gal. 5:22. John 15:8–10. 1 John 2:5. John 15:12. Rom. 5:8. 1 John 4:16.

JULY 23

MORNING

The end will come.

"No one knows about that day or hour, not even the angels in heaven, nor the Son, but only the Father. Be on guard! Be alert! You do not know when that time will come.... What I say to you, I say to everyone: 'Watch!'"—The Lord is not slow in keeping his promise, as some understand slowness. He is patient with you, not wanting anyone to perish, but everyone to come to repentance—The Lord's coming is near.... The Judge is standing at the door!—"Yes, I am coming soon."

Since everything will be destroyed in this way, what kind of people ought you to be? You ought to live holy and godly lives.

The end of all things is near. Therefore be clear minded and self-controlled so that you can pray.—"Be dressed ready for service and keep your lamps burning, like men waiting for their master to return from a wedding banquet, so that when he comes and knocks they can immediately open the door for him."

1 COR. 15:24. Mark 13:32–33, 37. 2 Peter 3:9. James 5:8–9. Rev. 22:20. 2 Peter 3:11. 1 Peter 4:7. Luke 12:35–36.

EVENING

Brothers, pray for us.

Is any one of you sick? He should call the elders of the church to pray over him and anoint him with oil in the name of the Lord. And the prayer offered in faith will make the sick person well; the Lord will raise him up. If he has sinned, he will be forgiven. Therefore confess your sins to each other and pray for each other so that you may be healed. The prayer of a righteous man is powerful and effective. Elijah was a man just like us. He prayed earnestly that it would not rain, and it did not rain on the land for three and a half years. Again he prayed, and the heavens gave rain, and the earth produced its crops.

Pray in the Spirit on all occasions with all kinds of prayers and requests. With this in mind, be alert and always keep on praying for all the saints.

I remember you in my prayers at all times.—Always wrestling in prayer for you, that you may stand firm in all the will of God.

1 THESS. 5:25. James 5:14–18. Eph. 6:18. Rom. 1:9. Col. 4:12.

JULY 24

MORNING

Patient in affliction.

"HE IS THE LORD; let him do what is good in his eyes." — "Though I were innocent, I could not answer him; I could only plead with my Judge for mercy." ...
"The LORD gave and the LORD has taken away; may the name of the LORD be
praised." ... "Shall we accept good from God, and not trouble?"

Jesus wept. — A man of sorrows, and familiar with suffering.... Surely he
took up our infirmities and carried our sorrows.

"The Lord disciplines those he loves, and he punishes everyone he accepts as a
son." ... No discipline seems pleasant at the time, but painful. Later on, however,
it produces a harvest of righteousness and peace for those who have been trained
by it. — Strengthened with all power according to his glorious might so that you
may have great endurance and patience — "In this world you will have trouble.
But take heart! I have overcome the world."

ROM. 12:12. 1 Sam. 3:18. Job 9:15; 1:21; 2:10. John 11:35. Isa. 53:3–4. Heb. 12:6, 11.
Col. 1:11. John 16:33.

EVENING

He did not waver through unbelief regarding the promise of God.

"HAVE FAITH IN God," Jesus answered. "I tell you the truth, if anyone says to this
mountian, 'Go, throw yourself into the sea,' and does not doubt in his heart but
believes that what he says will happen, it will be done for him. Therefore I tell
you, whatever you ask for in prayer, believe that you have received it, and it will be
yours." — Without faith it is impossible to please God, because anyone who comes
to him must believe that he exists and that he rewards those who earnestly seek him.

He who had received the promises was about to sacrifice his one and only son,
even though God had said to him, "It is through Isaac that your offspring will
be reckoned." Abraham reasoned that God could raise the dead. — Being fully
persuaded that God had power to do what he had promised.

"Is anything too hard for the Lord?" — "With God all things are possible." — "Increase our faith!"

ROM. 4:20. Mark 11:22–24. Heb. 11:6, 17–19. Rom. 4:21. Gen. 18:14. Matt. 19:26.
Luke 17:5.

JULY 25

MORNING

We know that we have passed from death to life.

"WHOEVER HEARS MY word and believes him who sent me has eternal life and will not be condemned; he has crossed over from death to life." — He who has the Son has life; he who does not have the Son of God does not have life.

Now it is God who makes both us and you stand firm in Christ. He anointed us, set his seal of ownership on us, and put his Spirit in our hearts. — This then is how we know that we belong to the truth, and how we set our hearts at rest in his presence.... Dear friends, if our hearts do not condemn us, we have confidence before God.... We know that we are children of God, and that the whole world is under the control of the evil one.

You were dead in your transgressions and sins.... Raised up with Christ. — For he has rescued us from the dominion of darkness and brought us into the kingdom of the Son he loves.

1 JOHN 3:14. John 5:24. 1 John 5:12. 2 Cor. 1:21 – 22. 1 John 3:19, 21; 5:19. Eph. 2:1, 5. Col. 1:13.

EVENING

You have made known to me the path of life.

"THIS IS WHAT the LORD says: See, I am setting before you the way of life and the way of death." — I will teach you the way that is good and right. — "I am the way and the truth and the life. No one comes to the Father except through me." — "Come, follow me."

There is a way that seems right to a man, but in the end it leads to death. — "Wide is the gate and broad is the road that leads to destruction, and many enter through it. But small is the gate and narrow the road that leads to life, and only a few find it."

And a highway will be there; it will be called the Way of Holiness. The unclean will not journey on it; it will be for those who walk in that Way; wicked fools will not go about on it. — Let us acknowledge the LORD; let us press on to acknowledge him.

"In my Father's house are many rooms; if it were not so, I would have told you. I am going there to prepare a place for you."

PS. 16:11. Jer. 21:8. 1 Sam. 12:23. John 14:6. Matt. 4:19. Prov. 14:12. Matt. 7:13 – 14. Isa. 35:8. Hos. 6:3. John 14:2.

JULY 26

MORNING

By faith Abraham, when called to go to a place he would
later receive as his inheritance, obeyed.

HE CHOSE OUR inheritance for us. — He guarded him as the apple of his eye, like an eagle that stirs up its nest and hovers over its young, that spreads its wings to catch them and carries them on its pinions. The LORD alone led him; no foreign god was with him.

"I am the LORD your God, who teaches you what is best for you, who directs you in the way you should go." — Who is a teacher like him?

We live by faith, not by sight. — Here we do not have an enduring city, but we are looking for the city that is to come. — Dear friends, I urge you, as aliens and strangers in the world, to abstain from sinful desires, which war against your soul. — Get up, go away! For this is not your resting place, because it is defiled, it is ruined, beyond all remedy.

HEB. 11:8. Ps. 47:4. Deut. 32:10–12. Isa. 48:17. Job 36:22. 2 Cor. 5:7. Heb. 13:14.
1 Peter 2:11. Mic. 2:10.

EVENING

Rejoice in the LORD, you who are righteous, and praise his holy name.

IF EVEN THE heavens are not pure in his eyes, how much less man, who is vile and corrupt, who drinks up evil like water!... "The stars are not pure in his eyes, how much less man, who is but a maggot—a son of man, who is only a worm!"

"Who among the gods is like you, O LORD? Who is like you—majestic in holiness?" — "Holy, holy, holy is the LORD Almighty."

But just as he who called you is holy, so be holy in all you do; for it is written: "Be holy, because I am holy." — Share in his holiness.

God's temple is sacred, and you are that temple. — What kind of people ought you to be? You ought to live holy and godly lives, ... spotless and blameless.

Do not let any unwholesome talk come out of your mouths, but only what is helpful for building others up according to their needs.... And do not grieve the Holy Spirit of God, with whom you were sealed for the day of redemption.

PS. 97:12. Job 15:15–16; 25:5–6. Exod. 15:11. Isa. 6:3. 1 Peter 1:15–16. Heb. 12:10.
1 Cor. 3:17. 2 Peter 3:11, 14. Eph. 4:29–30.

JULY 27

MORNING

Christ, who is the image of God.

THE GLORY OF the LORD will be revealed, and all mankind together will see it. — No one has ever seen God, but God the only Son, who is at the Father's side, has made him known.... The Word became flesh and lived for a while among us. We have seen his glory, the glory of the one and only Son, who came from the Father, full of grace and truth.... "Anyone who has seen me has seen the Father." — The Son is the radiance of God's glory and the exact representation of his being. — He appeared in a body.

In whom we have redemption, the forgiveness of sins. He is the image of the invisible God, the firstborn over all creation. — For those God foreknew he also predestined to be conformed to the likeness of his Son, that he might be the firstborn among many brothers.

And just as we have borne the likeness of the earthly man, so shall we bear the likeness of the man from heaven.

2 COR 4:4. Isa. 40:5. John 1:18, 14; 14:9. Heb. 1:3. 1 Tim. 3:16. Col. 1:14–15. Rom. 8:29. 1 Cor. 15:49.

EVENING

You armed me with strength for battle.

WHEN I AM weak, then I am strong.

Then Asa called to the LORD his God and said, "LORD, there is no one like you to help the powerless against the mighty. Help us, O LORD our God, for we rely on you, and in your name we have come against this vast army. O LORD, you are our God; do not let man prevail against you." ... Jehosaphat cried out, and the LORD helped him.

It is better to take refuge in the LORD than to trust in man. It is better to take refuge in the LORD than to trust in princes.

No king is saved by the size of his army; no warrior escapes by his great strength. A horse is a vain hope for deliverance; despite all its great strength it cannot save.

For our struggle is not against flesh and blood, but against the rulers, against the authorities, against the powers of this dark world and against the spiritual forces of evil in the heavenly realms. Therefore put on the full armor of God.

PS. 18:39. 2 Cor. 12:10. 2 Chron. 14:11; 18:31. Pss. 118:8–9; 33:16–17. Eph. 6:12–13.

JULY 28

MORNING

Live a life of love.

"A NEW COMMANDMENT I give you: Love one another. As I have loved you, so you must love one another." — Above all, love each other deeply, because love covers over a multitude of sins. — Love covers over all wrongs.

"And when you stand praying, if you hold anything against anyone, forgive him, so that your Father in heaven may forgive you your sins." — "But love your enemies, do good to them, and lend to them without expecting to get anything back." — Do not gloat when your enemy falls; when he stumbles, do not let your heart rejoice.

Do not repay evil with evil or insult with insult, but with blessing, because to this you were called so that you may inherit a blessing. — If it is possible, as far as it depends on you, live at peace with everyone. — Be kind and compassionate to one another, forgiving each other, just as in Christ God forgave you. — Dear children, let us not love with words or tongue but with actions and in truth.

EPH. 5:2. John 13:34. 1 Peter 4:8. Prov. 10:12. Mark 11:25. Luke 6:35. Prov. 24:17. 1 Peter 3:9. Rom. 12:18. Eph. 4:32. 1 John 3:18.

EVENING

Present your requests to God.

"ABBA, FATHER," he said, "everything is possible for you. Take this cup from me. Yet not what I will, but what you will." — There was given me a thorn in my flesh, a messenger of Satan, to torment me. Three times I pleaded with the Lord to take it away from me. But he said to me, "My grace is sufficient for you, for my power is made perfect in weakness." Therefore I will boast all the more gladly about my weaknesses.

I pour out my complaint before him; before him I tell my trouble. — In bitterness of soul Hannah wept much and prayed to the LORD. And she made a vow, saying, "O LORD Almighty, if you will only look upon your servant's misery and remember me, and not forget your servant but give her a son, then I will give him to the LORD for all the days of his life." ... The LORD remembered her.

We do not know what we ought to pray. — He chose our inheritance for us.

PHIL. 4:6. Mark 14:36. 2 Cor. 12:7–9. Ps. 142:2. 1 Sam. 1:10–11, 19. Rom. 8:26. Ps. 47:4.

JULY 29

MORNING

Oh, that you would rend the heavens and come down.

COME AWAY, MY lover, and be like a gazelle or like a young stag on the spice-laden mountains. — We ourselves, who have the firstfruits of the Spirit, groan inwardly as we wait eagerly for our adoption as sons, the redemption of our bodies. — Part your heavens, O LORD, and come down; touch the mountains, so that they smoke.

"This same Jesus, who has been taken from you into heaven, will come back in the same way you have seen him go into heaven." — He will appear a second time, not to bear sin, but to bring salvation to those who are waiting for him. — In that day they will say, "Surely this is our God; we trusted in him, and he saved us. This is the LORD, we trusted in him; let us rejoice and be glad in his salvation."

He who testifies to these things says, "Yes, I am coming soon." Amen. Come, Lord Jesus. — The blessed hope — the glorious appearing of our great God and Savior, Jesus Christ. — Our citizenship is in heaven.

ISA. 64:1. Song of Songs 8:14. Rom. 8:23. Ps. 144:5. Acts 1:11. Heb. 9:28. Isa. 25:9. Rev. 22:20. Titus 2:13. Phil. 3:20.

EVENING

You have given me the heritage of those who fear your name.

"NO WEAPON FORGED against you will prevail, and you will refute every tongue that accuses you. This is the heritage of the servants of the LORD, and this is their vindication from me," declares the LORD.

The angel of the LORD encamps around those who fear him, and he delivers them. Taste and see that the LORD is good; blessed is the man who takes refuge in him. Fear the LORD, you his saints, for those who fear him lack nothing. The lions may grow weak and hungry, but those who seek the LORD lack no good thing.... The boundary lines have fallen for me in pleasant places; surely I have a delightful inheritance.

But for you who revere my name, the sun of righteousness will rise with healing in its wings. And you will go out and leap like calves released from the stall. — He who did not spare his own Son, but gave him up for us all — how will he not also, along with him, graciously give us all things?

PS. 61:5. Isa. 54:17. Pss. 34:7–10; 16:6. Mal. 4:2. Rom. 8:32.

JULY 30

MORNING

Set your hearts on things above, where Christ is seated at the right hand of God.

GET WISDOM, GET understanding. — The wisdom that comes from heaven. — "The deep says, 'It is not in me'; the sea says, 'It is not with me.'" — We were therefore buried with him through baptism into death in order that, just as Christ was raised from the dead through the glory of the Father, we too may live a new life. If we have been united with him in his death, we will certainly also be united with him in his resurrection.

Let us throw off everything that hinders and the sin that so easily entangles, and let us run with perseverance the race marked out for us. — God ... made us alive with Christ.... God raised us up with Christ and seated us with him in the heavenly realms in Christ Jesus.

People who say such things show that they are looking for a country of their own. — Seek righteousness, seek humility, perhaps you will be sheltered on the day of the LORD's anger.

COL. 3:1. Prov. 4:5. James 3:17. Job 28:14. Rom. 6:4–5. Heb. 12:1. Eph. 2:4–6. Heb. 11:14. Zeph. 2:3.

EVENING

Nicodemus, who had gone to Jesus earlier.

PETER FOLLOWED HIM at a distance. — Many even among the leaders believed in him. But because of the Pharisees they would not confess their faith for fear they would be put out of the synagogue; for they loved praise from men more than praise from God. — Fear of man will prove to be a snare, but whoever trusts in the LORD is kept safe.

"Whoever comes to me I will never drive away." — A bruised reed he will not break, and a smoldering wick he will not snuff out. — "Faith as small as a mustard seed."

God did not give us a spirit of timidity, but a spirit of power, of love and of self-discipline. So do not be ashamed to testify about our Lord. — Dear children, continue in him, so that when he appears we may be confident and unashamed before him at his coming. — "Whoever acknowledges me before men, I will also acknowledge him before my Father in heaven."

JOHN 7:50. Matt. 26:58. John 12:42–43. Prov. 29:25. John 6:37. Isa. 42:3. Matt. 17:20. 2 Tim. 1:7–8. 1 John 2:28. Matt. 10:32.

July 31

Morning

Endure hardship with us like a good soldier of Christ Jesus.

"See, I have made him a witness to the peoples, a leader and commander of the peoples." — In bringing many sons to glory, it was fitting that God, for whom and through whom everything exists, should make the author of their salvation perfect through suffering. — "We must go through many hardships to enter the kingdom of God."

For our struggle is not against flesh and blood, but against the rulers, against the authorities, against the powers of this dark world and against the spiritual forces of evil in the heavenly realms. Therefore put on the full armor of God. — The weapons we fight with are not the weapons of the world. On the contrary, they have divine power to demolish strongholds.

The God of all grace, who called you to his eternal glory in Christ, after you have suffered a little while, will himself restore you and make you strong, firm and steadfast.

2 TIM. 2:3. Isa. 55:4. Heb. 2:10. Acts 14:22. Eph. 6:12 – 13. 2 Cor. 10:3 – 4. 1 Peter 5:10.

Evening

The unity of the Spirit.

There is one body and one Spirit.... For through him we both have access to the Father by one Spirit. Consequently, you are no longer foreigners and aliens, but fellow citizens with God's people and members of God's household, built on the foundation of the apostles and prophets, with Christ Jesus himself as the chief cornerstone. In him the whole building is joined together and rises to become a holy temple in the Lord. And in him you too are being built together to become a dwelling in which God lives by his Spirit.

How good and pleasant it is when brothers live together in unity! It is like precious oil poured on the head, running down on the beard, running down on Aaron's beard, down upon the collar of his robes.

Now that you have purified yourselves by obeying the truth so that you have sincere love for your brothers, love one another deeply, from the heart.

EPH. 4:3. Eph. 4:4; 2:18 – 22. Ps. 133:1 – 2. 1 Peter 1:22.

AUGUST 1

MORNING

The fruit of the Spirit is ... faithfulness.

BY GRACE YOU have been saved, through faith—and this not from yourselves, it is a gift of God.—Without faith it is impossible to please God.—"Whoever believes in him is not condemned, but whoever does not believe stands condemned already because he has not believed in the name of God's one and only Son."—"I do believe; help me overcome my unbelief!"

If anyone obeys his word, God's love is truly made complete in him.—Faith expresses itself through love.—Faith without deeds is useless.

We live by faith, not by sight.—I have been crucified with Christ and I no longer live, but Christ lives in me. The life I live in the body, I live by faith in the Son of God, who loved me and gave himself for me.—Though you have not seen him, you love him; and even though you do not see him now, you believe in him and are filled with an inexpressible and glorious joy, for you are receiving the goal of your faith, the salvation of your souls.

GAL. 5:22. Eph. 2:8. Heb. 11:6. John 3:18. Mark 9:24. 1 John 2:5. Gal. 5:6. James 2:20. 2 Cor. 5:7. Gal. 2:20. 1 Peter 1:8–9.

EVENING

The Lord is full of compassion and mercy.

AS A FATHER has compassion on his children, so the LORD has compassion on those who fear him.—The LORD is gracious and compassionate.... He remembers his covenant forever.

He who watches over you will not slumber, indeed, he who watches over Israel will neither slumber nor sleep.—Like an eagle that stirs up its nest and hovers over its young, that spreads its wings to catch them and carries them on its pinions. The LORD alone led him; no foreign god was with him.

His compassions never fail. They are new every morning; great is your faithfulness.

When Jesus landed and saw a large crowd, he had compassion on them and healed their sick.

"The very hairs of your head are all numbered." ... "Are not two sparrows sold for a penny? Yet not one of them will fall to the ground apart from the will of your Father." ... "So don't be afraid; you are worth more than many sparrows."

JAMES 5:11. Pss. 103:13; 111:4–5; 121:3–4. Deut. 32:11–12. Lam. 3:22–23. Matt. 14:14; 10:30, 29, 31.

August 2

Morning

The Lamb that was slain from the creation of the world.

"The animals you choose must be year-old males without defect.... All the people of the community of Israel must slaughter them at twilight. Then they are to take some of the blood and put it on the sides and tops of the doorframes of the houses where they eat the lambs.... When I see the blood, I will pass over you." — The sprinkled blood. — For Christ, our Passover lamb, has been sacrificed. — "This man was handed over to you by God's set purpose and foreknowledge." — This grace was given us in Christ Jesus before the beginning of time.

In him we have redemption through his blood, the forgiveness of sins.

Therefore, since Christ suffered in his body, arm yourselves also with the same attitude, because he who has suffered in his body is done with sin. As a result, he does not live the rest of his earthly life for evil human desires, but rather for the will of God.

REV. 13:8. Exod. 12:5–7, 13. Heb. 12:24. 1 Cor. 5:7. Acts 2:23. 2 Tim. 1:9. Eph. 1:7. 1 Peter 4:1–2.

Evening

"I have trodden the winepress alone."

"Who among the gods is like you, O Lord? Who is like you — majestic in holiness, awesome in glory, working wonders?" — He saw that there was no one, and he was appalled that there was no one to intercede; so his own arm worked salvation for him, and his own righteousness sustained him. — He himself bore our sins in his body on the tree. — Becoming a curse for us.

Sing to the Lord a new song, for he has done marvelous things; his right hand and his holy arm have worked salvation for him. — Having disarmed the powers and authorities, he made a public spectacle of them, triumphing over them by the cross. — After the suffering of his soul, he will see the light of life and be satisfied; by his knowledge my righteous servant will justify many, and he will bear their iniquities.

March on, my soul; be strong! — We are more than conquerors through him who loved us. — They overcame him by the blood of the Lamb and by the word of their testimony.

ISA. 63:3. Exod. 15:11. Isa. 59:16. 1 Peter 2:24. Gal. 3:13. Ps. 98:1. Col. 2:15. Isa. 53:11. Judg. 5:21. Rom. 8:37. Rev. 12:11.

AUGUST 3

MORNING

His mercy extends to those who fear him.

HOW GREAT IS your goodness, which you have stored up for those who fear you, which you bestow in the sight of men on those who take refuge in you. In the shelter of your presence you hide them from the intrigues of men; in your dwelling you keep them safe from the strife of tongues.

Since you call on a Father who judges each man's work impartially, live your lives as strangers here in reverent fear. — The LORD is near to all who call on him, to all who call on him in truth. He fulfills the desires of those who fear him; he hears their cry and saves them.

"Because your heart was responsive and you humbled yourself before the LORD, . . . and because you tore your robes and wept in my presence, I have heard you, declares the LORD." — "This is the one I esteem: he who is humble and contrite in spirit, and trembles at my word." — The LORD is close to the brokenhearted and saves those who are crushed in spirit.

LUKE 1:50. Ps. 31:19–20. 1 Peter 1:17. Ps. 145:18–19. 2 Kings 22:19. Isa. 66:2. Ps. 34:18.

EVENING

"Those who honor me I will honor."

"WHOEVER ACKNOWLEDGES ME before men, I will also acknowledge him before my Father in heaven."

"Anyone who loves his father or mother more than me is not worthy of me; anyone who loves his son or daughter more than me is not worthy of me; and anyone who does not take his cross and follow me is not worthy of me. Whoever finds his life will lose it, and whoever loses his life for my sake will find it."

Blessed is the man who perseveres under trial, because when he has stood the test, he will receive the crown of life that God has promised to those who love him.

"Do not be afraid of what you are about to suffer. . . . Be faithful, even to the point of death, and I will give you the crown of life."

For our light and momentary troubles are achieving for us an eternal glory that far outweighs them all. — Praise, glory and honor when Jesus Christ is revealed.

1 SAM. 2:30. Matt. 10:32, 37–39. James 1:12. Rev. 2:10. 2 Cor. 4:17. 1 Peter 1:7.

AUGUST 4

MORNING

"It is finished." With that, he bowed his head and gave up his spirit.

JESUS, THE AUTHOR and perfecter of our faith. — "I have brought you glory on earth by completing the work you gave me to do." — We have been made holy through the sacrifice of the body of Jesus Christ once for all. Day after day every priest stands and performs his religious duties; again and again he offers the same sacrifices, which can never take away sins. But when this priest had offered for all time one sacrifice for sins, he sat down at the right hand of God. Since that time he waits for his enemies to be made his footstool, because by one sacrifice he has made perfect forever those who are being made holy. — Having canceled the written code, with its regulations, that was against us and that stood opposed to us; he took it away, nailing it to the cross.

"I lay down my life — only to take it up again. No one takes it from me, but I lay it down of my own accord. I have authority to lay it down and authority to take it up again." ... "Greater love has no man than this, that one lay down his life for his friends."

JOHN 19:30. Heb. 12:2. John 17:4. Heb. 10:10 – 14. Col. 2:14. John 10:17 – 18; 15:13.

EVENING

He reached down from on high and took hold of me; he drew
me out of deep waters.

HE LIFTED ME out of the slimy pit, out of the mud and mire; he set my feet on a rock and gave me a firm place to stand. — You were dead in your transgressions and sins, in which you used to live when you followed the ways of this world.... All of us also lived among them at one time, gratifying the cravings of our sinful nature.

Hear my cry, O God; listen to my prayer. From the ends of the earth I call to you, I call as my heart grows faint. — "From the depths of the grave I called for help, and you listened to my cry. You hurled me into the deep, into the very heart of the seas, and the currents swirled about me; all your waves and breakers swept over me." — We went through fire and water, but you brought us to a place of abundance.

"When you pass through the waters, I will be with you; and when you pass through the rivers, they will not sweep over you."

PS. 18:16. Ps. 40:2. Eph. 2:1 – 3. Ps. 61:1 – 2. Jonah 2:2 – 3. Ps. 66:12. Isa. 43:2.

AUGUST 5

MORNING

Live a new life.

JUST AS YOU used to offer the parts of your body in slavery to impurity and to ever-increasing wickedness, so now offer them in slavery to righteousness leading to holiness.... Therefore, I urge you, brothers, in view of God's mercy, to offer your bodies as living sacrifices, holy and pleasing to God—which is your spiritual worship. Do not conform any longer to the pattern of this world, but be transformed by the renewing of your mind.

If anyone is in Christ, he is a new creation; the old has gone, the new has come!—Neither circumcision nor uncircumcision means anything; what counts is a new creation. Peace and mercy to all who follow this rule.—So I tell you this, and insist on it in the Lord, that you must no longer live as the Gentiles do, in the futility of their thinking.... You, however, did not come to know Christ that way. Surely you heard of him and were taught in him in accordance with the truth that is in Jesus.

Put on a new self, created to be like God in true righteousness and holiness.

ROM. 6:4. Rom. 6:19; 12:1–2. 2 Cor. 5:17. Gal. 6:15–16. Eph. 4:17, 20–21, 24.

EVENING

"May your will be done."

I KNOW, O LORD, that a man's life is not his own; it is not for man to direct his steps.—"Not as I will, but as you will."—But I have stilled and quieted my soul; like a weaned child with its mother, like a weaned child is my soul within me.

We do not know what we ought to pray, but the Spirit himself intercedes for us with groans that words cannot express. And he who searches our hearts knows the mind of the Spirit, because the Spirit intercedes for the saints, in accordance with God's will.

"You don't know what you are asking."—He gave them what they asked for, but sent a wasting disease upon them.—These things occurred as examples, to keep us from setting our hearts on evil things as they did.

I would like you to be free from concern.—You will keep in perfect peace him whose mind is steadfast, because he trusts in you.

MATT. 26:42. Jer. 10:23. Matt. 26:39. Ps. 131:2. Rom. 8:26–27. Matt. 20:22. Ps. 106:15. 1 Cor. 10:6; 7:32. Isa. 26:3.

AUGUST 6

MORNING

The LORD disciplines those he loves.

"SEE NOW THAT I myself am He! There is no god besides me. I put to death and I bring to life, I have wounded and I will heal, and no one can deliver from my hand." — "I know the plans I have for you," declares the LORD, "plans to prosper you and not to harm you, plans to give you hope and a future." — "For my thoughts are not your thoughts, neither are your ways my ways," declares the LORD.

"Therefore I am now going to allure her, I will lead her into the desert and speak tenderly to her." — As a man disciplines his son, so the LORD your God disciplines you. — No discipline seems pleasant at the time, but painful. Later on, however, it produces a harvest of righteousness and peace for those who have been trained by it. — Humble yourselves, therefore, under God's mighty hand, that he may lift you in due time.

I know, O LORD, that your laws are righteous, and in faithfulness you have afflicted me.

PROV. 3:12. Deut. 32:39. Jer. 29:11. Isa. 55:8. Hos. 2:14. Deut. 8:5. Heb. 12:11. 1 Peter 5:6. Ps. 119:75.

EVENING

The earth is the LORD'S, and everything in it.

"SHE HAS NOT acknowledged that I was the one who gave her the grain, the new wine and oil, who lavished on her the silver and gold — which they used for Baal. Therefore I will take away my grain when it ripens, and my new wine when it is ready. I will take back my wool and my linen."

"Everything comes from you, and we have given you only what comes from your hand. We are aliens and strangers in your sight, as were all our forefathers. Our days on earth are like a shadow, without hope. O LORD our God, as for all this abundance, ... it comes from your hand, and all of it belongs to you." — For from him and through him and to him are all things. To him be the glory forever! Amen.

God ... richly provides us with everything for our enjoyment.... For everything God created is good, and nothing is to be rejected if it is received with thanksgiving, because it is consecrated by the word of God and prayer.

And my God will meet all your needs according to his glorious riches in Christ Jesus.

PS. 24:1. Hos. 2:8–9. 1 Chron. 29:14–16. Rom. 11:36. 1 Tim. 6:17; 4:4–5. Phil. 4:19.

AUGUST 7

MORNING

"The Counselor, the Holy Spirit, whom the Father will send in my name."

"IF YOU KNEW the gift of God and who it is that asks you for a drink, you would have asked him and he would have given you living water." — "If you then, though you are evil, know how to give good gifts to your children, how much more will your Father in heaven give the Holy Spirit to those who ask him!" — "I tell you the truth, my Father will give you whatever you ask in my name. Until now you have not asked for anything in my name. Ask and you will receive, and your joy will be complete." — You do not have, because you do not ask God.

"But when he, the Spirit of truth, comes, he will guide you into all truth. He will not speak on his own; he will speak only what he hears, and he will tell you what is yet to come. He will bring glory to me by taking from what is mine and making it known to you."

They rebelled and grieved his Holy Spirit. So he turned and became their enemy and he himself fought against them.

JOHN 14:26. John 4:10. Luke 11:13. John 16:23–24. James 4:2. John 16:13–14. Isa. 63:10.

EVENING

"What do you think about Christ?"

LIFT UP YOUR heads, O you gates; lift them up, you ancient doors, that the King of glory may come in. Who is he, this King of glory? The LORD Almighty — he is the King of glory. — On his robe and on his thigh he has this name written: King of Kings and Lord of Lords.

Now to you who believe, this stone is precious. But to those who do not believe, "The stone the builders rejected has become the capstone." — Christ crucified: a stumbling block to Jews and foolishness to Gentiles, but to those whom God has called, both Jews and Greeks, Christ the power of God and the wisdom of God.

I consider everything a loss compared to the surpassing greatness of knowing Christ Jesus my Lord, for whose sake I have lost all things. I consider them rubbish, that I may gain Christ. — "Lord, you know all things; you know that I love you."

MATT. 22:42. Ps. 24:9–10. Rev. 19:16. 1 Peter 2:7. 1 Cor. 1:23–24. Phil. 3:8. John 21:17.

AUGUST 8

MORNING

The path of the righteous is like the first gleam of dawn,
shining ever brighter till the full light of day.

NOT THAT I have already obtained all this, or have already been made perfect, but I press on to take hold of that for which Christ Jesus took hold of me. — Let us acknowledge the LORD; let us press on to acknowledge him.

Then the righteous will shine like the sun in the kingdom of their Father. — We, who with unveiled faces all reflect the Lord's glory, are being transformed into his likeness with ever-increasing glory, which comes from the Lord, who is the Spirit. — But when perfection comes, the imperfect disappears.... Now we see but a poor reflection; then we shall see face to face. Now I know in part; then I shall know fully, even as I am fully known. — Dear friends, now we are children of God, and what we will be has not yet been made known. But we know that when he appears, we shall be like him, for we shall see him as he is. Everyone who has this hope in him purifies himself, just as he is pure.

PROV. 4:18. Phil. 3:12. Hos. 6:3. Matt. 13:43. 2 Cor. 3:18. 1 Cor. 13:10, 12. 1 John 3:2–3.

EVENING

"Everyone who calls on the name of the Lord will be saved."

"WHOEVER COMES TO me I will never drive away." — "Jesus, remember me when you come into your kingdom." Jesus answered him, "I tell you the truth, today you will be with me in paradise." — "What do you want me to do for you?" he asked. "Lord," they answered, "we want our sight." Jesus had compassion on them and touched their eyes. Immediately they received their sight and followed him.

"If you then, though you are evil, know how to give good gifts to your children, how much more will your Father in heaven give the Holy Spirit to those who ask him!" — "And I will put my Spirit in you." ... "This is what the Sovereign LORD says: Once again I will yield to the plea."

This is the assurance we have in approaching God: that if we ask anything according to his will, he hears us. And if we know that he hears us — whatever we ask — we know that we have what we asked of him.

**ROM. 10:13. John 6:37. Luke 23:42–43. Matt. 20:32–34. Luke 11:13. Ezek. 36:27, 37.
1 John 5:14–15.**

AUGUST 9

MORNING

All beautiful you are, my darling; there is no flaw in you.

YOUR WHOLE HEAD is injured, your whole heart afflicted. From the sole of your foot to the top of your head there is no soundness—only wounds and welts and open sores, not cleansed or bandaged or soothed with oil.... All of us have become like one who is unclean, and all our righteous acts are like filthy rags.—I know that nothing good lives in me, that is, in my sinful nature.—You were washed, you were sanctified, you were justified in the name of the Lord Jesus Christ and by the Spirit of our God.—All glorious is the princess within.—"The splendor I had given you made your beauty perfect, declares the Sovereign LORD."

May the favor of the Lord our God rest upon us.

"These are they who have ... washed their robes and made them white in the blood of the Lamb."—To present her to himself as a radiant church, without stain or wrinkle or any other blemish, but holy and blameless.

SONG OF SONGS 4:7. Isa. 1:5–6; 64:6. Rom. 7:18. 1 Cor. 6:11. Ps. 45:13. Ezek. 16:14. Ps. 90:17. Rev. 7:14. Eph. 5:27.

EVENING

Broken cisterns that cannot hold water.

SHE ... GAVE BIRTH to Cain. She said, "With the help of the LORD I have brought forth a man." ... "Come, let us build ourselves a city, with a tower that reaches to the heavens." ... The LORD scattered them.

Lot chose for himself the whole plain of the Jordan.... [It] was well watered, like the garden of the LORD.... The men of Sodom were wicked and were sinning greatly against the LORD.

Then I applied myself to the understanding of wisdom, and also of madness and folly, but I learned that this, too, is a chasing after the wind. For with much wisdom comes much sorrow; the more knowledge, the more grief.... I undertook great projects: I built houses for myself and planted vineyards.... I amassed silver and gold for myself.... Yet when I surveyed all that my hands had done and what I had toiled to achieve, everything was meaningless.

"If a man is thirsty, let him come to me and drink."

JER. 2:13. Gen. 4:1; 11:4. 8; 13:11, 10, 13. Eccl. 1:17–18; 2:4, 8, 11, John 7:37.

AUGUST 10

MORNING

> *"My prayer is not that you take them out of the world but that you protect them from the evil one."*

BLAMELESS AND PURE, children of God without fault in a crooked and depraved generation, in which you shine like stars in the universe. — "You are the salt of the earth.... You are the light of the world.... Let your light shine before men, that they may see your good deeds and praise your Father in heaven."

"I have kept you from sinning against me."

The Lord is faithful, and he will strengthen and protect you from the evil one. — But out of reverence for God I did not act like that. — Who gave himself for our sins to rescue us from the present evil age, according to the will of our God and Father. — To him who is able to keep you from falling and to present you before his glorious presence without fault and with great joy — to the only God our Savior be glory, majesty, power and authority, through Jesus Christ our Lord, before all ages, now and forevermore! Amen.

JOHN 17:15. Phil. 2:15. Matt. 5:13 – 14, 16. Gen. 20:6. 2 Thess. 3:3. Neh. 5:15. Gal. 1:4. Jude 24 – 25.

EVENING

> *Whoever trusts in the LORD is kept safe.*

THE LORD IS exalted, for he dwells on high. — The LORD is exalted over all the nations, his glory above the heavens.... He raises the poor from the dust and lifts the needy from the ash heap; he seats them with princes.

God, who is rich in mercy, made us alive with Christ even when we were dead in transgressions — it is by grace you have been saved. And God raised us up with Christ and seated us with him in the heavenly realms in Christ Jesus.

He who did not spare his own Son, but gave him up for us all — how will he not also, along with him, graciously give us all things? .... For I am convinced that neither death nor life, neither angels nor demons, neither the present nor the future, nor any powers, neither height nor depth, nor anything else in all creation, will be able to separate us from the love of God that is in Christ Jesus our Lord.

PROV. 29:25. Isa. 33:5. Ps. 113:4, 7 – 8. Eph. 2:4 – 6. Rom. 8:32, 38 – 39.

AUGUST 11

MORNING

By his death he might destroy him who holds the power of death.

OUR SAVIOR, CHRIST JESUS, ... has destroyed death and has brought life and immortality to light through the gospel. — He will swallow up death forever. The Sovereign LORD will wipe away the tears from all faces; he will remove the disgrace of his people from all the earth. The LORD has spoken. When the perishable has been clothed with the imperishable, and the mortal with immortality, then the saying that is written will come true: "Death has been swallowed up in victory. Where, O death, is your victory? Where, O death, is your sting?" The sting of death is sin, and the power of sin is the law. But thanks be to God! He gives us the victory through our Lord Jesus Christ.

For God did not give us a spirit of timidity, but a spirit of power, of love and of self-discipline. — Even though I walk through the valley of the shadow of death, I will fear no evil, for you are with me; your rod and your staff, they comfort me.

HEB. 2:14. 2 Tim. 1:10. Isa. 25:8. 1 Cor. 15:54 – 57. 2 Tim. 1:7. Ps. 23:4.

EVENING

"What is the way to the abode of light?"

GOD IS LIGHT; in him there is no darkness at all. — "While I am in the world, I am the light of the world."

If we claim to have fellowship with him yet walk in the darkness, we lie and do not live by the truth. But if we walk in the light, as he is in the light, we have fellowship with one another, and the blood of Jesus, his Son, purifies us from every sin. — The Father ... has qualified you to share in the inheritance of the saints in the kingdom of light. For he has rescued us from the dominion of darkness and brought us into the kingdom of the Son he loves, in whom we have redemption, the forgiveness of sins.

You are all sons of the light and sons of the day. We do not belong to the night or to the darkness. — "You are the light of the world. A city on a hill cannot be hidden.... Let your light shine before men, that they may see your good deeds and praise your Father in heaven."

JOB 38:19. 1 John 1:5. John 9:5. 1 John 1:6 – 7. Col. 1:12 – 14. 1 Thess. 5:5. Matt. 5:14, 16.

AUGUST 12

MORNING

*For men are not cast off by the Lord forever. Though he
brings grief, he will show compassion.*

"DO NOT FEAR, . . . for I am with you," declares the LORD. — "For a brief moment
I abandoned you, but with deep compassion I will bring you back. In a surge of
anger I hid my face from you for a moment, but with everlasting kindness I will
have compassion on you," says the LORD your Redeemer.

"Though the mountains be shaken and the hills be removed, yet my unfailing love for you will not be shaken nor my covenant of peace be removed," says
the LORD, who has compassion on you. "O afflicted city, lashed by storms and
not comforted, I will build you with stones of turquoise, your foundations with
sapphires."

I will bear the LORD's wrath, until he pleads my case and establishes my right.
He will bring me out into the light; I will see his justice.

LAM. 3:31 – 32. Jer. 46:28. Isa. 54:7 – 8, 10 – 11. Mic. 7:9.

EVENING

God chose the weak things of the world to shame the strong.

AGAIN THE ISRAELITES cried out to the LORD, and he gave them a deliverer — Ehud, a left-handed man. . . . After Ehud came Shamgar son of Anath,
who struck down six hundred Philistines with an oxgoad. He too saved Israel.

The LORD turned to him and said, "Go in the strength you have. . . . Am I
not sending you?" "But Lord," Gideon asked, "how can I save Israel? My clan is
the weakest in Manasseh, and I am the least in my family."

The LORD said to Gideon, "You have too many men for me to deliver Mid-
ian into their hands. In order that Israel may not boast against me that her own
strength has saved her. . . ."

"Not by might nor by power, but by my Spirit," says the LORD Almighty. — Be
strong in the Lord and in his mighty power.

1 COR. 1:27. Judg. 3:15, 31; 6:14 – 15; 7:2. Zech. 4:6. Eph. 6:10.

AUGUST 13

MORNING

He has prepared a city for them.

"IF I GO and prepare a place for you, I will come back and take you to be with me that you also may be where I am." — An inheritance that can never perish, spoil or fade — kept in heaven for you. — Here we do not have an enduring city, but we are looking for the city that is to come.

"This same Jesus, who has been taken from you into heaven, will come back in the same way you have seen him go into heaven." — Be patient, then, brothers, until the Lord's coming. See how the farmer waits for the land to yield its valuable crop and how patient he is for the fall and spring rains. — For in just a very little while, "He who is coming will come and will not delay."

We who are still alive and are left will be caught up with them in the clouds to meet the Lord in the air. And so we will be with the Lord forever. Therefore encourage each other with these words.

HEB. 11:16. John 14:3. 1 Peter 1:4. Heb. 13:14. Acts 1:11. James 5:7 – 8. Heb. 10:37. 1 Thess. 4:17 – 18.

EVENING

He chose the lowly things of this world.

DO NOT BE deceived: Neither the sexually immoral nor idolaters nor adulterers nor male prostitutes nor homosexual offenders nor thieves nor the greedy nor drunkards nor slanderers nor swindlers will inherit the kingdom of God. And that is what some of you were. But you were washed, you were sanctified, you were justified in the name of the Lord Jesus Christ and by the Spirit of our God.

You were dead in your transgressions and sins, in which you used to live when you followed the ways of this world and of the ruler of the kingdom of the air, the spirit who is now at work in those who are disobedient. All of us also lived among them at one time, gratifying the cravings of our sinful nature and following its desires and thoughts.

He saved us ... because of his mercy. He saved us through the washing of rebirth and renewal by the Holy Spirit, whom he poured out on us generously through Jesus Christ our Savior.

"For my thoughts are not your thoughts, neither are your ways my ways," declares the LORD.

1 COR. 1:28. 1 Cor. 6:9 – 11. Eph. 2:1 – 3. Titus 3:5 – 6. Isa. 55:8.

AUGUST 14

MORNING

"The joy of the LORD is your strength."

SHOUT FOR JOY, O heavens; rejoice, O earth; burst into song, O mountains! For the LORD comforts his people and will have compassion on his afflicted ones.... "Surely God is my salvation; I will trust and not be afraid. The LORD, the LORD, is my strength and my song; he has become my salvation." — The LORD is my strength and my shield; my heart trusts in him, and I am helped. My heart leaps for joy and I will give thanks to him in song. — My soul rejoices in my God. For he has clothed me with garments of salvation and arrayed me in a robe of righteousness, as a bridegroom adorns his head like a priest, and as a bride adorns herself with her jewels.

I glory in Christ Jesus in my service to God.... We also rejoice in God through our Lord Jesus Christ, through whom we have now received reconciliation. — I will be joyful in God my Savior.

NEH. 8:10. Isa. 49:13; 12:2. Ps. 28:7. Isa. 61:10. Rom. 15:17; 5:11. Hab. 3:18.

EVENING

Has he not made with me an everlasting covenant,
arranged and secured in every part?

I KNOW WHOM I have believed, and am convinced that he is able to guard what I have entrusted to him for that day.

Praise be to the God and Father of our Lord Jesus Christ, who has blessed us in the heavenly realms with every spiritual blessing in Christ. For he chose us in him before the creation of the world to be holy and blameless in his sight. In love he predestined us to be adopted as his sons through Jesus Christ, in accordance with his pleasure and will.

We know that in all things God works for the good of those who love him, who have been called according to his purpose. For those God foreknew he also predestined to be conformed to the likeness of his Son, that he might be the firstborn among many brothers. And those he predestined, he also called; those he called, he also justified; those he justified, he also glorified.

2 SAM. 23:5. 2 Tim. 1:12. Eph. 1:3–5. Rom. 9:28–30.

AUGUST 15

MORNING

May the God of peace ... equip you with everything good for doing his will.

AIM FOR PERFECTION, listen to my appeal, be of one mind, live in peace. And the God of love and peace will be with you.

By grace you have been saved, through faith — and this not from yourselves, it is the gift of God — not by works, so that no one can boast. — Every good and perfect gift is from above, coming down from the Father of the heavenly lights, who does not change like shifting shadows.

Work out your salvation with fear and trembling, for it is God who works in you to will and to act according to his good purpose. Do everything without complaining or arguing, so that you may become blameless and pure. — Be transformed by the renewing of your mind. Then you will be able to test and approve what God's will is — his good, pleasing and perfect will. — Filled with the fruit of righteousness that comes through Jesus Christ — to the glory and praise of God.

Not that we are competent to claim anything for ourselves, but our competence comes from God.

HEB. 13:20 – 21. 2 Cor. 13:11. Eph. 2:8 – 9. James 1:17. Phil. 2:12 – 13. Rom. 12:2. Phil. 1:11. 2 Cor. 3:5.

EVENING

I am now going to allure her; I will lead her into the desert and speak tenderly to her.

"THEREFORE COME OUT from them and be separate, says the Lord. Touch no unclean thing, and I will receive you." "I will be a Father to you, and you will be my sons and daughters, says the Lord Almighty." ... Since we have these promises, dear friends, let us purify ourselves from everything that contaminates body and spirit, perfecting holiness out of reverence for God.

Jesus also suffered outside the city gate to make the people holy through his own blood. Let us, then, go to him outside the camp, bearing the disgrace he bore.

[Jesus] said, ... "Come with me by yourselves to a quiet place and get some rest." — The LORD is my shepherd, I shall lack nothing. He makes me lie down in green pastures, he leads me beside quiet waters, he restores my soul. He guides me in paths of righteousness for his name's sake.

HOS: 2:14. 2 Cor. 6:17 – 18; 7:1. Heb. 13:12 – 13. Mark 6:31. Ps. 23:1 – 3.

AUGUST 16

MORNING

"The house to be built for the LORD should be of great magnificence."

YOU ALSO, LIKE living stones, are being built into a spiritual house. — Don't you know that you yourselves are God's temple and that God's Spirit lives in you? If anyone destroys God's temple, God will destroy him; for God's temple is sacred, and you are that temple.... Do you not know that your body is a temple of the Holy Spirit, who is in you, whom you have received from God? You are not your own; you were bought with a price. Therefore honor God with your body. — What agreement is there between the temple of God and idols? For we are the temple of the living God. As God has said: "I will live with them and walk among them, and I will be their God, and they will be my people." — You are ... built on the foundation of the apostles and prophets, with Christ Jesus himself as the chief cornerstone. In him the whole building is joined together and rises to become a holy temple in the Lord. And in him you too are being built together to become a dwelling in which God lives.

1 CHRON. 22:5. 1 Peter 2:5. 1 Cor. 3:16–17; 6:19–20. 2 Cor. 6:16. Eph. 2:19–22.

EVENING

He is before all things.

"THE AMEN, THE faithful and true witness, the ruler of God's creation." — The beginning and the firstborn from among the dead, so that in everything he might have the supremacy.

"The LORD possessed me at the beginning of his work, before his deeds of old; I was appointed from eternity, from the beginning, before the world began.... I was there when he set the heavens in place, when he marked out the horizon on the face of the deep, when he established the clouds above and fixed securely the fountains of the deep, when he gave the sea its boundary so the waters would not overstep his command, and when he marked out the foundations of the earth. Then I was the craftsman at his side. I was filled with delight day after day, rejoicing always in his presence." — "Yes, and from ancient days I am he."

The Lamb that was slain from the creation of the world. — The author and perfecter of our faith, who for the joy set before him endured the cross, scorning its shame, and sat down at the right hand of the throne of God.

COL. 1:17. Rev. 3:14. Col 1:18. Prov. 8:22–23, 27–30. Isa. 43:13. Rev. 13:8. Heb. 12:2.

AUGUST 17

MORNING

Pray for each other so that you may be healed.

ABRAHAM SPOKE UP again: "Now that I have been so bold as to speak to the Lord, though I am nothing but dust and ashes, what if the number of the righteous is five less than fifty? Will you destroy the whole city because of five people?" "If I find forty-five there, " he said, "I will not destroy it." — "Father, forgive them, for they do not know what they are doing." — "Pray for those who persecute you."

"I pray for them. I am not praying for the world, but for those you have given me, for they are yours. . . . My prayer is not for them alone. I pray also for those who will believe in me through their message." — Carry each other's burdens, and in this way you will fulfill the law of Christ.

The prayer of a righteous man is powerful and effective. Elijah was a man just like us. He prayed earnestly that it would not rain, and it did not rain on the land for three and a half years.

JAMES 5:16. Gen. 18:27 – 28. Luke 23:34. Matt. 5:44. John 17:9, 20. Gal. 6:2.
James 5:16 – 17.

EVENING

As for man, his days are like grass, he flourishes like a flower
of the field; the wind blows over it and it is gone, and its
place remembers it no more.

TEACH US TO number our days aright, that we may gain a heart of wisdom. — "What good is it for a man to gain the whole world, yet forfeit his soul?"

"The grass withers and the flowers fall, because the breath of the LORD blows on them. Surely the people are grass. The grass withers and the flowers fall, but the word of our God stands forever."

The world and its desires pass away, but the man who does the will of God lives forever.

I tell you, now is the time of God's favor, now is the day of salvation. — Use the things of the world, as if not engrossed in them. For this world in its present form is passing away. — Let us consider how we may spur one another on toward love and good deeds. Let us not give up meeting together, as some are in the habit of doing, but let us encourage one another — and all the more as you see the Day approaching.

PS. 103:15 – 16. Ps. 90:12. Mark 8:36. Isa. 40:7 – 8. 1 John 2:17. 2 Cor. 6:2. 1 Cor. 7:31.
Heb. 10:24 – 25.

August 18

Morning

*For what god is there in heaven or on earth who can do the
deeds and mighty works you do?*

For who in the skies above can compare with the Lord? Who is like the Lord among the heavenly beings? ... O Lord God Almighty, who is like you? You are mighty, O Lord, and your faithfulness surrounds you. — Among the gods there is none like you, O Lord; no deeds can compare with yours. — "For the sake of your word and according to your will, you have done this great thing and made it known to your servant. How great you are, O Sovereign Lord! There is no one like you, and there is no God but you, as we have heard with our own ears."

"No eye has seen, no ear has heard, no mind has conceived what God has prepared for those who love him" — but God has revealed it to us by his Spirit. — The secret things belong to the Lord our God, but the things revealed belong to us and to our children.

DEUT. 3:24. Pss. 89:6, 8; 86:8. 2 Sam. 7:21–22. 1 Cor. 2:9–10. Deut. 29:29.

Evening

"Let him who boasts boast in the Lord."

Let not the wise man boast of his wisdom or the strong man boast of his strength or the rich man boast of his riches, but let him who boasts boast about this: that he understands and knows me, that I am the Lord."

I consider everything a loss compared to the surpassing greatness of knowing Christ Jesus my Lord, for whose sake I have lost all things. I consider them rubbish, that I may gain Christ. — I am not ashamed of the gospel, because it is the power of God for the salvation of everyone who believes.... Therefore I glory in Christ Jesus in my service to God.

Whom have I in heaven but you? And being with you, I desire nothing on earth. — "My heart rejoices in the Lord.... I delight in your deliverance."

Not to us, O Lord, not to us but to your name be the glory, because of your love and faithfulness.

1 COR. 1:31. Jer. 9:23–24. Phil. 3:8. Rom. 1:16; 15:17. Ps. 73:25. 1 Sam. 2:1. Ps. 115:1.

AUGUST 19

MORNING

But just as he who called you is holy, so be holy in all you do.

WE DEALT WITH each of you ... urging you to live lives worthy of God, who calls you into his kingdom and glory. — You may declare the praises of him who called you out of darkness into his wonderful light.

For you were once darkness, but now you are light in the Lord. Live as children of light (for the fruit of the light consists in all goodness, righteousness and truth) and find out what pleases the Lord. Have nothing to do with the fruitless deeds of darkness, but rather expose them. — Filled with the fruit of righteousness that comes through Jesus Christ — to the glory and praise of God.

"Let your light shine before men, that they may see your good deeds and praise your Father in heaven." — So whether you eat or drink or whatever you do, do it all for the glory of God.

1 PETER 1:15. 1 Thess. 2:11–12. 1 Peter 2:9. Eph. 5:8–11. Phil. 1:11. Matt. 5:16.
   1 Cor. 10:31.

EVENING

"Concerning things to come, do you question me about my children, or give me orders about the work of my hands?"

"I WILL GIVE you a new heart and put a new spirit in you. And I will put my Spirit in you and move you to follow my decrees and be careful to keep my laws." ... "I will yield to the plea of the house of Israel and do this for them."

"If two of you on earth agree about anything you ask for, it will be done for you by my Father in heaven. For where two or three come together in my name, there am I with them."

"Have faith in God," Jesus answered. "I tell you the truth, if anyone says to this mountain, 'Go, throw yourself into the sea,' and does not doubt in his heart but believes that what he says will happen, it will be done for him."

ISA. 45:11. Ezek. 36:26–27, 37. Matt. 18:19–20. Mark 11:22–23.

August 20

Morning

*God is not a man, that he should lie, nor a son of man, that
he should change his mind.*

THE FATHER OF the heavenly lights, who does not change like shifting shadows. — Jesus Christ is the same yesterday and today and forever. — His faithfulness will be your shield and rampart.

Because God wanted to make the unchanging nature of his purpose very clear to the heirs of what was promised, he confirmed it with an oath. God did this so that, by two unchangeable things in which it is impossible for God to lie, we who have fled to take hold of the hope offered to us may be greatly encouraged.

The faithful God, keeping his covenant of love to a thousand generations. — All the ways of the LORD are loving and faithful for those who keep the demands of his covenant.... Blessed is he whose help is the God of Jacob, whose hope is in the LORD his God, ... who remains faithful forever.

NUM. 23:19. James 1:17. Heb. 13:8. Ps. 91:4. Heb. 6:17–18. Deut. 7:9.
Pss. 25:10; 146:5–6.

Evening

If you falter in times of trouble, how small is your strength!

HE GIVES STRENGTH to the weary and increases the power of the weak. — "My grace is sufficient for you, for my power is made perfect in weakness." — "He will call upon me, and I will answer him; I will be with him in trouble, I will deliver him." — The eternal God is your refuge, and underneath are the everlasting arms. He will drive out your enemy before you.

I looked for sympathy, but there was none, for comforters, but I found none.

Every high priest is selected from among men and is appointed to represent them in matters related to God.... He is able to deal gently with those who are ignorant and are going astray, since he himself is subject to weakness.... So Christ also, ... although he was a son, he learned obedience from what he suffered and, once made perfect, he became the source of eternal salvation for all who obey him. — Surely he took up our infirmities and carried our sorrows.

PROV. 24:10. Isa. 40:29. 2 Cor. 12:9. Ps. 91:15. Deut. 33:27. Ps. 69:20.
Heb. 5:1–2, 5, 8–9. Isa. 53:4.

AUGUST 21

MORNING

You are my portion, O LORD.

ALL THINGS ARE yours,... and you are of Christ, and Christ is of God. — Our great God and Savior, Jesus Christ... gave himself for us. — God placed all things under his feet and appointed him to be head over everything for the church.... Christ loved the church and gave himself up for her ... to present her to himself as a radiant church, without stain or wrinkle or any other blemish, but holy and blameless.

My soul will boast in the LORD. — I delight greatly in the LORD; my soul rejoices in my God. For he has clothed me with garments of salvation and arrayed me in a robe of righteousness.

Whom have I in heaven but you? And being with you, I desire nothing on earth. My flesh and my heart may fail, but God is the strength of my heart and my portion forever.... I said to the LORD, "You are my lord." ... LORD, you have assigned me my portion and my cup; you have made my lot secure. The boundary lines have fallen for me in pleasant places; surely I have a delightful inheritance.

PS. 119:57. 1 Cor. 3:21, 23. Titus 2:13–14. Eph. 1:22; 5:25, 27. Ps. 34:2. Isa. 61:10. Pss. 73:25–26; 16:2, 5–6.

EVENING

There is a way that seems right to a man, but in the end it leads to death.

HE WHO TRUSTS in himself is a fool.

Your word is a lamp to my feet and a light for my path.... As for the deeds of men — by the word of your lips I have kept myself from the ways of the violent.

If a prophet, or one who foretells by dreams, appears among you and announces to you a miraculous sign or wonder, and if the sign or wonder of which he has spoken takes place, and he says, "Let us follow other gods" (gods you have not known) "and let us worship them," you must not listen to the words of that prophet or dreamer. The LORD your God is testing you to find out whether you love him with all your heart and with all your soul. It is the LORD your God you must follow, and him you must revere. Keep his commands and obey him; serve him and hold fast to him.

I will instruct you and teach you in the way you should go; I will counsel you and watch over you.

PROV. 14:12. Prov. 28:26. Pss. 119:105; 17:4. Deut. 13:1–4. Ps. 32:8.

AUGUST 22

MORNING

For none of us lives to himself alone and none of us dies to himself alone.

IF WE LIVE, we live to the Lord; and if we die, we die to the Lord. So, whether we live or die, we belong to the Lord. — Nobody should seek his own good, but the good of others.... You were bought at a price. Therefore honor God with your body.

Christ will be exalted in my body, whether by life or by death. For to me, to live is Christ and to die is gain. If I am to go on living in the body, this will mean fruitful labor for me. Yet what shall I choose? I do not know! I am torn between the two: I desire to depart and be with Christ, which is better by far.

For through the law I died to the law so that I might live for God. I have been crucified with Christ and I no longer live, but Christ lives in me. The life I live in the body, I live by faith in the Son of God, who loved me and gave himself for me.

ROM. 14:7. Rom. 14:8. 1 Cor. 10:24; 6:20. Phil. 1:20–23. Gal. 2:19–20.

EVENING

God gave Solomon wisdom and very great insight, and a breadth of understanding as measureless as the sand on the seashore.

"ONE GREATER THAN Solomon is here." — Prince of Peace.

Very rarely will anyone die for a righteous man, though for a good man someone might possibly dare to die. But God demonstrates his own love for us in this: While we were still sinners, Christ died for us. — Who, being in very nature God, did not consider equality with God something to be grasped, but made himself nothing, taking the very nature of a servant, being made in human likeness. And being found in appearance as a man, he humbled himself and became obedient to death — even death on a cross! — This love ... surpasses knowledge.

Christ the power of God and the wisdom of God. — In whom are hidden all the treasures of wisdom and knowledge. — The unsearchable riches of Christ. — It is because of him that you are in Christ Jesus, who has become for us wisdom from God — that is, our righteousness, holiness and redemption.

1 KINGS 4:29. Matt. 12:42. Isa. 9:6. Rom. 5:7–8. Phil. 2:6–8. Eph. 3:19. 1 Cor. 1:24. Col. 2:3. Eph. 3:8. 1 Cor. 1:30.

August 23

Morning

*"I have loved you with an everlasting love; I have drawn you
with loving-kindness."*

But we ought always to thank God for you, brothers loved by the Lord, because from the beginning God chose you to be saved through the sanctifying work of the Spirit and through belief in the truth. He called you to this through our gospel, that you might share in the glory of our Lord Jesus Christ. — God, who has saved us and called us to a holy life — not because of anything we have done but because of his own purpose and grace. This grace was given us in Christ Jesus before the beginning of time. — Your eyes saw my unformed body. All the days ordained for me were written in your book before one of them came to be.

"For God so loved the world that he gave his one and only Son, that whoever believes in him shall not perish but have eternal life."

This is love: not that we loved God, but that he loved us and sent his Son as an atoning sacrifice for our sins.

JER. 31:3. 2 Thess. 2:13–14. 2 Tim. 1:9. Ps. 139:16. John 3:16. 1 John 4:10.

Evening

"I will sustain you and I will rescue you."

But now, this is what the Lord says — he who created you, O Jacob, he who formed you, O Israel: "Fear not, for I have redeemed you; I have called you by name; you are mine. When you pass through the waters, I will be with you; and when you pass through the rivers, they will not sweep over you." ... "Even to your old age and gray hairs I am he, I am he who will sustain you."

Like an eagle that stirs up its nest and hovers over its young, that spreads its wings to catch them and carries them on its pinions. The Lord alone led him; no foreign god was with him. — He lifted them up and carried mem all the days of old.

Jesus Christ is the same yesterday and today and forever. — For I am convinced that neither ... height nor depth, nor anything else in all creation, will be able to separate us from the love of God that is in Christ Jesus our Lord.

"Can a mother forget the baby at her breast and have no compassion on the child she has borne? Though she may forget, I will not forget you!"

**ISA. 46:4. Isa. 43:1–2; 46:4. Deut. 32:11–12. Isa. 63:9. Heb. 13:8. Rom. 8:38–39.
Isa. 49:15.**

AUGUST 24

MORNING

"I have indeed seen the misery of my people."

A MAN OF sorrows, and familiar with suffering. — One who has been tempted in every way, just as we are.

"He took up our infirmities and carried our diseases." — And Jesus, tired as he was from the journey, sat down by the well.

When Jesus saw her weeping, and the Jews who had come along with her also weeping, he was deeply moved in spirit and troubled.... Jesus wept. — Because he himself suffered when he was tempted, he is able to help those who are being tempted.

"The LORD looked down from his sanctuary on high, from heaven he viewed the earth, to hear the groans of the prisoners and release those condemned to death." — But he knows the way that I take; when he has tested me, I will come forth as gold. —

For whoever touches you touches the apple of his eye. — In all their distress he too was distressed, and the angel of his presence saved them.

EXOD. 3:7. Isa. 53:3. Heb. 4:15. Matt. 8:17. John 4:6; 11:33, 35. Heb. 2:18. Ps. 102:19 – 20. Job 23:10. Zech 2:8. Isa. 63:9.

EVENING

"As long as it is day, we must do the work of him who sent me."

THE SLUGGARD CRAVES and gets nothing, but the desires of the diligent are fully satisfied.... He who refreshes others will himself be refreshed.

"My food," said Jesus, "is to do the will of him who sent me and to finish his work. Do you not say, 'Four months more and then the harvest'? I tell you, open your eyes and look at the fields! They are ripe for harvest. Even now the reaper draws his wages, even now he harvests the crop for eternal life, so that the sower and the reaper may be glad together." — "The kingdom of heaven is like a land-owner who went out early in the morning to hire men to work in his vineyard. He agreed to pay them a denarius for the day and sent them into his vineyard."

Preach the Word; be prepared in season and out of season. — "Until I come back."

No, I worked harder than all of them — yet not I, but the grace of God that was with me.

JOHN 9:4. Prov. 13:4; 11:25. John 4:34 – 36. Matt. 20:1 – 2. 2 Tim. 4:2. Luke 19:13. 1 Cor. 15:10.

AUGUST 25

MORNING

*"Look to the rock from which you were cut and to the quarry
from which you were hewn."*

SURELY I HAVE been a sinner from birth. — "No one looked on you with pity.... You were thrown out into the open field, for on the day you were born you were despised. Then I passed by and saw you kicking about in your blood, and as you lay there in your blood I said to you, 'Live!' " — He lifted me out of the slimy pit, out of the mud and mire; he set my feet on a rock and gave me a firm place to stand. He put a new song in my mouth, a hymn of praise to our God.

You see, at just the right time, when we were still powerless, Christ died for the ungodly. Very rarely will anyone die for a righteous man, though for a good man someone might possibly dare to die. But God demonstrates his own love for us in this: While we were still sinners, Christ died for us. — God, who is rich in mercy, made us alive with Christ even when we were dead in transgressions — it is by grace you have been saved.

ISA. 51:1. Ps. 51:5. Ezek. 16:5 – 6. Ps. 40:2 – 3. Rom. 5:6 – 8. Eph. 2:4 – 5.

EVENING

I delight greatly in the LORD; my soul rejoices in my God.

I WILL EXTOL the LORD at all times; his praise will always be on my lips. My soul will boast in the LORD; let the afflicted hear and rejoice. Glorify the LORD with me; let us exalt his name together.... The LORD bestows favor and honor; no good thing does he withhold.... Praise the LORD, O my soul; all my inmost being, praise his holy name.

Is anyone happy? Let him sing songs of praise. — Be filled with the Spirit. Speak to one another with psalms, hymns and spiritual songs. Sing and make music in your heart to the Lord, always giving thanks to God the Father for everything. — Sing psalms, hymns and spiritual songs with gratitude in your hearts to God.

About midnight Paul and Silas were praying and singing hymns to God, and the other prisoners were listening to them. — Rejoice in the Lord always. I will say it again: Rejoice!

ISA. 61:10. Pss. 34:1 – 3; 84:11 – 12; 103:1. James 5:13. Eph. 5:18 – 20. Col. 3:16.
    Acts 16:25. Phil. 4:4.

AUGUST 26

MORNING

*"Make a plate of pure gold and engrave on it as on a seal:
Holy to the LORD."*

WITHOUT HOLINESS NO one will see the Lord. — "God is spirit, and his worshipers must worship in spirit and in truth." — All of us have become like one who is unclean, and all our righteous acts are like filthy rags. — "Among those who approach me I will show myself holy; in the sight of all the people I will be honored."

"This is the law of the temple: All the surrounding area on top of the mountain will be most holy." — Holiness adorns your house for endless days, O LORD.

"For them I sanctify myself, that they too may be truly sanctified." — Therefore, since we have a great high priest who has gone through the heavens, Jesus the Son of God, let us ... then approach the throne of grace with confidence, so that we may receive mercy and find grace to help us in our time of need.

EXOD. 28:36. Heb. 12:14. John 4:24. Isa. 64:6. Lev. 10:3. Ezek. 43:12. Ps. 93:5. John 17:19. Heb. 4:14, 16.

EVENING

My cup overflows.

TASTE AND SEE that the LORD is good; blessed is the man who takes refuge in him. Fear the LORD, you his saints, for those who fear him lack nothing. The lions may grow weak and hungry, but those who seek the LORD lack no good thing. — His compassions never fail. They are new every morning; great is your faithfulness.

LORD, you have assigned me my portion and my cup; you have made my lot secure. The boundary lines have fallen for me in pleasant places; surely I have a delightful inheritance. — Whether Paul or Apollos or Cephas or the world or life or death or the present or the future — all are yours. — Praise be to the God and Father of our Lord Jesus Christ, who has blessed us in the heavenly realms with every spiritual blessing in Christ.

I have learned to be content whatever the circumstances. — Godliness with contentment is great gain. — My God will meet all your needs according to his glorious riches in Christ Jesus.

PS. 23:5. Ps. 34:8–10. Lam. 3:22–23. Ps. 16:5–6. 1 Cor. 3:22. Eph. 1:3. Phil. 4:11. 1 Tim. 6:6. Phil. 4:19.

AUGUST 27

MORNING

Your word is a lamp to my feet and a light for my path.

BY THE WORD of your lips I have kept myself from the ways of the violent. My steps have held to your paths; my feet have not slipped. — When you walk, they will guide you; when you sleep, they will watch over you; when you awake, they will speak to you. For these commands are a lamp, this teaching is a light. — Whether you turn to the right or to the left, your ears will hear a voice behind you, saying, "This is the way; walk in it."

"I am the light of the world. Whoever follows me will never walk in darkness, but will have the light of life." — We have the word of the prophets made more certain, and you will do well to pay attention to it, as to a light shining in a dark place. — Now we see but a poor reflection; then we shall see face to face. Now I know in part; then I shall know fully, even as I am fully known.

PS. 119:105. Ps. 17:4–5. Prov. 6:22–23. Isa. 30:21. John 8:12. 2 Peter 1:19. 1 Cor. 13:12.

EVENING

"How can you sleep? Get up."

FOR THIS IS not your resting place, because it is defiled, it is ruined, beyond all remedy. — Set your minds on things above, not on earthly things. — Though your riches increase, do not set your heart on them. — Now devote your heart and soul to seeking the LORD your God.

"Why are you sleeping?" he asked them. "Get up and pray so that you will not fall into temptation." ... "Be careful, or your hearts will be weighed down with dissipation, drunkenness and the anxieties of life, and that day will close on you unexpectedly."

The bridegroom was a long time in coming, and they all became drowsy and fell asleep. — For in just a very little while, "He who is coming will come and will not delay." — The hour has come for you to wake up from your slumber, because our salvation is nearer now than when we first believed. — "Watch because you do not know when the owner of the house will come back—whether in the evening, or at midnight, or when the rooster crows, or at dawn. If he comes suddenly, do not let him find you sleeping."

JONAH 1:6. Mic. 2:10. Col. 3:2. Ps. 62:10. 1 Chron. 22:19. Luke 22:46; 21:34. Matt. 25:5. Heb. 10:37. Rom. 13:11. Mark 13:35–36.

AUGUST 28

MORNING

"For the accuser of our brothers, who accuses them before our
God day and night, has been hurled down."

"THEY OVERCAME HIM by the blood of the Lamb and by the word of their testimony." — Who will bring any charge against those whom God has chosen? It
is God who justifies. Who is he that condemns? Christ Jesus, who died — more
than that, who was raised to life — is at the right hand of God and is also interceding for us.

Having disarmed the powers and authorities, he made a public spectacle of
them. — So that by his death he might destroy him who holds the power of
death — that is, the devil — and free those who all their lives were held in slavery
by their fear of death. — In all these things we are more than conquerors through
him who loved us. — Put on the full armor of God so that you can take your
stand against the devil's schemes.... Take the helmet of salvation and the sword
of the Spirit, which is the word of God.

Thanks be to God! He gives us the victory through our Lord Jesus Christ.

REV. 12:10. Rev. 12:11. Rom. 8:33–34. Col. 2:15. Heb. 2:14–15. Rom. 8:37. Eph. 6:11,
17. 1 Cor. 15:57.

EVENING

The tree of life.

GOD HAS GIVEN us eternal life, and this life is in his Son. — "He gave his one
and only Son, that whoever believes in him shall not perish but have eternal life."
... "As the Father raises the dead and gives them life, even so the Son gives life
to whom he is pleased to give it.... As the Father has life in himself, so he has
granted the Son to have life in himself."

"To him who overcomes, I will give the right to eat from the tree of life, which
is in the paradise of God." ... On each side of the river stood the tree of life, bearing twelve crops of fruit, yielding its fruit every month. And the leaves of the tree
are for the healing of the nations.

Blessed is the man who finds wisdom, the man who gains understanding....
Long life is in her right hand.... She is a tree of life to those who embrace her, those
who lay hold of her will be blessed. — Christ Jesus ... has become for us wisdom.

GEN. 2:9. 1 John 5:11. John 3:16; 5:21, 26. Rev. 2:7; 22:2. Prov. 3:13, 16, 18. 1 Cor. 1:30.

August 29

Morning

Blessed is he who trusts in the LORD.

[ABRAHAM] DID NOT waver through unbelief regarding the promise of God, but was strengthened in his faith and gave glory to God, being fully persuaded that God had power to do what he had promised. — The men of Judah were victorious because they relied on the LORD, the God of their fathers.

God is our refuge and strength, an ever present help in trouble. Therefore we will not fear, though the earth give way and the mountains fall into the heart of the sea.... It is better to take refuge in the LORD than to trust in man. It is better to take refuge in the LORD than to trust in princes.... The LORD delights in the way of the man whose steps he has made firm; though he stumble, he will not fall, for the LORD upholds him with his hand.

Taste and see that the LORD is good; blessed is the man who takes refuge in him. Fear the LORD, you his saints, for those who fear him lack nothing.

PROV. 16:20. Rom. 4:20–21. 2 Chron. 13:18. Pss. 46:1–2; 118:8–9; 37:23–24; 34:8–9.

Evening

I will lie down and sleep in peace, for you alone, O LORD,
make me dwell in safety.

YOU WILL NOT fear the terror of night, nor the arrow that flies by day.... He will cover you with his feathers, and under his wings you will find refuge. — "As a hen gathers her chicks under her wings." — He will not let your foot slip — he who watches over you will not slumber; indeed, he who watches over Israel will neither slumber nor sleep. The LORD watches over you — the LORD is your shade at your right hand.

I long to dwell in your tent forever and take refuge in the shelter of your wings.... The darkness will not be dark to you; the night will shine like the day, for darkness is as light to you.

He who did not spare his own Son, but gave him up for us all — how will he not also, along with him, graciously give us all things? — You are of Christ, and Christ is of God. — I will trust and not be afraid.

PS. 4:8. Ps. 91:5, 4. Matt. 23:37. Pss. 121:3–5; 61:4; 139:12. Rom. 8:32. 1 Cor. 3:23.
Isa. 12:2.

AUGUST 30

MORNING

[The king] held out to her the gold scepter that was in his hand. So Esther approached and touched the tip of the scepter.

WHEN HE CRIES out to me, I will hear, for I am compassionate.

We know and rely on the love God has for us. God is love. Whoever lives in love lives in God, and God in him. Love is made complete among us so that we will have confidence on the day of judgment, because in this world we are like him. There is no fear in love. But perfect love drives out fear, because fear has to do with punishment. The man who fears is not made perfect in love. We love because he first loved us.

Let us draw near to God with a sincere heart in full assurance of faith, having our hearts sprinkled to cleanse us from a guilty conscience and having our bodies washed with pure water. — For through him we both have access to the Father by one Spirit.... In him and through faith in him we may approach God with freedom and confidence.

ESTH. 5:2. Exod. 22:27. 1 John 4:16 – 19. Heb. 10:22. Eph. 2:18; 3:12.

EVENING

They said to each other, "What is it?" For they did not know what it was.

BEYOND ALL QUESTION, the mystery of godliness is great: He appeared in a body. — "For the bread of God is he who comes down from heaven and gives life to the world."

"Your forefathers ate the manna in the desert, yet they died.... If a man eats of this bread, he will live forever.... This bread is my flesh, which I will give for the life of the world." ... "My flesh is real food and my blood is real drink."

The Israelites did as they were told; some gathered much, some little..... He who gathered much did not have too much, and he who gathered little did not have too little.... Each morning everyone gathered as much as he needed.

"So do not worry, saying, 'What shall we eat?' or 'What shall we drink?' or 'What shall we wear?' For the pagans run after all these things, and your heavenly Father knows that you need them. But seek first his kingdom and his righteousness, and all these things will be given to you as well."

EXOD. 16:15. 1 Tim. 3:16. John 6:33. 49, 51, 55. Exod. 16:17 – 18, 21. Matt. 6:31 – 33.

AUGUST 31

MORNING

The gift followed many trespasses and brought justification.

"THOUGH YOUR SINS are like scarlet, they shall be as white as snow; though they are red as crimson, they shall be like wool." ... "I, even I, am he who blots out your transgressions, for my own sake, and remembers your sins no more. Review the past for me, let us argue the matter together; state the case for your innocence." ... "Return to me, for I have redeemed you."

"God so loved the world that he gave his one and only Son, that whoever believes in him shall not perish but have eternal life." — But the gift is not like the trespass. For if the many died by the trespass of the one man, how much more did God's grace and the gift that came by the grace of the one man, Jesus Christ, overflow to the many! — And that is what some of you were. But you were washed, you were sanctified, you were justified in the name of the Lord Jesus Christ and by the Spirit of our God.

ROM. 5:16. Isa. 1:18; 43:25–26; 44:22. John 3:16. Rom. 5:15. 1 Cor. 6:11.

EVENING

"Put this money to work ... until I come back."

"IT'S LIKE A man going away: He leaves his house in charge of his servants, each with his assigned task, and tells the one at the door to keep watch." — "To one he gave five talents of money, to another two talents, and to another one talent, each according to his ability. Then he went on his journey."

"As long as it is day, we must do the work of him who sent me. Night is coming, when no one can work." — "Didn't you know I had to be in my Father's house?" — Leaving you an example, that you should follow in his steps.

Preach the Word; be prepared in season and out of season; correct, rebuke and encourage — with great patience and careful instruction. — His work will be shown for what it is, because the Day will bring it to light.... Therefore, my dear brothers, stand firm. Let nothing move you. Always give yourselves fully to the work of the Lord, because you know that your labor in the Lord is not in vain.

**LUKE 19:13. Mark 13:34. Matt. 25:15. John 9:4. Luke 2:49. 1 Peter 2:21. 2 Tim. 4:2.
1 Cor. 3:13; 15:58.**

SEPTEMBER 1

MORNING

The fruit of the Spirit is ... gentleness.

THE HUMBLE WILL rejoice in the LORD; the needy will rejoice in the Holy One of Israel. — "Unless you change and become like little children, you will never enter the kingdom of heaven. Therefore, whoever humbles himself like this child is the greatest in the kingdom of heaven." — The unfading beauty of a gentle and quiet spirit ... is of great worth in God's sight. — Love ... does not boast, it is not proud.

Pursue gentleness. — "Take my yoke upon you and learn from me, for I am gentle and humble in heart." — He was oppressed and afflicted, yet he did not open his mouth; he was led like a lamb to the slaughter, and as a sheep before her shearers is silent, so he did not open his mouth. — Christ suffered for you, leaving you an example, that you should follow in his steps. "He committed no sin, and no deceit was found in his mouth." When they hurled their insults at him, he did not retaliate. . . . Instead, he entrusted himself to him who judges justly.

GAL. 5:22. Isa. 29:19. Matt. 18:3–4. 1 Peter 3:4. 1 Cor. 13:4. 1 Tim. 6:11. Matt. 11:29. Isa. 53:7. 1 Peter 2:21–23.

EVENING

"If anyone would come after me, he must deny himself and take up his cross daily and follow me."

THROUGH GLORY AND dishonor, bad report and good report. — Everyone who wants to live a godly life in Christ Jesus will be persecuted. — The offense of the cross.

If I were still trying to please men, I would not be a servant of Christ. — If you are insulted because of the name of Christ, you are blessed, for the Spirit of glory and of God rests on you. If you suffer, it should not be as a murderer or thief or any other kind of criminal, or even as a meddler. However, if you suffer as a Christian, do not be ashamed, but praise God that you bear that name.

For it has been granted to you on behalf of Christ not only to believe on him, but also to suffer for him. — That one died for all, and therefore all died. And he died for all, that those who live should no longer live for themselves but for him who died for them and was raised again. — If we endure, we will also reign with him.

LUKE 9:23. 2 Cor. 6:8. 2 Tim. 3:12. Gal. 5:11; 1:10. 1 Peter 4:14–16. Phil. 1:29. 2 Cor. 5:14–15. 2 Tim. 2:12.

SEPTEMBER 2

MORNING

Wait for the LORD, be strong and take heart and wait for the LORD.

DO YOU NOT know? Have you not heard? The LORD is the everlasting God, the Creator of the ends of the earth. He will not grow tired or weary. He gives strength to the weary and increases the power of the weak.... "So do not fear, for I am with you; do not be dismayed, for I am your God. I will strengthen you and help you; I will uphold you with my righteous right hand." ... You have been a refuge for the poor, a refuge for the needy in his distress, a shelter from the storm and a shade from the heat: For the breath of the ruthless is like a storm driving against a wall.

The testing of your faith develops perseverance. Perseverance must finish its work so that you may be mature and complete, not lacking anything. — Do not throw away your confidence; it will be richly rewarded. You need to persevere so that when you have done the will of God, you will receive what he has promised.

PS. 27:14. Isa. 40:28 – 29; 41:10; 25:4. James 1:3 – 4. Heb. 10:35 – 36.

EVENING

He makes me lie down in green pastures.

BUT THE WICKED are like the tossing sea, which cannot rest. "There is no peace," says my God, "for the wicked."

"Come to me, all you who are weary and burdened, and I will give you rest." — Be still before the LORD. — Anyone who enters God's rest also rests from his own work, just as God did from his.

Do not be carried away by all kinds of strange teachings. It is good for our hearts to be strengthened by grace. — Then we will no longer be infants, tossed back and forth by the waves, and blown here and there by every wind of teaching and by the cunning and craftiness of men in their deceitful scheming. Instead, speaking the truth in love, we will in all things grow up into him who is the Head, that is, Christ.

I delight to sit in his shade, and his fruit is sweet to my taste. He has taken me to the banquet hall, and his banner over me is love.

PS. 23:2. Isa. 57:20 – 21. Matt. 11:28. Ps. 37:7. Heb. 4:10; 13:9. Eph. 4:14 – 15.
Song of Songs 2:3 – 4.

SEPTEMBER 3

MORNING

"Nor shall any yeast be seen anywhere within your borders."

To fear the Lord is to hate evil. — Hate what is evil. — Avoid every kind of evil. — See to it that no one misses the grace of God and that no bitter root grows up to cause trouble and defile many. If I had cherished sin in my heart, the Lord would not have listened.

Don't you know that a little yeast works through the whole batch of dough? Get rid of the old yeast that you may be a new batch without yeast—as you really are. For Christ, our Passover lamb, has been sacrificed. Therefore let us keep the Festival, not with the old yeast, the yeast of malice and wickedness, but with bread without yeast, the bread of sincerity and truth.... A man ought to examine himself before he eats of the bread and drinks of the cup.

"Everyone who confesses the name of the Lord must turn away from wickedness."

EXOD. 13:7. Prov. 8:13. Rom. 12:9. 1 Thess. 5:22. Heb. 12:15. Ps. 66:18.
1 Cor. 5:6–8; 11:28. 2 Tim. 2:19.

EVENING

"You will not surely die," the serpent said to the woman. "For God knows that when you eat of it your eyes will be opened, and you will be like God, knowing good and evil."

I am afraid that just as Eve was deceived by the serpent's cunning, your minds may somehow be led astray from your sincere and pure devotion to Christ.

Finally, be strong in the Lord and in his mighty power. Put on the full armor of God so that you can take your stand against the devil's schemes.... Therefore put on the full armor of God, so that when the day of evil comes, you may be able to stand your ground, and after you have done everything, to stand. Stand firm then, with the belt of truth buckled around your waist, with the breastplate of righteousness in place, and with your feet fitted with the readiness that comes from the gospel of peace. In addition to all this, take up the shield of faith, with which you can extinguish all the flaming arrows of the evil one. Take the helmet of salvation and the sword of the Spirit, which is the word of God. — In order that Satan might not outwit us. For we are not unaware of his schemes.

GEN. 3:4–5. 2 Cor. 11:3. Eph. 6:10–11, 13–17. 2 Cor. 2:11.

SEPTEMBER 4

MORNING

"Wait, my daughter."

"BE CAREFUL, KEEP calm and don't be afraid. Do not lose heart." — "Be still, and know that I am God." — "Did I not tell you that if you believed, you would see the glory of God?" — The arrogance of man will be brought low and the pride of men humbled; the LORD alone will be exalted in that day.

Mary ... sat at the Lord's feet listening to what he said. "Mary has chosen what is better, and it will not be taken away from her." — "In repentance and rest is your salvation, in quietness and trust is your strength." — When you are on your beds, search your hearts and be silent.

Be still before the LORD and wait patiently for him; do not fret when men succeed in their ways, when they carry out their wicked schemes.... He will have no fear of bad news; his heart is steadfast, trusting in the LORD. His heart is secure. — The one who trusts will never be dismayed.

RUTH 3:18. Isa. 7:4. Ps. 46:10. John 11:40. Isa. 2:17. Luke 10:39, 42. Isa. 30:15. Pss. 4:4; 37:7; 112:7 – 8. Isa. 28:16.

EVENING

"You do not realize now what I am doing, but later you will understand."

REMEMBER HOW THE LORD your God led you all the way in the desert these forty years, to humble you and to test you in order to know what was in your heart, whether or not you would keep his commands.

"Later I passed by, and when I looked at you and saw that you were old enough for love, I spread the corner of my garment over you and covered your nakedness. I gave you my solemn oath and entered into a covenant with you, declares the Sovereign LORD, and you became mine." — The Lord disciplines those he loves.

Dear friends, do not be surprised at the painful trial you are suffering, as though something strange were happening to you. But rejoice that you participate in the sufferings of Christ, so that you may be overjoyed when his glory is revealed. — For our light and momentary troubles are achieving for us an eternal glory that far outweighs them all. So we fix our eyes not on what is seen, but on what is unseen. For what is seen is temporary, but what is unseen is eternal.

JOHN 13:7. Deut. 8:2. Ezek. 16:8. Heb. 12:6. 1 Peter 4:12 – 13. 2 Cor. 4:17 – 18.

SEPTEMBER 5

MORNING

The body is a unit, though it is made up of many parts....
So it is with Christ.

HE IS THE head of the body, the church.—The head over everything for the church, which is his body, the fullness of him who fills everything in every way.... For we are members of his body.

A body you prepared for me.—Your eyes saw my unformed body. All the days ordained for me were written in your book before one of them came to be.

"They were yours; you gave them to me."—He chose us in him before the creation of the world.—For those God foreknew he also predestined to be conformed to the likeness of his Son.

Grow up into him who is the Head, that is, Christ. From him the whole body, joined and held together by every supporting ligament, grows and builds itself up in love.

1 COR. 12:12. Col. 1:18. Eph. 1:22–23; 5:30. Heb. 10:5. Ps. 139:16. John 17:6. Eph. 1:4. Rom. 8:29. Eph. 4:15–16.

EVENING

The spring of living water.

HOW PRICELESS IS your unfailing love! Both high and low among men find refuge in the shadow of your wings. They feast on the abundance of your house; you give them drink from your river of delights. For with you is the fountain of life.

Therefore this is what the Sovereign LORD says: "My servants will eat, but you will go hungry; my servants will drink, but you will go thirsty."—"But whoever drinks the water I give him will never thirst. Indeed, the water I give him will become in him a spring of water welling up to eternal life." ... By this he meant the Spirit, whom those who believed in him were later to receive.

"Come, all you who are thirsty, come to the waters."—The Spirit and the bride say, "Come!" And let him who hears say, "Come!" Whoever is thirsty, let him come; and whoever wishes, let him take the free gift of the water of life.

JER. 2:13. Ps. 36:7–9. Isa. 65:13. John 4:14; 7:39. Isa. 55:1. Rev. 22:17.

SEPTEMBER 6

MORNING

Let us lift up our hearts and our hands to God in heaven.

WHO IS LIKE the LORD our God, the One who sits enthroned on high, who stoops down to look on the heavens and the earth?... To you, O LORD, I lift up my soul.... I spread out my hands to you; my soul thirsts for you like a parched land. Answer me quickly, O LORD; my spirit faints with longing. Do not hide your face from me or I will be like those who go down to the pit. Let the morning bring me word of your unfailing love, for I have put my trust in you. Show me the way I should go, for to you I lift up my soul.

Because your love is better than life, my lips will glorify you. I will praise you as long as I live, and in your name I will lift up my hands.... Bring joy to your servant, for to you, O Lord, I lift up my soul. You are kind and forgiving, O Lord, abounding in love to all who call to you. — "And I will do whatever you ask in my name."

LAM. 3:41. Pss. 113:5 – 6; 25:1; 143:6 – 8; 63:3 – 4; 86:4 – 5. John 14:13.

EVENING

"Watchman, what is left of the night?"

THE HOUR HAS come for you to wake up from your slumber, because our salvation is nearer now than when we first believed. The night is nearly over; the day is almost here. So let us put aside the deeds of darkness and put on the armor of light.

"Now learn this lesson from the fig tree: As soon as its twigs get tender and its leaves come out, you know that summer is near. Even so, when you see all these things, you know that it is near, right at the door.... Heaven and earth will pass away, but my words will never pass away."

I wait for the LORD, my soul waits, and in his word I put my hope. My soul waits for the Lord more than watchmen wait for the morning, more than watchmen wait for the morning.

He who testifies to these things says, "Yes, I am coming soon." Amen. Come, Lord Jesus. — "Therefore keep watch, because you do not know the day or the hour."

ISA. 21:11. Rom. 13:11 – 12. Matt. 24:32 – 33, 35. Ps. 130:5 – 6. Rev. 22:20. Matt. 25:13.

SEPTEMBER 7

MORNING

Be joyful in hope.

THE HOPE THAT is stored up for you in heaven. — If only for this life we have hope in Christ, we are to be pitied more than all men. — "We must go through many hardships to enter the kingdom of God." — "Anyone who does not carry his cross and follow me cannot be my disciple." — No one would be unsettled by these trials. You know quite well that we were destined for them.

Rejoice in the Lord always. I will say it again: Rejoice! — The God of hope fill you with all joy and peace as you trust in him, so that you may overflow with hope by the power of the Holy Spirit. — Praise be to the God and Father of our Lord Jesus Christ! In his great mercy he has given us new birth into a living hope through the resurrection of Jesus Christ from the dead. . . . Though you have not seen him, you love him; and even though you do not see him now, you believe in him and are filled with an inexpressible and glorious joy. — Through whom we have gained access by faith into this grace in which we now stand. And we rejoice in the hope of the glory of God.

ROM. 12:12. Col. 1:5. 1 Cor. 15:19. Acts 14:22. Luke 14:27. 1 Thess. 3:3. Phil. 4:4. Rom. 15:13. 1 Peter 1:3, 8. Rom. 5:2.

EVENING

Yet I am poor and needy; may the Lord think of me.

"FOR I KNOW the plans I have for you," declares the LORD, "plans to prosper you and not to harm you." — "For my thoughts are not your thoughts, neither are your ways my ways," declares the LORD. "As the heavens are higher than the earth, so are my ways higher than your ways and my thoughts than your thoughts."

How precious to me are your thoughts, O God! How vast is the sum of them! Were I to count them, they would outnumber the grains of sand. When I awake, I am still with you. . . . O LORD, how profound your thoughts! . . . Many, O LORD my God, are the wonders you have done. The things you planned for us.

Not many were influential; not many were of noble birth. — Has not God chosen those who are poor in the eyes of the world to be rich in faith and to inherit the kingdom? — Having nothing, and yet possessing everything. — The unsearchable riches of Christ.

PS. 40:17. Jer. 29:11. Isa. 55:8–9. Pss. 139:17–18; 92:5; 40:5. 1 Cor. 1:26. James 2:5. 2 Cor. 6:10. Eph. 3:8.

SEPTEMBER 8

MORNING

"You have been weighed on the scales and found wanting."

THE LORD IS a God who knows, and by him deeds are weighed. — You are the ones who justify yourselves in the eyes of men, but God knows your hearts. — "The LORD does not look at the things man looks at. Man looks at the outward appearance, but the LORD looks at the heart." — Do not be deceived: God cannot be mocked. A man reaps what he sows. The one who sows to please his sinful nature, from that nature will reap destruction; the one who sows to please the Spirit, from the Spirit will reap eternal life.

"What good will it be for a man if he gains the whole world, yet forfeits his soul? Or what can a man give in exchange for his soul?" — Whatever was to my profit I now consider loss for the sake of Christ.

Surely you desire truth in the inner parts.... Though you probe my heart and examine me at night, though you test me, you will find nothing.

DAN. 5:27. 1 Sam. 2:3. Luke 16:15. 1 Sam. 16:7. Gal. 6:7 – 8. Matt. 16:26. Phil. 3:7. Pss. 51:6; 17:3.

EVENING

Christ, the firstfruits.

"UNLESS A KERNEL of wheat falls to the ground and dies, it remains only a single seed. But if it dies, it produces many seeds." — If the part of the dough offered as firstfruits is holy, then the whole batch is holy; if the root is holy, so are the branches. — But Christ has indeed been raised from the dead, the firstfruits of those who have fallen asleep. — If we have been united with him in his death, we will certainly also be united with him in his resurrection. — The Lord Jesus Christ, who, by the power that enables him to bring everything under his control, will transform our lowly bodies so that they will be like his glorious body.

The firstborn from among the dead. — If the Spirit of him who raised Jesus from the dead is living in you, he who raised Christ from the dead will also give life to your mortal bodies through his Spirit, who lives in you.

"I am the resurrection and the life. He who believes in me will live, even though he dies."

1 COR. 15:23. John 12:24. Rom. 11:16. 1 Cor. 15:20. Rom. 6:5. Phil. 3:20 – 21. Col. 1:18. Rom. 8:11. John 11:25.

SEPTEMBER 9

MORNING

He has filled the hungry with good things but has sent the
rich away empty.

"YOU SAY, 'I am rich; I have acquired wealth and do not need a thing.' But you do not realize that you are wretched, pitiful, poor, blind and naked. I counsel you to buy from me gold refined in the fire, so you can become rich; and white clothes to wear, so you can cover your shameful nakedness; and salve to put on your eyes, so you can see. Those whom I love I rebuke and discipline. So be earnest, and repent."

"Blessed are those who hunger and thirst for righteousness, for they will be filled." — "The poor and needy search for water, but there is none; their tongues are parched with thirst. But I the LORD will answer them; I, the God of Israel, will not forsake them." — "I am the LORD your God.... Open wide your mouth and I will fill it."

"Why spend money on what is not bread, and your labor on what does not satisfy? Listen, listen to me, and eat what is good, and your soul will delight in the richest of fare." — "I am the bread of life. He who comes to me will never go hungry, and he who believes in me will never be thirsty."

LUKE 1:53. Rev. 3:17 – 19. Matt. 5:6. Isa. 41:17. Ps. 81:10. Isa. 55:2. John 6:35.

EVENING

My feet had almost slipped; I had nearly lost my foothold.

WHEN I SAID, "My foot is slipping," your love, O LORD, supported me.

"Simon, Simon, Satan has asked to sift you as wheat. But I have prayed for you, Simon, that your faith may not fail." — For though a righteous man falls seven times, he rises again. — Though he stumble, he will not fall, for the LORD upholds him with his hand.

Do not gloat over me, my enemy! Though I have fallen, I will rise. Though I sit in darkness, the LORD will be my light. — From six calamities he will rescue you; in seven no harm will befall you.

But if anybody does sin, we have one who speaks to the Father in our defense — Jesus Christ, the Righteous One. — Therefore he is able to save completely those who come to God through him, because he always lives to intercede for them.

PS. 73:2. Ps. 94:18. Luke 22:31 – 32. Prov. 24:16. Ps. 37:24. Mic. 7:8. Job 5:19. 1 John 2:1. Heb. 7:25.

SEPTEMBER 10

MORNING

I will give them singleness of heart and action, so that they will always fear me for their own good and the good of their children after them.

I WILL GIVE you a new heart and put a new spirit in you. — Good and upright is the LORD; therefore he instructs sinners in his ways. He guides the humble in what is right and teaches them his way. All the ways of the LORD are loving and faithful for those who keep the demands of his covenant.

"That all of them may be one, Father, just as you are in me and I am in you. May they also be in us so that the world may believe that you have sent me."

I urge you to live a life worthy of the calling you have received. Be completely humble and gentle; be patient, bearing with one another in love. Make every effort to keep the unity of the Spirit through the bond of peace. There is one body and one Spirit — just as you were called to one hope when you were called — one Lord, one faith, one baptism; one God and Father of all, who is over all and through all and in all.

JER. 32:39. Ezek. 36:26. Ps. 25:8 – 10. John 17:21. Eph. 4:1 – 6.

EVENING

Those who hope in the LORD will renew their strength.

FOR WHEN I am weak, then I am strong. — My God has been my strength. — He said to me, "My grace is sufficient for you, for my power is made perfect in weakness." Therefore I will boast all the more gladly about my weaknesses, so that Christ's power may rest on me. — "Let them come to me for refuge."

Cast your cares on the LORD and he will sustain you. — "His strong arms stayed limber, because of the hand of the Mighty One of Jacob." ... "I will not let you go unless you bless me."

"You come against me with sword and spear and javelin, but I come against you in the name of the LORD Almighty, the God of the armies of Israel, whom you have defied." — Contend, O LORD, with those who contend with me; fight against those who fight against me. Take up shield and buckler; arise and come to my aid.

ISA. 40:31. 2 Cor. 12:10. Isa. 49:5. 2 Cor. 12:9. Isa. 27:5. Ps. 55:22. Gen. 49:24; 32:26.
1 Sam. 17:45. Ps. 35:1 – 2.

SEPTEMBER 11

MORNING

*Do not conform any longer to the pattern of this world, but
be transformed by the renewing of your mind.*

"Do not follow the crowd in doing wrong."—Don't you know that friendship
with the world is hatred toward God? Anyone who chooses to be a friend of the
world becomes an enemy of God.

For what do righteousness and wickedness have in common? Or what fellowship can light have with darkness? What harmony is there between Christ and
Belial? What does a believer have in common with an unbeliever? What agreement
is there between the temple of God and idols?—Do not love the world or anything
in the world. If anyone loves the world, the love of the Father is not in him.... The
world and its desires pass away, but the man who does the will of God lives forever.

In which you used to live when you followed the ways of this world and of the
ruler of the kingdom of the air, the spirit who is now at work in those who are
disobedient.... You, however, did not come to know Christ that way. Surely you
heard of him and were taught in him in accordance with the truth that is in Jesus.

ROM. 12:2. Exod. 23:2. James 4:4. 2 Cor. 6:14–16. 1 John 2:15, 17. Eph. 2:2; 4:20–21.

EVENING

Then man goes out to his work, to his labor until evening.

By the sweat of your brow you will eat your food until you return to the
ground.—We gave you this rule: "If a man will not work, he shall not
eat."—Make it your ambition to lead a quiet life, to mind your own business
and to work with your hands.

Whatever your hand finds to do, do it with all your might, for in the grave,
where you are going, there is neither working nor planning nor knowledge nor
wisdom.—"Night is coming, when no one can work."—Let us not become
weary in doing good, for at the proper time we will reap a harvest if we do not
give up.—Always give yourselves fully to the work of the Lord, because you
know that your labor in the Lord is not in vain.

There remains, then, a Sabbath-rest for the people of God.—"And you have
made them equal to us who have borne the burden of the work and the heat of
the day."

**PS. 104:23. Gen. 3:19. 2 Thess. 3:10. 1 Thess. 4:11. Eccl. 9:10. John 9:4. Gal. 6:9.
1 Cor. 15:58. Heb. 4:9. Matt. 20:12.**

SEPTEMBER 12

MORNING

"I have seen his ways, but I will heal him."

"I AM THE LORD who heals you." — O LORD, you have searched me and you know me. You know when I sit and when I rise; you perceive my thoughts from afar. You discern my going out and my lying down; you are familiar with all my ways.... You have set our iniquities before you, our secret sins in the light of your presence. — Everything is uncovered and laid bare before the eyes of him to whom we must give account.

"Come now, let us reason together," says the LORD. "Though your sins are like scarlet, they shall be as white as snow; though they are red as crimson, they shall be like wool." — "To be gracious to him and say, 'Spare him from going down to the pit; I have found a ransom for him.'" — But he was pierced for our transgressions, he was crushed for our iniquities; the punishment that brought us peace was upon him, and by his wounds we are healed.... He has sent me to bind up the brokenhearted.

"Your faith has healed you. Go in peace and be freed from your suffering."

ISA. 57:18. Exod. 15:26. Pss. 139:1–3; 90:8. Heb. 4:13. Isa. 1:18. Job 33:24. Isa. 53:5; 61:1. Mark 5:34.

EVENING

The LORD is with me; he is my helper.

MAY THE LORD answer you when you are in distress; may the name of the God of Jacob protect you. May he send you help from the sanctuary and grant you support from Zion.... We will shout for joy when you are victorious and will lift up our banners in the name of our God.... Some trust in chariots and some in horses, but we trust in the name of the LORD our God. They are brought to their knees and fall, but we rise up and stand firm.

For he will come like a pent-up flood that the breath of the LORD drives along. — No temptation has seized you except what is common to man. And God is faithful; he will not let you be tempted beyond what you can bear. But when you are tempted, he will also provide a way out so that you can stand up under it.

If God is for us, who can be against us? — The LORD is with me; I will not be afraid. — The God we serve is able to save us from it, and he will rescue us.

PS. 118:7; Ps. 20:1–2, 5, 7–8. Isa. 59:19. 1 Cor. 10:13. Rom. 8:31. Ps. 118:6. Dan. 3:17.

SEPTEMBER 13

MORNING

"If a man is thirsty, let him come to me and drink."

MY SOUL YEARNS, even faints for the courts of the LORD; my heart and my flesh cry out for the living God.... O God, you are my God, earnestly I seek you; my soul thirsts for you, my body longs for you, in a dry and weary land where there is no water. I have seen you in the sanctuary.

"Come, all you who are thirsty, come to the waters; and you who have no money, come, buy and eat! Come, buy wine and milk without money and without cost."—The Spirit and the bride say, "Come!" And let him who hears say, "Come!" Whoever is thirsty, let him come; and whoever wishes, let him take the free gift of the water of life.—"Whoever drinks the water I give him will never thirst. Indeed, the water I give him will become in him a spring of water welling up to eternal life."... "My blood is real drink."

Eat, O friends, and drink; drink your fill, O lovers.

JOHN 7:37. Pss. 84:2; 63:1–2. Isa. 55:1. Rev. 22:17. John 4:14; 6:55. Song of Songs 5:1.

EVENING

"You are the salt of the earth."

UNFADING BEAUTY.... For you have been born again, not of perishable seed, but of imperishable, through the living and enduring word of God.—"He who believes in me will live, even though he dies; and whoever lives and believes in me will never die."—"They are God's children, since they are children of the resurrection."—Immortal God.

If anyone does not have the Spirit of Christ, he does not belong to Christ. But if Christ is in you, your body is dead because of sin, yet your spirit is alive because of righteousness. And if the Spirit of him who raised Jesus from the dead is living in you, he who raised Christ from the dead will also give life to your mortal bodies through his Spirit, who lives in you.—The body that is sown is perishable, it is raised imperishable.

"Have salt in yourselves, and be at peace with each other."—Do not let any unwholesome talk come out of your mouths, but only what is helpful for building others up according to their needs, that it may benefit those who listen.

MATT. 5:13. 1 Peter 3:4; 1:23. John 11:25–26. Luke 20:36. Rom. 1:23; 8:9–11. 1 Cor. 15:42. Mark 9:50. Eph. 4:29.

SEPTEMBER 14

MORNING

"I, even I, am he who comforts you."

PRAISE BE TO the God and Father of our Lord Jesus Christ, the Father of compassion and the God of all comfort, who comforts us in all our troubles, so that we can comfort those in any trouble with the comfort we ourselves have received from God. — As a father has compassion on his children, so the LORD has compassion on those who fear him; for he knows how we are formed, he remembers that we are dust. — "As a mother comforts her child, so will I comfort you." — Cast all your anxiety on him because he cares for you.

You, O Lord, are a compassionate and gracious God, slow to anger, abounding in love and faithfulness.

"Another Counselor ... the Spirit of truth." — The Spirit helps us in our weakness. — "He will wipe every tear from their eyes. There will be no more death or mourning or crying or pain, for the old order of things has passed away."

ISA. 51:12. 2 Cor. 1:3–4. Ps. 103:13–14. Isa. 66:13. 1 Peter 5:7. Ps. 86:15. John 14:16–17. Rom. 8:26. Rev. 21:4.

EVENING

God ... has called you into fellowship with his Son.

FOR HE RECEIVED honor and glory from God the Father when the voice came to him from the Majestic Glory, saying, "This is my Son, whom I love, with him I am well pleased." — How great is the love the Father has lavished on us, that we should be called children of God!

Be imitators of God, therefore, as dearly loved children. — Now if we are children, then we are heirs — heirs of God and co-heirs with Christ. — The Son is the radiance of God's glory and the exact representation of his being. — "Let your light shine before men, that they may see your good deeds and praise your Father in heaven."

Jesus, the author and perfecter of our faith, who for the joy set before him endured the cross, scorning its shame. — "I say these things while I am still in the world, so that they may have the full measure of my joy within them." — For just as the sufferings of Christ flow over into our lives, so also through Christ our comfort overflows.

1 COR. 1:9. 2 Peter 1:17. 1 John 3:1. Eph. 5:1. Rom. 8:17. Heb. 1:3. Matt. 5:16. Heb. 12:2. John 17:13. 2 Cor. 1:5.

SEPTEMBER 15

MORNING

For sin shall not be your master, because you are not under law, but under grace.

WHAT THEN? SHALL we sin because we are not under law but under grace? By no means!... My brothers, you also died to the law through the body of Christ, that you might belong to another, to him who was raised from the dead, in order that we might bear fruit. — (I am not free from God's law but am under Christ's law.) ... The sting of death is sin, and the power of sin is the law. But thanks be to God! He gives us the victory through our Lord Jesus Christ.

The law of the Spirit of life set me free from the law of sin and death. — "Everyone who sins is a slave to sin.... So if the Son sets you free, you will be free indeed."

Stand firm, then, and do not let yourselves be burdened again by a yoke of slavery.

ROM. 6:14. Rom. 6:15; 7:4. 1 Cor. 9:21; 15:56–57. Rom. 8:2. John 8:34, 36. Gal. 5:1.

EVENING

He is a double-minded man, unstable in all he does.

"NO ONE WHO puts his hand to the plow and looks back is fit for service in the kingdom of God."

Anyone who comes to him must believe that he exists and that he rewards those who earnestly seek him. — But when he asks, he must believe and not doubt, because he who doubts is like a wave of the sea, blown and tossed by the wind. That man should not think he will receive anything from the Lord. — "Whatever you ask for in prayer, believe that you have received it, and it will be yours."

We will no longer be infants, tossed back and forth by the waves, and blown here and there by every wind of teaching and by the cunning and craftiness of men in their deceitful scheming. Instead, speaking the truth in love, we will in all things grow up into him who is the Head, that is, Christ.

"Remain in me." — Stand firm. Let nothing move you. Always give yourselves fully to the work of the Lord, because you know that your labor in the Lord is not in vain.

JAMES 1:8. Luke 9:62. Heb. 11:6. James 1:6–7. Mark 11:24. Eph. 4:14–15. John 15:4. 1 Cor. 15:58.

SEPTEMBER 16

MORNING

The LORD weighs the heart.

FOR THE LORD watches over the way of the righteous, but the way of the wicked shall perish. — The LORD will show who belongs to him and who is holy. — "Then your Father, who sees what is done in secret, will reward you."

Search me, O God, and know my heart; test me and know my anxious thoughts. See if there is any offensive way in me, and lead me in the way everlasting. — There is no fear in love. But perfect love drives out fear.

All my longings lie open before you, O Lord; my sighing is not hidden from you.... When my spirit grows faint within me, it is you who know my way. — He who searches our hearts knows the mind of the Spirit, because the Spirit intercedes for the saints in accordance with God's will.

God's solid foundation stands firm, sealed with this inscription: "The Lord knows those who are his," and, "Everyone who confesses the name of the Lord must turn away from wickedness."

PROV. 21:2. Ps. 1:6. Num. 16:5. Matt. 6:4. Ps. 139:23–24. 1 John 4:18. Pss. 38:9; 142:3. Rom. 8:27. 2 Tim. 2:19.

EVENING

Weeping may remain for a night, but rejoicing comes in the morning.

SO THAT NO one would be unsettled by these trials. You know quite well that we are destined for them. In fact, when we were with you, we kept telling you that we would be persecuted. — "In me you may have peace. In this world you will have trouble. But take heart! I have overcome the world."

When I awake, I will be satisfied with seeing your likeness. — The night is nearly over; the day is almost here. — He is like the light of morning at sunrise on a cloudless morning, like the brightness after rain.

He will swallow up death forever. The Sovereign LORD will wipe away the tears from all faces. — "There will be no more death or mourning or crying or pain, for the old order of things has passed away." — We who are still alive and are left will be caught up with them in the clouds to meet the Lord in the air. And so we will be with the Lord forever. Therefore encourage each other with these words.

PS. 30:5. 1 Thess. 3:3–4. John 16:33. Ps. 17:15. Rom. 13:12. 2 Sam. 23:4. Isa. 25:8. Rev. 21:4. 1 Thess. 4:17–18.

SEPTEMBER 17

MORNING

A bruised reed he will not break.

THE SACRIFICES OF God are a broken spirit; a broken and contrite heart, O God, you will not despise.... He heals the brokenhearted and binds up their wounds. — For this is what the high and lofty One says — he who lives forever, whose name is holy: "I live in a high and holy place, but also with him who is contrite and lowly in spirit, to revive the spirit of the lowly and to revive the heart of the contrite. I will not accuse forever, nor will I always be angry, for then the spirit of man would grow faint before me — the breath of man that I have created."

"I will search for the lost and bring back the strays. I will bind up the injured and strengthen the weak." — Therefore, strengthen your feeble arms and weak knees. "Make level paths for your feet," so that the lame may not be disabled, but rather healed. — "Your God will come,... He will come to save you."

MATT. 12:20. Pss. 51:17; 147:3. Isa. 57:15 – 16. Ezek. 34:16. Heb. 12:12 – 13. Isa. 35:4.

EVENING

Taste and see that the LORD is good; blessed is the man who takes refuge in him.

THE MASTER OF the banquet tasted the water that had been turned into wine. He did not realize where it had come from,... and said, "Everyone brings out the choice wine first and then the cheaper wine after the guests have had too much to drink; but you have saved the best till now."

For the ear tests words as the tongue tastes food. — "I believed; therefore I have spoken." — I know whom I have believed. — I delight to sit in his shade, and his fruit is sweet to my taste.

God's kindness.... He who did not spare his own Son, but gave him up for us all — how will he not also, along with him, graciously give us all things? — Like newborn babies, crave pure spiritual milk, so that by it you may grow up in your salvation, now that you have tasted that the Lord is good.

Let all who take refuge in you be glad; let them ever sing for joy.

PS. 34:8. John 2:9 – 10. Job 34:3. 2 Cor. 4:13. 2 Tim. 1:12. Song of Songs 2:3. Rom. 2:4; 8:32. 1 Peter 2:2 – 3. Ps. 5:11.

SEPTEMBER 18

MORNING

Open my eyes that I may see wonderful things in your law.

THEN HE OPENED their minds so they could understand the Scriptures. — "The knowledge of the secrets of the kingdom of heaven has been given to you, but not to them." ..."I praise you, Father, Lord of heaven and earth, because you have hidden these things from the wise and learned, and revealed them to little children. Yes, Father, for this was your good pleasure." — We have not received the spirit of the world but the Spirit who is from God, that we may understand what God has freely given us.

How precious to me are your thoughts, O God! How vast is the sum of them! Were I to count them, they would outnumber the grains of sand. — Oh, the depth of the riches of the wisdom and knowledge of God! How unsearchable his judgments, and his paths beyond tracing out! "Who has known the mind of the Lord? Or who has been his counselor?" ... For from him and through him and to him are all things. To him be the glory forever! Amen.

PS. 119:18. Luke 24:45. Matt. 13:11; 11:25–26. 1 Cor. 2:12. Ps. 139:17–18. Rom. 11:33–34, 36.

EVENING

So the spring was called En Hakkore.

"IF YOU KNEW the gift of God and who it is that asks you for a drink, you would have asked him and he would have given you living water." ... "If a man is thirsty, let him come to me and drink." ... By this he meant the Spirit, whom those who believed in him were later to receive.

"Test me in this," says the LORD Almighty, "and see if I will not throw open the floodgates of heaven and pour out so much blessing that you will not have room enough for it." — "If you then, though you are evil, know how to give good gifts to your children, how much more will your Father in heaven give the Holy Spirit to those who ask him!" ... "Ask and it will be given to you; seek and you will find."

Because you are sons, God sent the Spirit of his Son into our hearts, the Spirit who calls out, *"Abba,* Father." — For you did not receive a spirit that makes you a slave again to fear, but you received the Spirit of sonship. And by him we cry, *"Abba,* Father."

JUDG. 15:19. John 4:10; 7:37, 39. Mal. 3:10. Luke 11:13, 9. Gal. 4:6. Rom. 8:15.

SEPTEMBER 19

MORNING

The God of all grace.

"I WILL PROCLAIM my name, the LORD, in your presence. I will have mercy on whom I will have mercy." — "To be gracious to him and say, 'Spare him from going down to the pit; I have found a ransom for him.' " — Justified freely by his grace through the redemption that came by Christ Jesus. God presented him as a sacrifice of atonement, through faith in his blood. He did this to demonstrate his justice, because in his forbearance he had left the sins committed beforehand unpunished. — Grace and truth came through Jesus Christ.

For it is by grace you have been saved, through faith — and this not from yourselves. — Grace, mercy and peace from God the Father and Christ Jesus our Lord. — But to each one of us grace has been given as Christ apportioned it. — Each one should use whatever gift he has received to serve others, faithfully administering God's grace in its various forms. — He gives us more grace.

Grow in the grace and knowledge of our Lord and Savior Jesus Christ. To him be glory both now and forever! Amen.

1 PETER 5:10. Exod. 33:19. Job. 33:24. Rom. 3:24–25. John 1:17. Eph. 2:8. 1 Tim. 1:2. Eph. 4:7. 1 Peter 4:10. James 4:6. 2 Peter 3:18.

EVENING

I lift up my eyes to the hills — where does my help come from?
My help comes from the LORD.

As THE MOUNTAINS surround Jerusalem, so the LORD surrounds his people both now and forevermore.

I lift up my eyes to you, to you whose throne is in heaven. As the eyes of slaves look to the hand of their master, as the eyes of a maid look to the hand of her mistress, so our eyes look to the LORD our God, till he shows us his mercy.... Because you are my help, I sing in the shadow of your wings.

"O our God, will you not judge them? For we have no power to face this vast army that is attacking us. We do not know what to do, but our eyes are upon you." — My eyes are ever on the LORD, for only he will release my feet from the snare.... Our help is in the name of the LORD, the Maker of heaven and earth.

PS. 121:1–2. Pss. 125:2; 123:1–2; 63:7. 2 Chron. 20:12. Pss. 25:15; 124:8.

SEPTEMBER 20

MORNING

Blessed is the man who finds wisdom, the man who gains understanding.

WHOEVER FINDS ME finds life and receives favor from the LORD. — This is what the LORD says: "Let not the wise man boast of his wisdom or the strong man boast of his strength.... But let him who boasts boast about this: that he understands and knows me, that I am the LORD." — "The fear of the LORD is the beginning of wisdom."

Whatever was to my profit I now consider loss for the sake of Christ. What is more, I consider everything a loss compared to the surpassing greatness of knowing Christ Jesus my Lord, for whose sake I have lost all things. I consider them rubbish, that I may gain Christ. — In whom are hidden all the treasures of wisdom and knowledge. — Counsel and sound judgment are mine; I have understanding and power.

Christ Jesus ... has become for us our righteousness, holiness and redemption. — He who wins souls is wise.

PROV. 3:13. Prov. 8:35. Jer. 9:23–24. Prov. 9:10. Phil. 3:7–8. Col. 2:3. Prov. 8:14. 1 Cor. 1:30. Prov. 11:30.

EVENING

Poor, yet making many rich.

YOU KNOW THE grace of our Lord Jesus Christ, that though he was rich, yet for your sakes he became poor, so that you through his poverty might become rich. — From the fullness of his grace we have all received one blessing after another. — My God will meet all your needs according to his glorious riches in Christ Jesus. — God is able to make all grace abound to you, so that in all things at all times, having all that you need, you will abound in every good work.

Has not God chosen those who are poor in the eyes of the world to be rich in faith and to inherit the kingdom he promised those who love him? — Not many of you were wise by human standards; not many were influential; not many were of noble birth. But God chose the foolish things of the world to shame the wise; God chose the weak things of the world to shame the strong. — We have this treasure in jars of clay to show that this all-surpassing power is from God and not from us.

2 COR. 6:10. 2 Cor. 8:9. John 1:16. Phil. 4:19. 2 Cor. 9:8. James 2:5. 1 Cor. 1:26–27. 2 Cor. 4:7.

SEPTEMBER 21

MORNING

We know that in all things God works for the good of those who love him.

SURELY YOUR WRATH against men brings you praise, and the survivors of your wrath are restrained. — You intended to harm me, but God intended it for good.

All things are yours, whether ... the world or life or death or the present or the future — all are yours, and you are of Christ, and Christ is of God. — All this is for your benefit, so that the grace that is reaching more and more people may cause thanksgiving to overflow to the glory of God.

Therefore we do not lose heart. Though outwardly we are wasting away, yet inwardly we are being renewed day by day. For our light and momentary troubles are achieving for us an eternal glory that far outweighs them all.

Consider it pure joy, my brothers, whenever you face trials of many kinds, because you know that the testing of your faith develops perseverance. Perseverance must finish its work so that you may be mature and complete, not lacking anything.

ROM. 8:28. Ps. 76:10. Gen. 50:20. 1 Cor. 3:21–23. 2 Cor. 4:15–17. James 1:2–4.

EVENING

The fellowship of the Holy Spirit be with you all.

"I WILL ASK the Father, and he will give you another Counselor to be with you forever — the Spirit of truth. The world cannot accept him, because it neither sees him nor knows him. But you know him, for he lives with you and will be in you." ... "He will not speak on his own; he will speak only what he hears, and he will tell you what is yet to come. He will bring glory to me by taking from what is mine and making it known to you."

God has poured out his love into our hearts by the Holy Spirit, whom he has given us. — He who unites himself with the Lord is one with him in spirit.... Do you not know that your body is a temple of the Holy Spirit, who is in you, whom you have received from God? You are not your own.

Do not grieve the Holy Spirit of God, with whom you were sealed for the day of redemption. — The Spirit helps us in our weakness. We do not know what we ought to pray, but the Spirit himself intercedes for us with groans that words cannot express.

2 COR. 13:14. John 14:16–17; 16:13–14. Rom. 5:5. 1 Cor. 6:17, 19. Eph. 4:30. Rom. 8:26.

SEPTEMBER 22

MORNING

May my meditation be pleasing to him, as I rejoice in the LORD.

LIKE AN APPLE tree among the trees of the forest is my lover among the young men. I delight to sit in his shade, and his fruit is sweet to my taste.—For who in the skies above can compare with the LORD? Who is like the LORD among the heavenly beings?

My lover is radiant and ruddy, outstanding among ten thousand.—"One [pearl] of great value."—The ruler of the kings of the earth.

His head is purest gold; his hair is wavy and black as a raven.—Head over everything.—He is the head of the body, the church.

His lips are like lilies dripping with myrrh.—"No one ever spoke the way this man does."

His appearance is like Lebanon, choice as its cedars.—Let your face shine on your servants.... Let the light of your face shine upon us, O LORD.

PS. 104:34. Song of Songs 2:3. Ps. 89:6. Song of Songs 5:10. Matt. 13:46. Rev. 1:5. Song of Songs 5:11. Eph. 1:22. Col. 1:18. Song of Songs 5:13. John 7:46. Song of Songs 5:15. Pss. 31:16; 4:6.

EVENING

"My Father, if it is possible, may this cup be taken from me.
Yet not as I will, but as you will."

"NOW MY HEART is troubled, and what shall I say? 'Father, save me from this hour'? No, it was for this very reason I came to this hour." ... "I have come down from heaven not to do my will but to do the will of him who sent me."—He ... became obedient to death—even death on a cross!—During the days of Jesus' life on earth, he offered up prayers and petitions with loud cries and tears to the one who could save him from death, and he was heard because of his reverent submission. Although he was a son, he learned obedience from what he suffered.

"Do you think I cannot call on my Father, and he will at once put at my disposal more than twelve legions of angels?"—"This is what is written: The Christ will suffer and rise from the dead on the third day, and repentance and forgiveness of sins will be preached in his name to all nations, beginning at Jerusalem."

MATT. 26:39. John 12:27; 6:38. Phil. 2:8. Heb. 5:7–8. Matt. 26:53. Luke 24:46–47.

SEPTEMBER 23

MORNING

God has not deserted us.

DEAR FRIENDS, DO not be surprised at the painful trial you are suffering, as though something strange were happening to you. — Endure hardship as discipline; God is treating you as sons. For what son is not disciplined by his father? If you are not disciplined (and everyone undergoes discipline), then you are illegitimate children and not true sons. — The LORD your God is testing you to find out whether you love him with all your heart and with all your soul.

For the sake of his great name the LORD will not reject his people, because the LORD was pleased to make you his own. — "Can a mother forget the baby at her breast and have no compassion on the child she has borne? Though she may forget, I will not forget you!" — Blessed is he whose help is the God of Jacob, whose hope is in the LORD his God.

"Will not God bring about justice for his chosen ones, who cry out to htm day and night? Will he keep putting them off? I tell you, he will see that they get justice, and quickly."

EZRA 9:9. 1 Peter 4:12. Heb. 12:7 – 8. Deut. 13:3. 1 Sam. 12:22. Isa. 49:15. Ps. 146:5. Luke 18:7 – 8.

EVENING

"He who overcomes will inherit all this."

IF ONLY FOR this life we have hope in Christ, we are to be pitied more than all men. — They were longing for a better country — a heavenly one. Therefore God is not ashamed to be called their God, for he has prepared a city for them. — An inheritance that can never perish, spoil or fade — kept in heaven for you.

All things are yours, ... the world or life or death or the present or the future — all are yours. ... "No eye has seen, no ear has heard, no mind has conceived what God has prepared for those who love him" — but God has revealed it to us by his Spirit.

Watch out that you do not lose what you have worked for, but that you may be rewarded fully. — Let us throw off everything that hinders and the sin that so easily entangles, and let us run with perseverance the race marked out for us.

REV. 21:7. 1 Cor. 15:19. Heb. 11:16. 1 Peter 1:4. 1 Cor. 3:21 – 22; 2:9 – 10. 2 John 8. Heb. 12:1.

SEPTEMBER 24

MORNING

As for me, it is good to be near God.

I LOVE THE house where you live, O LORD, the place where your glory dwells.... Better is one day in your courts than a thousand elsewhere; I would rather be a doorkeeper in the house of my God than dwell in the tents of the wicked.... Blessed is the man you choose and bring near to live in your courts! We are filled with the good things of your house, of your holy temple.

The LORD is good to those whose hope is in him, to the one who seeks him. — Yet the LORD longs to be gracious to you; he rises to show you compassion. For the LORD is a God of justice. Blessed are all who wait for him!

Therefore, brothers, since we have confidence to enter the Most Holy Place by the blood of Jesus, by a new and living way opened for us through the curtain, that is, his body, ... let us draw near to God with a sincere heart in full assurance of faith, having our hearts sprinkled to cleanse us from a guilty conscience.

PS. 73:28. Pss. 26:8; 84:10; 65:4. Lam. 3:25. Isa. 30:18. Heb. 10:19–20, 22.

EVENING

You know the grace of our Lord Jesus Christ.

THE WORD BECAME flesh and lived for a while among us. We have seen his glory, the glory of the one and only Son, who came from the Father, full of grace and truth. — You are the most excellent of men and your lips have been anointed with grace. — All spoke well of him and were amazed at the gracious words that came from his lips.

You have tasted that the Lord is good. — Anyone who believes in the Son of God has this testimony in his heart. — We speak of what we know, and we testify to what we have seen.

Taste and see that the LORD is good; blessed is the man who takes refuge in him. — I delight to sit in his shade, and his fruit is sweet to my taste.

He said to me, "My grace is sufficient for you, for my power is made perfect in weakness." — But to each one of us grace has been given as Christ apportioned it. — Each one should use whatever gift he has received to serve others, faithfully administering God's grace in its various forms.

2 COR. 8:9. John 1:14. Ps. 45:2. Luke 4:22. 1 Peter 2:3. 1 John 5:10. John 3:11. Ps. 34:8. Song of Songs 2:3. 2 Cor. 12:9. Eph. 4:7. 1 Peter 4:10.

September 25

Morning

*Perseverance must finish its work so that you may be mature
and complete, not lacking anything.*

Though now for a little while you may have had to suffer grief in all kinds of trials. These have come so that your faith — of greater worth than gold, which perishes even though refined by fire — may be proved genuine and may result in praise, glory and honor when Jesus Christ is revealed. — We also rejoice in our sufferings, because we know that suffering produces perseverance; perseverance, character; and character, hope.

It is good to wait quietly for the salvation of the LORD. — You knew that you yourselves had better and lasting possessions. So do not throw away your confidence; it will be richly rewarded. You need to persevere so that when you have done the will of God, you will receive what he has promised. — May our Lord Jesus Christ himself and God our Father, who loved us and by his grace gave us eternal encouragement and good hope, encourage your hearts.

JAMES 1:4. 1 Peter 1:6 – 7. Rom. 5:3 – 4. Lam. 3:26. Heb. 10:34 – 36. 2 Thess. 2:16 – 17.

Evening

God will judge men's secrets through Jesus Christ.

Judge nothing before the appointed time; wait till the Lord comes. He will bring to light what is hidden in darkness and will expose the motives of men's hearts. At that time each will receive his praise from God. — "The Father judges no one, but has entrusted all judgment to the Son. . . . Because he is the Son of Man." — "The Son of God, whose eyes are like blazing fire."

They say, "How can God know? Does the Most High have knowledge?" . . . "These things you have done and I kept silent; you thought I was altogether like you. But I will rebuke you and accuse you to your face." — "There is nothing concealed that will not be disclosed, or hidden that will not be made known."

All my longings lie open before you, O Lord; my sighing is not hidden from you. . . . Test me, O LORD, and try me, examine my heart and my mind.

ROM. 2:16. 1 Cor. 4:5. John 5:22, 27. Rev. 2:18. Pss. 73:11; 50:21. Luke 12:2.
Pss. 38:9; 26:2.

SEPTEMBER 26

MORNING

A faithful God who does no wrong, upright and just is he.

Him who judges justly. — For we must all appear before the judgment seat of Christ, that each one may receive what is due him for the things done while in the body, whether good or bad. — So then, each of us will give an account of himself to God. — The soul who sins is the one who will die.

"Awake, O sword, against my shepherd, against the man who is close to me!" declares the Lord Almighty. "Strike the shepherd." — The Lord has laid on him the iniquity of us all. — Love and faithfulness meet together; righteousness and peace kiss each other. — Mercy triumphs over judgment! — For the wages of sin is death, but the gift of God is eternal life in Christ Jesus our Lord.

"A righteous God and a Savior; there is none but me." — To be just and the one who justifies the man who has faith in Jesus. . . . Justified freely by his grace through the redemption that came by Christ Jesus.

DEUT. 32:4. 1 Peter 2:23. 2 Cor. 5:10. Rom. 14:12. Ezek. 18:4. Zech. 13:7. Isa. 53:6. Ps. 85:10. James 2:13. Rom. 6:23. Isa. 45:21. Rom. 3:26, 24.

EVENING

"Death has been swallowed up in victory."

But thanks be to God! He gives us the victory through our Lord Jesus Christ.

Since the children have flesh and blood, he too shared in their humanity so that by his death he might destroy him who holds the power of death — that is, the devil — and free those who all their lives were held in slavery by their fear of death.

If we died with Christ, we believe that we will also live with him. For we know that since Christ was raised from the dead, he cannot die again; death no longer has mastery over him. The death he died, he died to sin once for all; but the life he lives, he lives to God.

In the same way, count yourselves dead to sin but alive to God in Christ Jesus. . . . In all things we are more than conquerors through him who loved us.

1 COR. 15:54. 1 Cor. 15:57. Heb. 2:14–15. Rom. 6:8–11; 8:37.

SEPTEMBER 27

MORNING

*Humble yourselves, therefore, under God's mighty hand, that
he may lift you up in due time.*

THE LORD DETESTS all the proud of heart. Be sure of this: They will not go
unpunished.

O LORD, you are our Father. We are the clay, you are the potter; we are all the
work of your hand. Do not be angry beyond measure, O LORD; do not remember
our sins forever. Oh, look upon us, we pray, for we are all your people. — "You disciplined me like an unruly calf, and I have been disciplined. Restore me, and I will
return, because you are the LORD my God. After I strayed, I repented; after I came
to understand, I beat my breast. I was ashamed and humiliated because I bore the
disgrace of my youth." — It is good for a man to bear the yoke while he is young.

For hardship does not spring from the soil, nor does trouble sprout from the
ground. Yet man is born to trouble as surely as sparks fly upward.

1 PETER 5:6. Prov. 16:5. Isa. 64:8–9. Jer. 31:18–19. Lam. 3:27. Job 5:6–7.

EVENING

"Did God really say ...?"

THE TEMPTER CAME to him and said, "If you are the Son of God." ... Jesus
answered, "It is written." ... "It is also written:" ... "For it is written." ... Then
the devil left him.

"I cannot turn back and go with you, nor can I eat bread or drink water with
you in this place. I have been told by the word of the LORD: 'You must not eat
bread or drink water there or return by the way you came.'" The old prophet
answered, "I too am a prophet, as you are. And an angel said to me by the word
of the LORD: 'Bring him back with you to your house so that he may eat bread
and drink water.'" (But he was lying to him.) So the man of God ... "defied the
word of the LORD. The LORD has given him over to the lion, which has mauled
him and killed him, as the word of the LORD had warned him." — But even if we
or an angel from heaven should preach a gospel other than the one we preached
to you, let him be eternally condemned! — I have hidden your word in my heart
that I might not sin against you.

GEN. 3:1. Matt. 4:3–4, 7, 10–11. 1 Kings 13:16–19, 26. Gal. 1:8. Ps. 119:11.

SEPTEMBER 28

MORNING

"So they will put my name on the Israelites, and I will bless them."

O LORD, OUR God, other lords besides you have ruled over us, but your name alone do we honor.... We are yours from of old; but you have not ruled over them, they have not been called by your name.

All the peoples on earth will see that you are called by the name of the LORD, and they will fear you. — The LORD will not reject his people, because the LORD was pleased to make you his own.

"O Lord, listen! O Lord, forgive! O Lord, hear and act! For your sake, O my God, do not delay, because your city and your people bear your Name." — Help us, O God our Savior, for the glory of your name; deliver us and atone for our sins for your name's sake. Why should the nations say, "Where is their God?" — The name of the LORD is a strong tower; the righteous run to it and are safe.

NUM. 6:27. Isa. 26:13; 63:19. Deut. 28:10. 1 Sam. 12:22. Dan. 9:19. Ps. 79:9–10. Prov. 18:10.

EVENING

The heavens declare the glory of God; the skies proclaim the work of his hands.

FOR SINCE THE creation of the world God's invisible qualities — his eternal power and divine nature — have been clearly seen, being understood from what has been made. — "He has not left himself without testimony." — Day after day they pour forth speech; night after night they display knowledge. There is no speech or language where their voice is not heard.

When I consider your heavens, the work of your fingers, the moon and the stars, which you have set in place, what is man that you are mindful of him, the son of man that you care for him?

The sun has one kind of splendor, the moon another and the stars another; and star differs from star in splendor. So will it be with the resurrection of the dead. — Those who are wise will shine like the brightness of the heavens, and those who lead many to righteousness, tike the stars for ever and ever.

PS. 19:1. Rom. 1:20. Acts 14:17. Pss. 19:2–3; 8:3–4. 1 Cor. 15:41–42. Dan. 12:3.

SEPTEMBER 29

MORNING

This is how we know what love is: Jesus Christ laid down his life for us.

THIS LOVE THAT surpasses knowledge. — Greater love has no one than this, that one lay down his life for his friends. — You know the grace of our Lord Jesus Christ, that though he was rich, yet for your sakes he became poor, so that you through his poverty might become rich. — Dear friends, since God so loved us, we also ought to love one another. — Be kind and compassionate to one another, forgiving each other, just as in Christ God forgave you. — Bear with each other and forgive whatever grievances you may have against one another. Forgive as the Lord forgave you. — "For even the Son of Man did not come to be served, but to serve, and to give his life as a ransom for many." — Christ suffered for you, leaving you an example, that you should follow in his steps.

"You also should wash one another's feet. I have set you an example that you should do as I have done for you." — We ought to lay down our lives for our brothers.

1 JOHN 3:16. Eph. 3:19. John 15:13. 2 Cor. 8:9. 1 John 4:11. Eph. 4:32. Col. 3:13. Mark 10:45. 1 Peter 2:21. John 13:14–15. 1 John 3:16.

EVENING

"Whatever the Father does the Son also does."

FOR THE LORD gives wisdom, and from his mouth come knowledge and understanding. — "For I will give you words and wisdom that none of your adversaries will be able to resist or contradict." Wait for the LORD; be strong and take heart and wait for the LORD. — "My grace is sufficient for you, for my power is made perfect in weakness."

Who are loved by God the Father. — Both the one who makes men holy and those who are made holy are of the same family. So Jesus is not ashamed to call them brothers. — "Do not I fill heaven and earth?" declares the LORD. — The fullness of him who fills eeverything in every way.

"I, even I, am the LORD, and apart from me there is no savior." — "This man really is the Savior of the world." — Grace and peace from God the Father and Christ Jesus our Savior.

JOHN 5:19. Prov. 2:6. Luke 21:15. Ps. 27:14. 2 Cor. 12:9. Jude 1. Heb. 2:11. Jer. 23:24. Eph. 1:23. Isa. 43:11. John 4:42. Titus 1:4.

SEPTEMBER 30

MORNING

He knows the way that I take; when he has tested me,
I will come forth as gold.

HE KNOWS HOW we are formed. — For he does not willingly bring affliction or grief to the children of men.

God's solid foundation stands firm, sealed with this inscription: "The Lord knows those who are his," and, "Everyone who confesses the name of the Lord must turn away from wickedness." In a large house there are articles not only of gold and silver, but also of wood and clay; some are for noble purposes and some for ignoble. If a man cleanses himself from the latter, he will be an instrument for noble purposes, made holy, useful to the Master and prepared to do any good work.

He will sit as a refiner and purifier of silver; he will purify the Levites and refine them like gold and silver. Then the LORD will have men who will bring offerings in righteousness. — "I will refine them like silver and test them like gold. They will call on my name and I will answer them; I will say, 'They are my people,' and they will say, 'The LORD is our God.'"

JOB 23:10. Ps. 103:14. Lam. 3:33. 2 Tim. 2:19–21. Mal. 3:3. Zech. 13:9.

EVENING

Show me your ways, O LORD, teach me your paths.

MOSES SAID TO the LORD, . . . "If I have found favor in your eyes, teach me your ways so I may know you." . . . The LORD replied, "My Presence will go with you, and I will give you rest." — He made known his ways to Moses, his deeds to the people of Israel.

He guides the humble in what is right and teaches them his way. . . . Who, then, is the man that fears the LORD? He will instruct him in the way chosen for him. — Trust in the LORD with all your heart and lean not on your own understanding; in all your ways acknowledge him, and he will make your paths straight.

You have made known to me the path of life; you will fill me with joy in your presence. . . . I will instruct you and teach you in the way you should go; I will counsel you and watch over you. — The path of the righteous is like the first gleam of dawn, shining ever brighter till the full light of day.

PS. 25:4. Exod. 33:12–14. Pss. 103:7; 25:9, 12. Prov. 3:5–6. Pss. 16:11; 32:8.
Prov. 4:18.

OCTOBER 1

MORNING

The fruit of the Spirit is ... self-control.

EVERYONE WHO COMPETES in the games goes into strict training. They do it to get a crown that will not last; but we do it to get a crown that will last forever. Therefore I do not run like a man running aimlessly; I do not fight like a man beating the air. No, I beat my body and make it my slave so that after I have preached to others, I myself will not be disqualified for the prize.

Do not get drunk on wine, which leads to debauchery. Instead, be filled with the Spirit. — "If anyone would come after me, he must deny himself and take up his cross and follow me."

Let us not be like others, who are asleep, but let us be alert and self-controlled. For those who sleep, sleep at night, and those who get drunk, get drunk at night. But since we belong to the day, let us be self-controlled. — Say "No" to ungodliness and worldly passions, and ... live self-controlled, upright and godly lives in this present age, while we wait for the blessed hope — the glorious appearing of our great God and Savior, Jesus Christ.

GAL. 5:22. 1 Cor. 9:25 – 27. Eph. 5:18. Matt. 16:24. 1 Thess. 5:6 – 8. Titus 2:12 – 13.

EVENING

Grow up into him who is the Head, that is, Christ.

"FIRST THE STALK, then the head, then the full kernel in the head." — Until we all reach unity in the faith and in the knowledge of the Son of God and become mature, attaining to the whole measure of the fullness of Christ.

When they measure themselves by themselves and compare themselves with themselves, they are not wise.... "Let him who boasts boast in the Lord." For it is not the man who commends himself who is approved, but the man whom the Lord commends.

Found in Christ. Do not let anyone who delights in false humility and the worship of angels disqualify you for the prize. Such a person goes into great detail about what he has seen, and his unspiritual mind puffs him up with idle notions. He has lost connection with the Head, from whom the whole body, supported and held together by its ligaments and sinews, grows as God causes it to grow. — Grow in the grace and knowledge of our Lord and Savior Jesus Christ.

EPH. 4:15. Mark 4:28. Eph. 4:13. 2 Cor. 10:12, 17 – 18. Col. 2:17 – 19. 2 Peter 3:18.

OCTOBER 2

MORNING

"The goat will carry on itself all their sins to a solitary place;
and the man shall release it in the desert."

AS FAR AS the east is from the west, so far has he removed our transgressions from us. — "In those days, at that time," declares the LORD, "search will be made for Israel's guilt, but there will be none, and for the sins of Judah, but none will be found, for I will forgive the remnant I spare." — You will tread our sins underfoot and hurl all our iniquities into the depths of the sea.... Who is a God like you, who pardons sin?

We all, like sheep, have gone astray, each of us has turned to his own way; and the LORD has laid on him the iniquity of us all.... After the suffering of his soul, he will see the light of life and be satisfied; by his knowledge my righteous servant will justify many, and he will bear their iniquities. Therefore I will give him a portion among the great, and he will divide the spoils with the strong, because he poured out his life unto death, and was numbered with the transgressors. — "Look, the Lamb of God, who takes away the sin of the world!"

LEV. 16:22. Ps. 103:12. Jer. 50:20. Mic. 7:19, 18. Isa. 53:6, 11–12. John 1:29.

EVENING

For who makes you different from anyone else? What do you
have that you did not receive?

BY THE GRACE of God I am what I am. — He chose to give us birth through the word of truth. — It does not, therefore, depend on man's desire or effort, but on God's mercy.... Where, then, is boasting? It is excluded. — Christ Jesus ... has become for us wisdom from God — that is, our righteousness, holiness and redemption.... "Let him who boasts boast in the Lord."

You were dead in your transgressions and sins, in which you used to live when you followed the ways of this world and the ruler of the kingdom of the air, the spirit who is now at work in those who are disobedient. All of us also lived among them at one time, gratifying the cravings of our sinful nature and following its desires and thoughts. Like the rest, we were by nature objects of wrath. — You were washed, you were sanctified, you were justified in the name of the Lord Jesus Christ and by the Spirit of our God.

1 COR. 4:7. 1 Cor. 15:10. James 1:18. Rom. 9:16; 3:27. 1 Cor. 1:30–31. Eph. 2:1–3.
   1 Cor. 6:11.

OCTOBER 3

MORNING

To him who loves us and has freed us from our sins by his blood.

MANY WATERS CANNOT quench love; rivers cannot wash it away.... For love is as strong as death. — "Greater love has no one than this, that one lay down his life for his friends."

He himself bore our sins in his body on the tree, so that we might die to sins and live for righteousness; by his wounds you have been healed.

You were washed, you were sanctified, you were justified in the name of the Lord Jesus Christ and by the Spirit of our God. — You are a chosen people, a royal priesthood, a holy nation, a people belonging to God, that you may declare the praises of him who called you out of darkness into his wonderful light.

Therefore, I urge you, brothers, in view of God's mercy, to offer your bodies as living sacrifices, holy and pleasing to God — which is your spiritual worship.

REV. 1:5. Song of Songs 8:7, 6. John 15:13. 1 Peter 2:24. 1 Cor. 6:11. 1 Peter 2:9. Rom. 12:1.

EVENING

There are different kinds of service, but the same Lord.

AZMAVETH SON OF Adiel was in charge of the royal storehouses. Jonathan son of Uzziah was in charge of the storehouses in the outlying districts, in the towns, the villages and the watchtowers. Ezri son of Kelub was in charge of the field workers who farmed the land. Shimei the Ramathite was in charge of the vineyards.... All these were the officials in charge of King David's property.

And in the church God has appointed first of all apostles, second prophets, third teachers, then workers of miracles, also those having gifts of healing, those able to help others, those with gifts of administration, and those speaking in different kinds of tongues.... All these are the work of one and the same Spirit, and he gives them to each man, just as he determines.

Each one should use whatever gift he has received to serve others, faithfully administering God's grace in its various forms. If anyone speaks, he should do it as one speaking the very words of God. If anyone serves, he should do it with the strength God provides, so that in all things God may be praised through Jesus Christ. To him be the glory and the power for ever and ever.

1 COR. 12:5. 1 Chron. 27:25–27, 31. 1 Cor. 12:28, 11. 1 Peter 4:10–11.

OCTOBER 4

MORNING

*He was not aware that his face was radiant because he had
spoken with the LORD.*

NOT TO US, O LORD, not to us but to your name be the glory. — "Lord, when did we
see you hungry and feed you, or thirsty and give you something to drink?" — But in
humility consider others better than yourselves. — Clothe yourselves with humility.

There he [Jesus] was transfigured before them. His face shone like the sun,
and his clothes became as white as the light. — All who were sitting in the Sanhedrin looked intently at Stephen, and they saw that his face was like the face of an
angel. — "I have given them the glory that you gave me." — We, who with unveiled
faces all reflect the Lord's glory, are being transformed into his likeness with ever-
increasing glory, which comes from the Lord.

"You are the light of the world. A city on a hill cannot be hidden. Neither do
people light a lamp and put it under a bowl. Instead they put it on its stand, and it
gives light to everyone in the house."

**EXOD. 34:29. Ps. 115:1. Matt. 25:37. Phil. 2:3. 1 Peter 5:5. Matt. 17:2. Acts 6:15. John
17:22. 2 Cor. 3:18. Matt. 5:14–15.**

EVENING

*There are different kinds of working, but the same God works
all of them in all men.*

SOME OF THE men of Manasseh defected to David.... They helped David
against raiding bands, for all of them were brave warriors. — Now to each one
the manifestation of the Spirit is given for the common good.

Men of Issachar, who understood the times and knew what Israel should
do — 200 chiefs, with all their relatives under their command. — To one there
is given through the Spirit the message of wisdom, to another the message of
knowledge by means of the same Spirit.

Men of Zebulun, experienced soldiers prepared for battle with every type
of weapon, to help David with undivided loyalty — 50,000. — He is a double-
minded man, unstable in all he does.

There should be no division in the body, but ... its parts should have equal
concern for each other. If one part suffers, every part suffers with it; if one part
is honored, every part rejoices with it. — One Lord, one faith, one baptism.

**1 COR. 12:6. 1 Chron. 12:19, 21. 1 Cor. 12:7. 1 Chron. 12:32. 1 Cor. 12:8. 1 Chron.
12:33. James 1:8. 1 Cor. 12:25–26. Eph. 4:5.**

OCTOBER 5

MORNING

"Call upon me in the day of trouble; I will deliver you,
and you will honor me."

WHY ARE YOU downcast, O my soul? Why so disturbed within me? Put your hope in God, for I will yet praise him, my Savior and my God.... You hear, O LORD, the desire of the afflicted; you encourage them, and you listen to their cry.... You are kind and forgiving, O Lord, abounding in love to all who call to you.

So Jacob said to his household, ... "Let us go up to Bethel, where I will build an altar to God, who answered me in the day of my distress and who has been with me wherever I have gone." — Praise the LORD, O my soul, and forget not all his benefits.

I love the LORD, for he heard my voice; he heard my cry for mercy. Because he turned his ear to me, I will call on him as long as I live. The cords of death entangled me, the anguish of the grave came upon me; I was overcome by trouble and sorrow. Then I called on the name of the LORD.

PS. 50:15. Pss. 42:11; 10:17; 86:5. Gen. 35:2–3. Pss. 103:2; 116:1–4.

EVENING

For in just a very little while, "He who is coming will come
and will not delay."

"WRITE DOWN THE revelation and make it plain on tablets so that a herald may run with it. For the revelation awaits an appointed time; it speaks of the end and will not prove false. Though it linger, wait for it; it will certainly come and will not delay."

But do not forget this one thing, dear friends: With the Lord a day is like a thousand years, and a thousand years are like a day. The Lord is not slow in keeping his promise, as some understand slowness. He is patient with you, not wanting anyone to perish, but everyone to come to repentance. — But you, O Lord, are a compassionate and gracious God, slow to anger, abounding in love and faithfulness. — Oh, that you would rend the heavens and come down.... Since ancient times no one has heard, no ear has perceived, no eye has seen any God besides you, who acts on behalf of those who wait for him.

HEB. 10:37. Hab. 2:2–3. 2 Peter 3:8–9. Ps. 86:15. Isa. 64:1, 4.

OCTOBER 6

MORNING

For our Lord God Almighty reigns.

"I KNOW THAT you can do all things."

"What is impossible with men is possible with God." — He does as he pleases with the powers of heaven and the peoples of the earth. No one can hold back his hand or say to him: "What have you done?" — "No one can deliver out of my hand. When I act, who can reverse it?" — "*Abba,* Father," he said, "everything is possible for you."

"Do you believe that I am able to do this?" "Yes, Lord," they replied. Then he touched their eyes and said, "According to your faith will it be done to you." ... "Lord, if you are willing, you can make me clean." Jesus reached out his hand and touched the man. "I am willing," he said. "Be clean!" — Mighty God. — "All authority in heaven and on earth has been given to me."

Some trust in chariots and some in horses, but we trust in the name of the LORD our God. — "Be strong and courageous. Do not be afraid or discouraged, ... there is a greater power with us than with him."

**REV. 19:6. Job 42:2. Luke 18:27. Dan. 4:35. Isa. 43:13. Mark 14:36.
Matt. 9:28 – 29; 8:2 – 3. Isa. 9:6. Matt. 28:18. Ps. 20:7. 2 Chron. 32:7.**

EVENING

"What was it he said to you?"

HE HAS SHOWED you, O man, what is good. And what does the LORD require of you? To act justly and to love mercy and to walk humbly with your God. — To observe the LORD's commands and decrees that I am giving you today for your own good. — All who rely on observing the law are under a curse, for it is written: "Cursed is everyone who does not continue to do everything written in the Book of the Law." Clearly no one is justified before God by the law, because, "The righteous will live by faith." ... What, then, was the purpose of the law? It was added because of transgressions until the Seed to whom the promise referred had come.

In the past God spoke to our forefathers through the prophets at many times and in various ways, but in these last days he has spoken to us by his Son. — "Speak, LORD, for your servant is listening."

1 SAM. 3:17. Mic. 6:8. Deut. 10:13. Gal. 3:10 – 11, 19. Heb. 1:1 – 2. 1 Sam. 3:9.

OCTOBER 7

MORNING

He guides the humble in what is right and teaches them his way.

"BLESSED ARE THE meek."—I have seen something else under the sun: The race is not to the swift or the battle to the strong, nor does food come to the wise or wealth to the brilliant or favor to the learned.—In his heart a man plans his course, but the LORD determines his steps.

I lift up my eyes to you, to you whose throne is in heaven. As the eyes of slaves look to the hand of their master, as the eyes of a maid look to the hand of her mistress, so our eyes look to the LORD our God.... Show me the way I should go, for to you I lift up my soul.

"O our God, will you not judge them? For we have no power to face this vast army that is attacking us. We do not know what to do, but our eyes are upon you."—If any of you lacks wisdom, he should ask God, who gives generously to all without finding fault, and it will be given to him.—"But when he, the Spirit of truth, comes, he will guide you into all truth."

PS. 25:9. Matt. 5:5. Eccl. 9:11. Prov. 16:9. Pss. 123:1–2; 143:8. 2 Chron. 20:12. James 1:5. John 16:13.

EVENING

"O Sovereign LORD, ... with your blessing the house of your servant will be blessed forever."

"You, O LORD, have blessed it, and it will be blessed forever."—The blessing of the LORD brings wealth, and he adds no trouble to it.

"Remembering the words the Lord Jesus himself said: 'It is more blessed to give than to receive.'"—"But when you give a banquet, invite the poor, the crippled, the lame, the blind, and you will be blessed. Although they cannot repay you, you will be repaid at the resurrection of the righteous."—"'Come, you who are blessed by my father; take your inheritance, the kingdom prepared for you since the creation of the world. For I was hungry and you gave me something to eat, I was thirsty and you gave me something to drink, I was a stranger and you invited me in, I needed clothes and you clothed me, I was sick and you looked after me, I was in prison and you came to visit me.'"

Blessed is he who has regard for the weak; the LORD delivers him in times of trouble.... For the LORD God is a sun and shield.

2 SAM. 7:29. 1 Chron. 17:27. Prov. 10:22. Acts 20:35. Luke 14:13–14. Matt. 25:34–36. Pss. 41:1; 84:11.

OCTOBER 8

MORNING

"I will not be afraid. What can man do to me?"

WHO SHALL SEPARATE us from the love of Christ? Shall trouble or hardship or persecution or famine or nakedness or danger or sword?... No, in all these things we are more than conquerors through him who loved us.

"Do not be afraid of those who kill the body and after that can do no more. But I will show you whom you should fear: Fear him who, after the killing of the body, has power to throw you into hell. Yes, I tell you, fear him."

"Blessed are those who are persecuted because of righteousness, for theirs is the kingdom of heaven. Blessed are you when people insult you, persecute you and falsely say all kinds of evil against you because of me. Rejoice and be glad, because great is your reward in heaven." — "However, I consider my life worth nothing to me, if only I may finish the race and complete the task." — I will speak of your statutes before kings and will not be put to shame.

HEB. 13:6. Rom. 8:35, 37. Luke 12:4 – 5. Matt. 5:10 – 12. Acts 20:24. Ps. 119:46.

EVENING

He set my feet on a rock.

THAT ROCK WAS Christ. — Simon Peter answered, "You are the Christ, the Son of the living God." ... "On this rock I will build my church, and the gates of Hades will not overcome it." — "Salvation is found in no one else, for there is no other name under heaven given to men by which we must be saved."

Full assurance of faith.... Hold unswervingly to the hope. — He must believe and not doubt, because he who doubts is like a wave of the sea, blown and tossed by the wind.

Who shall separate us from the love of Christ? Shall trouble or hardship or persecution or famine or nakedness or danger or sword?... In all these things we are more than conquerors through him who loved us.... Neither height nor depth, nor anything else in all creation, will be able to separate us from the love of God that is in Christ Jesus our Lord.

PS. 40:2. 1 Cor. 10:4. Matt. 16:16, 18. Acts 4:12. Heb. 10:22 – 23. James 1:6. Rom. 8:35, 37, 39.

OCTOBER 9

MORNING

But you are a forgiving God, gracious and compassionate,
slow to anger and abounding in love.

THE LORD IS not slow in keeping his promise, as some understand slowness. He is patient with you, not wanting anyone to perish, but everyone to come to repentance.... Bear in mind that our Lord's patience means salvation.

For that very reason I was shown mercy so that in me, the worst of sinners, Christ Jesus might display his unlimited patience as an example for those who would believe on him and receive eternal life. — For everything that was written in the past was written to teach us, so that through endurance and the encouragement of the Scriptures we might have hope.

Do you show contempt for the riches of his kindness, tolerance and patience, not realizing that God's kindness leads you toward repentance? — Rend your heart and not your garments. Return to the LORD your God, for he is gracious and compassionate, slow to anger and abounding in love, and he relents from sending calamity.

NEH. 9:17. 2 Peter 3:9, 15. 1 Tim. 1:16. Rom. 15:4; 2:4. Joel 2:13.

EVENING

And the words of the LORD are flawless.

YOUR PROMISES HAVE been thoroughly tested, and your servant loves them.... The precepts of the LORD are right, giving joy to the heart. The commands of the LORD are radiant, giving light to the eyes. — "Every word of God is flawless; he is a shield to those who take refuge in him. Do not add to his words, or he will rebuke you and prove you a liar.

I have hidden your word in my heart that I might not sin against you.... I meditate on your precepts and consider your ways. — Finally, brothers, whatever is true, whatever is noble, whatever is right, whatever is pure, whatever is lovely, whatever is admirable — if anything is excellent or praiseworthy — think about such things. — Like newborn babies, crave pure spiritual milk, so that by it you may grow up in your salvation.

Unlike so many, we do not peddle the word of God for profit. On the contrary, in Christ we speak before God with sincerity, like men sent from God.... Nor do we distort the word of God.

PS. 12:6. Pss. 119:140; 19:8. Prov. 30:5 – 6. Ps. 119:11, 15. Phil. 4:8. 1 Peter 2:2.
2 Cor. 2:17; 4:2.

OCTOBER 10

MORNING

His whole family in heaven and on earth.

ONE GOD AND Father of all, who is over all and through all and in all. — You are all sons of God through faith in Christ Jesus. — To be put into effect when the times will have reached their fulfillment — to bring all things in heaven and on earth together under one head, even Christ.

Jesus is not ashamed to call them brothers. — "Here are my mother and my brothers. For whoever does the will of my Father in heaven is my brother and sister and mother." — "Go instead to my brothers and tell them, 'I am returning to my Father and your Father, to my God and your God.'"

I saw under the altar the souls of those who had been slain because of the word of God and the testimony they had maintained. They called out in a loud voice, "How long, Sovereign Lord, holy and true, until you judge the inhabitants of the earth and avenge our blood?" Then each of them was given a white robe, and they were told to wait a little longer, until the number of their fellow servants and brothers who were to be killed as they had been was completed. — That only together with us would they be made perfect.

EPH. 3:15. Eph. 4:6. Gal. 3:26. Eph. 1:10. Heb. 2:11. Matt. 12:49–50. John 20:17.
Rev. 6:9–11. Heb. 11:40.

EVENING

"This is how you should pray: 'Our Father in heaven.'"

AFTER JESUS SAID this, he looked toward heaven and prayed: "Father." ... "My Father and your Father."

You are all sons of God through faith in Christ Jesus. — For you did not receive a spirit that makes you a slave again to fear, but you received the Spirit of son-ship. And by him we cry, *"Abba,* Father." The Spirit himself testifies with our spirit that we are God's children.

Because you are sons, God sent the Spirit of his Son into our hearts, the Spirit who calls out, *"Abba,* Father." So you are no longer a slave, but a son. — "I tell you the truth, my Father will give you whatever you ask in my name. Until now you have not asked for anything in my name. Ask and you will receive, and your joy will be complete."

"I will receive you. I will be a Father to you, and you will be my sons and daughters, says the Lord Almighty."

MATT. 6:9. John 17:1; 20:17. Gal. 3:26. Rom. 8:15–16. Gal. 4:6–7. John 16:23–24.
2 Cor. 6:17–18.

OCTOBER 11

MORNING

Do not be far from me, for trouble is near.

HOW LONG, O LORD? Will you forget me forever? How long will you hide your face from me? How long must I wrestle with my thoughts and every day have sorrow in my heart?... Do not hide your face from me, do not turn your servant away in anger; you have been my helper. Do not reject me or forsake me, O God my Savior.

"He will call upon me, and I will answer him; I will be with him in trouble, I will deliver him and honor him." ... The LORD is near to all who call on him, to all who call on him in truth. He fulfills the desires of those who fear him; he hears their cry and saves them.

"I will not leave you as orphans; I will come to you." — "And surely I will be with you always, to the very end of the age."

God is our refuge and strength, an ever present help in trouble.... My soul finds rest in God alone; my salvation comes from him.... My hope comes from him.

PS. 22:11. Pss. 13:1–2; 27:9; 91:15; 145:18–19. John 14:18. Matt. 28:20. Pss. 46:1; 62:1, 5.

EVENING

"Hallowed be your name."

"DO NOT WORSHIP any other god, for the LORD, whose name is Jealous, is a jealous God." ... "Who among the gods is like you, O LORD? Who is like you — majestic in holiness, awesome in glory, working wonders?" — "Holy, holy, holy is the Lord God Almighty."

Worship the LORD in the splendor of his holiness. — I saw the Lord seated on a throne, high and exalted, and the train of his robe filled the temple. Above him were seraphs, each with six wings: With two wings they covered their faces, with two they covered their feet, and with two they were flying. And they were calling to one another: "Holy, holy, holy is the LORD Almighty; the whole earth is full of his glory." ..."Woe to me!" I cried. "I am ruined!"

My ears had heard of you but now my eyes have seen you. Therefore I despise myself. — The blood of Jesus, his son, purifies us from every sin. — But God disciplines us for our good, that we may share in his holiness.... Therefore, brothers, since we have confidence to enter the Most Holy Place by the blood of Jesus,... let us draw near to God with a sincere heart.

MATT. 6:9. Exod. 34:14; 15:11. Rev. 4:8. 1 Chron. 16:29. Isa. 6:1–3, 5. Job 42:5–6.
1 John 1:7. Heb. 12:10; 10:19, 22.

OCTOBER 12

MORNING

God was reconciling the world to himself in Christ, not
counting men's sins against them.

FOR GOD WAS pleased to have all his fullness dwell in him, and through him
to reconcile to himself all things, whether things on earth or things in heaven,
by making peace through his blood, shed on the cross. — Love and faithfulness
meet together; righteousness and peace kiss each other.

"I know the plans I have for you," declares the LORD, "plans to prosper you
and not to harm you, plans to give you hope and a future." — "Come now, let
us reason together," says the LORD. "Though your sins are like scarlet, they shall
be as white as snow; though they are red as crimson, they shall be like wool."

Who is a God like you, who pardons sin? — "Submit to God and be at peace
with him." — Work out your salvation with fear and trembling, for it is God
who works in you to will and to act according to his good purpose. — LORD,
you establish peace for us; all that we have accomplished you have done for us.

2 COR. 5:19. Col. 1:19 – 20. Ps. 85:10. Jer. 29:11. Isa. 1:18. Mic. 7:18. Job 22:21. Phil.
2:12 – 13. Isa. 26:12.

EVENING

"Your kingdom come."

"IN THE TIME of those kings, the God of heaven will set up a kingdom that will
never be destroyed, nor will it be left to another people. It will crush all those kingdoms and bring them to an end, but it will itself endure forever." ... A rock was cut
out, but not by human hands. — "Not by might nor by power, but by my Spirit,"
says the LORD Almighty. — "The kingdom of God does not come visibly, nor will
people say, 'Here it is,' or 'There it is,' because the kingdom of God is within you."

"The secret of the kingdom of God has been given to you." ... He also said,
"This is what the kingdom of God is like. A man scatters seed on the ground.
Night and day, whether he sleeps or gets up, the seed sprouts and grows, though
he does not know how.... As soon as the grain is ripe, he puts the sickle to it,
because the harvest has come."

"So you also must be ready, because the Son of Man will come at an hour
when you do not expect him." — The Spirit and the bride say, "Come!" And let
him who hears say, "Come!"

MATT. 6:10. Dan. 2:44, 34. Zech. 4:6. Luke 17:20 – 21. Mark 4:11, 26 – 27, 29.
Matt. 24:44. Rev. 22:17.

OCTOBER 13

MORNING

"Since the first day that you set your mind to gain understanding and to humble yourself before your God, your words were heard."

FOR THIS IS what the high and lofty One says—he who lives forever, whose name is holy: "I live in a high and holy place, but also with him who is contrite and lowly in spirit, to revive the spirit of the lowly and to revive the heart of the contrite."—The sacrifices of God are a broken spirit; a broken and contrite heart, O God, you will not despise.... Though the LORD is on high, he looks upon the lowly, but the proud he knows from afar.

Humble yourselves, therefore, under God's mighty hand, that he may lift you up in due time.... "God opposes the proud but gives grace to the humble." Submit yourselves, then, to God.—You are kind and forgiving, O Lord, abounding in love to all who call to you. Hear my prayer, O LORD; listen to my cry for mercy. In the day of my trouble I will call to you, for you will answer me.

DAN. 10:12. Isa. 57:15. Pss. 51:17; 138:6. 1 Peter 5:5–6. James 4:6–7. Ps. 86:5–7.

EVENING

"Your will be done on earth as it is in heaven."

UNDERSTAND WHAT THE Lord's will is.—"Your Father in heaven is not willing that any of these little ones should be lost."

It is God's will that you should be holy.—As a result, he does not live the rest of his earthly life for evil human desires, but rather for the will of God.—He chose to give us birth through the word of truth.... Therefore, get rid of all moral filth.

"Be holy, because I am holy."—Jesus said, "Here are my mother and my brothers! Whoever does God's will is my brother and sister and mother."—"Therefore everyone who hears these words of mine and puts them into practice is like a wise man who built his house on the rock. The rain came down, the streams rose, and the winds blew and beat against that house; yet it did not fall, because it had its foundation on the rock."—The world and its desires pass away, but the man who does the will of God lives forever.

MATT. 6:10. Eph. 5:17. Matt. 18:14. 1 Thess. 4:3. 1 Peter 4:2. James 1:18, 21.
1 Peter 1:16. Mark 3:34–35. Matt. 7:24–25. 1 John 2:17.

OCTOBER 14

MORNING

*Christ died and returned to life so that he might be the Lord
of both the dead and the living.*

IT WAS THE LORD'S will to crush him and cause him to suffer, and though the LORD makes his life a guilt offering, he will see his offspring and prolong his days, and the will of the LORD will prosper in his hand. After the suffering of his soul, he will see the light of life and be satisfied; by his knowledge my righteous servant will justify many, and he will bear their iniquities. — "Did not the Christ have to suffer these things and then enter his glory?" — We are convinced that one died for all, and therefore all died. And he died for all, that those who live should no longer live for themselves but for him who died for them and was raised again.

"Let all Israel be assured of this: God has made this Jesus, whom you crucified, both Lord and Christ." — He was chosen before the creation of the world, but was revealed in these last times for your sake. Through him you believe in God.

ROM. 14:9. Isa. 53:10–11. Luke 24:26. 2 Cor. 5:14–15. Acts 2:36. 1 Peter 1:20–21.

EVENING

"Give us today our daily bread."

I WAS YOUNG and now I am old, yet I have never seen the righteous forsaken or their children begging bread. — His bread will be supplied, and water will not fail him. — The ravens brought him bread and meat in the morning and bread and meat in the evening, and he drank from the brook.

My God will meet all your needs according to his glorious riches in Christ Jesus. — Be content with what you have, because God has said, "Never will I leave you; never will I forsake you."

He humbled you, causing you to hunger and then feeding you with manna, which neither you nor your fathers had known, to teach you that man does not live on bread alone but on every word that comes from the mouth of the LORD — "I tell you the truth, it is not Moses who has given you the bread from heaven, but it is my Father who gives you the true bread from heaven. For the bread of God is he who comes down from heaven and gives life to the world." "Sir," they said, "from now on give us this bread."

**MATT. 6:11. Ps. 37:25. Isa. 33:16. 1 Kings 17:6. Phil. 4:19. Heb. 13:5. Deut. 8:3.
John 6:32–34.**

OCTOBER 15

MORNING

O God, . . . my fortress.

"THE LORD IS my rock, my fortress and my deliverer; my God is my rock, in whom I take refuge, my shield and the horn of my salvation. He is my stronghold, my refuge and my savior." — The LORD is my strength and my shield; my heart trusts in him, and I am helped. My heart leaps for joy and I will give thanks to him in song.

For he will come like a pent-up flood that the breath of the LORD drives along. — "The Lord is my helper; I will not be afraid. What can man do to me?"

The LORD is my light and my salvation — whom shall I fear? . . . As the mountains surround Jerusalem so the LORD surrounds his people both now and forevermore. . . . Because you are my help, I sing in the shadow of your wings. . . . For the sake of your name lead and guide me.

PS. 59:9. 2 Sam. 22:2–3. Ps. 28:7. Isa. 59:19. Heb. 13:6. Pss. 27:1; 125:2; 63:7; 31:3.

EVENING

"Forgive us our debts, as we also have forgiven our debtors."

"LORD, HOW MANY times shall I forgive my brother when he sins against me? Up to seven times?" Jesus answered, "I tell you, not seven times, but seventy-seven times." . . . " 'You wicked servant,' he said, 'I canceled all that debt of yours because you begged me to. Shouldn't you have had mercy on your fellow servant just as I had on you?' In anger his master turned him over to the jailers until he should pay back all he owed. This is how my heavenly Father will treat each of you unless you forgive your brother from your heart." — Be kind and compassionate to one another, forgiving each other, just as in Christ God forgave you.

When you were dead in your sins and in the uncircumcision of your sinful nature, God made you alive with Christ. He forgave us all our sins, having canceled the written code, with its regulations, that was against us and that stood opposed to us; he took it away, nailing it to the cross. . . . Forgive as the Lord forgave you.

MATT. 6:12. Matt. 18:21–22, 32–35. Eph. 4:32. Col. 2:13–14; 3:13.

OCTOBER 16

MORNING

Never be lacking in zeal, but keep your spiritual fervor, serving the Lord.

WHATEVER YOUR HAND finds to do, do it with all your might, for in the grave, where you are going, there is neither working nor planning nor knowledge nor wisdom. — Whatever you do, work at it with all your heart, as working for the Lord, not for men, since you know that you will receive an inheritance from the Lord as a reward. It is the Lord Christ you are serving. — Because you know that the Lord will reward everyone for whatever good he does.

"As long as it is day, we must do the work of him who sent me. Night is coming, when no one can work." — "Didn't you know I had to be in my Father's house?" — "Zeal for your house will consume me."

My brothers, be all the more eager to make your calling and election sure. For if you do these things, you will never fall. — We want each of you to show this same diligence to the very end, in order to make your hope sure. We do not want you to become lazy, but to imitate those who through faith and patience inherit what has been promised.

ROM. 12:11. Eccl. 9:10. Col. 3:23–24. Eph. 6:8. John 9:4. Luke 2:49. John 2:17.
2 Peter 1:10. Heb. 6:11–12.

EVENING

"And lead us not into temptation, but deliver us from the evil one."

HE WHO TRUSTS in himself is a fool, but he who walks in wisdom is kept safe.

When tempted, no one should say, "God is tempting me." For God cannot be tempted by evil, nor does he tempt anyone; but each one is tempted when, by his own evil desire, he is dragged away and enticed. — "Therefore come out from them and be separate, Touch no unclean thing, and I will receive you."

Lot looked up and saw that the whole plain of the Jordan was well watered, like the garden of the LORD.... So Lot chose for himself the whole plain of the Jordan.... Now the men of Sodom were wicked and were sinning greatly against the LORD. — [The Lord] rescued Lot, a righteous man, who was distressed by the filthy lives of lawless men.... The Lord knows how to rescue godly men from trials. — And he will stand, for the Lord is able to make him stand.

MATT. 6:13. Prov. 28:26. James 1:13–14. 2 Cor. 6:17. Gen. 13:10–11, 13. 2 Peter 2:7, 9.
Rom. 14:4.

OCTOBER 17

MORNING

They rejoice in your name all day long; they exult in your righteousness.

"'IN THE LORD are righteousness and strength.'" All who have raged against him will come to him and be put to shame. But in the LORD all the descendants of Israel will be found righteous and will exult. — Rejoice in the LORD and be glad, you righteous; sing, all you who are upright in heart!

But now a righteousness from God, apart from law, has been made known, to which the Law and the Prophets testify. This righteousness from God comes through faith in Jesus Christ to all who believe.... He did it to demonstrate his justice at the present time, so as to be just and the one who justifies the man who has faith in Jesus.

Rejoice in the Lord always. I will say it again: Rejoice! — Though you have not seen him, you love him; and even though you do not see him now, you believe in him and are filled with an inexpressible and glorious joy.

PS. 89:16. Isa. 45:24 – 25. Ps. 32:11. Rom. 3:21 – 22, 26. Phil. 4:4. 1 Peter 1:8.

EVENING

"He will reign over the house of Jacob forever; his kingdom will never end."

THE LORD REIGNS, he is robed in majesty; the LORD is robed in majesty.... Your throne was established long ago; you are from all eternity.

The LORD is ... great in power. — If God is for us, who can be against us? — "The God we serve is able to save us." — "My Father, who has given them to me, is greater than all; no one can snatch them out of my Father's hand." — "The one who is in you is greater than the one who is in the world."

Not to us, O LORD, not to us but to your name be the glory. — Yours, O LORD, is the greatness and the power and the glory and the majesty and the splendor, for everything in heaven and earth is yours. Yours, O LORD, is the kingdom.... Now, our God, we give you thanks and praise your glorious name. "But who am I, and who are my people, that we should be able to give as generously as this?" Everything comes from you, and we have given you only what comes from your hand.

LUKE 1:33. Ps. 93:1 – 2. Nah. 1:3. Rom. 8:31. Dan. 3:17. John 10:29. 1 John 4:4. Ps. 115:1. 1 Chron. 29:11, 13 – 14.

OCTOBER 18

MORNING

One of the soldiers pierced Jesus' side with a spear, bringing a
sudden flow of blood and water.

"THIS IS THE blood of the covenant that the LORD has made with you." — "For
the life of a creature is in the blood, and I have given it to you to make atonement for yourselves on the altar; it is the blood that makes atonement for one's
life." — It is impossible for the blood of bulls and goats to take away sins.

"This is my blood of the covenant, which is poured out for many," he [Jesus]
said to them. — He entered the Most Holy Place once for all by his own blood,
having obtained eternal redemption. — Peace through his blood, shed on the cross.

For you know that it was not with perishable things such as silver or gold, that
you were redeemed, ... but with the precious blood of Christ, a lamb without
blemish or defect, ... revealed in these last times for your sake.

JOHN 19:34. Exod. 24:8. Lev. 17:11. Heb. 10:4. Mark 14:24. Heb. 9:12. Col. 1:20.
1 Peter 1:18 – 20.

EVENING

"Amen."

"AMEN! MAY THE LORD, the God of my lord the king, so declare it." — Whoever
invokes a blessing in the land will do so by the God of truth; he who takes an
oath in the land will swear by the God of truth.

When God made his promise to Abraham, since there was no one greater for
him to swear by, he swore by himself. ... Men swear by someone greater than
themselves, and the oath confirms what is said and puts an end to all argument.
Because God wanted to make the unchanging nature of his purpose very clear
to the heirs of what was promised, he confirmed it with an oath. God did this
so that, by two unchangeable things in which it is impossible for God to lie, we
who have fled to take hold of the hope offered to us may be greatly encouraged.

"These are the words of the Amen, the faithful and true witness." — For no matter how many promises God has made, they are "Yes" in Christ. — Praise be to the
LORD God, the God of Israel, who alone does marvelous deeds. Praise be to his glorious name forever; may the whole earth be filled with his glory. Amen and Amen.

MATT. 6:13. 1 Kings 1:36. Isa. 65:16. Heb. 6:13, 16 – 18. Rev. 3:14. 2 Cor. 1:20.
Ps. 72:18 – 19.

OCTOBER 19

MORNING

*For the LORD will be your confidence and will keep your foot
from being snared.*

SURELY YOUR WRATH against men brings you praise, and the survivors of your wrath are restrained. — The king's heart is in the hand of the LORD; he directs it like a watercourse wherever he pleases. . . . When a man's ways are pleasing to the LORD, he makes even his enemies live at peace with him.

I wait for the LORD, my soul waits, and in his word I put my hope. My soul waits for the Lord more than watchmen wait for the morning, more than watchmen wait for the morning. . . . I sought the LORD, and he answered me; he delivered me from all my fears.

"The eternal God is your refuge, and underneath are the everlasting arms. He will drive out your enemy before you, saying, 'Destroy him!' " — "But blessed is the man who trusts in the LORD, whose confidence is in him." — What, then, shall we say in response to this? If God is for us, who can be against us?

PROV. 3:26. Ps. 76:10. Prov. 21:1; 16:7. Pss. 130:5 – 6; 34:4. Deut. 33:27. Jer. 17:7. Rom. 8:31.

EVENING

*If you have any encouragement from being united with Christ, if any
comfort from his love, if any fellowship with the Spirit.*

"MAN BORN OF woman is of few days and full of trouble. He springs up like a flower and withers away; like a fleeting shadow, he does not endure." — My flesh and my heart may fail, but God is the strength of my heart and my portion forever.

"The Father . . . will give you another Counselor to be with you forever. . . . The Counselor, the Holy Spirit, whom the Father will send in my name." — Praise be to the God and Father of our Lord Jesus Christ, the Father of compassion and the God of all comfort, who comforts us in all our troubles, so that we can comfort those in any trouble with the comfort we ourselves have received from God.

We believe that Jesus died and rose again and so we believe that God will bring with Jesus those who have fallen asleep in him. . . . And so we will be with the Lord forever. Therefore encourage each other with these words.

PHIL. 2:1. Job. 14:1 – 2. Ps. 73:26. John 14:16, 26. 2 Cor. 1:3 – 4. 1 Thess. 4:14, 17 – 18.

OCTOBER 20

MORNING

For in my inner being I delight in God's law.

OH HOW I love your law! I meditate on it all day long. — When your words came, I ate them; they were my joy and my heart's delight. — I delight to sit in his shade, and his fruit is sweet to my taste. — "I have treasured the words of his mouth more than my daily bread."

"To do your will, O my God, is my desire; your law is within my heart." — "My food," said Jesus, "is to do the will of him who sent me and to finish his work."

The precepts of the LORD are right, giving joy to the heart. The commands of the LORD are radiant.... They are more precious than gold, than much pure gold; they are sweeter than honey, than honey from the comb. — Do not merely listen to the word, and so deceive yourselves. Do what it says. Anyone who listens to the word but does not do what it says is like a man who looks at his face in a mirror and ... goes away and immediately forgets what he looks like.

ROM. 7:22. Ps. 119:97. Jer. 15:16. Song of Songs 2:3. Job 23:12. Ps. 40:8. John 4:34. Ps. 19:8, 10. James 1:22–24.

EVENING

"May the LORD your God accept you."

WITH WHAT SHALL I come before the LORD and bow down before the exalted God? Shall I come before him with burnt offerings, with calves a year old? Will the LORD be pleased with thousands of rams, with ten thousand rivers of oil? Shall I offer my firstborn for my transgression, the fruit of my body for the sin of my soul? He has showed you, O man, what is good. And what does the LORD require of you? To act justly and to love mercy and to walk humbly with your God.

All of us have become like one who is unclean, and all our righteous acts are like filthy rags. — "There is no one righteous, not even one." ... For all have sinned and fall short of the glory of God, and are justified freely by his grace through the redemption that came by Christ Jesus. God presented him as a sacrifice of atonement, through faith in his blood. He did this to demonstrate his justice, because in his forbearance he had left the sins committed beforehand unpunished — he did it to demonstrate his justice at the present time, so as to be just and the one who justifies the man who has faith in Jesus.

2 SAM. 24:23. Mic. 6:6–8. Isa. 64:6. Rom. 3:10, 23–26.

MORNING

From the fullness of his grace we have all received
one blessing after another.

"THIS IS MY Son, whom I love; with him I am well pleased."—How great is the love the Father has lavished on us, that we should be called children of God!—His Son, whom he appointed heir of all things.—Now if we are children, then we are heirs—heirs of God and co-heirs with Christ, if indeed we share in his sufferings in order that we may also share in his glory.

"I and the Father are one." ... "The Father is in me, and I in the Father." ... "My Father and your Father,... my God and your God." ... "I in them and you in me. May they be brought to complete unity."

The church, which is his body, the fullness of him who fills everything in every way.—Since we have these promises, dear friends, let us purify ourselves from everything that contaminates body and spirit, perfecting holiness out of reverence for God.

JOHN 1:16. Matt. 17:5. 1 John 3:1. Heb. 1:2. Rom. 8:17. John 10:30, 38; 20:17; 17:23. Eph. 1:22–23. 2 Cor. 7:1.

EVENING

"No servant is greater than his master, nor is a messenger greater than
the one who sent him. Now that you know these things, you will be
blessed if you do them."

A DISPUTE AROSE among them as to which of them was considered to be greatest. Jesus said to them, "The kings of the Gentiles lord it over them; and those who exercise authority over them call themselves Benefactors. But you are not to be like that. Instead, the greatest among you should be like the youngest, and the one who rules like the one who serves. For who is greater, the one who is at the table or the one who serves? Is it not the one who is at the table? But I am among you as one who serves."—"Just as the Son of Man did not come to be served, but to serve, and to give his life as a ransom for many."

[Jesus] got up from the meal, took off his outer clothing, and wrapped a towel around his waist. After that, he poured water into a basin and began to wash his disciples' feet, drying them with the towel that was wrapped around him.

JOHN 13:16–17. Luke 22:24–27. Matt. 20:28. John 13:3–5.

OCTOBER 22

MORNING

My heart is steadfast, O God.

THE LORD IS my light and my salvation—whom shall I fear? The LORD is the stronghold of my life—of whom shall I be afraid?

You will keep in perfect peace him whose mind is steadfast, because he trusts in you.—He will have no fear of bad news; his heart is steadfast, trusting in the LORD. His heart is secure, he will have no fear; in the end he will look in triumph on his foes.

When I am afraid, I will trust in you.... For in the day of trouble he will keep me safe in his dwelling; he will hide me in the shelter of his tabernacle and set me high upon a rock. Then my head will be exalted above the enemies who surround me; at his tabernacle will I sacrifice with shouts of joy; I will sing and make music to the LORD.

The God of all grace, who called you to his eternal glory in Christ, after you have suffered a little while, will himself restore you and make you strong, firm and steadfast. To him be the power for ever and ever.

PS. 108:1. Ps. 27:1. Isa. 26:3. Pss. 112:7–8; 56:3; 27:5–6. 1 Peter 5:10–11.

EVENING

The LORD has established his throne in heaven, and his
kingdom rules over all.

THE LOT IS cast into the lap, but its every decision is from the LORD.—When disaster comes to a city, has not the LORD caused it?—"I am the LORD, and there is no other; apart from me there is no God. I will strengthen you, though you have not acknowledged me, so that from the rising of the sun to the place of its setting men may know there is none besides me. I am the LORD, and there is no other. I form the light and create darkness, I bring prosperity and create disaster; I, the LORD, do all these things."

He does as he pleases with the powers of heaven and the peoples of the earth. No one can hold back his hand or say to him: "What have you done?"—If God is for us, who can be against us?

For he must reign until he has put all his enemies under his feet.—"Do not be afraid, little flock, for your Father has been pleased to give you the kingdom."

PS. 103:19. Prov. 16:33. Amos 3:6. Isa. 45:5–7. Dan. 4:35. Rom. 8:31. 1 Cor. 15:25.
   Luke 12:32.

OCTOBER 23

MORNING

"A man's life does not consist in the abundance of his possessions."

BETTER THE LITTLE that the righteous have than the wealth of many wicked. — Better a little with the fear of the LORD than great wealth with turmoil. — Godliness with contentment is great gain.... If we have food and clothing, we will be content with that.

"Give me neither poverty nor riches, but give me only my daily bread. Otherwise, I may have too much and disown you and say, 'Who is the LORD?' Or I may become poor and steal, and so dishonor the name of my God."

"Give us today our daily bread." ... "Do not worry about your life, what you will eat or drink; or about your body, what you will wear. Is not life more important than food, and the body more important than clothes?" ... "When I sent you without purse, bag or sandals, did you lack anything?" — Keep your lives free from the love of money and be content with what you have, because God has said, "Never will I leave you; never will I forsake you."

LUKE 12:15. Ps. 37:16. Prov. 15:16. 1 Tim. 6:6, 8. Prov. 30:8 – 9. Matt. 6:11, 25. Luke 22:35. Heb. 13:5.

EVENING

"The Spirit gives life."

"THE FIRST MAN Adam became a living being"; the last Adam, a life-giving spirit. — "Flesh gives birth to flesh, but the Spirit gives birth to spirit." — He saved us, not because of righteous things we had done, but because of his mercy. He saved us through the washing of rebirth and renewal by the Holy Spirit.

If anyone does not have the Spirit of Christ, he does not belong to Christ. But if Christ is in you, your body is dead because of sin, yet your spirit is alive because of righteousness.... If the Spirit of him who raised Jesus from the dead is living in you, he who raised Christ from the dead will also give life to your mortal bodies through his Spirit, who lives in you.

I no longer live, but Christ lives in me. The life I live in the body, I live by faith in the Son of God. — In the same way, count yourselves dead to sin but alive to God in Christ Jesus.

JOHN 6:63. 1 Cor. 15:45. John 3:6. Titus 3:5. Rom. 8:9 – 11. Gal. 2:20. Rom. 6:11.

OCTOBER 24

MORNING

"I have been banished from your sight; yet I will look again toward your holy temple."

BUT ZION SAID, "The LORD has forsaken me, the Lord has forgotten me. Can a mother forget the baby at her breast and have no compassion on the child she has borne? Though she may forget, I will not forget you!"

I have forgotten what prosperity is. So I say, "My splendor is gone and all that I had hoped from the LORD." — Awake, O Lord! Why do you sleep? Rouse yourself! Do not reject us forever. — Why do you say, O Jacob, and complain, O Israel, "My way is hidden from the LORD; my cause is disregarded by my God"? ... "In a surge of anger I hid my face from you for a moment, but with everlasting kindness I will have compassion on you," says the LORD your Redeemer.

Why are you downcast, O my soul? Why so disturbed within me? Put your hope in God, for I will yet praise him, my Savior and my God. — We are hard pressed on every side, but not crushed; perplexed, but not in despair; persecuted, but not abandoned; struck down, but not destroyed.

JONAH 2:4. Isa. 49:14 – 15. Lam. 3:17 – 18. Ps. 44:23. Isa. 40:27; 54:8. Ps. 43:5.
2 Cor. 4:8 – 9.

EVENING

"The poor and needy search for water, but there is none; their tongues are parched with thirst. But I the LORD will answer them."

MANY ARE ASKING, "Who can show us any good?" — What does a man get for the toil and anxious striving with which he labors under the sun? All his days his work is pain and grief; even at night his mind does not rest. ... All of it is meaningless, a chasing after the wind. — "They have forsaken me, the spring of living water, and have dug their own cisterns, broken cisterns that cannot hold water."

"Whoever comes to me I will never drive away." — "For I will pour water on the thirsty land." — "Blessed are those who hunger and thirst for righteousness, for they will be filled."

O God, you are my God, earnestly I seek you; my soul thirsts for you, my body longs for you, in a dry and weary land where there is no water.

ISA. 41:17. Ps. 4:6. Eccl. 2:22 – 23, 17. Jer. 2:13. John 6:37. Isa. 44:3. Matt. 5:6. Ps. 63:1.

October 25

Morning

"Surely I will be with you always, to the very end of the age."

"If two of you on earth agree about anything you ask for, it will be done for you by my Father in heaven. For where two or three come together in my name, there am I with them." — "Whoever has my commands and obeys them, he is the one who loves me. He who loves me will be loved by my Father, and I too will love him and show myself to him." ... "But, Lord, why do you intend to show yourself to us and not to the world?" ... "If anyone loves me, he will obey my teaching. My Father will love him, and we will come to him and make our home with him."

To him who is able to keep you from falling and to present you before his glorious presence without fault and with great joy — to the only God our Savior be glory, majesty, power and authority, through Jesus Christ our Lord, before all ages, now and forevermore! Amen.

MATT. 28:20. Matt. 18:19–20. John 14:21–23. Jude 24–25.

Evening

The end of all things is near.

I saw a great white throne and him who was seated on it. Earth and sky fled from his presence. — The present heavens and earth are reserved for fire, being kept for the day of judgment.

God is our refuge and strength, an ever present help in trouble. Therefore we will not fear, though the earth give way and the mountains fall into the heart of the sea, though its waters roar and foam and the mountains quake with their surging. — "You will hear of wars and rumors of wars, but see to it that you are not alarmed."

We have a building from God, an eternal house in heaven, not built by human hands. — We are looking forward to a new heaven and a new earth, the home of righteousness. So then, dear friends, since you are looking forward to this, make every effort to be found spotless, blameless and at peace with him.

1 PETER 4:7. Rev. 20:11. 2 Peter 3:7. Ps. 46:1–3. Matt. 24:6. 2 Cor. 5:1. 2 Peter 3:13–14.

OCTOBER 26

MORNING

The LORD reigns.

"SHOULD YOU NOT fear me?" declares the LORD. "Should you not tremble in my presence? I made the sand a boundary for the sea, an everlasting barrier it cannot cross. The waves may roll, but they cannot prevail; they may roar, but they cannot cross it." — No one from the east or the west or from the desert can exalt a man. But it is God who judges: He brings one down, he exalts another.

He changes times and seasons; he sets up kings and deposes them. He gives wisdom to the wise and knowledge to the discerning. — "You will hear of wars and rumors of wars, but see to it that you are not alarmed."

If God is for us, who can be against us? — "Are not two sparrows sold for a penny? Yet not one of them will fall to the ground apart from the will of your Father. And even the very hairs of your head are all numbered. So don't be afraid; you are worth more than many sparrows."

PS. 99:1. Jer. 5:22. Ps. 75:6 – 7. Dan 2:21. Matt. 24:6. Rom. 8:31. Matt. 10:29 – 31.

EVENING

So guard yourself in your spirit.

"MASTER," SAID JOHN, "we saw a man driving out demons in your name and we tried to stop him, because he is not one of us." "Do not stop him," Jesus said, "for whoever is not against you is for you." ... "Lord, do you want us to call fire down from heaven to destroy them?" But Jesus turned and rebuked them.

"Eldad and Medad are prophesying in the camp." Joshua ... spoke up and said, "Moses, my lord, stop them!" But Moses replied, "Are you jealous for my sake? I wish that all the LORD's people were prophets and that the LORD would put his Spirit on them!"

But the fruit of the Spirit is love, joy, peace, patience, kindness, goodness, faithfulness, gentleness and self-control.... Those who belong to Christ Jesus have crucified the sinful nature with its passions and desires. Since we live by the Spirit, let us keep in step with the Spirit. Let us not become conceited, provoking and envying each other.

MAL. 2:15. Luke 9:49 – 50, 54 – 55. Num. 11:27 – 29. Gal. 5:22 – 26.

OCTOBER 27

MORNING

"He took up our infirmities and carried our diseases."

"THE PRIEST SHALL order that two live clean birds and some cedar wood, scarlet yarn and hyssop be brought for the one to be cleansed. Then the priest shall order that one of the birds be killed over fresh water in a clay pot. He is then to take the live bird and dip it, together with the cedar wood, the scarlet yarn and the hyssop, into the blood of the bird that was killed over the fresh water. Seven times he shall sprinkle the one to be cleansed of the infectious disease and pronounce him clean. Then he is to release the live bird in the open fields."

A man came along who was covered with leprosy. When he saw Jesus, he fell with his face to the ground and begged him, "Lord, if you are willing, you can make me clean." — Filled with compassion, Jesus reached out his hand and touched the man. "I am willing," he said. "Be clean!" Immediately the leprosy left him and he was cured.

MATT. 8:17. Lev. 14:4–7. Luke 5:12. Mark 1:41–42.

EVENING

Those you bless are blessed.

"BLESSED ARE THE poor in spirit, for theirs is the kingdom of heaven. Blessed are those who mourn, for they will be comforted. Blessed are the meek, for they will inherit the earth. Blessed are those who hunger and thirst for righteousness, for they will be filled. Blessed are the merciful, for they will be shown mercy. Blessed are the pure in heart, for they will see God. Blessed are the peacemakers, for they will be called sons of God. Blessed are those who are persecuted because of righteousness, for theirs is the kingdom of heaven."

"Blessed are you when people insult you, persecute you and falsely say all kinds of evil against you because of me. Rejoice and be glad, because great is your reward in heaven." — "Blessed rather are those who hear the word of God and obey it." — "Blessed are those who wash their robes, that they may have the right to the tree of life and may go through the gates into the city."

NUM. 22:6. Matt. 5:3–12. Luke 11:28. Rev. 22:14.

OCTOBER 28

MORNING

*He saw that there was no one, and he was appalled that there was no one
to intercede; so his own arm worked salvation for him.*

SACRIFICE AND OFFERING you did not desire, but my ears you have pierced;
burnt offerings and sin offerings you did not require. Then I said, "Here I am, I
have come — it is written about me in the scroll. To do your will, O my God, is
my desire; your law is within my heart." — "I lay down my life — only to take it
up again. No one takes it from me, but I lay it down of my own accord. I have
authority to lay it down and authority to take it up again."

"And there is no God apart from me, a righteous God and a Savior; there is
none but me. Turn to me and be saved, all you ends of the earth; for I am God,
and there is no other." By myself I have sworn, my mouth has uttered in all
integrity. — "There is no other name under heaven given to men by which we
must be saved."

ISA. 59:16. Ps. 40:6 – 8. John 10:17 – 18. Isa. 45:23. Acts 4:12.

EVENING

"The enemy."

BE SELF-CONTROLLED AND alert. Your enemy the devil prowls around like a roaring
lion looking for someone to devour. — Resist the devil, and he will flee from you.

Put on the full armor of God so that you can take your stand against the
devil's schemes. For our struggle is not against flesh and blood, but against the
rulers, against the authorities, against the powers of this dark world and against
the spiritual forces of evil in the heavenly realms. Therefore put on the full
armor of God, so that when the day of evil comes, you may be able to stand your
ground, and after you have done everything, to stand. Stand firm then, with the
belt of truth buckled around your waist, with the breastplate of righteousness in
place, and with your feet fitted with the readiness that comes from the gospel
of peace. In addition to all this, take up the shield of faith, with which you can
extinguish all the flaming arrows of the evil one.

Do not gloat over me, my enemy! Though I have fallen, I will rise. Though I
sit in darkness, the LORD will be my light.

LUKE 10:19. 1 Peter 5:8. James 4:7. Eph. 6:11 – 16. Mic. 7:8.

MORNING

He is altogether lovely.

MAY MY MEDITATION be pleasing to him. — My lover is outstanding among ten thousand. — "A chosen and precious cornerstone, and the one who trusts in him will never be put to shame." — You are the most excellent of men and your lips have been anointed with grace. — Therefore God exalted him to the highest place and gave him the name that is above every name. — For God was pleased to have all his fullness dwell in him.

Though you have not seen him, you love him; and even though you do not see him now, you believe in him and are filled with an inexpressible and glorious joy. — I consider everything a loss compared to the surpassing greatness of knowing Christ Jesus my Lord, for whose sake I have lost all things. I consider them rubbish, that I may gain Christ and be found in him, not having a righteousness of my own that comes from the law, but that which is through faith in Christ — the righteousness that comes from God and is by faith.

SONG OF SONGS 5:16. Ps. 104:34. Song of Songs 5:10. 1 Peter 2:6. Ps. 45:2. Phil. 2:9. Col. 1:19. 1 Peter 1:8. Phil. 3:8–9.

EVENING

David found strength in the LORD his God.

"LORD, TO WHOM shall we go? You have the words of eternal life." — I know whom I have believed, and am convinced that he is able to guard what I have entrusted to him for that day.

In my distress I called to the LORD; I cried to my God for help. From his temple he heard my voice; my cry came before him, into his ears.... They confronted me in the day of my disaster, but the LORD was my support. He brought me out into a spacious place; he rescued me because he delighted in me.

I will extol the LORD at all times; his praise will always be on my lips. My soul will boast in the LORD; let the afflicted hear and rejoice. Glorify the LORD with me; let us exalt his name together. I sought the LORD, and he answered me; he delivered me from all my fears.... Taste and see that the LORD is good; blessed is the man who takes refuge in him.

1 SAM. 30:6. John 6:68. 2 Tim. 1:12. Pss. 18:6, 18–19; 34:1–4, 8.

OCTOBER 30

MORNING

It is good to wait quietly for the salvation of the LORD.

"HAS GOD FORGOTTEN to be merciful? Has he in anger withheld his compassion?" … In my alarm I said, "I am cut off from your sight!" Yet you heard my cry for mercy when I called to you for help.

"Will not God bring about justice for his chosen ones, who cry out to him day and night? Will he keep putting them off? I tell you, he will see that they get justice, and quickly." — Wait for the LORD, and he will deliver you. — Be still before the LORD and wait patiently for him; do not fret when men succeed in their ways, when they carry out their wicked schemes.

You will not have to fight this battle. Take up your positions; stand firm and see the deliverance the LORD will give you. — Let us not become weary in doing good, for at the proper time we will reap a harvest if we do not give up. — See how the farmer waits for the land to yield its valuable crop and how patient he is for the fall and spring rains.

LAM. 3:26. Pss. 77:9; 31:22. Luke 18:7–8. Prov. 20:22. Ps. 37:7. 2 Chron. 20:17. Gal. 6:9. James 5:7.

EVENING

Catch for us the foxes, the little foxes that ruin the vineyards,
our vineyards that are in bloom.

WHO CAN DISCERN his errors? Forgive my hidden faults. — See to it that no one misses the grace of God and that no bitter root grows up to cause trouble and defile many. — You were running a good race. Who cut in on you and kept you from obeying the truth?

He who began a good work in you will carry it on to completion until the day of Christ Jesus…. Conduct yourselves in a manner worthy of the gospel of Christ. — The tongue is a small part of the body, but it makes great boasts. Consider what a great forest is set on fire by a small spark. The tongue also is a fire, a world of evil among the parts of the body. It corrupts the whole person, sets the whole course of his life on fire, and is itself set on fire by hell…. But no man can tame the tongue. It is a restless evil, full of deadly poison. — Let your conversation be always full of grace, seasoned with salt.

SONG OF SONGS 2:15. Ps. 19:12. Heb. 12:15. Gal. 5:7. Phil. 1:6, 27. James 3:5–6, 8. Col. 4:6.

OCTOBER 31

MORNING

"Not by might nor by power, but by my Spirit," says the LORD Almighty.

WHO HAS UNDERSTOOD the Spirit of the LORD, or instructed him as his counselor?—But God chose the foolish things of the world to shame the wise; God chose the weak things of the world to shame the strong. He chose the lowly things of this world and the despised things—and the things that are not—to nullify the things that are, so that no one may boast before him.

"The wind blows wherever it pleases. You hear its sound, but you cannot tell where it comes from or where it is going. So it is with everyone born of the Spirit." ... Born not of natural descent, nor of human decision or a husband's will, but born of God.

"And my Spirit remains among you. Do not fear."—For the battle is not yours, but God's.—It is not by sword or spear that the LORD saves; for the battle is the LORD's.

ZECH. 4:6. Isa. 40:13. 1 Cor. 1:27–29. John 3:8; 1:13. Hag. 2:5. 2 Chron. 20:15. 1 Sam. 17:47.

EVENING

"Do as you promised."

FULFILL YOUR PROMISE to your servant, so that you may be feared.... Then I will answer the one who taunts me, for I trust in your word.... Remember your word to your servant, for you have given me hope.... Your decrees are the theme of my song wherever I lodge.

The law from your mouth is more precious to me than thousands of pieces of silver and gold.... Your word, O LORD, is eternal; it stands firm in the heavens. Your faithfulness continues through all generations.

Because God wanted to make the unchanging nature of his purpose very clear to the heirs of what was promised, he confirmed it with an oath. God did this so that, by two unchangeable things in which it is impossible for God to lie, we who have fled to take hold of the hope offered to us may be greatly encouraged. We have this hope as an anchor for the soul, firm and secure. It enters the inner sanctuary behind the curtain, where Jesus, who went before us, has entered on our behalf.—Very great and precious promises.

2 SAM 7:25. Ps. 119:38, 42, 49, 54, 72, 89–90. Heb. 6:17–20. 2 Peter 1:4.

NOVEMBER 1

MORNING

Blessed is the man who listens to me, watching daily at my doors, waiting at my doorway.

AS THE EYES of slaves look to the hand of their master, as the eyes of a maid look to the hand of her mistress, so our eyes look to the LORD our God, till he shows us his mercy.

"For the generations to come this burnt offering is to be made regularly at the entrance to the Tent of Meeting before the LORD. There I will meet you and speak to you." ... "Wherever I cause my name to be honored, I will come to you and bless you."

"For where two or three come together in my name, there am I with them." — "Yet a time is coming and has now come when the true worshipers will worship the Father in spirit and truth, for they are the kind of worshipers the Father seeks. God is spirit, and his worshipers must worship in spirit and in truth."

Pray in the Spirit on all occasions with all kinds of prayers and requests. — Pray continually.

PROV. 8:34. Ps. 123:2. Exod. 29:42; 20:24. Matt. 18:20. John 4:23–24. Eph. 6:18.
1 Thess. 5:17.

EVENING

He will be called Wonderful Counselor.

THE SPIRIT OF the LORD will rest on him — the Spirit of wisdom and of understanding, the Spirit of counsel and of power, the Spirit of knowledge and of the fear of the LORD — and he will delight in the fear of the LORD. Does not wisdom call out? Does not understanding raise her voice?... "To you, O men, I call out; I raise my voice to all mankind." You who are simple, gain prudence; you who are foolish, gain understanding. Listen, for I have worthy things to say; I open my lips to speak what is right.... Counsel and sound judgment are mine; I have understanding and power.

The LORD Almighty, wonderful in counsel and magnificent in wisdom. — If any of you lacks wisdom, he should ask God, who gives generously to all without finding fault, and it will be given to him. — Trust in the LORD with all your heart and lean not on your own understanding. In all your ways acknowledge him, and he will make your paths straight.

ISA. 9:6. Isa. 11:2–3. Prov. 8:1, 4–6, 14. Isa. 28:29. James 1:5. Prov. 3:5–6.

November 2

Morning

Always try to be kind.

To THIS YOU were called, because Christ suffered for you, leaving you an example, that you should follow in his steps. "He committed no sin, and no deceit was found in his mouth." When they hurled their insults at him, he did not retaliate; when he suffered he made no threats. Instead, he entrusted himself to him who judges justly. — Consider him who endured such opposition from sinful men, so that you will not grow weary and lose heart.

Let us throw off everything that hinders and the sin that so easily entangles, and let us run with perseverance the race marked out for us. Let us fix our eyes on Jesus, the author and perfecter of our faith, who for the joy set before him endured the cross, scorning its shame, and sat down at the right hand of the throne of God.

Finally, brothers, whatever is true, whatever is noble, whatever is right, whatever is pure, whatever is lovely, whatever is admirable—if anything is excellent or praiseworthy—think about such things.

1 THESS. 5:15. 1 Peter 2:21–23. Heb. 12:3, 1–2. Phil. 4:8.

Evening

The Mighty God.

You ARE THE most excellent of men and your lips have been anointed with grace, since God has blessed you forever. Gird your sword upon your side, O mighty one; clothe yourself with splendor and majesty. In your majesty ride forth victoriously.... Your throne, O God, will last for ever and ever; a scepter of justice will be the scepter of your kingdom.... Once you spoke in a vision, to your faithful people you said: "I have bestowed strength on a warrior."—"The man who is close to me!"

"Surely God is my salvation; I will trust and not be afraid. The LORD, the LORD, is my strength and my song; he has become my salvation."—Thanks be to God, who always leads us in triumphal procession in Christ.—To him who is able to keep you from falling and to present you before his glorious presence without fault and with great joy—to the only God our Savior be glory, majesty, power and authority, through Jesus Christ our Lord, before all ages, now and forevermore!

ISA. 9:6. Pss. 45:2–4, 6; 89:19. Zech. 13:7. Isa. 12:2. 2 Cor. 2:14. Jude 24–25.

NOVEMBER 3

MORNING

The ways of the LORD are right; the righteous walk in them,
but the rebellious stumble in them.

NOW TO YOU who believe, this stone is precious. But to those who do not believe, "The stone the builders rejected has become the capstone." — The way of the LORD is a refuge for the righteous, but it is the ruin of those who do evil.

"He who has ears, let him hear." — Whoever is wise, let him heed these things and consider the great love of the LORD. — "The eye is the lamp of the body. If your eyes are good, your whole body will be full of light." — "If any one chooses to do God's will, he will find out whether my teaching comes from God." — "Whoever has will be given more, and he will have an abundance."

"He who belongs to God hears what God says. The reason you do not hear is that you do not belong to God." ... "Yet you refuse to come to me to have life." ... "My sheep listen to my voice; I know them, and they follow me."

HOS. 14:9. 1 Peter 2:7 – 8. Prov. 10:29. Matt. 11:15. Ps. 107:43. Matt. 6:22. John 7:17. Matt. 13:12. John 8:47; 5:40; 10:27.

EVENING

Everlasting Father.

HEAR. O ISRAEL: The LORD our God, the LORD is one.

"I and the Father are one.... The Father is in me, and I in the Father." ... "If you knew me, you would know my Father also." ... Philip said, "Lord, show us the Father and that will be enough for us." Jesus answered: "Don't you know me, Philip, even after I have been among you such a long time? Anyone who has seen me has seen the Father." — "Here am I, and the children God has given me."

After the suffering of his soul, he will see the light of life and be satisfied. — "I am the Alpha and the Omega," says the Lord God, "who is, and who was, and who is to come, the Almighty." — "Before Abraham was born, I am!" — God said to Moses, "I am who I am. This is what you are to say to the Israelites: 'I AM has sent me to you.'"

About the Son he says, "Your throne, O God, will last for ever and ever." — He is before all things, and in him all things hold together.... In Christ all the fullness of the Deity lives in bodily form.

ISA. 9:6. Deut. 6:4. John 10:30, 38; 8:19; 14:8 – 9. Heb. 2:13. Isa. 53:11. Rev. 1:8. John 8:58. Exod. 3:14. Heb. 1:8. Col. 1:17; 2:9.

NOVEMBER 4

MORNING

*In this you greatly rejoice, though now for a little while you
may have had to suffer grief in all kinds of trials.*

DEAR FRIENDS, DO not be surprised at the painful trial you are suffering, as
though something strange were happening to you. But rejoice that you participate in the sufferings of Christ, so that you may be overjoyed when his glory
is revealed. — That word of encouragement that addresses you as sons: "My
son, do not make light of the Lord's discipline, and do not lose heart when he
rebukes you." ... No discipline seems pleasant at the time, but painful. Later on,
however, it produces a harvest of righteousness and peace for those who have
been trained by it.

For we do not have a high priest who is unable to sympathize with our weaknesses, but we have one who has been tempted in every way, just as we are — yet
was without sin.... Because he himself suffered when he was tempted, he is able
to help those who are being tempted.

1 PETER 1:6. 1 Peter 4:12–13. Heb. 12:5, 11; 4:15; 2:18.

EVENING

Prince of Peace.

HE WILL JUDGE your people in righteousness, your afflicted ones with justice. The
mountains will bring prosperity to the people, the hills the fruit of righteousness.
He will defend the afflicted among the people and save the children of the needy;
he will crush the oppressor. He will endure as long as the sun, as long as the moon,
through all generations. He will be like rain falling on a mown field, like showers
watering the earth. In his days the righteous will flourish; prosperity will abound till
the moon is no more. — "Glory to God in the highest, and on earth peace to men."

"Because of the tender mercy of our God, by which the rising sun will come to
us from heaven to shine on those living in darkness and in the shadow of death, to
guide our feet into the path of peace." — Peace through Jesus Christ, who is Lord
of all.

"I have told you these things, so that in me you may have peace. In this world
you will have trouble. But take heart! I have overcome the world." ... "Peace I
leave with you; my peace I give you. I do not give to you as the world gives."

ISA. 9:6. Ps. 72:2–7. Luke 2:14; 1:78–79. Acts 10:36. John 16:33; 14:27.

NOVEMBER 5

MORNING

"Take the following fine spices.... Make these into a sacred anointing oil."

Do not pour it on men's bodies and do not make any oil with the same formula. It is sacred, and you are to consider it sacred. — One Spirit. — There are different kinds of gifts, but the same Spirit.

Therefore God, your God, has set you above your companions by anointing you with the oil of joy. — "God anointed Jesus of Nazareth with the Holy Spirit and power." — "God gives the Spirit without limit."

From the fullness of his grace we have all received. — The anointing you received from him remains in you, and you do not need anyone to teach you. But as his anointing teaches you about all things and as that anointing is real, not counterfeit — just as it has taught you, remain in him. — God who ... anointed us, set his seal of ownership on us, and put his Spirit in our hearts.

But the fruit of the Spirit is love, joy, peace, patience, kindness, goodness, faithfulness, gentleness and self-control. Against such things there is no law.

EXOD. 30:23, 25. Exod. 30:32. Eph. 4:4. 1 Cor. 12:4. Ps. 45:7. Acts 10:38. John 3:34; 1:16. 1 John 2:27. 2 Cor. 1:21–22. Gal. 5:22–23.

EVENING

For this world in its present form is passing away.

Altogether, Methuselah lived 969 years, and then he died. — The brother in humble circumstances ought to take pride in his high position. But the one who is rich should take pride in his low position, because he will pass away like a wild flower. For the sun rises with scorching heat and withers the plant; its blossom falls and its beauty is destroyed. In the same way, the rich man will fade away even while he goes about his business.... What is your life? You are a mist that appears for a little while and then vanishes. — The world and its desires pass away, but the man who does the will of God lives forever.

"Show me, O Lord, my life's end and the number of my days; let me know how fleeting is my life." — While people are saying, "Peace and safety," destruction will come on them suddenly, as labor pains on a pregnant woman, and they will not escape. But you, brothers, are not in darkness so that this day should surprise you like a thief.

1 COR. 7:31. Gen. 5:27. James 1:9–11; 4:14. 1 John 2:17. Ps. 39:4. 1 Thess. 5:3–4.

NOVEMBER 6

MORNING

When Christ, who is your life, appears, then you also will
appear with him in glory.

"I AM THE resurrection and the life. He who believes in me will live, even though he dies." — God has given us eternal life, and this life is in his Son. He who has the Son has life; he who does not have the Son of God does not have life.

For the Lord himself will come down from heaven, with a loud command, with the voice of the archangel and with the trumpet call of God, and the dead in Christ will rise first. After that, we who are still alive and are left will be caught up with them in the clouds to meet the Lord in the air. And so we will be with the Lord forever. Therefore encourage each other with these words. — But we know that when he appears, we shall be like him, for we shall see him as he is. — It is sown in dishonor, it is raised in glory; it is sown in weakness, it is raised in power.

"And if I go and prepare a place for you, I will come back and take you to be with me that you also may be where I am."

COL. 3:4. John 11:25. 1 John 5:11–12. 1 Thess. 4:16–18. 1 John 3:2. 1 Cor. 15:43. John 14:3.

EVENING

Guide me in your truth and teach me.

"BUT WHEN HE, the Spirit of truth, comes, he will guide you into all truth." — But you have an anointing from the Holy One, and all of you know the truth.

To the law and to the testimony! If they do not speak according to this word, they have no light of dawn. — All Scripture is God-breathed and is useful for teaching, rebuking, correcting and training in righteousness, so that the man of God may be thoroughly equipped for every good work.... The holy Scriptures ... are able to make you wise for salvation through faith in Christ Jesus.

I will instruct you and teach you in the way you should go; I will counsel you and watch over you. — "The eye is the lamp of the body. If your eyes are good, your whole body will be full of light." — "If any one chooses to do God's will, he will find out whether my teaching comes from God." — Wicked fools will not go about on it.

PS. 25:5. John 16:13. 1 John 2:20. Isa. 8:20. 2 Tim. 3:16–17, 15. Ps. 32:8. Matt. 6:22. John 7:17. Isa. 35:8.

NOVEMBER 7

MORNING

*Let them give thanks to the LORD for his unfailing love and
his wonderful deeds for men.*

TASTE AND SEE that the LORD is good; blessed is the man who takes refuge in him.... How great is your goodness, which you have stored up for those who fear you.

"The people I formed for myself that they may proclaim my praise."—He predestined us to be adopted as his sons through Jesus Christ, in accordance with his pleasure and will—to the praise of his glorious grace, which he has freely given us in the One he loves.... In order that we, who were the first to hope in Christ, might be for the praise of his glory.

How attractive and beautiful they will be!—The LORD is good to all; he has compassion on all he has made. All you have made will praise you, O LORD; your saints will extol you. They will tell of the glory of your kingdom and speak of your might, so that all men may know of your mighty acts and the glorious splendor of your kingdom.

PS. 107:8. Pss. 34:8; 31:19. Isa. 43:21. Eph. 1:5–6, 12. Zech. 9:17. Ps. 145:9–12.

EVENING

We consider blessed those who have persevered.

WE ALSO REJOICE in our sufferings, because we know that suffering produces perseverance; perseverance, character; and character, hope. And hope does not disappoint us, because God has poured out his love into our hearts by the Holy Spirit, whom he has given us.—No discipline seems pleasant at the time, but painful. Later on, however, it produces a harvest of righteousness and peace for those who have been trained by it.

Consider it pure joy, my brothers, whenever you face trials of many kinds, because you know that the testing of your faith develops perseverance. Perseverance must finish its work so that you may be mature and complete, not lacking anything.... Blessed is the man who perseveres under trial, because when he has stood the test, he will receive the crown of life that God has promised to those who love him.—Therefore I will boast all the more gladly about my weaknesses, so that Christ's power may rest on me. That is why, for Christ's sake, I delight in weaknesses, in insults, in hardships, in persecutions, in difficulties. For when I am weak, then I am strong.

JAMES 5:11. Rom. 5:3–5. Heb. 12:11. James 1:2–4, 12. 2 Cor. 12:9–10.

NOVEMBER 8

MORNING

Since we belong to the day, let us be self-controlled, putting on faith and hue as a breastplate, and the hope of salvation as a helmet.

THEREFORE, PREPARE YOUR minds for action; be self-controlled; set your hope fully on the grace to be given you when Jesus Christ is revealed. — Stand firm then, with the belt of truth buckled around your waist, with the breastplate of righteousness in place.... In addition to all this, take up the shield of faith, with which you can extinguish all the flaming arrows of the evil one. Take the helmet of salvation and the sword of the Spirit, which is the word of God.

He will swallow up death forever. The Sovereign LORD will wipe away the tears from all faces; he will remove the disgrace of his people from all the earth. The LORD has spoken. In that day they will say, "Surely this is our God; we trusted in him, and he saved us. This is the LORD, we trusted in him; let us rejoice and be glad in his salvation."

Now faith is being sure of what we hope for and certain of what we do not see.

1 THESS. 5:8. 1 Peter 1:13. Eph. 6:14, 16–17. Isa. 25:8–9. Heb. 11:1.

EVENING

The Israelites camped opposite them like two small flocks of goats, while the Arameans covered the countryside.

"THIS IS WHAT the LORD says: 'Because the Arameans think the LORD is a god of the hills and not a god of the valleys, I will deliver this vast army into your hands, and you will know that I am the LORD.'" For seven days they camped opposite each other, and on the seventh day the battle was joined. The Israelites inflicted a hundred thousand casualties on the Aramean foot soldiers in one day. — You, dear children, are from God and have overcome them, because the one who is in you is greater than the one who is in the world.

"So do not fear, for I am with you; do not be dismayed, for I am your God. I will strengthen you and help you; I will uphold you with my righteous right hand." — "They will fight against you but will not overcome you, for I am with you and will rescue you," declares the LORD.

1 KINGS 20:27. 1 Kings 20:28–29. 1 John 4:4. Isa. 41:10. Jer. 1:19.

NOVEMBER 9

MORNING

*"I have bestowed strength on a warrior; I have exalted a
young man from among the people."*

"I, EVEN I, am the LORD, and apart from me there is no savior." — For there is one God and one mediator between God and men, the man Christ Jesus. — "There is no other name under heaven given to men by which we must be saved."

Mighty God. — But made himself nothing, taking the very nature of a servant, being made in human likeness. And being found in appearance as a man, he humbled himself and became obedient to death — even death on a cross! Therefore God exalted him to the highest place and gave him the name that is above every name. — But we see Jesus, who was made a little lower than the angels, now crowned with glory and honor because he suffered death, so that by the grace of God he might taste death for everyone.... Since the children have flesh and blood, he too shared in their humanity.

PS. 89:19. Isa. 43:11. 1 Tim. 2:5. Acts 4:12. Isa. 9:6. Phil. 2:7–9. Heb. 2:9, 14.

EVENING

*"Gather to me my consecrated ones, who made a covenant
with me by sacrifice."*

So CHRIST WAS sacrificed once to take away the sins of many people; and he will appear a second time, not to bear sin, but to bring salvation.... For this reason Christ is the mediator of a new covenant, that those who are called may receive the promised eternal inheritance.

"Father, I want those you have given me to be with me where I am." — "And he will send his angels and gather his elect from the four winds, from the ends of the earth to the ends of the heavens." — Even if you have been banished to the most distant land under the heavens, from there the LORD your God will gather you and bring you back.

The dead in Christ will rise first. After that, we who are still alive and are left will be caught up with them in the clouds to meet the Lord in the air. And so we will be with the Lord forever.

PS. 50:5. Heb. 9:28, 15. John 17:24. Mark 13:27. Deut. 30:4. 1 Thess. 4:16–17.

November 10

Morning

Bearing fruit in every good work, growing in the knowledge of God.

Therefore, I urge you, brothers, in view of God's mercy, to offer your bodies as living sacrifices, holy and pleasing to God—which is your spiritual worship. Do not conform any longer to the pattern of this world, but be transformed by the renewing of your mind. Then you will be able to test and approve what God's will is—his good, pleasing and perfect will.... Just as you used to offer the parts of your body in slavery to impurity and to ever-increasing wickedness, so now offer them in slavery to righteousness leading to holiness.

Neither circumcision nor uncircumcision means anything; what counts is a new creation. Peace and mercy to all who follow this rule, even to the Israel of God.—"This is my Father's glory, that you bear much fruit, showing yourselves to be my disciples.... I chose you to go and bear fruit—fruit that will last. Then the Father will give you whatever you ask in my name. This is my command: Love each other."

COL. 1:10. Rom. 12:1–2; 6:19. Gal. 6:15–16. John 15:8, 16–17.

Evening

I looked for him but did not find him.

Return, O Israel, to the Lord your God. Your sins have been your downfall! Take words with you and return to the Lord. Say to him: "Forgive all our sins and receive us graciously."

When tempted, no one should say, "God is tempting me." For God cannot be tempted by evil, nor does he tempt anyone; but each one is tempted when, by his own evil desire, he is dragged away and enticed. Then, after desire has conceived, it gives birth to sin; and sin, when it is full-grown, gives birth to death. Don't be deceived, my dear brothers. Every good and perfect gift is from above, coming down from the Father of the heavenly lights, who does not change like shifting shadows.

Wait for the Lord; be strong and take heart and wait for the Lord.—It is good to wait quietly for the salvation of the Lord.—And will not God bring about justice for his chosen ones, who cry out to him day and night? Will he keep putting them off?

My soul finds rest in God alone; my salvation comes from him.... Find rest, O my soul, in God alone; my hope comes from him.

SONG OF SONGS 3:1. Hos. 14:1–2. James 1:13–17. Ps. 27:14. Lam. 3:26. Luke 18:7. Ps. 62:1, 5.

November 11

Morning

He guided them safely.

I WALK IN the way of righteousness, along the paths of justice. — "See, I am sending an angel ahead of you to guard you along the way and to bring you to the place I have prepared." — In all their distress he too was distressed, and the angel of his presence saved them. In his love and mercy he redeemed them; he lifted them up and carried them all the days of old.

It was not by their sword that they won the land, nor did their arm bring them victory; it was your right hand, your arm, and the light of your face, for you loved them. — This is how you guided your people to make for yourself a glorious name.

Lead me, O LORD, in your righteousness because of my enemies — make straight your way before me.... Send forth your light and your truth, let them guide me; let them bring me to your holy mountain, to the place where you dwell. Then will I go to the altar of God, to God, my joy and my delight. I will praise you with the harp, O God, my God.

PS. 78:53. Prov. 8:20. Exod. 23:20. Isa. 63:9. Ps. 44:3. Isa. 63:14. Pss. 5:8; 43:3–4.

Evening

But you were washed, you were sanctified, you were justified.

THE BLOOD OF Jesus, his Son, purifies us from every sin. — The punishment that brought us peace was upon him, and by his wounds we are healed.

Christ loved the church and gave himself up for her to make her holy, cleansing her by the washing with water through the word, and to present her to himself as a radiant church, without stain or wrinkle or any other blemish, but holy and blameless. — "Fine linen, bright and clean, was given her to wear." (Fine linen stands for the righteous acts of the saints.) — Let us draw near to God with a sincere heart in full assurance of faith, having our hearts sprinkled to cleanse us from a guilty conscience and having our bodies washed with pure water.

Who will bring any charge against those whom God has chosen? It is God who justifies. — Blessed is he whose transgressions are forgiven, whose sins are covered. Blessed is the man whose sin the LORD does not count against him and in whose spirit is no deceit.

1 COR. 6:11. 1 John 1:7. Isa. 53:5. Eph. 5:25–27. Rev. 19:8. Heb. 10:22. Rom. 8:33. Ps. 32:1–2.

November 12

Morning

Godly sorrow brings repentance that leads to salvation and leaves no regret.

Then Peter remembered the word Jesus had spoken: "Before the rooster crows, you will disown me three times." And he went outside and wept bitterly. — If we confess our sins, he is faithful and just and will forgive us our sins and purify us from all unrighteousness.... The blood of Jesus, his Son, purifies us from every sin.

For troubles without number surround me; my sins have overtaken me, and I cannot see. They are more than the hairs of my head, and my heart fails within me. Be pleased, O Lord, to save me; O Lord, come quickly to help me. — But you must return to your God; maintain love and justice, and wait for your God always.

The sacrifices of God are a broken spirit; a broken and contrite heart, O God, you will not despise.... He heals the brokenhearted and binds up their wounds. — He has showed you, O man, what is good. And what does the Lord require of you? To act justly and to love mercy and to walk humbly with your God.

2 COR. 7:10. Matt. 26:75. 1 John 1:9, 7. Ps. 40:12 – 13. Hos. 12:6. Pss. 51:17; 147:3. Mic. 6:8.

Evening

"Are you all right?" ... "Everything is all right," she said.

With that same spirit of faith.... Beaten, and yet not killed; sorrowful, yet always rejoicing; poor, yet making many rich; having nothing, and yet possessing everything.

We are hard pressed on every side, but not crushed; perplexed, but not in despair; persecuted, but not abandoned; struck down, but not destroyed. We always carry around in our body the death of Jesus, so that the life of Jesus may also be revealed in our body.... Therefore we do not lose heart. Though outwardly we are wasting away, yet inwardly we are being renewed day by day. For our light and momentary troubles are achieving for us an eternal glory that far outweighs them all. So we fix our eyes not on what is seen, but on what is unseen.

Dear friend, I pray that you may enjoy good health and that all may go well with you, even as your soul is getting along well.

2 KINGS 4:26. 2 Cor. 4:13; 6:9 – 10; 4:8 – 10, 16 – 18. 3 John 2.

NOVEMBER 13

MORNING

Christ loved the church and gave himself up for her to make her holy,
cleansing her by the washing with water through the word.

AND LIVE A life of love, just as Christ loved us and gave himself up for us as a fragrant offering and sacrifice to God.

For you have been born again, not of perishable seed, but of imperishable, through the living and enduring word of God. — Sanctify them by the truth; your word is truth.... Unless a man is born of water and the Spirit, he cannot enter the kingdom of God. — Not because of righteous things we had done, but because of his mercy. He saved us through the washing of rebirth and renewal by the Holy Spirit.

Your promise renews my life.... The law of the LORD is perfect, reviving the soul. The statutes of the LORD are trustworthy, making wise the simple. The precepts of the LORD are right, giving joy to the heart. The commands of the LORD are radiant, giving light to the eyes.

EPH. 5:25 – 26. Eph. 5:2. 1 Peter 1:23. John 17:17; 3:5. Titus 3:5. Pss. 119:50; 19:7 – 8.

EVENING

For through him we both have access to the Father by one Spirit.

"I IN THEM and you in me. May they be brought to complete unity." ... "And I will do whatever you ask in my name, so that the Son may bring glory to the Father. You may ask me for anything in my name, and I will do it.... And I will ask the Father, and he will give you another Counselor to be with you forever — the Spirit of truth. The world cannot accept him, because it neither sees him nor knows him. But you know him, for he lives with you and will be in you."

There is one body and one Spirit — just as you were called to one hope when you were called — one Lord, one faith, one baptism; one God and Father of all, who is over all and through all and in all. — "When you pray, say: 'Father, hallowed be your name, your kingdom come.'"

Therefore, brothers, since we have confidence to enter the Most Holy Place by the blood of Jesus, by a new and living way,... let us draw near.

EPH. 2:18. John 17:23; 14:13 – 14, 16 – 17. Eph. 4:4 – 6. Luke 11:2. Heb. 10:19 – 20, 22.

NOVEMBER 14

MORNING

You are my help and my deliverer; O my God, do not delay.

THE LORD DELIGHTS in the way of the man whose steps he has made firm; though he stumble, he will not fall, for the LORD upholds him with his hand.—He who fears the LORD has a secure fortress, and for his children it will be a refuge.—Who are you that you fear mortal men, the sons of men, who are but grass, that you forget the LORD your Maker?

"I am with you and will rescue you," declares the LORD.—"Be strong and courageous. Do not be afraid or terrified because of them, for the LORD your God goes with you; he will never leave you nor forsake you."

But I will sing of your strength, in the morning I will sing of your love; for you are my fortress, my refuge in times of trouble.... You are my hiding place; you will protect me from trouble and surround me with songs of deliverance.

PS. 40:17. Ps. 37:23–24. Prov. 14:26. Isa. 51:12–13. Jer. 1:8. Deut. 31:6. Pss. 59:16; 32:7.

EVENING

How will you manage in the thickets by the Jordan?

NOW THE JORDAN is at flood stage all during harvest.... The priests who carried the ark of the covenant of the LORD stood firm on dry ground in the middle of the Jordan, while all Israel passed by until the whole nation had completed the crossing on dry ground.

But we see Jesus, who was made a little lower than the angels, now crowned with glory and honor because he suffered death, so that by the grace of God he might taste death for everyone.

Even though I walk through the valley of the shadow of death, I will fear no evil, for you are with me; your rod and your staff, they comfort me.—"When you pass through the waters, I will be with you; and when you pass through the rivers, they will not sweep over you."

"Do not be afraid. I am the First and the Last. I am the Living One; I was dead, and behold I am alive for ever and ever! And I hold the keys of death and Hades."

JER. 12:5. Josh. 3:15, 17. Heb. 2:9. Ps. 23:4. Isa. 43:2. Rev. 1:17–18.

NOVEMBER 15

MORNING

God, who has called you into fellowship with his Son Jesus Christ our Lord, is faithful.

LET US HOLD unswervingly to the hope we profess, for he who promised is faithful. — As God has said: "I will live with them and walk among them, and I will be their God, and they will be my people." — And our fellowship is with the Father and with his Son, Jesus Christ. — But rejoice that you participate in the sufferings of Christ, so that you may be overjoyed when his glory is revealed.

And I pray that you, being rooted and established in love, may have power, together with all the saints, to grasp how wide and long and high and deep is the love of Christ, and to know this love that surpasses knowledge — that you may be filled to the measure of all the fullness of God.

If anyone acknowledges that Jesus is the Son of God, God lives in him and he in God.... Those who obey his commands live in him, and he in them.

1 COR. 1:9. Heb. 10:23. 2 Cor. 6:16. 1 John 1:3. 1 Peter 4:13. Eph. 3:17–19.
1 John 4:15; 3:24.

EVENING

We are God's workmanship.

THEY REMOVED FROM the quarry large blocks of quality stone to provide a foundation of dressed stone for the temple.... In building the temple, only blocks dressed at the quarry were used, and no hammer, chisel or any other iron tool was heard at the temple site while it was being built.

You also, like living stones, are being built into a spiritual house. — Built on the foundation of the apostles and prophets, with Christ Jesus himself as the chief cornerstone. In him the whole building is joined together and rises to become a holy temple in the Lord. And in him you too are being built together to become a dwelling in which God lives by his Spirit. — Once you were not a people, but now you are the people of God.

You are ... God's building. — Therefore, if anyone is in Christ, he is a new creation; the old has gone, the new has come!... Now it is God who has made us for this very purpose and has given us the Spirit as a deposit, guaranteeing what is to come.

EPH. 2:10. 1 Kings 5:17; 6:7. 1 Peter 2:5. Eph. 2:20–22. 1 Peter 2:10. 1 Cor. 3:9.
2 Cor. 5:17, 5.

NOVEMBER 16

MORNING

"Sanctify them by the truth; your word is truth."

"YOU ARE ALREADY clean because of the word I have spoken to you." — Let the word of Christ dwell in you richly as you teach and admonish one another with all wisdom. — How can a young man keep his way pure? By living according to your word. I seek you with all my heart; do not let me stray from your commands.

For wisdom will enter your heart, and knowledge will be pleasant to your soul. Discretion will protect you, and understanding will guard you. — My feet have closely followed his steps; I have kept to his way without turning aside. I have not departed from the commands of his lips; I have treasured the words of his mouth more than my daily bread. — I have more insight than all my teachers, for I meditate on your statutes. — "If you hold to my teaching, you are really my disciples. Then you will know the truth, and the truth will set you free."

JOHN 17:17. John 15:3. Col. 3:16. Ps. 119:9 – 10. Prov. 2:10 – 11. Job 23:11 – 12. Ps. 119:99. John 8:31 – 32.

EVENING

Fellow citizens with God's people

BUT YOU HAVE come to Mount Zion, to the heavenly Jerusalem, the city of the living God. You have come to thousands upon thousands of angels in joyful assembly, to the church of the firstborn, whose names are written in heaven. You have come to God, the judge of all men, to the spirits of righteous men made perfect.... All these people were still living by faith when they died. They did not receive the things promised; they only saw them and welcomed them from a distance. And they admitted that they were aliens and strangers on earth.

But our citizenship is in heaven. And we eagerly await a Savior from there, the Lord Jesus Christ, who, by the power that enables him to bring everything under his control, will transform our lowly bodies so that they will be like his glorious body. — The Father ... has rescued us from the dominion of darkness and brought us into the kingdom of the Son he loves.

As aliens and strangers in the world,... abstain from sinful desires, which war against your soul.

EPH. 2:19. Heb. 12:22 – 23; 11:13. Phil. 3:20 – 21. Col 1:12 – 13. 1 Peter 2:11.

November 17

Morning

How profound your thoughts!

We have not stopped praying for you and asking God to fill you with the knowledge of his will through all spiritual wisdom and understanding. — That you, being rooted and established in love, may have power, together with all the saints, to grasp how wide and long and high and deep is the love of Christ, and to know this love that surpasses knowledge — that you may be filled to the measure of all the fullness of God.

Oh, the depth of the riches of the wisdom and knowledge of God! How unsearchable his judgments, and his paths beyond tracing out! — "For my thoughts are not your thoughts, neither are your ways my ways," declares the Lord. "As the heavens are higher than the earth, so are my ways higher than your ways and my thoughts than your thoughts." — Many, O Lord my God, are the wonders you have done. The things you planned for us no one can recount to you; were I to speak and tell of them, they would be too many to declare.

PS. 92:5. Col. 1:9. Eph. 3:17 – 19. Rom. 11:33. Isa. 55:8 – 9. Ps. 40:5.

Evening

A man reaps what he sows.

As I have observed, those who plow evil and those who sow trouble reap it. — "They sow the wind and reap the whirlwind." — One who sows to please his sinful nature, from that nature will reap destruction.

But he who sows righteousness reaps a sure reward. — The one who sows to please the Spirit, from the Spirit will reap eternal life. Let us not become weary in doing good, for at the proper time we will reap a harvest if we do not give up. Therefore, as we have opportunity, let us do good to all people, especially to those who belong to the family of believers.

One man gives freely, yet gains even more; another withholds unduly, but comes to poverty. A generous man will prosper; he who refreshes others will himself be refreshed. — Whoever sows sparingly will also reap sparingly, and whoever sows generously will also reap generously.

GAL. 6:7. Job 4:8. Hos. 8:7. Gal. 6:8. Prov. 11:18. Gal. 6:8 – 10. Prov. 11:24 – 25. 2 Cor. 9:6.

NOVEMBER 18

MORNING

With his fierce blast he drives her out, as on a day the east wind blows.

"LET US FALL into the hands of the LORD, for his mercy is great; but do not let me fall into the hands of men." — "I am with you and will save you," declares the LORD.... "I will discipline you but only with justice; I will not let you go entirely unpunished." — He will not always accuse, nor will he harbor his anger forever; he does not treat us as our sins deserve or repay us according to our iniquities.... For he knows how we are formed, he remembers that we are dust. — "I will spare them, just as in compassion a man spares his son who serves him."

God is faithful; he will not let you be tempted beyond what you can bear. But when you are tempted, he will also provide a way out so that you can stand up under it. — "Satan has asked to sift you as wheat. But I have prayed for you, Simon, that your faith may not fail."

You have been a refuge for the poor, a refuge for the needy in his distress, a shelter from the storm and a shade from the heat: For the breath of the ruthless is like a storm driving against a wall.

ISA. 27:8. 2 Sam. 24:14. Jer. 30:11. Ps. 103:9 – 10, 14. Mal. 3:17. 1 Cor. 10:13. Luke 22:31 – 32. Isa. 25:4.

EVENING

"I did not believe these things until I came and saw with my own eyes. Indeed, not even half was told me."

"THE QUEEN OF the South will rise at the judgment with this generation and condemn it; for she came from the ends of the earth to listen to Solomon's wisdom, and now one greater than Solomon is here." — We have seen his glory, the glory of the one and only Son, who came from the Father, full of grace and truth.

My message and my preaching were not with wise and persuasive words, but with a demonstration of the Spirit's power, so that your faith might not rest on men's wisdom, but on God's power.... However, as it is written: "No eye has seen, no ear has heard, no mind has conceived what God has prepared for those who love him" — but God has revealed it to us by his Spirit. The Spirit searches all things, even the deep things of God.

Your eyes will see the king in his beauty. — In my flesh I will see God; I will be satisfied.

1 KINGS 10:7. Matt. 12:42. John 1:14. 1 Cor. 2:4 – 5, 9 – 10. Isa. 33:17. 1 John 3:2. Job 19:26. Ps. 17:15.

November 19

Morning

"By their fruits you will recognize them."

Dear children, do not let anyone lead you astray. He who does what is right is righteous, just as he is righteous. — Can both fresh water and salt water flow from the same spring? My brothers, can a fig tree bear olives, or a grapevine bear figs? Neither can a salt spring produce fresh water. Who is wise and understanding among you? Let him show it by his good life, by deeds done in the humility that comes from wisdom. — Live such good lives among the pagans that, though they accuse you of doing wrong, they may see your good deeds and glorify God on the day he visits us.

"Make a tree good and its fruit will be good, or make a tree bad and its fruit will be bad, for a tree is recognized by its fruit.... The good man brings good things out of the good stored up in him, and the evil man brings evil things out of the evil stored up in him."

"What more could have been done for my vineyard than I have done for it?"

Matt. 7:20. 1 John 3:7. James 3:11–13. 1 Peter 2:12. Matt. 12:33, 35. Isa. 5:4.

Evening

"I will glorify the place of my feet."

This is what the Lord says: "Heaven is my throne and the earth is my footstool."

"Will God really dwell on earth with men? The heavens, even the highest heavens, cannot contain you. How much less this temple I have built."

"This is what the Lord Almighty says: In a little while I will once more shake the heavens and the earth, the sea and the dry land. I will shake all nations, and the desired of all nations will come, and I will fill this house with glory,' says the Lord Almighty.... "The glory of this present house will be greater than the glory of the former house,' says the Lord Almighty."

I saw a new heaven and a new earth, for the first heaven and the first earth had passed away, and there was no longer any sea.... And I heard a loud voice from the throne saying, "Now the dwelling of God is with men, and he will live with them. They will be his people, and God himself will be with them and be their God."

Isa. 60:13. Isa. 66:1. 2 Chron. 6:18. Hag. 2:6–7, 9. Rev. 21:1, 3.

November 20

Morning

Though I sit in darkness, the LORD will be my light.

"When you pass through the waters, I will be with you; and when you pass through the rivers they will not sweep over you. When you walk through the fire, you will not be burned; the flames will not set you ablaze. For I am the LORD, your God, the Holy One of Israel, your Savior." ... "I will lead the blind by ways they have not known, along unfamiliar paths I will guide them; I will turn the darkness into light before them and make the rough places smooth. These are the things I will do; I will not forsake them."

Even though I walk through the valley of the shadow of death, I will fear no evil, for you are with me; your rod and your staff, they comfort me.... When I am afraid, I will trust in you. In God, whose word I praise, in God I trust; I will not be afraid. What can mortal man do to me?... The LORD is my light and my salvation—whom shall I fear? The LORD is the stronghold of my life—of whom shall I be afraid?

MIC. 7:8. Isa. 43:2–3; 42:16. Pss. 23:4; 56:3–4; 27:1.

Evening

For there is one God and one mediator between God and men, the man Christ Jesus.

Hear, O Israel: The LORD our God, the LORD is one. — A mediator, however, does not represent just one party; but God is one.

We have sinned, even as our fathers did; we have done wrong and acted wickedly. When our fathers were in Egypt, they gave no thought to your miracles; they did not remember your many kindnesses.... So he said he would destroy them—had not Moses, his chosen one, stood in the breach before him to keep his wrath from destroying them.

Therefore, holy brothers, who share in the heavenly calling, fix your thoughts on Jesus, the apostle and high priest whom we confess. He was faithful to the one who appointed him, just as Moses was faithful in all God's house. Jesus has been found worthy of greater honor than Moses, just as the builder of a house has greater honor than the house itself.... The covenant of which he is mediator is superior to the old one, and it is founded on better promises.... "For I will forgive their wickedness and will remember their sins no more."

1 TIM. 2:5. Deut. 6:4. Gal. 3:20. Ps. 106:6–7, 23. Heb. 3:1–3; 8:6, 12.

November 21

Morning

"Whoever comes to me I will never drive away."

"When he cries out to me, I will hear, for I am compassionate."—"I will not reject them or abhor them so as to destroy them completely, breaking my covenant with them. I am the Lord their God."—"I will remember the covenant I made with you in the days of your youth, and I will establish an everlasting covenant with you."

"Come now, let us reason together," says the Lord. "Though your sins are like scarlet, they shall be as white as snow; though they are red as crimson, they shall be like wool." ... Let the wicked forsake his way and the evil man his thoughts. Let him turn to the Lord, and he will have mercy on him, and to our God, for he will freely pardon.—"Jesus, remember me when you come into your kingdom." Jesus answered him, "I tell you the truth, today you will be with me in paradise."

A bruised reed he will not break, and a smoldering wick he will not snuff out.

JOHN 6:37. Exod. 22:27. Lev. 26:44. Ezek. 16:60. Isa. 1:18; 55:7. Luke 23:42–43. Isa. 42:3.

Evening

The Son he loves.

"This is my Son, whom I love; with him I am well pleased."—"Here is my servant, whom I uphold. My chosen one in whom I delight."—God, the only Son ... is at the Father's side.

This is how God showed his love among us: He sent his one and only Son into the world that we might live through him. This is love: not that we loved God, but that he loved us and sent his Son as an atoning sacrifice for our sins.... And so we know and rely on the love God has for us. God is love.

"I have given them the glory that you gave me, that they may be one as we are one: I in them and you in me. May they be brought to complete unity to let the world know that you sent me and have loved them even as you have loved me."—How great is the love the Father has lavished on us, that we should be called children of God!

COL. 1:13. Matt. 3:17. Isa. 42:1. John 1:18. 1 John 4:9–10, 16. John 17:22–23. 1 John 3:1.

NOVEMBER 22

MORNING

Pray in the Holy Spirit.

"GOD IS SPIRIT, and his worshipers must worship in spirit and in truth." — For through him we both have access to the Father by one Spirit. — "My Father, if it is possible, may this cup be taken from me. Yet not as I will, but as you will."

In the same way, the Spirit helps us in our weakness. We do not know what we ought to pray, but the Spirit himself intercedes for us with groans that words cannot express. And he who searches our hearts knows the mind of the Spirit, because the Spirit intercedes for the saints in accordance with God's will. — This is the assurance we have in approaching God: that if we ask anything according to his will, he hears us. — "But when he, the Spirit of truth, comes, he will guide you into all truth."

And pray in the Spirit on all occasions with all kinds of prayers and requests.

JUDE 20. John 4:24. Eph. 2:18. Matt. 26:39. Rom. 8:26–27. 1 John 5:14. John 16:13. Eph. 6:18.

EVENING

At least there is hope for a tree: If it is cut down, it will sprout
again, and its new shoots will not fail.

A BRUISED REED he will not break. — He restores my soul. — Godly sorrow brings repentance that leads to salvation and leaves no regret, but worldly sorrow brings death. — No discipline seems pleasant at the time, but painful. Later on, however, it produces a harvest of righteousness and peace for those who have been trained by it.

Before I was afflicted I went astray, but now I obey your word. — "What has happened to us is a result of our evil deeds and our great guilt, and yet, our God, you have punished us less than our sins have deserved and have given us a remnant like this."

Do not gloat over me, my enemy! Though I have fallen, I will rise. Though I sit in darkness, the LORD will be my light.... He will bring me out into the light; I will see his justice.

JOB 14:7. Isa. 42:3. Ps. 23:3. 2 Cor. 7:10. Heb. 12:11. Ps. 119:67. Ezra 9:13. Mic. 7:8–9.

NOVEMBER 23

MORNING

*"But whoever listens to me will live in safety and be at ease,
without fear of harm."*

LORD, YOU HAVE been our dwelling place throughout all generations.... He who dwells in the shelter of the Most High will rest in the shadow of the Almighty.... His faithfulness will be your shield and rampart.

Your life is now hidden with Christ in God.—For whoever touches you touches the apple of his eye.—"Do not be afraid. Stand firm and you will see the deliverance the LORD will bring you today. The Egyptians you see today you will never see again. The LORD will fight for you; you need only to be still."—God is our refuge and strength, an ever present help in trouble. Therefore we will not fear.

But Jesus immediately said to them: "Take courage! It is I. Don't be afraid."—"Why are you troubled, and why do doubts rise in your minds? Look at my hands and my feet. It is I myself! Touch me and see; a ghost does not have flesh and bones, as you see I have."—I know whom I have believed, and am convinced that he is able to guard what I have entrusted to him for that day.

PROV. 1:33. Pss. 90:1; 91:1, 4. Col. 3:3. Zech. 2:8. Exod. 14:13–14. Ps. 46:1–2.
Matt. 14:27. Luke 24:38–39. 2 Tim. 1:12.

EVENING

"My kingdom is not of this world."

BUT WHEN THIS priest had offered for all time one sacrifice for sins, he sat down at the right hand of God. Since that time he waits for his enemies to be made his footstool.—"In the future you will see the Son of Man sitting at the right hand of the Mighty One and coming on the clouds of heaven."—For he must reign until he has put all his enemies under his feet.

But thanks be to God! He gives us the victory through our Lord Jesus Christ.—He [God] raised him [Christ] from the dead and seated him at his right hand in the heavenly realms, far above all rule and authority, power and dominion, and every title that can be given, not only in the present age but also in the one to come. And God placed all things under his feet and appointed him to be head over everything for the church, which is his body, the fullness of him who fills everything in every way.—God, the blessed and only Ruler, the King of kings and Lord of lords.

JOHN 18:36. Heb. 10:12–13. Matt. 26:64. 1 Cor. 15:25, 57. Eph. 1:20–23. 1 Tim. 6:15.

November 24

Morning

"My mother and brothers are those who hear God's word and put it into practice."

Both the one who makes men holy and those who are made holy are of the same family. So Jesus is not ashamed to call them brothers. He says, "I will declare your name to my brothers; in the presence of the congregation I will sing your praises."—For in Christ Jesus neither circumcision nor uncircumcision has any value. The only thing that counts is faith expressing itself through love.—"You are my friends if you do what I command."

"Blessed rather are those who hear the word of God and obey it."—"Not everyone who says to me, 'Lord, Lord,' will enter the kingdom of heaven, but only he who does the will of my Father who is in heaven."—"My food," said Jesus, "is to do the will of him who sent me."

If we claim to have fellowship with him yet walk in the darkness, we lie and do not live by the truth.... But if anyone obeys his word, God's love is truly made complete in him. This is how we know we are in him.

LUKE 8:21. Heb. 2:11–12. Gal. 5:6. John 15:14. Luke 11:28. Matt. 7:21. John 4:34. 1 John 1:6; 2:5.

Evening

"What are you doing here, Elijah?"

He knows the way that I take.—O Lord, you have searched me and you know me. You know when I sit and when I rise; you perceive my thoughts from afar. You discern my going out and my lying down; you are familiar with all my ways.... Where can I go from your Spirit? Where can I flee from your presence?... If I rise on the wings of the dawn, if I settle on the far side of the sea, even there your hand will guide me, your right hand will hold me fast.

Elijah was a man just like us.—Fear of man will prove to be a snare, but whoever trusts in the Lord is kept safe.—Though he stumble, he will not fall, for the Lord upholds him with his hand.—For though a righteous man falls seven times, he rises again.

Let us not become weary in doing good, for at the proper time we will reap a harvest if we do not give up.—"Watch and pray so that you will not fall into temptation. The spirit is willing, but the body is weak."

1 KINGS 19:9. Job. 23:10. Ps. 139:1–3, 7, 9–10. James 5:17. Prov. 29:25. Ps. 37:24. Prov. 24:16. Gal. 6:9. Matt. 26:41.

November 25

Morning

You have been set free from sin and have become slaves to righteousness.

"You cannot serve both God and Money." — When you were slaves to sin, you were free from the control of righteousness. What benefit did you reap at that time from the things you are now ashamed of? Those things result in death! But now that you have been set free from sin and have become slaves to God, the benefit you reap leads to holiness, and the result is eternal life.... Christ is the end of the law so that there may be righteousness for everyone who believes.

"Whoever serves me must follow me; and where I am, my servant also will be. My Father will honor the one who serves me." — "Take my yoke upon you and learn from me, for I am gentle and humble in heart, and you will find rest for your souls. For my yoke is easy and my burden is light."

O Lord, our God, other lords besides you have ruled over us, but your name alone do we honor. — I run in the path of your commands, for you have set my heart free.

ROM. 6:18. Matt. 6:24. Rom. 6:20–22; 10:4. John 12:26. Matt. 11:29–30. Isa. 26:13. Ps. 119:32.

Evening

"And everyone who calls on the name of the Lord will be saved."

[Manasseh] did evil in the eyes of the Lord, following the detestable practices of the nations the Lord had driven out before the Israelites. He rebuilt the high places his father Hezekiah had destroyed.... He bowed down to all the starry hosts and worshiped them.... In both courts of the temple of the Lord, he built altars to all the starry hosts. He sacrificed his own son in the fire, practiced sorcery and divination, and consulted mediums and spiritists. He did much evil in the eyes of the Lord, provoking him to anger. — In his distress he sought the favor of the Lord his God and humbled himself greatly before the God of his fathers. And when he prayed to him, the Lord was moved by his entreaty and listened to his plea.

"Come now, let us reason together," says the Lord. "Though your sins are like scarlet, they shall be as white as snow; though they are red as crimson, they shall be like wool." — He is patient with you, not wanting anyone to perish.

ACTS 2:21. 2 Kings 21:2–3, 5–6. 2 Chron. 33:12–13. Isa. 1:18. 2 Peter 3:9.

NOVEMBER 26

MORNING

For the LORD will take delight in you.

THIS IS WHAT the LORD says—he who created you,... "Fear not, for I have redeemed you; I have called you by name; you are mine." ... "Can a mother forget the baby at her breast and have no compassion on the child she has borne? Though she may forget, I will not forget you! See, I have engraved you on the palms of my hands; your walls are ever before me."

The LORD delights in the way of the man whose steps he has made firm.—Delighting in mankind.—The LORD delights in those who fear him, who put their hope in his unfailing love.—"They will be mine," says the LORD Almighty, "in the day when I make up my treasured possession. I will spare them, just as in compassion a man spares his son who serves him."

Once you were alienated from God and were enemies in your minds because of your evil behavior. But now he has reconciled you by Christ's physical body through death to present you holy in his sight, without blemish and free from accusation.

ISA. 62:4. Isa. 43:1; 49:15–16. Ps. 37:23. Prov. 8:31. Ps. 147:11. Mal. 3:17.
Col. 1:21–22.

EVENING

Worldly sorrow brings death.

WHEN AHITHOPHEL SAW that his advice had not been followed, he saddled his donkey and set out for his house in his home town. He put his house in order and then hanged himself.—A crushed spirit who can bear?

Is there no balm in Gilead? Is there no physician there? Why then is there no healing for the wound of my people?—The LORD has anointed me to preach good news to the poor. He has sent me to bind up the brokenhearted, to proclaim freedom for the captives and release for the prisoners, to proclaim the year of the LORD's favor and the day of vengeance of our God, to comfort all who mourn, and provide for those who grieve in Zion—to bestow on them a crown of beauty instead of ashes, the oil of gladness instead of mourning, and a garment of praise instead of a spirit of despair.

"Come to me, all you who are weary and burdened, and I will give you rest. Take my yoke upon you and learn from me, for I am gentle and humble in heart, and you will find rest for your souls. For my yoke is easy and my burden is light."

2 COR. 7:10. 2 Sam. 17:23. Prov. 18:14. Jer. 8:22. Isa. 61:1–3. Matt. 11:28–30.

NOVEMBER 27

MORNING

"I have given them the glory that you gave me."

I SAW THE LORD seated on a throne, high and exalted, and the train of his robe filled the temple. Above him were seraphs.... And they were calling to one another: "Holy, holy, holy is the LORD Almighty; the whole earth is full of his glory." — Isaiah said this because he saw Jesus' glory and spoke about man.... Like the appearance of a rainbow in the clouds on a rainy day, so was the radiance around him. This was the appearance of the likeness of the glory of the LORD.

Then Moses said, "Now show me your glory." ... "But," he said, "you cannot see my face, for no one may see me and live." — No one has ever seen God, but God the only Son, who is at the Father's side, has made him known. — For God, who said, "Let light shine out of darkness," made his light shine in our hearts to give us the light of the knowledge of the glory of God in the face of Christ.

JOHN 17:22. Isa. 6:1–3. John 12:41. Ezek. 1:26, 28. Exod. 33:18, 20. John 1:18. 2 Cor. 4:6.

EVENING

My son, if sinners entice you, do not give in to them.

SHE TOOK SOME [fruit] and ate. She also gave some to her husband, who was with her, and he ate it. — "When Achan son of Zerah acted unfaithfully regarding the devoted things, did not wrath come upon the whole community of Israel? He was not the only one who died for his sin." — "Do not follow the crowd in doing wrong."

"For wide is the gate and broad is the road that leads to destruction, and many enter through it." — For none of us lives to himself alone. — You, my brothers, were called to be free. But do not use your freedom to indulge the sinful nature; rather, serve one another in love. — Be careful, however, that the exercise of your freedom does not become a stumbling block to the weak.... When you sin against your brothers in this way and wound their weak conscience, you sin against Christ.

We all, like sheep, have gone astray, each of us has turned to his own way; and the LORD has laid on him the iniquity of us all.

PROV. 1:1. Gen. 3:6. Josh. 22:20. Exod. 23:2. Matt. 7:13. Rom. 14:7. Gal. 5:13.
1 Cor. 8:9, 12. Isa. 53:6.

NOVEMBER 28

MORNING

As the body without the spirit is dead, so faith without deeds is dead.

"NOT EVERYONE WHO says to me, 'Lord, Lord,' will enter the kingdom of heaven, but only he who does the will of my Father who is in heaven." —Without holiness no one will see the Lord.—Add to your faith goodness; and to goodness, knowledge; and to knowledge, self-control; and to self-control, perseverance; and to perseverance, godliness; and to godliness, brotherly kindness; and to brotherly kindness, love. For if you possess these qualities in increasing measure, they will keep you from being ineffective and unproductive in your knowledge of our Lord Jesus Christ. But if anyone does not have them, he is nearsighted and blind, and has forgotten that he has been cleansed from his past sins. Therefore, my brothers, be all the more eager to make your calling and election sure. For if you do these things, you will never fall.

JAMES 2:26. Matt. 7:21. Heb. 12:14. 2 Peter 1:5–10.

EVENING

Since the children have flesh and blood, he too shared in their humanity;
so that by his death he might destroy him who holds the power of
death—that is, the devil—and free those who all their lives were held in
slavery by their fear of death.

THE STING OF death is sin, and the power of sin is the law.... Thanks be to God! He gives us the victory through our Lord Jesus Christ.—Therefore we do not lose heart. Though outwardly we are wasting away, yet inwardly we are being renewed day by day.... Now we know that if the earthly tent we live in is destroyed, we have a building from God, an eternal house in heaven, not built by human hands.... Therefore we are always confident and know that as long as we are at home in the body we are away from the Lord. We live by faith, not by sight. We are confident, I say, and would prefer to be away from the body and at home with the Lord.

"Do not let your hearts be troubled. Trust in God; trust also in me. In my Father's house are many rooms; if it were not so, I would have told you. I am going there to prepare a place for you."

HEB. 2:14–15. 1 Cor. 15:55, 57. 2 Cor. 4:16; 5:1, 6–8. John 14:1–3.

NOVEMBER 29

MORNING

We are filled with the good things of your house.

ONE THING I ask of the LORD, this is what I seek: that I may dwell in the house of the LORD all the days of my life, to gaze upon the beauty of the LORD and to seek him in his temple.

"Blessed are those who hunger and thirst for righteousness, for they will be filled." — "He has filled the hungry with good things but has sent the rich away empty."

For he satisfies the thirsty and fills the hungry with good things. — "I am the bread of life. He who comes to me will never go hungry, and he who believes in me will never be thirsty." — How priceless is your unfailing love! Both high and low among men find refuge in the shadow of your wings. They feast on the abundance of your house; you give them drink from your river of delights. For with you is the fountain of life; in your light we see light.

PS. 65:4. Ps. 27:4. Matt. 5:6. Luke 1:53. Ps. 107:9. John 6:35. Ps. 36:7 – 9.

EVENING

"You believe at last!"

WHAT GOOD IS it, my brothers, if a man claims to have faith but has no deeds? Can such faith save him? . . . Faith by itself, if it is not accompanied by action, is dead.

By faith Abraham, when God tested him, offered Isaac as a sacrifice. He who had received the promises was about to sacrifice his one and only son, even though God had said to him, "It is through Isaac that your offspring will be reckoned." Abraham reasoned that God could raise the dead. — Was not our ancestor Abraham considered righteous for what he did when he offered his son Isaac on the altar? . . . You see that a person is justified by what he does and not by faith alone. . . . But the man who looks intently into the perfect law that gives freedom, and continues to do this, not forgetting what he has heard, but doing it — he will be blessed in what he does.

"Thus, by their fruit you will recognize them. Not everyone who says to me, 'Lord, Lord,' will enter the kingdom of heaven, but only he who does the will of my Father who is in heaven." — "Now that you know these things, you will be blessed if you do them."

JOHN 16:31. James 2:14, 17. Heb. 11:17 – 19. James 2:21, 24; 1:25. Matt. 7:20 – 21. John 13:17.

NOVEMBER 30

MORNING

Now may the Lord of peace himself give you peace at all times and in every way. The Lord be with all of you.

GRACE AND PEACE to you from him who is, and who was, and who is to come. — The peace of God, which transcends all understanding, will guard your hearts and your minds in Christ Jesus. Jesus himself stood among them and said to them, "Peace be with you." — "Peace I leave with you; my peace I give you. I do not give to you as the world gives. Do not let your hearts be troubled and do not be afraid.... The Counselor ... Spirit of truth."

But the fruit of the Spirit is love, joy, peace. — The Spirit himself testifies with our spirit that we are God's children.

"My Presence will go with you, and I will give you rest." Then Moses said to him, "If your Presence does not go with us, do not send us up from here. How will anyone know that you are pleased with me and with your people unless you go with us?"

2 THESS. 3:16. Rev. 1:4. Phil. 4:7. Luke 24:36. John 14:27; 15:26. Gal. 5:22. Rom. 8:16. Exod. 33:14–16.

EVENING

We ... rejoice in our sufferings.

IF ONLY FOR this life we have hope in Christ, we are to be pitied more than all men. — Dear friends, do not be surprised at the painful trial you are suffering, as though something strange were happening to you. But rejoice that you participate in the sufferings of Christ, so that you may be overjoyed when his glory is revealed. — Sorrowful, yet always rejoicing.

Rejoice in the Lord always. I will say it again: Rejoice! — The apostles left the Sanhedrin, rejoicing because they had been counted worthy of suffering disgrace for the Name. — May the God of hope fill you with all joy and peace as you trust in him.

Though the fig tree does not bud and there are no grapes on the vines, though the olive crop fails and the fields produce no food, though there are no sheep in the pen and no cattle in the stalls, yet I will rejoice in the LORD, I will be joyful in God my Savior.

ROM. 5:3. 1 Cor. 15:19. 1 Peter 4:12–13. 2 Cor. 6:10. Phil. 4:4. Acts 5:41. Rom. 15:13. Hab. 3:17–18.

DECEMBER 1

MORNING

Each man will be like a shelter from the wind and a refuge from the storm.

SINCE THE CHILDREN have flesh and blood, he too shared in their humanity. — "The man who is close to me!" declares the LORD Almighty. — "I and the Father are one."

He who dwells in the shelter of the Most High will rest in the shadow of the Almighty. — It will be a shelter and shade from the heat of the day, and a refuge and hiding place from the storm and rain. — The LORD is your shade at your right hand; the sun will not harm you by day, nor the moon by night.

I call as my heart grows faint; lead me to the rock that is higher than I. . . . You are my hiding place; you will protect me from trouble. — You have been a refuge for the poor, a refuge for the needy in his distress, a shelter from the storm and a shade from the heat: For the breath of the ruthless is like a storm driving against a wall.

ISA. 32:2. Heb. 2:14. Zech. 13:7. John 10:30. Ps. 91:1. Isa. 4:6. Pss. 121:5 – 6; 61:2; 32:7. Isa. 25:4.

EVENING

"Behold, I will create new heavens and a new earth."

"As THE NEW heavens and the new earth that I make will endure before me, . . . so will your name and descendants endure." — In keeping with his promise we are looking forward to a new heaven and a new earth, the home of righteousness.

Then I saw a new heaven and a new earth, for the first heaven and the first earth had passed away, and there was no longer any sea. I saw the Holy City, the new Jerusalem, coming down out of heaven from God, prepared as a bride beautifully dressed for her husband. And I heard a loud voice from the throne saying, "Now the dwelling of God is with men, and he will live with them. They will be his people, and God himself will be with them and be their God. He will wipe every tear from their eyes. There will be no more death or mourning or crying or pain, for the old order of things has passed away." He who was seated on the throne said, "I am making everything new!"

ISA. 65:17. Isa. 66:22. 2 Peter 3:13. Rev. 21:1 – 5.

DECEMBER 2

MORNING

But you have an anointing from the Holy One, and all of you know the truth.

"GOD ANOINTED JESUS of Nazareth with the Holy Spirit and power." — For God was pleased to have all his fullness dwell in him. — From the fullness of his grace we have all received one blessing after another.

You anoint my head with oil. — The anointing you received from him remains in you, and you do not need anyone to teach you. But as his anointing teaches you about all things and as that anointing is real, not counterfeit — just as it has taught you, remain in him.

"The Counselor, the Holy Spirit, whom the Father will send in my name, will teach you all things and will remind you of everything I have said to you." — The Spirit helps us in our weakness. We do not know what we ought to pray, but the Spirit himself intercedes for us with groans that words cannot express.

1 JOHN 2:20. Acts 10:38. Col. 1:19. John 1:16. Ps. 23:5. 1 John 2:27. John 14:26.
Rom. 8:26.

EVENING

Having our hearts sprinkled to cleanse us from a guilty conscience.

THE BLOOD OF goats and bulls and the ashes of a heifer sprinkled on those who are ceremonially unclean sanctify them so that they are outwardly clean. How much more, then, will the blood of Christ, who through the eternal Spirit offered himself unblemished to God, cleanse our consciences from acts that lead to death, so that we may serve the living God!... The sprinkled blood that speaks a better word than the blood of Abel.

In him we have redemption through his blood, the forgiveness of sins, in accordance with the riches of God's grace.

When Moses had proclaimed every commandment of the law to all the people, he took the blood of calves, together with water, scarlet wool and branches of hyssop, and sprinkled the scroll and all the people.... In the same way, he sprinkled with the blood both the tabernacle and everything used in its ceremonies. In fact, the law requires that nearly everything be cleansed with blood, and without the shedding of blood there is no forgiveness.

HEB. 10:22. Heb. 9:13–14; 12:24. Eph. 1:7. Heb. 9:19, 21–22.

DECEMBER 3

MORNING

"But if it were I, I would appeal to God; I would lay my cause before him."

IS ANYTHING TOO hard for the LORD?—Commit your way to the LORD; trust in him and he will do this.—Do not be anxious about anything, but in everything, by prayer and petition, with thanksgiving, present your requests to God.—Cast all your anxiety on him because he cares for you.

Hezekiah received the letter from the messengers and read it. Then he went up to the temple of the LORD and spread it out before the LORD. And Hezekiah prayed to the LORD. . . . "Before they call I will answer; while they are still speaking I will hear."—The prayer of a righteous man is powerful and effective.

I love the LORD, for he heard my voice; he heard my cry for mercy. Because he turned his ear to me, I will call on him as long as I live.

JOB 5:8. Gen. 18:14. Ps. 37:5. Phil. 4:6. 1 Peter 5:7. Isa. 37:14–15; 65:24. James 5:16. Ps. 116:1–2.

EVENING

Our bodies washed with pure water.

"MAKE A BRONZE basin, with its bronze stand, for washing. Place it between the Tent of Meeting and the altar, and put water in it. Aaron and his sons are to wash their hands and feet with water from it. Whenever they enter the Tent of Meeting, they shall wash with water so that they will not die. Also, when they approach the altar to minister by presenting an offering made to the LORD by fire, they shall wash their hands and feet so that they will not die."—Your body is a temple of the Holy Spirit, who is in you. . . . If anyone destroys God's temple, God will destroy him; for God's temple is sacred, and you are that temple.

Yet in my flesh I will see God; myself will see him with my own eyes—I, and not another.—Nothing impure will ever enter it.—Your eyes are too pure to look on evil; you cannot tolerate wrong.—Therefore, I urge you, brothers, in view of God's mercy, to offer your bodies as living sacrifices, holy and pleasing to God—which is your spiritual worship.

HEB. 10:22. Exod. 30:18–21. 1 Cor. 6:19; 3:17. Job 19:26–27. Rev. 21:27. Hab. 1:13. Rom. 12:1.

DECEMBER 4

MORNING

"But where can wisdom be found?"

IF ANY OF you lacks wisdom, he should ask God, who gives generously to all without finding fault, and it will be given to him. But when he asks, he must believe and not doubt. — Trust in the LORD with all your heart and lean not on your own understanding; in all your ways acknowledge him, and he will make your paths straight. — The only God. — Do not be wise in your own eyes.

"Ah, Sovereign LORD," I said, "I do not know how to speak; I am only a child." But the LORD said to me, "Do not say, 'I am only a child.' You must go to everyone I send you to and say whatever I command you. Do not be afraid of them, for I am with you and will rescue you," declares the LORD.

"My Father will give you whatever you ask in my name. Until now you have not asked for anything in my name. Ask and you will receive, and your joy will be complete." — "If you believe, you will receive whatever you ask for in prayer."

JOB 28:12. James 1:5–6. Prov. 3:5–6. 1 Tim. 1:17. Prov. 3:7. Jer. 1:6–8. John 16:23–24. Matt. 21:22.

EVENING

I would not live forever.

I SAID, "OH, that I had the wings of a dove! I would fly away and be at rest.... I would hurry to my place of shelter, far from the tempest and storm."

Meanwhile we groan, longing to be clothed with our heavenly dwelling.... For while we are in this tent, we groan and are burdened, because we do not wish to be unclothed but to be clothed with our heavenly dwelling, so that what is mortal may be swallowed up by life. — I desire to depart and be with Christ, which is better by far.

Let us run with perseverance the race marked out for us. Let us fix our eyes on Jesus, the author and perfecter of our faith, who for the joy set before him endured the cross, scorning its shame, and sat down at the right hand of the throne of God. Consider him who endured such opposition from sinful men, so that you will not grow weary and lose heart. — "Do not let your hearts be troubled and do not be afraid."

JOB 7:16. Ps. 55:6, 8. 2 Cor. 5:2, 4. Phil. 1:23. Heb. 12:1–3. John 14:27.

DECEMBER 5

MORNING

It was good for me to be afflicted so that I might learn your decrees.

ALTHOUGH HE WAS a son, he learned obedience from what he suffered. — We share in his sufferings in order that we may also share in his glory. I consider that our present sufferings are not worth comparing with the glory that will be revealed in us.

But he knows the way that I take; when he has tested me, I will come forth as gold. My feet have closely followed his steps; I have kept to his way without turning aside.

Remember how the LORD your God led you all the way in the desert these forty years, to humble you and to test you in order to know what was in your heart, whether or not you would keep his commands.... Know then in your heart that as a man disciplines his son, so the LORD your God disciplines you. Observe the commands of the LORD your God, walking in his ways and revering him.

PS. 119:71. Heb. 5:8. Rom. 8:17–18. Job 23:10–11. Deut. 8:2, 5–6.

EVENING

"It is not by strength that one prevails."

DAVID SAID TO the Philistine, "You come against me with sword and spear and javelin, but I come against you in the name of the LORD Almighty, the God of the armies of Israel, whom you have defied.... Reaching into his bag and taking out a stone, he slung it and struck the Philistine on the forehead. The stone sank into his forehead, and he fell facedown on the ground. So David triumphed over the Philistine with a sling and a stone.

No king is saved by the size of his army; no warrior escapes by his great strength.... But the eyes of the LORD are on those who fear him, on those whose hope is in his unfailing love. — Wealth and honor come from you; you are the ruler of all things. In your hands are strength and power to exalt and give strength to all.

Therefore I will boast all the more gladly about my weaknesses, so that Christ's power may rest on me. That is why, for Christ's sake, I delight in weaknesses, in insults, in hardships, in persecutions, in difficulties. For when I am weak, then I am strong.

1 SAM. 2:9. 1 Sam. 17:45, 49–50. Ps. 33:16, 18. 1 Chron. 29:12. 2 Cor. 12:9–10.

DECEMBER 6

MORNING

For it is God who works in you.

NOT THAT WE are competent to claim anything for ourselves, but our competence comes from God. — "A man can receive only what is given him from heaven." ... "No one can come to me unless the Father who sent me draws him, and I will raise him up at the last day." — "I will give them singleness of heart and action, so that they will always fear me."

Don't be deceived, my dear brothers. Every good and perfect gift is from above, coming down from the Father of the heavenly lights, who does not change like shifting shadows. He chose to give us birth through the word of truth, that we might be a kind of firstfruits of all he created. — For we are God's workmanship, created in Christ Jesus to do good works, which God prepared in advance for us to do.

LORD, you establish peace for us; all that we have accomplished you have done for us.

PHIL. 2:13. 2 Cor. 3:5. John 3:27; 6:44. Jer. 32:39. James 1:16–18. Eph. 2:10. Isa. 26:12.

EVENING

"The spirit is willing, but the body is weak."

YES, LORD, WALKING in the way of your laws, we wait for you; your name and renown are the desire of our hearts. My soul yearns for you in the night; in the morning my spirit longs for you.

I know that nothing good lives in me, that is, in my sinful nature. For I have the desire to do what is good, but I cannot carry it out.... For in my inner being I delight in God's law; but I see another law at work in the members of my body, waging war against the law of my mind and making me a prisoner of the law of sin at work within my members. — For the sinful nature desires what is contrary to the Spirit, and the Spirit what is contrary to the sinful nature. They are in conflict with each other, so that you do not do what you want.

I can do everything through him who gives me strength. — Our competence comes from God.... "My grace is sufficient for you."

MATT. 26:41. Isa. 26:8–9. Rom. 7:18, 22–23. Gal 5:17. Phil. 4:13. 2 Cor. 3:5; 12:9.

DECEMBER 7

MORNING

God made him who had no sin to be sin for us, so that in him
we might become the righteousness of God.

THE LORD HAS laid on him the iniquity of us all. — He himself bore our sins in his body on the tree, so that we might die to sins and live for righteousness; by his wounds you have been healed. — Just as through the disobedience of the one man the many were made sinners, so also through the obedience of the one man the many will be made righteous.

But when the kindness and love of God our Savior appeared, he saved us, not because of righteous things we had done, but because of his mercy. He saved us through the washing of rebirth and renewal by the Holy Spirit, whom he poured out on us generously through Jesus Christ our Savior, so that, having been justified by his grace, we might become heirs having the hope of eternal life. — Therefore, there is now no condemnation for those who are in Christ Jesus. — The LORD Our Righteousness.

2 COR. 5:21. Isa. 53:6. 1 Peter 2:24. Rom. 5:19. Titus 3:4–7. Rom. 8:1. Jer. 23:6.

EVENING

I will be like the dew to Israel.

THE MEEKNESS AND gentleness of Christ. — A bruised reed he will not break, and a smoldering wick he will not snuff out.

"The Spirit of the Lord is on me, because he has anointed me to preach good news to the poor. He has sent me to proclaim freedom for the prisoners and recovery of sight for the blind, to release the oppressed, to proclaim the year of the Lord's favor." ... And he said to them, "Today this scripture is fulfilled in your hearing." All spoke well of him and were amazed at the gracious words that came from his lips.

The Lord turned and looked straight at Peter. Then Peter remembered the word the Lord had spoken to him: "Before the rooster crows today, you will disown me three times." And he went outside and wept bitterly. — He tends his flock like a shepherd: He gathers the lambs in his arms and carries them close to his heart; he gently leads those that have young.

HOS. 14:5. 2 Cor. 10:1. Isa. 42:3. Luke 4:18–19, 21–22; 22:61–62. Isa. 40:11.

December 8

Morning

Serve one another in love.

Brothers, if someone is caught in a sin, you who are spiritual should restore him gently. But watch yourself, or you also may be tempted. Carry each other's burdens, and in this way you will fulfill the law of Christ.

My brothers, if one of you should wander from the truth and someone should bring him back, remember this: Whoever turns a sinner away from his error will save him from death and cover over a multitude of sins. — Now that you have purified yourselves by obeying the truth so that you have sincere love for your brothers, love one another deeply, from the heart.

Let no debt remain outstanding, except the continuing debt to love one another, for he who loves his fellow man has fulfilled the law.... Be devoted to one another in brotherly love. Honor one another above yourselves. — Young men, in the same way be submissive to those who are older. Clothe yourselves with humility toward one another, because, "God opposes the proud."

GAL. 5:13. Gal. 6:1–2. James 5:19–20. 1 Peter 1:22. Rom. 13:8; 12:10. 1 Peter 5:5.

Evening

The dust returns to the ground it came from.

The body that is sown is perishable, it is raised imperishable; it is sown in dishonor, it is raised in glory; it is sown in weakness, it is raised in power; it is sown a natural body, it is raised a spiritual body.... The first man was of the dust of the earth, the second man from heaven.

"For dust you are and to dust you will return." — One man dies in full vigor, completely secure and at ease.... Another man dies in bitterness of soul, never having enjoyed anything good. Side by side they lie in the dust, and worms cover them both.

My body also will rest secure. — And after my skin has been destroyed, yet in my flesh I will see God. — The Lord Jesus Christ, who, by the power that enables him to bring everything under his control, will transform our lowly bodies so that they will be like his glorious body.

"Show me, O LORD, my life's end and the number of my days; let me know how fleeting is my life." ... Teach us to number our days aright, that we may gain a heart of wisdom.

ECCL. 12:7. 1 Cor. 15:42–44, 47. Gen. 3:19. Job 21:23, 25–26. Ps. 16:9. Job 19:26. Phil. 3:20–21. Pss. 39:4; 90:12.

DECEMBER 9

MORNING

To do what is right and just is more acceptable to the LORD than sacrifice.

HE HAS SHOWED you, O man, what is good. And what does the LORD require of you? To act justly and to love mercy and to walk humbly with your God. — "Does the LORD delight in burnt offerings and sacrifices as much as in obeying the voice of the LORD? To obey is better than sacrifice, and to heed is better than the fat of rams." — "To love him with all your heart, with all your understanding and with all your strength, and to love your neighbor as yourself is more important than all burnt offerings and sacrifices."

But you must return to your God; maintain love and justice, and wait for your God always. — Mary ... sat at the Lord's feet listening to what he said. ... "But only one thing is needed. Mary has chosen what is better, and it will not be taken away from her."

For it is God who works in you to will and to act according to his good purpose.

PROV. 21:3. Mic. 6:8. 1 Sam. 15:22. Mark 12:33. Hos. 12:6. Luke 10:39, 42. Phil. 2:13.

EVENING

The spirit returns to God who gave it.

THE LORD GOD formed man from the dust of the ground and breathed into his nostrils the breath of life, and man became a living being. — But it is the spirit in a man, the breath of the Almighty, that gives him understanding. — "The first man Adam became a living being." — The spirit of man rises upward.

We are always confident and know that as long as we are at home in the body we are away from the Lord. ... We are confident, I say, and would prefer to be away from the body and at home with the Lord. — With Christ, which is better by far. — Brothers, we do not want you to be ignorant about those who fall asleep, or grieve like the rest of men, who have no hope. We believe that Jesus died and rose again and so we believe that God will bring with Jesus those who have fallen asleep in him.

"I am going there to prepare a place for you. And if I go and prepare a place for you, I will come back and take you to be with me that you also may be where I am."

ECCL. 12:7. Gen. 2:7. Job 32:8. 1 Cor. 15:45. Eccl. 3:21. 2 Cor. 5:6, 8. Phil. 1:23.
1 Thess. 4:13 – 14. John 14:2 – 3.

December 10

Morning

"No one can snatch them out of my Father's hand."

I know whom I have believed, and am convinced that he is able to guard what I have entrusted to him for that day.... The Lord will rescue me from every evil attack and will bring me safely to his heavenly kingdom. — We are more than conquerors through him who loved us. For I am convinced that neither death nor life, neither angels nor demons, neither the present nor the future, nor any powers, neither height nor depth, nor anything else in all creation, will be able to separate us from the love of God that is in Christ Jesus our Lord. — For you died, and your life is now hidden with Christ in God.

Has not God chosen those who are poor in the eyes of the world to be rich in faith and to inherit the kingdom he promised those who love him?

May our Lord Jesus Christ himself and God our Father, who loved us and by his grace gave us eternal encouragement and good hope, encourage your hearts and strengthen you in every good deed and word.

JOHN 10:29. 2 Tim. 1:12; 4:18. Rom. 8:37–39. Col. 3:3. James 2:5. 2 Thess. 2:16–17.

Evening

Perfect law that gives freedom.

"Then you will know the truth, and the truth will set you free." They answered him, "We are Abraham's descendants and have never been slaves of anyone. How can you say that we shall be set free?" Jesus replied, "I tell you the truth, everyone who sins is a slave to sin.... So if the Son sets you free, you will be free indeed."

Stand firm, then, and do not let yourselves be burdened again by a yoke of slavery.... You, my brothers, were called to be free. But do not use your freedom to indulge the sinful nature; rather, serve one another in love. The entire law is summed up in a single command: "Love your neighbor as yourself." — You have been set free from sin and have become slaves to righteousness.... For example, by law a married woman is bound to her husband as long as he is alive, but if her husband dies, she is released from the law of marriage.

Through Christ Jesus the law of the Spirit of life set me free from the law of sin and death. — I will walk about in freedom, for I have sought out your precepts.

JAMES 1:25. John 8:32–34, 36. Gal. 5:1, 13–14. Rom. 6:18; 7:2; 8:2. Ps. 119:45.

DECEMBER 11

MORNING

Do not allow what you consider good to be spoken of as evil.

AVOID EVERY KIND of evil. — For we are taking pains to do what is right, not only in the eyes of the Lord but also in the eyes of men. — For it is God's will that by doing good you should silence the ignorant talk of foolish men. . . . If you suffer, it should not be as a murderer or thief or any other kind of criminal, or even as a meddler. However, if you suffer as a Christian, do not be ashamed, but praise God that you bear that name.

You, my brothers, were called to be free. But do not use your freedom to indulge the sinful nature; rather, serve one another in love. — Be careful, however, that the exercise of your freedom does not become a stumbling block to the weak. — "But if anyone causes one of these little ones who believe in me to sin, it would be better for him to have a large millstone hung around his neck and to be drowned in the depths of the sea." . . . "Whatever you did for one of the least of these brothers of mine, you did for me."

ROM. 14:16. 1 Thess. 5:22. 2 Cor. 8:21. 1 Peter 2:15; 4:15 – 16. Gal. 5:13. 1 Cor. 8:9. Matt. 18:6; 25:40.

EVENING

"Wake up, O sleeper, rise from the dead, and Christ will shine on you."

THE HOUR HAS come for you to wake up from your slumber, because our salvation is nearer now than when we first believed. — Let us not be like others, who are asleep, but let us be alert and self-controlled. For those who sleep, sleep at night, and those who get drunk, get drunk at night. But since we belong to the day, let us be self-controlled, putting on faith and love as a breastplate, and the hope of salvation as a helmet.

"Arise, shine, for your light has come, and the glory of the LORD rises upon you. See, darkness covers the earth and thick darkness is over the peoples, but the LORD rises upon, you and his glory appears over you."

Therefore, prepare your minds for action; be self-controlled; set your hope fully on the grace to be given you when Jesus Christ is revealed. — "Be dressed ready for service and keep your lamps burning, like men waiting for their master."

EPH. 5:14. Rom. 13:11. 1 Thess. 5:6 – 8. Isa. 60:1 – 2. 1 Peter 1:13. Luke 12:35 – 36.

DECEMBER 12

MORNING

The LORD, the King of Israel, is with you.

"So DO NOT fear, for I am with you; do not be dismayed, for I am your God. I will strengthen you and help you; I will uphold you with my righteous right hand." ... Strengthen the feeble hands, steady the knees that give way; say to those with fearful hearts, "Be strong, do not fear; your God will come, he will come with vengeance; with divine retribution he will come to save you." — "The LORD your God is with you, he is mighty to save. He will take great delight in you, he will quiet you with his love, he will rejoice over you with singing." — Wait for the LORD; be strong and take heart and wait for the LORD.

And I heard a loud voice from the throne saying, "Now the dwelling of God is with men, and he will live with them. They will be his people, and God himself will be with them and be their God. He will wipe every tear from their eyes. There will be no more death or mourning or crying or pain."

ZEPH. 3:15. Isa. 41:10; 35:3 – 4. Zeph. 3:17. Ps. 27:14. Rev. 21:3 – 4.

EVENING

"Why are you crying out to me? Tell the Israelites to move on."

"BE STRONG AND let us fight bravely for our people and the cities of our God. The LORD will do what is good in his sight." — But we prayed to our God and posted a guard day and night to meet this threat. — "Not everyone who says to me, 'Lord, Lord,' will enter the kingdom of heaven, but only he who does the will of my Father who is in heaven." — "If any one chooses to do God's will, he will find out whether my teaching comes from God." — Let us acknowledge the LORD; let us press on to acknowledge him.

"Watch and pray so that you will not fall into temptation." — Be on your guard; stand firm in the faith; be men of courage; be strong. — Never be lacking in zeal, but keep your spiritual fervor, serving the Lord.

Strengthen the feeble hands, steady the knees that give way; say to those with fearful hearts, "Be strong, do not fear."

EXOD. 14:15. 1 Chron. 19:13. Neh. 4:9. Matt. 7:21. John 7:17. Hos. 6:3. Matt. 26:41. 1 Cor. 16:13. Rom. 12:11. Isa. 35:3 – 4.

DECEMBER 13

MORNING

Be strong in the grace that is in Christ Jesus.

BEING STRENGTHENED WITH all power according to his glorious might.... So then, just as you received Christ Jesus as Lord, continue to live in him, rooted and built up in him, strengthened in the faith as you were taught, and overflowing with thankfulness. — They will be called oaks of righteousness, a planting of the LORD for the display of his splendor. — Built on the foundation of the apostles and prophets, with Christ Jesus himself as the chief cornerstone. In him the whole building is joined together and rises to become a holy temple in the Lord. And in him you too are being built together to become a dwelling in which God lives by his Spirit.

"Now I commit you to God and to the word of his grace, which can build you up and give you an inheritance among all those who are sanctified." — Filled with the fruit of righteousness that comes through Jesus Christ — to the glory and praise of God.

Fight the good fight of the faith. — Without being frightened in any way by those who oppose you.

2 TIM. 2:1. Col. 1:11; 2:6 – 7. Isa. 61:3. Eph. 2:20 – 22. Acts 20:32. Phil. 1:11.
1 Tim. 6:12. Phil. 1:28.

EVENING

Surely you will reward each person according to what he has done.

FOR NO ONE can lay any foundation other than the one already laid, which is Jesus Christ.... If what he has built survives, he will receive his reward. If it is burned up, he will suffer loss; he himself will be saved, but only as one escaping through the flames. — For we must all appear before the judgment seat of Christ, that each one may receive what is due him for the things done while in the body, whether good or bad.

But when you give to the needy, do not let your left hand know what your right hand is doing, so that your giving may be in secret. Then your Father, who sees what is done in secret, will reward you." ... "After a long time the master of those servants returned and settled accounts with them."

Not that we are competent to claim anything for ourselves, but our competence comes from God. — LORD, you establish peace for us; all that we have accomplished you have done for us.

PS. 62:12. 1 Cor. 3:11, 14 – 15. 2 Cor. 5:10. Matt. 6:3 – 4; 25:19. 2 Cor. 3:5. Isa. 26:12.

DECEMBER 14

MORNING

Sing to the glory of his name; offer him glory and praise!

"THE PEOPLE I formed for myself that they may proclaim my praise." — "I will cleanse them from all the sin they have committed against me and will forgive all their sins of rebellion against me. Then this city will bring me renown, joy, praise and honor before all nations on earth." — Through Jesus, therefore, let is continually offer to God a sacrifice of praise — the fruit of lips that confess his name.

I will praise you, O Lord my God, with all my heart; I will glorify your name forever. For great is your love toward me; you have delivered my soul from the depths of the grave. — "Who among the gods is like you, LORD? Who is like you — majestic in holiness, awesome in glory, working wonders?" — I will praise God's name in song and glorify him with thanksgiving. — [They] sang the song of Moses the servant of God and the song of the Lamb: "Great and marvelous are your deeds, Lord God Almighty."

PS. 66:2. Isa. 43:21. Jer. 33:8–9. Heb. 13:15. Ps. 86:12–13. Exod. 15:11. Ps. 69:30. Rev. 15:3.

EVENING

Like the rest, we were by nature objects of wrath.

AT ONE TIME we too were foolish, disobedient, deceived and enslaved by all kinds of passions and pleasures. We lived in malice and envy, being hated and hating one another. — "You should not be surprised at my saying, 'You must be born again.'"

Then Job answered the LORD: "I am unworthy — how can I reply to you? I put my hand over my mouth." ... Then the LORD said to Satan, "Have you considered my servant Job? There is no one on earth like him; he is blameless and upright, a man who fears God and shuns evil."

Surely I have been a sinner from birth, sinful from the time my mother conceived me. — He testified concerning him [David]: "I have found David son of Jesse a man after my own heart; he will do everything I want him to do."

Even though I was once a blasphemer and a persecutor and a violent man, I was shown mercy because I acted in ignorance and unbelief. — Flesh gives birth to flesh, but the Spirit gives birth to spirit.

EPH. 2:3. Titus 3:3. John 3:7. Job 40:3–4; 1:8. Ps. 51:5. Acts. 13:22. 1 Tim. 1:13. John 3:6.

DECEMBER 15

MORNING

Carry each other's burdens, and in this way you will fulfill the law of Christ.

EACH OF YOU should look not only to your own interests, but also to the interests of others. Your attitude should be the same as that of Christ Jesus.... [He] made himself nothing, taking the very nature of a servant. — "Even the Son of Man did not come to be served, but to serve, and to give his life as a ransom for many." — He died for all, that those who live should no longer live for themselves but for him who died for them and was raised again.

When Jesus saw her weeping, and the Jews who had come along with her also weeping, he was deeply moved in spirit and troubled.... Jesus wept. — Rejoice with those who rejoice; mourn with those who mourn.

All of you live in harmony with one another; be sympathetic, love as brothers, be compassionate and humble. Do not repay evil with evil or insult with insult, but with blessing, because to this you were called so that you may inherit a blessing.

GAL. 6:2. Phil. 2:4–5, 7. Mark 10:45. 2 Cor. 5:15. John 11:33, 35. Rom. 12:15.
1 Peter 3:8–9.

EVENING

"Son, go and work today in the vineyard."

"SO YOU ARE no longer a slave, but a son; and since you are a son, God has made you also an heir."

In the same way, count yourselves dead to sin but alive to God in Christ Jesus. Therefore do not let sin reign in your mortal body so that you obey its evil desires. Do not offer the parts of your body to sin, as instruments of wickedness, but rather offer yourselves to God. — As obedient children, do not conform to the evil desires you had when you lived in ignorance. But just as he who called you is holy, so be holy in all you do. — Made holy, useful to the Master and prepared to do any good work.

Therefore, my dear brothers, stand firm. Let nothing move you. Always give yourselves fully to the work of the Lord, because you know that your labor in the Lord is not in vain.

MATT. 21:28. Gal. 4:7. Rom. 6:11–13. 1 Peter 1:14–15. 2 Tim. 2:21. 1 Cor. 15:58.

DECEMBER 16

MORNING

Having loved his own who were in the world, he now showed
them the full extent of his love.

"I PRAY FOR them. I am not praying for the world, but for those you have given me, for they are yours. All I have is yours, and all you have is mine. And glory has come to me through them.... My prayer is not that you take them out of the world but that you protect them from the evil one. They are not of the world, even as I am not of it."

"As the Father has loved me, so have I loved you. Now remain in my love.... Greater love has no one than this, that one lay down his life for his friends. You are my friends if you do what I command." ... "A new commandment I give you: Love one another. As I have loved you, so you must love one another."

He who began a good work in you will carry it on to completion until the day of Christ Jesus. — Christ loved the church and gave himself up for her to make her holy, cleansing her by the washing with water through the word.

JOHN 13:1. John 17:9–10, 15–16; 15:9, 13–14; 13:54. Phil. 1:6. Eph. 5:25–26.

EVENING

God has revealed it to us by his Spirit.

"I NO LONGER call you servants, because a servant does not know his master's business. Instead, I have called you friends, for everything that I learned from my Father I have made known to you." — "The knowledge of the secrets of the kingdom of heaven has been given to you."

We have not received the spirit of the world but the Spirit who is from God, that we may understand what God has freely given us.

For this reason I kneel before the Father, from whom his whole family in heaven and on earth derives its name. I pray that out of his glorious riches he may strengthen you with power through his Spirit in your inner being, so that Christ may dwell in your hearts through faith. And I pray that you, being rooted and established in love, may have power, together with all the saints, to grasp how wide and long and high and deep is the love of Christ, and to know this love that surpasses knowledge — that you may be filled to the measure of all the fullness of God.

1 COR. 2:10. John 15:15. Matt. 13:11. 1 Cor. 2:12. Eph. 3:14–19.

DECEMBER 17

MORNING

Revive us, and we will call on your name.

THE SPIRIT GIVES life. — In the same way, the Spirit helps us in our weakness. We do not know what we ought to pray, but the Spirit himself intercedes for us with groans that words cannot express. And he who searches our hearts knows the mind of the Spirit, because the Spirit intercedes for the saints in accordance with God's will. — And pray in the Spirit on all occasions with all kinds of prayers and requests. With this in mind, be alert and always keep on praying for all the saints.

I will never forget your precepts, for by them you have renewed my life. — "The flesh counts for nothing. The words I have spoken to you are spirit and they are life." — For the letter kills, but the Spirit gives life. — "If you remain in me and my words remain in you, ask whatever you wish, and it will be given you." — This is the assurance we have in approaching God: that if we ask anything according to his will, he hears us.

And no one can say, "Jesus is Lord," except by the Holy Spirit.

PS. 80:18. John 6:63. Rom. 8:26–27. Eph. 6:18. Ps. 119:93. John 6:63. 2 Cor. 3:6. John 15:7. 1 John 5:14. 1 Cor. 12:3.

EVENING

Have nothing to do with the fruitless deeds of darkness,
but rather expose them.

DO NOT BE misled: "Bad company corrupts good character." . . . Don't you know that a little yeast works through the whole batch of dough? Get rid of the old yeast that you may be a new batch without yeast — as you really are. . . . I have written you in my letter not to associate with sexually immoral people — not at all meaning the people of this world who are immoral, or the greedy and swindlers, or idolaters. In that case you would have to leave this world. But now I am writing you that you must not associate with anyone who calls himself a brother but is sexually immoral or greedy, an idolater or a slanderer, a drunkard or a swindler. With such a man do not even eat. — So that you may become blameless and pure, children of God without fault in a crooked and depraved generation, in which you shine like stars in the universe.

In a large house there are articles not only of gold and silver, but also of wood and clay; some are for noble purposes and some for ignoble.

EPH. 5:11. 1 Cor. 15:33; 5:6–7, 9–11. Phil. 2:15. 2 Tim. 2:20.

DECEMBER 18

MORNING

Let us then approach the throne of grace with confidence, so that we may receive mercy and find grace to help us in our time of need.

DO NOT BE anxious about anything, but in everything, by prayer and petition, with thanksgiving, present your requests to God. And the peace of God, which transcends all understanding, will guard your hearts and your minds in Christ Jesus. — For you did not receive a spirit that makes you a slave again to fear, but you received the Spirit of sonship. And by him we cry, *"Abba,* Father."

"I have not said to Jacob's descendants, 'Seek me in vain.' " — Therefore, brothers, since we have confidence to enter the Most Holy Place by the blood of Jesus,... let us draw near to God with a sincere heart in full assurance of faith, having our hearts sprinkled to cleanse us from a guilty conscience and having our bodies washed with pure water.... So we say with confidence, "The Lord is my helper, I will not be afraid. What can man do to me?"

HEB. 4:16. Phil. 4:6–7. Rom. 8:15. Isa. 45:19. Heb. 10:19, 22; 13:6.

EVENING

"Then you will know the truth, and the truth will set you free."

WHERE THE SPIRIT of the Lord is, there is freedom. — Because through Christ Jesus the law of the Spirit of life set me free from the law of sin and death. — "So if the Son sets you free, you will be free indeed."

Therefore, brothers, we are not children of the slave woman, but of the free woman.... Know that a man is not justified by observing the law, but by faith in Jesus Christ. So we, too, have put our faith in Christ Jesus that we may be justified by faith in Christ and not by observing the law, because by observing the law no one will be justified.

But the man who looks intently into the perfect law that gives freedom, and continues to do this, not forgetting what he has heard, but doing it — he will be blessed in what he does. — It is for freedom that Christ has set us free. Stand firm, then, and do not let yourselves be burdened again by a yoke of slavery.

JOHN 8:32. 2 Cor. 3:17. Rom. 8:2. John 8:36. Gal. 4:31; 2:16. James 1:25. Gal. 5:1.

DECEMBER 19

MORNING

Even in darkness light dawns for the upright.

WHO AMONG YOU fears the LORD and obeys the word of his servant? Let him who walks in the dark, who has no light, trust in the name of the LORD and rely on his God. — Though he stumble, he will not fall, for the LORD upholds him with his hand. — For these commands are a lamp, this teaching is a light.

Do not gloat over me, my enemy! Though I have fallen, I will rise. Though I sit in darkness, the LORD will be my light. Because I have sinned against him, I will bear the LORD's wrath, until he pleads my case and establishes my right. He will bring me out into the light; I will see his justice.

"The eye is the lamp of the body. If your eyes are good, your whole body will be full of light. But if your eyes are bad, your whole body will be full of darkness. If then the light within you is darkness, how great is that darkness!"

PS. 112:4. Isa. 50:10. Ps. 37:24. Prov. 6:23. Mic. 7:8–9. Matt. 6:22–23.

EVENING

He tends his flock like a shepherd: He gathers the lambs in his arms and carries them close to his heart; he gently leads those that have young.

"I HAVE COMPASSION for these people; they have already been with me three days and have nothing to eat. I do not want to send them away hungry, or they may collapse on the way." — For we do not have a high priest who is unable to sympathize with our weaknesses.

People were bringing little children to Jesus to have him touch them.... And he took the children in his arms, put his hands on them and blessed them.

I have strayed like a lost sheep. Seek your servant. — "For the Son of Man came to seek and to save what was lost." — For you were like sheep going astray, but now you have returned to the Shepherd and Overseer of your souls.

"Do not be afraid, little flock, for your Father has been pleased to give you the kingdom." — I myself will tend my sheep and have them lie down, declares the Sovereign LORD.

ISA. 40:11. Matt. 15:32. Heb. 4:15. Mark 10:13, 16. Ps. 119:176. Luke 19:10. 1 Peter 2:25. Luke 12:32. Ezek. 34:15.

DECEMBER 20

MORNING

*For he chose us in him before the creation of the world to be
holy and blameless in his sight.*

FROM THE BEGINNING God chose you to be saved through the sanctifying work of the Spirit and through belief in the truth. He called you to this through our gospel, that you might share in the glory of our Lord Jesus Christ. — For those God foreknew he also predestined to be conformed to the likeness of his Son, that he might be the firstborn among many brothers. And those he predestined, he also called; those he called, he also justified; those he justified, he also glorified. — Who have been chosen according to the foreknowledge of God the Father, by the sanctifying work of the Spirit, for obedience to Jesus Christ and sprinkling by his blood.

I will give you a new heart and put a new spirit in you; I will remove from you your heart of stone and give you a heart of flesh. — For God did not call us to be impure, but to live a holy life.

EPH. 1:4. 2 Thess. 2:13 – 14. Rom. 8:29 – 30. 1 Peter 1:2. Ezek. 36:26. 1 Thess. 4:7.

EVENING

*"Look, even if the LORD should open the floodgates of the
heavens, could this happen?"*

"HAVE FAITH IN God." — Without faith it is impossible to please God. — "With God all things are possible."

"Was my arm too short to ransom you? Do I lack the strength to rescue you?" ... "For my thoughts are not your thoughts, neither are your ways my ways," declares the LORD. "As the heavens are higher than the earth, so are my ways higher than your ways and my thoughts than your thoughts." — "Test me in this," says the LORD Almighty, "and see if I will not throw open the floodgates of heaven and pour out so much blessing that you will not have room enough for it."

Surely the arm of the LORD is not too short to save, nor his ear too dull to hear. — "LORD, there is no one like you to help the powerless against the mighty."

We might not rely on ourselves but on God, who raises the dead.

**2 KINGS 7:2. Mark 11:22. Heb. 11:6. Matt. 19:26. Isa. 50:2; 55:8 – 9. Mal. 3:10. Isa. 59:1.
2 Chron. 14:11. 2 Cor. 1:9.**

DECEMBER 21

MORNING

"And your days of sorrow will end."

"IN THIS WORLD you will have trouble." — We know that the whole creation has been groaning as in the pains of childbirth right up to the present time. Not only so, but we ourselves, who have the firstfruits of the Spirit, groan inwardly as we wait eagerly for our adoption as sons, the redemption of our bodies. — For while we are in this tent, we groan and are burdened, because we do not wish to be unclothed but to be clothed with our heavenly dwelling, so that what is mortal may be swallowed up by life.

"These are they who have come out of the great tribulation; they have washed their robes and made them white in the blood of the Lamb. Therefore they are before the throne of God and serve him day and night in his temple; and he who sits on the throne will spread his tent over them. Never again will they hunger, never again will they thirst. The sun will not beat upon them, nor any scorching heat. For the Lamb at the center of the throne will be their shepherd; he will lead them to springs of living water. And God will wipe away every tear from their eyes."

ISA. 60:20. John 16:33. Rom. 8:22–23. 2 Cor. 5:4. Rev. 7:14–17.

EVENING

"Teacher, don't you care if we drown?"

THE LORD IS good to all; he has compassion on all he has made.

"Everything that lives and moves will be food for you. Just as I gave you the green plants, I now give you everything." ... "As long as the earth endures, seedtime and harvest, cold and heat, summer and winter, day and night will never cease."

The LORD is good, a refuge in times of trouble. He cares for those who trust in him. — God heard the boy crying, and the angel of God called to Hagar from heaven and said to her, "What is the matter, Hagar? Do not be afraid; God has heard the boy crying as he lies there." ... Then God opened her eyes and she saw a well of water. So she went and filled the skin with water and gave the boy a drink.

"So do not worry, saying, 'What shall we eat?' or 'What shall we drink?' or 'What shall we wear?' ... Your heavenly Father knows that you need them." — Hope in God, who richly provides us with everything for our enjoyment.

MARK 4:38. Ps. 145:9. Gen. 9:3; 8:22. Nah. 1:7. Gen. 21:17, 19. Matt. 6:31–32. 1 Tim. 6:17.

DECEMBER 22

MORNING

Your work produced by faith.

"THE WORK OF God is this: to believe in the one he has sent." — Faith by itself, if it is not accompanied by action, is dead. — Faith expressing itself through love.... The one who sows to please his sinful nature, from that nature will reap destruction; the one who sows to please the Spirit, from the Spirit will reap eternal life.

For we are God's workmanship, created in Christ Jesus to do good works, which God prepared in advance for us to do. — Who gave himself for us to redeem us from all wickedness and to purify for himself a people that are his very own, eager to do what is good.

We ought always to thank God for you, brothers, and rightly so, because your faith is growing more and more, and the love every one of you has for each other is increasing.... With this in mind, we constantly pray for you, that our God may count you worthy of his calling, and that by his power he may fulfill every good purpose of yours and every act prompted by your faith.

1 THESS. 1:3. John 6:29. James 2:17. Gal. 5:6; 6:8. Eph. 2:10. Titus 2:14. 2 Thess. 1:3, 11.

EVENING

"Where is this 'coming' he promised?"

ENOCH, THE SEVENTH from Adam, prophesied about these men: "See, the Lord is coming with thousands upon thousands of his holy ones to judge everyone, and to convict all the ungodly of all the ungodly acts they have done in the ungodly way, and of all the harsh words ungodly sinners have spoken against him." — Look, he is coming with the clouds, and every eye will see him, even those who pierced him; and all the peoples of the earth will mourn because of him.

For the Lord himself will come down from heaven, with a loud command, with the voice of the archangel and with the trumpet call of God, and the dead in Christ will rise first. After that, we who are still alive and are left will be caught up with them in the clouds to meet the Lord in the air. And so we will be with the Lord forever.

For the grace of God that brings salvation has appeared to all men. It teaches us to say "No" to ungodliness and worldly passions, and to live self-controlled, upright and godly lives in this present age, while we wait for the blessed hope — the glorious appearing of our great God and Savior, Jesus Christ.

2 PETER 3:4. Jude 14 – 15. Rev. 1:7. 1 Thess. 4:16 – 17. Titus 2:11 – 13.

DECEMBER 23

MORNING

"Let them come to me for refuge; let them make peace with me."

"For I KNOW the plans I have for you," declares the LORD, "plans to prosper you and not to harm you, plans to give you hope and a future." — "There is no peace," says the LORD, "for the wicked." — But now in Christ Jesus you who once were far away have been brought near through the blood of Christ. For he himself is our peace.

For God was pleased to have all his fullness dwell in him, and through him to reconcile to himself all things. — Christ Jesus. God presented him as a sacrifice of atonement, through faith in his blood. He did this to demonstrate his justice, because in his forbearance he had left the sins committed beforehand unpunished — he did it to demonstrate his justice at the present time, so as to be just and the one who justifies the man who has faith in Jesus. — If we confess our sins, he is faithful and just and will forgive us our sins and purify us from all unrighteousness.

Trust in the LORD forever, for the LORD, the LORD, is the Rock eternal.

ISA. 27:5. Jer. 29:11. Isa. 48:22. Eph. 2:13–14. Col. 1:19–20. Rom. 3:24–26. 1 John 1:9. Isa. 26:4.

EVENING

God has given us eternal life, and this life is in his Son.

"For AS THE Father has life in himself, so he has granted the Son to have life in himself." ... "For just as the Father raises the dead and gives them life, even so the Son gives life to whom he is pleased to give it."

"I am the resurrection and the life. He who believes in me will live, even though he dies; and whoever lives and believes in me will never die." ... "I am the good shepherd. The good shepherd lays down his life for the sheep.... I lay down my life — only to take it up again. No one takes it from me, but I lay it down of my own accord. I have authority to lay it down and authority to take it up again. This command I received from my Father." ... "No one comes to the Father except through me."

He who has the Son has life; he who does not have the Son of God does not have life. — For you died, and your life is now hidden with Christ in God. When Christ, who is your life, appears, then you also will appear with him in glory.

1 JOHN 5:11. John 5:26, 21; 11:25–26; 10:11, 17–18; 14:6. 1 John 5:12. Col. 3:3–4.

DECEMBER 24

MORNING

For if you live according to the sinful nature, you will die; but if by the Spirit you put to death the misdeeds of the body, you will live.

THE ACTS OF the sinful nature are obvious: sexual immorality, impurity and debauchery; ... and the like. I warn you, as I did before, that those who live like this will not inherit the kingdom of God. But the fruit of the Spirit is love, joy, peace, patience, kindness, goodness, faithfulness, gentleness and self-control. Against such things there is no law. Those who belong to Christ Jesus have crucified the sinful nature with its passions and desires. Since we live by the Spirit, let us keep in step with the Spirit.

For the grace of God that brings salvation has appeared to all men. It teaches us to say "No" to ungodliness and worldly passions, and to live self-controlled, upright and godly lives in this present age, while we wait for the blessed hope—the glorious appearing of our great God and Savior, Jesus Christ, who gave himself for us to redeem us from all wickedness and to purify for himself a people that are his very own, eager to do what is good.

ROM. 8:13. Gal. 5:19, 21–25. Titus 2:11–14.

EVENING

The commanders of the Philistines asked, "What about these Hebrews?"

IF YOU ARE insulted because of the name of Christ, you are blessed, for the Spirit of glory and of God rests on you. If you suffer, it should not be as a murderer or thief or any other kind of criminal, or even as a meddler.—Do not allow what you consider good to be spoken of as evil.—Live such good lives among the pagans.

Do not be yoked together with unbelievers. For what do righteousness and wickedness have in common? Or what fellowship can light have with darkness?... For we are the temple of the living God.... "Therefore come out from them and be separate, says the Lord. Touch no unclean thing."

But you are a chosen people, a royal priesthood, a holy nation, a people belonging to God, that you may declare the praises of him who called you out of darkness into his wonderful light.

1 SAM. 29:3. 1 Peter 4:14–15. Rom. 14:16. 1 Peter 2:12. 2 Cor. 6:14, 16–17. 1 Peter 2:9.

DECEMBER 25

MORNING

When the kindness and love of God our Savior appeared.

"I HAVE LOVED you with an everlasting love." — This is how God showed his love among us: He sent his one and only Son into the world that we might live through Him. This is love: not that we loved God, but that he loved us and sent his Son as an atoning sacrifice for our sins.

But when the time had fully come, God sent his Son, born of a woman, born under law, to redeem those under law, that we might receive the full rights of sons. — The Word became flesh and lived for a while among us. We have seen his glory, the glory of the one and only Son, who came from the Father, full of grace and truth. — Beyond all question, the mystery of godliness is great: He appeared in a body, was vindicated by the Spirit.

Since the children have flesh and blood, he too shared in their humanity so that by his death he might destroy him who holds the power of death — that is, the devil.

TITUS 3:4. Jer. 31:3. 1 John 4:9 – 10. Gal. 4:4 – 5. John 1:14. 1 Tim. 3:16. Heb. 2:14.

EVENING

Thanks be to God for his indescribable gift!

SHOUT FOR JOY to the LORD, all the earth. Serve the LORD with gladness; come before him with joyful songs.... Enter his gates with thanksgiving and his courts with praise; give thanks to him and praise his name. — For to us a child is born, to us a son is given, and the government will be on his shoulders. And he will be called Wonderful Counselor, Mighty God, Everlasting Father, Prince of Peace.

He ... did not spare his own Son, but gave him up for us all. — "He had one left to send, a son, whom he loved."

Let them give thanks to the LORD for his unfailing love and his wonderful deeds for men.... Praise the LORD, O my soul; all my inmost being, praise his holy name. — "My soul praises the Lord and my spirit rejoices in God my Savior."

2 COR. 9:15. Ps. 100:1 – 2, 4. Isa. 9:6 – 7. Rom. 8:32. Mark 12:6. Pss. 107:21; 103:1.
Luke 1:46 – 47.

DECEMBER 26

MORNING

Stand firm. Let nothing move you. Always give yourselves fully to the work of the Lord.

BECAUSE YOU KNOW that your labor in the Lord is not in vain. — So then, just as you received Christ Jesus as Lord, continue to live in him, rooted and built up in him, strengthened in the faith as you were taught, and overflowing with thankfulness. — "But he who stands firm to the end will be saved." — "But the seed on good soil stands for those with a noble and good heart, who hear the word, retain it, and by persevering produce a crop."

By faith you stand firm. — "As long as it is day, we must do the work of him who sent me. Night is coming, when no one can work."

The one who sows to please his sinful nature, from that nature will reap destruction; the one who sows to please the Spirit, from the Spirit will reap eternal life. Let us not become weary in doing good, for at the proper time we will reap a harvest if we do not give up. Therefore, as we have opportunity, let us do good to all people, especially to those who belong to the family of believers.

1 COR. 15:58. 1 Cor. 15:58. Col. 2:6–7. Matt. 24:13. Luke 8:15. 2 Cor. 1:24. John 9:4. Gal. 6:8–10.

EVENING

He is able to save completely those who come to God through him.

"I AM THE way and the truth and the life. No one comes to the Father except through me." — "Salvation is found in no one else, for there is no other name under heaven given to men by which we must be saved."

"My sheep listen to my voice; I know them, and they follow me. I give them eternal life, and they shall never perish; no one can snatch them out of my hand." — He who began a good work in you will carry it on to completion until the day of Christ Jesus. — Is anything too hard for the LORD?

To him who is able to keep you from falling and to present you before his glorious presence without fault and with great joy — to the only God our Savior be glory, majesty, power and authority, through Jesus Christ our Lord, before all ages, now and forevermore! Amen.

HEB. 7:25. John 14:6. Acts 4:12. John 10:27–28. Phil. 1:6. Gen. 18:14. Jude 24–25.

DECEMBER 27

MORNING

We fix our eyes not on what is seen but on what is unseen. For what is seen is temporary, but what is unseen is eternal.

FOR HERE WE do not have an enduring city.... You knew that you yourselves had better and lasting possessions.

"Do not be afraid, little flock, for your Father has been pleased to give you the kingdom."—For a little while you may have had to suffer grief in all kinds of trials.—There the wicked cease from turmoil, and there the weary are at rest.

For while we are in this tent, we groan and are burdened.—"He will wipe every tear from their eyes. There will be no more death or mourning or crying or pain, for the old order of things has passed away."—I consider that our present sufferings are not worth comparing with the glory that will be revealed in us.—For our light and momentary troubles are achieving for us an eternal glory that far outweighs them all.

2 COR. 4:18. Heb. 13:14; 10:34. Luke 12:32. 1 Peter 1:6. Job 3:17. 2 Cor. 5:4. Rev. 21:4. Rom. 8:18. 2 Cor. 4:17.

EVENING

He himself is our peace.

GOD WAS RECONCILING the world to himself in Christ, not counting men's sins against them.... God made him who had no sin to be sin for us, so that in him we might become the righteousness of God.—And through him to reconcile to himself all things, whether things on earth or things in heaven, by making peace through his blood, shed on the cross. Once you were alienated from God and were enemies in your minds because of your evil behavior. But now he has reconciled you by Christ's physical body through death to present you holy in his sight, without blemish and free from accusation.... Having canceled the written code, with its regulations, that was against us and that stood opposed to us; he took it away, nailing it to the cross.

By abolishing in his flesh the law with its commandments and regulations. His purpose was to create in himself one new man out of the two, thus making peace.—"Peace I leave with you; my peace I give you. I do not give to you as the world gives. Do not let your hearts be troubled and do not be afraid."

EPH. 2:14. 2 Cor. 5:19, 21. Col 1:20–22; 2:14. Eph. 2:15. John 14:27.

DECEMBER 28

MORNING

"Son, your sins are forgiven."

"FOR I WILL forgive their wickedness and will remember their sins no more." — "Who can forgive sins but God alone?"

"I, even I, am he who blots out your transgressions, for my own sake, and remembers your sins no more." — Blessed is he whose transgressions are forgiven, whose sins are covered. Blessed is the man whose sin the LORD does not count against him. — Who is a God like you, who pardons sin and forgives the transgression?

In Christ God forgave you. — The blood of Jesus, his Son, purifies us from every sin. If we claim to be without sin, we deceive ourselves and the truth is not in us. If we confess our sins, he is faithful and just and will forgive us our sins and purify us from all unrighteousness.

As far as the east is from the west, so far has he removed our transgressions from us. — For sin shall not be your master, because you are not under law, but under grace.... You have been set free from sin and have become slaves to righteousness.

MARK 2:5. Jer. 31:34. Mark 2:7. Isa. 43:25. Ps. 32:1–2. Mic. 7:18. Eph. 4:32. 1 John 1:7–9. Ps. 103:12. Rom. 6:14, 18.

EVENING

"We would like to see Jesus."

YES, LORD, WALKING in the way of your laws, we wait for you; your name and renown are the desire of our hearts. — The LORD is near to all who call on him, to all who call on him in truth.

"For where two or three come together in my name, there am I with them." — "I will not leave you as orphans; I will come to you." — "And surely I will be with you always, to the very end of the age."

Let us run with perseverance the race marked out for us. Let us fix our eyes on Jesus, the author and perfecter of our faith. — Now we see but a poor reflection; then we shall see face to face. — I desire to depart and be with Christ, which is better by far.

Dear friends, now we are children of God, and what we will be has not yet been made known. But we know that when he appears, we shall be like him, for we shall see him as he is. Everyone who has this hope in him purifies himself, just as he is pure.

JOHN 12:21. Isa. 26:8. Ps. 145:18. Matt. 18:20. John 14:18. Matt. 28:20. Heb. 12:1–2. 1 Cor. 13:12. Phil. 1:23. 1 John 3:2–3.

DECEMBER 29

MORNING

Understand what the Lord's will is.

IT IS GOD's will that you should be holy. — "Submit to God and be at peace with him; in this way prosperity will come to you." — "Now this is eternal life: that they may know you, the only true God, and Jesus Christ, whom you have sent." — We know also that the Son of God has come and has given us understanding, so that we may know him who is true. And we are in him who is true — even in his Son Jesus Christ. He is the true God and eternal life.

We have not stopped praying for you and asking God to fill you with the knowledge of his will through all spiritual wisdom and understanding. — I keep asking that the God of our Lord Jesus Christ, the glorious Father, may give you the Spirit of wisdom and revelation, so that you may know him better. I pray also that the eyes of your heart may be enlightened in order that you may know the hope to which he has called you, the riches of his glorious inheritance in the saints, and his incomparably great power for us who believe.

EPH. 5:17. 1 Thess. 4:3. Job 22:21. John 17:3. 1 John 5:20. Col. 1:9. Eph. 1:17 – 19.

EVENING

Come near to God and he will come near to you.

ENOCH WALKED WITH God. — Do two walk together unless they have agreed to do so? — But as for me, it is good to be near God.

The LORD is with you when you are with him. If you seek him, he will be found by you, but if you forsake him, he will forsake you.... In their distress they turned to the LORD, the God of Israel, and sought him, and he was found by them.

"For I know the plans I have for you," declares the LORD, "plans to prosper you and not to harm you, plans to give you hope and a future. Then you will call upon me and come and pray to me, and I will listen to you. You will seek me and find me when you seek me with all your heart."

Therefore, brothers, since we have confidence to enter the Most Holy Place by the blood of Jesus, by a new and living way opened for us through the curtain, that is, his body, and since we have a great priest over the house of God, let us draw near to God with a sincere heart in full assurance of faith.

JAMES 4:8. Gen. 5:24. Amos 3:3. Ps. 73:28. 2 Chron. 15:2, 4. Jer. 29:11 – 13. Heb. 10:19 – 22.

DECEMBER 30

MORNING

Blameless on the day of our Lord Jesus Christ.

ONCE YOU WERE alienated from God and were enemies in your minds because of your evil behavior. But now he has reconciled you by Christ's physical body through death to present you holy in his sight, without blemish and free from accusation—if you continue in your faith, established and firm, not moved from the hope held out in the gospel.—So that you may become blameless and pure, children of God without fault in a crooked and depraved generation, in which you shine like stars in the universe.

So then, dear friends, since you are looking forward to this, make every effort to be found spotless, blameless and at peace with him.—Pure and blameless until the day of Christ.

To him who is able to keep you from falling and to present you before his glorious presence without fault and with great joy—to the only God our Savior be glory, majesty, power and authority, through Jesus Christ our Lord, before all ages, now and forevermore!

1 COR. 1:8. Col. 1:21–23. Phil. 2:15. 2 Peter 3:14. Phil. 1:10. Jude 24–25.

EVENING

He will guard the feet of his saints.

IF WE CLAIM to have fellowship with him yet walk in the darkness, we lie and do not live by the truth. But if we walk in the light, as he is in the light, we have fellowship with one another, and the blood of Jesus, his Son, purifies us from every sin.—"A person who has had a bath needs only to wash his feet; his whole body is clean."

I guide you in the way of wisdom and lead you along straight paths. When you walk, your steps will not be hampered; when you run, you will not stumble.... Do not set foot on the path of the wicked or walk in the way of evil men. Avoid it, do not travel on it; turn from it and go on your way.... Let your eyes look straight ahead, fix your gaze directly before you. Make level paths for your feet and take only ways that are firm. Do not swerve to the right or the left; keep your foot from evil.

The Lord will rescue me from every evil attack and will bring me safely to his heavenly kingdom. To him be glory for ever and ever. Amen.

1 SAM. 2:9. 1 John 1:6–7. John 13:10. Prov. 4:11–12, 14–15, 25–27. 2 Tim. 4:18.

DECEMBER 31

MORNING

*"The LORD your God carried you, as a father carries his son,
all the way you went until you reached this place."*

"I CARRIED YOU on eagles' wings and brought you to myself." — In all their
distress he too was distressed, and the angel of his presence saved them. In his
love and mercy he redeemed them; he lifted them up and carried them all the
days of old. — Like an eagle that stirs up its nest and hovers over its young, that
spreads its wings to catch them and carries them on its pinions. The LORD alone
led him; no foreign god was with him.

"Even to your old age and gray hairs I am he, I am he who will sustain you. I
have made you and I will carry you; I will sustain you and I will rescue you." — For
this God is our God for ever and ever, he will be our guide even to the end.

Cast your cares on the LORD and he will sustain you. — "Do not worry about
your life, what you will eat or drink; or about your body, what you will wear....
Your heavenly father knows that you need them." — "Thus far has the LORD
helped us."

DEUT. 1:31. Exod. 19:4. Isa. 63:9. Deut. 32:11–12. Isa. 46:4 Pss. 48:14; 55:22.
   Matt. 6:25, 32. 1 Sam. 7:12.

EVENING

"There are still very large areas of land to be taken over."

NOT THAT I have already obtained all this, or have already been made perfect,
but I press on to take hold of that for which Christ Jesus took hold of me.

"Be perfect." — Make every effort to add to your faith goodness; and to goodness, knowledge; and to knowledge, self-control; and to self-control, perseverance; and to perseverance, godliness; and to godliness, brotherly kindness; and
to brotherly kindness, love.

And this is my prayer, that your love may abound more and more in knowledge
and depth of insight. — "No eye has seen, no ear has heard, no mind has conceived
what God has prepared for those who love him" — but God has revealed it to us
by his Spirit. — There remains, then a Sabbath-rest for the people of God. — Your
eyes will see the king in his beauty and view a land that stretches afar.

JOSH. 13:1. Phil. 3:12. Matt. 5:48. 2 Peter 1:5–7. Phil. 1:9. 1 Cor. 2:9–10. Heb. 4:9.
   Isa. 33:17.

Share Your Thoughts

With the Author: Your comments will be forwarded to the author when you send them to *zauthor@zondervan.com*.

With Zondervan: Submit your review of this book by writing to *zreview@zondervan.com*.

Free Online Resources at
www.zondervan.com

Zondervan AuthorTracker: Be notified whenever your favorite authors publish new books, go on tour, or post an update about what's happening in their lives at www.zondervan.com/authortracker.

Daily Bible Verses and Devotions: Enrich your life with daily Bible verses or devotions that help you start every morning focused on God. Visit www.zondervan.com/newsletters.

Free Email Publications: Sign up for newsletters on Christian living, academic resources, church ministry, fiction, children's resources, and more. Visit www.zondervan.com/newsletters.

Zondervan Bible Search: Find and compare Bible passages in a variety of translations at www.zondervanbiblesearch.com.

Other Benefits: Register yourself to receive online benefits like coupons and special offers, or to participate in research.

ZONDERVAN

ZONDERVAN.com/
AUTHORTRACKER
follow your favorite authors